How Ottawa Spends, 2(

THE SCHOOL OF PUBLIC POLICY AND ADMINISTRATION at Carleton University is a national center for the study of public policy and public management.

The School's Centre for Policy and Program Assessment provides research services and courses to interest groups, businesses, unions, and governments in the evaluation of public policies, programs and activities.

School of Public Policy and Administration
Carleton University
10th Floor Dunton Tower
1125 Colonel By Drive
Ottawa, ON
Canada K1S 5B6
www.carleton.ca/sppa

How Ottawa Spends, 2009–2010

Economic Upheaval and Political Dysfunction

Edited by
ALLAN M. MASLOVE

Published for
The School of Public Policy and Administration
Carleton University
by
McGill-Queen's University Press
Montreal & Kingston · London · Ithaca

© McGill-Queen's University Press 2009
ISBN 978-0-7735-3612-8

Legal deposit third quarter 2009
Bibliothèque nationale du Québec

Printed in Canada on acid-free paper that is 100 % ancient forest free
(100 % post-consumer recycled), processed chlorine free.

McGill-Queen's University Press acknowledges the support of the Canada
Council for the Arts for our publishing program. We also acknowledge
the financial support of the Government of Canada through the Book Publishing
Industry Development Program (BPIDP) for our publishing activities.

Library and Archives Canada has catalogued this publication as follows:

How Ottawa spends.
    1983–
    Imprint varies.
    Includes bibliographical references.
    Continues: How Ottawa spends your tax dollars, ISSN 0711-4990.
    ISSN 0822-6482
    ISBN 978-0-7735-3612-8 (2009/2010 edition)

    1. Canada – Appropriations and expenditures – Periodicals.
    I. Carleton University. School of Public Policy and Administration

HJ7663.H69   354.710072'2   C84-030303-3

This book was typeset by Interscript in 10/12 Minion.

Contents

Preface   vii

1 Introduction   3
  Allan M. Maslove

2 Evolving Budgetary Policies and Experiments: 1980 to 2009–2010   14
  Bruce Doern

  PART ONE: ISSUES OF STRUCTURE AND PROCESS

3 How Ottawa Assesses Department/Agency Performance: Treasury Board's Management Accountability Framework   47
  Evert Lindquist

4 Design Challenges for the Strategic State: Bricolage and Sabotage   89
  Ruth Hubbard and Gilles Paquet

5 Evaluating the Rationale of the New Federal *Lobbying Act*: Making Lobbying Transparent or Regulating the Industry?   115
  Robert Shepherd

  PART TWO: SELECTED POLICY FIELDS

6 Could the Senate Be Right? Should CIDA Be Abolished?   151
  Chris Brown and Edward T. Jackson

7 Federal Gas Tax Transfers: Politics and Perverse Policy   175
  Robert Hilton and Christopher Stoney

8 How Ottawa Spends and How Canadians Save: "Asset-Based" Approaches in Uncertain Times   194
   Jennifer Robson, Richard Shillington, and Peter Nares

9 Communication by Stealth: The New Common Sense in Government Communication   222
   Kirsten Kozolanka

10 Framing the Harper Government: "Gender-Neutral" Electoral Appeals While Being Gender-Negative in Caucus   241
    Melissa Haussman and L. Pauline Rankin

11 Where Is VIA Going? A Case Study of Managing a Commercial Crown Corporation   263
    Malcolm G. Bird

Appendix A: Canadian Political Facts and Trends   283

Appendix B: Fiscal Facts and Trends   291

Contributors   307

Preface

This is the thirtieth annual edition of *How Ottawa Spends*, a milestone none of us had in mind when the series began in 1980. This edition, as all the others, would not be realized without the contributions of our authors; they are its essential input.[1]

This volume, and those of the last several years have benefited enormously from the organizational and technical support of Kimberly Huang of the School of Public Policy and Administration. I also thank Joan McGilvray and the team at McGill-Queen's University Press for their continuing help and support. Thanks as well to Genevieve Harte for her research assistance.

Finally, on behalf of all the editors of *How Ottawa Spends* over the years I want to acknowledge and thank our colleagues at Carleton University and across the country who have generously contributed (always without remuneration) their insights and analyses over the past thirty years.

Allan M. Maslove
Ottawa
March 2009

NOTE

1 The views and opinions expressed by the authors in this volume are their own and do not necessarily reflect the views of the editor or of the School of Public Policy and Administration at Carleton University.

How Ottawa Spends, 2009–2010

1 Introduction: How Ottawa Spends 2009–10: Economic Upheaval and Political Dysfunction

ALLAN M. MASLOVE

This volume of *How Ottawa Spends* is the thirtieth annual edition in the series. It is arguable that never over that period of time have Canadians faced a period of economic upheaval and political dysfunction as serious as what is now before us. We have seen dramatic and seemingly sudden changes in the economy and in financial markets, and at the same time, a series of political dramas that are largely disassociated with these real and pressing economic challenges.

At the beginning of 2009, the United States economy had been in recession for a full year. In Canada, the economy entered recession in the fourth quarter of 2008. During the last half of the year, global financial markets all but collapsed. Petroleum prices were in major retreat, as were the prices of most resources. On the political front, in 2008 Canadians went through an election called because the Prime Minister perceived that Parliament was dysfunctional, which if true, was largely a circumstance of the government's own making. This was quickly followed by an actual dysfunction of the new Parliament created by a government so hyper-partisan that it chose to use the fall economic statement to pursue a political agenda while largely ignoring the rapidly developing economic crisis. As a result 2009 (and beyond?) will witness a minority government, working under the severe handicaps of lack of trust and goodwill in Parliament, attempting to implement an agenda to deal with the recession, the problems in the financial markets, and economic restructuring.

In this introduction to the volume, we present an overview of the economic circumstances and the political maneuvering of 2008 and the first months of 2009 as a background and lead-in to the more focused analyses in the following chapters.

A BIT OF HISTORICAL PERSPECTIVE

To provide some insight to current economic conditions and to current federal policy moves, some historical perspective is in order. Behind the headline events are certain long-standing fundamentals of the Canadian economic and political structure (as well as some profound changes) that are important to understanding current policy issues. Many of these issues have been recurring subjects over the thirty years of *How Ottawa Spends*. The following chapter in this volume, written by Bruce Doern, the founding editor of the series, reviews many of these themes.

There have been three fundamental constants throughout the economic history of Canada. The Canadian economy has always been resource-based, internationally open, and regionally diverse. Resources have been the driving forces of Canadian economic fortunes from the earliest days of fish and furs[1], to timber and agriculture, to the modern era of oil, gas and other primary commodities. External markets for Canadian products have primarily been markets for our resources. While over time Canada developed other sectors of economic growth – an important manufacturing sector being the most notable – the importance of natural resource based growth has been a constant.

The openness of the Canadian economy is directly related to its resource-based nature. Foreign markets have been crucial to economic progress from the earliest days and continue to be so today. Globalization, and the emergence of new markets in countries such as China and India have created new opportunities for Canadian exporters, but somewhat ironically, at the same time the FTA/NAFTA has actually increased our reliance on the US as our primary market.

The third aspect, regionalism, is also closely related. Resources and indeed other bases of economic activity are not evenly distributed across the country, leading to regionally differing paces of development, differing needs in terms of government policy, and differing trading interests. The recent rise (and fall) of oil prices in recent years illustrates this point well. Rising prices were a huge stimulus to economic growth in Alberta, Saskatchewan and Newfoundland, and were a major factor behind the rising exchange value of the Canadian dollar. These two factors (increasing energy prices and the high exchange rate) contributed significantly to the stresses facing the manufacturing sector centered largely in Ontario and Quebec, ultimately helping to push Ontario into equalization receiving status as of 2009–10. The regional dimensions of this shift in economic activity and economic clout are profound.

That leads us to the dominant governance question that has existed at least since the Confederation debates: how should we structure ourselves politically to manage and develop the Canadian economy effectively. In large part this question is about the federal structure – the roles and authorities allocated to the two orders of government and to the fiscal balances between them. To this long-standing issue we may now be adding learning how to operate minority (and possibly coalition) governments in Ottawa. The last three elections have all produced minority governments; there is a real possibility that this type of electoral outcome will become a more regular event in the future than it has been in the past. The events of the closing weeks of 2008 suggest that our political system may not be up to the task.

THE CURRENT SITUATION

The onset of what threatens to be a serious recession may in fact be more than another cyclical event, at least in Canada. It may also be a time of realization that the Canadian economy is in the midst of a major restructuring. To start, there are structural changes occurring in the manufacturing sector. Most prominent of course is the auto industry; even if the North American Big Three survive, the auto industry will look fundamentally different than it has in the past. The need to recognize and address our reliance on fossil energy, including the environmental impacts it creates, is becoming increasingly pressing. The changes in the resource and manufacturing sectors of the economy have created major shifts in the regional distribution of wealth and income. If that is the case, the task facing Ottawa is not only one of stimulating a slow economy, but more fundamentally of addressing the longer-term shifts that are underway.

The government will have to decide what role Ottawa should play in the process of restructuring underway in the auto industry and elsewhere in the manufacturing sector. Ottawa will have to decide what policies it wishes to put in place to assist workers displaced from long-standing, high-paying jobs. It will have to decide what long-term response is called for to deal with the large regional shifts in relative wealth and income that have occurred and will likely continue (possibly at a slower pace as resource prices slowly rise again over time).

Other issues that have been on the table for some time remain unresolved and feed into the current economic situation. Prominent among these are the need to address energy consumption and climate change.

RECENT GOVERNMENT ACTIONS

In the face of this increasingly pressing list of economic problems, the approach of the government in Ottawa since the October 2008 election is contained in a number of official statements and documents. The first was the Speech from the Throne, opening the new parliament on 19 November. Unlike the sharply focused set of priorities of the Harper government's first Throne Speech in 2006, the November 2008 speech identifies no fewer than ten priority areas. While acknowledging the economic situation, the relevant proposals in the speech curiously lacked any sense of urgency. For example, the first theme, about restoring confidence and stability to the world financial system, was vague – even for a Throne Speech – as to what measures the government was contemplating to help bring this about. The second theme (sound budgeting) spoke of the need to avoid structural budget deficits, controlling spending and public sector compensation, and limiting growth of fiscal equalization payments to the provinces; none of these measures suggests a government seized with the idea that fiscal stimulation is the order of the day.

Other themes in the speech relating to economic concerns included: jobs (support for education and training, hints of support for various sectors, and public infrastructure investment); investment and trade (new international trade agreements, removing internal trade barriers); and energy (developing cleaner sources such as natural gas and nuclear). Rounding out the priority list were: more effective government (streamlining processes, expenditure review); climate change and the environment; helping Canadians "participate" (measures relating to the universal child benefit, maternity/parental employment insurance benefits, caregiver benefits, and first-time home buyers); security (stiffer criminal penalties, food, medicine and toy safety); and stronger public institutions (adjusting seats in the House of Commons, elected Senators with eight year terms, public service renewal, and a promised Charter of Open Federalism which appears largely to mirror the Social Union Framework Agreement signed by the provinces and Prime Minister Chrétien in 1999).

On 27 November 2008 the government produced its fall Economic and Fiscal Statement which was notable for two things. First, it painted an unrealistic picture of the economic situation and of the fiscal position of the government. On the latter point it projected balanced budgets (actually surpluses of $100 million) for the next two fiscal years (2009–10 and 2010–11) with recovering surpluses thereafter to 2013–14. Secondly, the statement introduced the government's plans to eliminate political party subsidies, to suspend collective bargaining and strike rights of public servants, and revise pay equity policies while proposing essentially nothing to directly address the economic recession.

The government's fiscal projections were in striking contrast to the forecasts of virtually all private sector predictions as well as those of the Parliamentary Budget Officer. The PBO projected, based on an average scenario of other publicly available forecasts, deficits of $3.9 billion in 2009–10 and $1.4 billion in 2010–11, followed by a return to modest surpluses thereafter. The PBO numbers assumed the fiscal policy stance in place in 2008 while the government's forecasts included the impact of several actions, the largest being "effective management of government spending" which was to realize $4.3 billion in savings in 2009–10. However, the statement was virtually silent on how these efficiencies would be realized or from which programs they would come.

Meanwhile the other items in the statement were largely in pursuit of a purely partisan agenda, doing nothing to address the actual economic circumstances confronting Canadians. The direct attack on the opposition parties combined with the unrealistic economic assessment and the complete lack of any significant measures to address the economic downturn led the Liberal and New Democratic parties declare their intention to vote non-confidence in the government and to propose a coalition to replace it (with promised support from the Bloc Quebecois). Mr Harper sought and succeeded in obtaining a prorogation of parliament to avoid the non-confidence vote.

On 26 January 2009 a new parliamentary session was launched followed by an official budget speech the next day. In the "do-over" Throne Speech the government struck a better tone, recognizing that addressing the state of the economy was urgent, promising non-partisan consultation and co-operation and noting that a stimulus package would be included in the new budget.

On 27 January the budget was delivered. It presented fiscal projections dramatically at odds with those in the November statement. The government attributed the changes to the rapidly developing global economic situation; in fact, the more realistic budget projections only served to further discredit the November figures. For example, the federal budgetary balance difference between the two projections for fiscal year 2009–10 was about $16 billion[2]; it is difficult to believe that the underlying economic projections changed sufficiently to generate a fiscal difference of this magnitude.

Nonetheless, the budget contained enough in the way of stimulus to end, for the moment, the threat of parliamentary non-confidence (and the possible installation of a Liberal-NDP coalition government). The budget included a mixture of tax relief and direct spending measures. Prominent among the former were increases in the basic personal exemption and top limits of the first two personal income tax brackets, increases in the Child Tax Benefit and the Working Income Tax Benefit, and a temporary Home Renovation Tax Credit. Among the main spending initiatives were investments in housing and infrastructure, some of which required matching funds from provinces, municipalities and others. Among the purely federal infrastructure investments were a long list of projects scattered across the country.

The federal deficit before the budget measures was projected to be $15.7 billion for 2009–10; after the budget measures were factored in the projection was $33.7 billion. While the federal measures amounted to $18 billion for 2009–10, the government projected that the total stimulus would be just under $30 billion for the year. The latter estimate, however, anticipated the provinces and municipalities fully taking up all the sharing arrangements on offer.

ADDRESSING THE CANADIAN RECESSION

At the time of writing it is still not clear how severe the recession will be, what long-term structural changes will occur, and how the government's initiatives will affect the course of the economy. However, it is possible to suggest some initial impressions and raise issues to monitor. We organize this preliminary assessment around three questions.

1 Does the Harper government's 2009 budget contain enough stimulus to significantly moderate the recession? On the surface the budget measures meet the informal international agreement to develop stimulus packages amounting to 2 per cent of national GDP. However, there are at least two reasons to be concerned that the budget package will be inadequate on this score. The first is the already mentioned reliance on provincial and municipal take-ups to generate the full amount of fiscal stimulus. Provincial governments are now facing their own budget deficits for the first time in a decade, and several are struggling to maintain their existing program spending. Municipal governments are even more constrained. It is likely that at least some of the federal money will be left on the table, and possibly a great deal of it. Second, the Harper government itself seems distinctly unenthusiastic about its own budget. Certainly compared to the active promotion of the Obama economic stimulus measures in the United States, Prime Minister Harper and his Cabinet have been notably subdued in their promotion of the January budget. In itself that may not be significant, but it does raise the question of how aggressive they will be in ensuring that the promised spending actually occurs in a timely fashion.

The recession in Canada has mainly been imported – that is, it is caused by the deep recession in the rest of the world and especially by the collapsing American market. Fully replacing that external demand for Canadian resources, manufactured goods and services for a significant length of time is likely beyond the capacity of governments. But moderating the downturn in a meaningful way is not. Whether the Harper government has the will to do so remains an open question.

2 Does the budget open the door to long-term structural deficits? Conservatives, Liberals, and New Democrats all seem to agree that any deficits incurred during the recession should be short-term. Certainly, the Conservatives' reluctance to incur deficits of any variety is not hidden. The infrastructure spending measures in this budget appear, for the most part, to be one-time items (though they may last for several years), and therefore they would not move Ottawa's fiscal position towards structural deficits. The tax measures, on the other hand, are more likely to be long-standing and thus move the fiscal position about $5 billion annually towards structural deficit.

3 Do the budget measures address the more fundamental structural adjustments discussed earlier? An argument might be constructed to the effect that investments are required to rebuild the manufacturing sector of the economy (and to a lesser extent the resource sector) to put it into an advantageous position as the global economy recovers. Alternatively, it might be argued that a renewal strategy should focus not on restructuring the "old economy," but on developing new sectors that seek to exploit Canada's human resource and technology advantages.

The Harper government has not clearly articulated any overall strategy. Certainly, there are measures to save and promote restructuring of parts of the manufacturing sector – most notably the aid packages offered to the auto companies. To some extent, the proposed investments in physical infrastructure and in training are also consistent with this strategy. But many of the infrastructure projects listed in the budget are quite unimaginative; rather they resemble a sprinkling of money across the country. As for a "new economy" strategy, there is virtually nothing in the budget. For example, there is little to address issues like energy consumption and the environment, the development of renewable energy sources, or the development of new high value-added sectors.

With this background, the following ten chapters explore in more depth aspects of Ottawa's spending policies and governing processes and structures.

OVERVIEW OF THE CHAPTERS

In the next chapter, Bruce Doern, the founding editor of the *How Ottawa Spends* series, reviews changes in budgetary design over the thirty years that the volume has been produced by the Carleton University's School of Public Policy and Administration. Doern traces four budgetary periods: the Trudeau years (characterized by deficits and stagflation); Mulroney (untamed deficits); Chrétien/Martin (deficit elimination and budget surpluses); and Harper (the return to deficits). He identifies and reviews the numerous changes in budget design and budget experiments that occurred during this period. For those who monitor federal budgets and budgeting this was anything but a quiet period, as successive governments attempted to design the system to confront the most pressing issues they faced and to generate the outcomes they desired.

The sponsorship affair led governments to strengthen the accountability of ministers and deputy ministers, improve financial management, regularize reviews and evaluations of programs, and increase monitoring of departments and agencies. In chapter 3, Evert Lindquist focuses on the Management Accountability Framework administered by the Treasury Board Secretariat, which employs quantitative and non-quantitative indicators to gauge the performance and capabilities of departments and agencies. Lindquist explores the origins of MAF and how it gathered steam in the "hyper-accountability" environment that descended on Ottawa. He observes that MAF elicits strong reactions because of its broad approach to reviewing performance, and the resources required to operate it. But, he notes that citizens and elected representatives would be surprised if such assessments were not undertaken. He also notes that MAF has played an important role in establishing a new identity for the Treasury Board Secretariat, allowing Treasury Board to finally live up to the designation of "management board."

In chapter 4, Ruth Hubbard and Gilles Paquet address questions of organizational design at a fundamental level. They first explore the problem in general in a world where nobody is in charge due to ongoing complexity, turbulence and surprises. They then apply their model to two recent federal cases. In the case of the Canadian Nuclear Safety Commission the Hubbard/Paquet analysis sheds light on the regulatory "fiasco" of late 2007, and explains why and how "passive sabotage" has prevented meaningful organizational improvement since then. In the case of Service Canada they explain how an initially promising initiative to deliver government services and information more adeptly to citizens fails because of "active sabotage" from within the bureaucracy. Hubbard and Paquet conclude with three reform suggestions which, in order, hold some promise. First the government requires a better and fuller appreciation of the organizational design function and the development of competencies in this area. Second, there should be organizational performance oversight and adjustment in real time, rather than an auditor (ex post) type of oversight. Third, the Office of the Auditor General should pay more attention to organizational design matters instead of creeping into issues of government policy.

Robert Shepherd examines the new federal Lobbying Act in chapter 5. He traces the change in focus from the original act, dating from the late 1980s, which was intended primarily to promote transparency in lobbying, to the new act of the Harper government which is about regulating lobbying activity. The 2006 changes, being based on rules and the regulation of behaviour, shifts from broad ethics guiding principles to "ethical silos" which focus on rules to regulate specific lobbying activities. Shepherd raises the question of whether the rules interfere with what is really important – better people building better public organizations. Do rules impede the inculcation of ideals?

A recent Senate Committee recommended that the Canadian International Development Agency (CIDA) be abolished because it was ineffective and seemed to have lost its way. Chris Brown and Edward Jackson examine CIDA in light of the Senate report in chapter 6. They argue that there is a need for a fundamental review of the agency but that leadership in this area from the Harper government is lacking. CIDA is spread too thinly – geographically and sectorally – and combined with its relatively modest budget, it has had no real impact anywhere, with the possible exception of Haiti. Brown and Jackson examine CIDA from three perspectives. As a member of the international development community, CIDA is a relatively small player in most of its recipient countries, and the move towards donor consortia approaches within a country leave little room for CIDA to have a profile. Within the Canadian political scene there is general good will towards development assistance, but there is no strong constituency for this spending and no strong domestic voice for CIDA. Within the federal government, there has been a succession of relatively weak ministers in charge of CIDA, their tenures at the agency have been short, and the nature of CIDA's programming does not fit well with the new public management initiatives that have been so prominent of late. Brown and Jackson also note that post-9/11, the primary focus on Afghanistan has distorted CIDA's already troubled mission. They conclude that Canadian international development assistance should be more focused (geographically and sectorally), have a longer-term orientation and that more money will be required if we are to have any meaningful impact.

Robert Hilton and Christopher Stoney examine Ottawa's decision to proceed with the so-called gas tax transfer to municipalities to fund infrastructure investments (chapter 7). The transfer, announced as a five year program in 2004 by the Martin Liberal government, was later extended and then made permanent by the Harper conservatives after they came to office. The gas tax transfer stands in contrast to the long history of largely one-off funding and loan programs to support municipal infrastructure, programs that have waxed and waned with changing economic and political circumstances. Hilton and Stoney argue that the gas tax program is inconsistent with Harper's commitment to "open federalism," and they argue that it reflects good politics more than good policy. It involves Ottawa in local decisions and may well distort local priorities and accountability links. They argue that turning over unencumbered tax room to the municipalities would be a preferred alternative.

Ottawa spends money directly, but Ottawa also spends money indirectly through tax preferences and incentives. Jennifer Robson, Richard Shillington, and Peter Nares examine federal tax incentives to support personal wealth accumulation (chapter 8). The benefits of these programs, the most important of which provide incentives for home ownership and retirement saving, are directly related to incomes; higher income taxpayers derive proportionally greater benefits than lower income individuals. While there are more recent programs ostensibly directed at small savers (such as the Canada Learning Bond and the Registered Disabilities Savings Plan) Robson, Shillington and Nares argue that there are barriers that inhibit their take-up by low income individuals and families and that most of the benefits go to middle and upper income groups. The newest such measure is the Tax Free Savings Account (TFSA) introduced in the 2008 budget. The authors point out that on its own it has some attractive properties, but that it is not yet clear how the assets in these accounts will be regarded by provincial social assistance programs.

In chapter 9, Kirsten Kozolanka examines Ottawa's communications policies and programs. She contrasts the approaches of recent Liberal governments with that of the Harper Conservatives. Kozolanka argues that while the Chrétien and Martin Liberals tended to be overt in their deployment of communications strategies to advance their political and policy goals, the

Conservatives' strategy is more hidden. It is "communications by stealth." The ultimate objective is to have the government's priorities and thinking accepted as "common sense." Part of this strategy, Kozolanka argues, was the aggressive manner in which the Harper government centralized and limited the media's access to ministers and to the prime minister himself.

In chapter 10, Melissa Haussman and Pauline Rankin examine the government's stance on a number of social and gender issues. They argue the Conservative government and party is a balancing act between economic conservatives (concerned mainly with restrained government spending, lower taxes, and economic regulation) and social conservatives (whose main issues are abortion, stem cell research, and gay rights). Haussman and Rankin argue that Harper has tried to bury the social conservative agenda while permitting this wing of his base enough room to move to keep them happy. The authors trace through how this balancing act has played itself out on a number of fronts including abortion, the Board of the Assisted Human Reproduction Agency of Canada, and funding for Status of Women Canada.

Government policies also emerge through their interventions with federal agencies outside the ministries. Malcolm Bird examines this impact in the case of VIA Rail. He argues that VIA's main problems over its 30 year history are not primarily ones of management (though they are certainly present) but of neglect, underfunding and political interference by successive governments. He sees a purpose in Ottawa's stance towards VIA that is intended to undermine its viability as a means of transportation. Bird argues that if VIA is to succeed in the mandate it has been given Ottawa must refrain from interfering in its operations and confine itself to setting general policy goals and directives in return for its subsidization of the service. Further there must be significant reform of VIA's governance structure and it must have a team of competent managers who have adequate capital to work with. The financial infusions from the government announced in 2007 and in the 2009 budget are helpful but do not address the fundamental problems that VIA faces.

CONCLUSION

The recession that hit Canada in 2008 may, in time, be seen as a major turning point. While most of the downturn was caused by events in the rest of the world, especially the United States, the cyclical economic weakness has served to shine a spotlight on more several structural problems in the Canadian economy. At the same time, the policy responses have served to raise some disquieting questions both about the current Conservative government and the capacity of governance in Ottawa.

The chapters in this thirtieth annual edition of *How Ottawa Spends*, while varied in the topics they cover, all speak to these important questions.

NOTES

1 This pattern was most notably studied by Harold Innis in *The Fur Trade in Canada: An Introduction to Canadian Economic History*, first published in 1930.
2 The November statement projected a surplus of $100 million while the January budget projected a deficit of $15.7 billion (before any budgetary measures were included).

2 Evolving Budgetary Policies and Experiments: 1980 to 2009–2010

G. BRUCE DOERN

This chapter provides a personal reflection on evolving federal budgetary policies and developments as revealed in 30 years of *How Ottawa Spends* (*HOS*) as an annual commentary on Canadian fiscal dynamics, politics and policy.[1] It is personal in the sense that my colleagues and I initiated *HOS* in 1980 when I was director of the School of Public Administration and then I was its editor for the first four editions in the early 1980s and then again for five further editions from 2001–2002 on. But overall, *HOS* is very much a collective analytical effort in two senses, first among colleagues in the School and, even more importantly, among a range of about 200 academics (including graduate students) across Canada and abroad from varied academic disciplines and political perspectives.

The structure of the chapter is quite straightforward. The first section comments briefly on the origins and coverage of *HOS* as an annual review of federal spending and policy. This is followed by a broad summary view of four macro budgetary-political epochs from 1980 to the present, which more or less coincide with four prime ministerial eras, namely those of the Trudeau, Mulroney, Chrétien-Martin and Harper periods in office. These tended to be the focus of the lead chapter by successive editors of *HOS* but these macro features invariably are the context for virtually every chapter by other *HOS* authors as well. The final section then looks at several efforts at mezzo-level budgetary design and experimentation across the 30 year period.[2] Conclusions then follow.

15 Evolving Budgetary Policies and Experiments

ORIGINS AND COVERAGE

The idea for an annual *How Ottawa Spends* commentary on federal fiscal and policy issues emerged in 1979. We had one model in the U.S. for such a publication, which we knew we could not replicate. This was the annual Washington-based Brookings Institution annual review of U.S. budgets. It not only reviewed particular areas of departmental spending but it also, crucially, produced its own counter-budget and fiscal forecast. Our hardy band of policy and budgetary analysts did not have the funding resources to produce the latter but we did feel, in alliance with others, that we could do the former.

Thus, from the outset, the purpose of *How Ottawa Spends* has been to provide an informed independent commentary and analysis of federal spending and of the underlying political-economy of factors and forces that were driving federal spending and taxation and the changing federal priority agenda.[3] We saw HOS as being aimed at an informed audience consisting of ministers, MPs, civil servants, journalists, interest group and NGO lobbyists, and others. We also saw potential in it as a supplementary text in basic university courses in Canadian politics and policy. Our preferred modus operandi has been to publish HOS as quickly as possible after the tabling of the federal Budget and estimates in February or March of each year.

From the outset it was clear that HOS would be about spending but also would go without question beyond spending into areas of taxation for certain, but also regulation (both spending on regulation, rules that regulate spending, and also the mandated private sector "spending" required by new federal rules) and exhortation or suasion.[4] It short, we followed the public money trail and the power of the purse wherever it lead into many diverse policy instruments and public policy fields. The authors' analyses, though focused on the contemporary scene, also provided important historical context for the fiscal and policy issues being reviewed.

We sought to be non-partisan and to bring to public debate a wide range of opinions from the full political spectrum of views. While the editor each year identified three or four core topics/fields, which he or she planned to cover in that edition of HOS, the larger number of chapters in each addition came from our annual call for chapters sent out to academics and other potential informed contributors and analysts across Canada. Frequently the team of authors also met in an author's workshop to discuss draft chapters or chapter outlines and key lines of argument.

Across the last 30 years the policy fields and aspects of budgeting covered by HOS authors' chapters are roughly as follows:

- 22 per cent on social policy (the largest area of federal public spending by far);
- 16 per cent on energy and environmental policy;
- 15 per cent on public service/bureaucracy reform issues;

- 14.5 per cent on varied aspects of taxation, tax reform, and the nature of the expenditure estimates;
- 12.5 per cent on international affairs and trade issues;
- 12 per cent on federalism, federal-provincial fiscal arrangements and regional policy;
- 6 per cent on Aboriginal policy; and
- 5 per cent on innovation/industrial policy.

This is quite reasonable coverage overall but obviously, some areas such as transportation, northern development, policing and corrections, immigration, procurement, and national defence, though examined, were not consistently covered over the 30 year period. Some of the cumulative analysis from the first eight years of HOS did find its way into an integrated text book on public budgeting written by the first three editors of HOS.[5]

MACRO BUDGETARY-POLITICAL EPOCHS: 1980 TO 2009–10

Clearly, the telling and interpretation of the macro budgetary-political story of the last 30 years was central both to the purposes of HOS and, even more importantly, to the actual functioning and policy steering of the Government of Canada and of the overall Canadian polity. This section profiles four macro budgetary-political epochs. Macro refers here to classic notions of broad overall economic policy (the tax and spending interactions of fiscal policy with some references to monetary policy and inflation). It also refers to the always-linked macro calculations of prime ministerial political and policy agendas, as successive prime ministers and their political party interpret and try to manage effectively both global and national political and socio-economic forces, plus also unexpected crises.

The four prime ministerial epochs are by no means watertight periods for the narrative. Overlaps across these periods are numerous and there are also often gaps between the rhetorical claims and flourish of political debate compared to the actual patterns of spending and taxation. For example, there are some similarities between the Martin and Harper eras, not only because of their close proximity time-wise but also because they were both minority governments with shortened electoral cycles and strong distributive needs and appetites. Nonetheless, there is a sufficiently accurate core fiscal and policy story to each period. For example, the three charts in Appendix 1 of this chapter show clearly the overall patterns for deficits/surpluses; national debt, and federal spending. The chart on deficits and surpluses shows the burgeoning of deficits in the 1980 to 1984 period under the Trudeau Liberals but also the overall inability of the Mulroney Conservatives to grapple with it and reduce it. Deficits quickly disappear under the Chrétien-Martin Liberals and then from 1997 to 2007, large though variable surpluses are the norm. The chart on the national debt mirrors the fiscal changes with national debt increasing six-fold between 1980 and 1996 and gradually reducing as parts of the surplus were explicitly targeted to debt reduction. The chart on federal spending shows a steady growth of spending under the Trudeau Liberals and Mulroney Conservatives, then a modest decline in 1996–98 period under the Chrétien-Martin Liberals, and finally a fairly sharp growth under both the Martin Liberals and in the early Harper Conservative years.

A further feature of the 30 year macro story is the way in which overriding macro economic policy theories and paradigms were changing as revealed in various Budget Speeches and as captured in debate among economists. Thus, the demise of Keynesian macro economic policy was already evident as the final Trudeau years of the early 1980s played out. Monetarism and a greater focus on low inflation and on securing a manageable non-inflationary rate of unemployment emerged from the mid- 1980s on. Once surpluses became the norm in the late 1990s, any return to deficits was viewed as the ultimate fiscal political-economic sin. However, following the banking/financial crash of 2008 and the deep 2008–09 global and Canadian recession, neo-Keynesian views are reemerging in political and economic discourse as well as in policy and fiscal actions in Canada and abroad.

The Trudeau Era (1980–1984): Deficits and Stagflation

Pierre Trudeau had of course been in power from 1968 to 1979 when the short-lived Joe Clark-led Conservative government won power in a minority government. But Trudeau was quickly back in power in 1980 and, in the 1980 to 1984 period, launched an aggressive activist agenda that included constitutional change centered on the *Canadian Charter of Rights and Freedoms*, the highly interventionist and divisive National Energy Program (NEP) and a natural resource-driven industrial policy mega projects strategy, among other initiatives.[6] But the background rolling of the political-economic drums during this period was manifest in massively increased fiscal deficits, combined with high structural unemployment and the presence of high inflation, in a word, stagflation.

Deficits had begun to emerge and grow in the late 1970s but they were mild compared to what was to follow as the 1980s began. Some growth in deficits was undoubtedly due to the energy crises of 1973 and 1979, and policy responses to them, especially the 1979 crisis. Fiscal political debate quickly came up with other causes of the huge fiscal gap between revenues and expenditures in the Trudeau era. Uncontrolled spending via the NEP and other programs was certainly one. So also was the indexation of major statutory spending and of the tax system overall. [7]Another was the emerging debate about growing tax expenditures, the deductions from taxation whose value to taxpayers increased with the wealth of such taxpayers and which by the mid 1980s was draining revenue from the federal purse and hence contributing to increased deficits.[8] In other words, both excessive spending and the failure to tax were becoming a part of the debate over cause(s) of federal government deficits.

Also growing in prominence in national debate were the then burgeoning new paradigms of macro policy centered variously on the criticism of traditional 1960s-style Keynesian macro economic and fiscal policy, the emergence of monetarism under Margaret Thatcher in particular, and the Ronald Reagan-led ideological views about both the need for less government but also the economic value of supply-side economics which held that tax cuts and resultant growth would create new wealth and jobs, enriching the tax coffers of the state at the same time.

The Mulroney Era (1984–1993): The Failure to Tame the Deficit

Conservative Prime Minister Brian Mulroney's eight year tenure was characterized overall by a failure to tame or reduce the fiscal deficit.[9] Indeed, federal deficits stayed at virtually the same high level during the entire period. This stasis occurred despite early electoral and rhetorical emphasis by the Conservatives on the need to right the fiscal ship and also to reduce the size of the state and its level of renewed interventionism in the Trudeau era. There was early evidence in the first Mulroney term in office of action on both fronts mainly by the work of the Nielson Task Force on Program Review, the reversal of the Liberal NEP energy spending and tax levies, and its replacement by a Conservative energy policy that was far more market-oriented and decentralized in keeping with the strong Alberta-centred part of the Western Canada-Québec coalition that underpinned the Mulroney electoral-political base. There was also considerable initial suspicion in the Mulroney Cabinet of federal regional spending as regional welfare rather than as development.[10] In addition, the Mulroney Tories launched one of the first regulatory reform reviews tied eventually to plans for both deregulation and also the privatization of some federal Crown Corporation as was beginning to happen in Thatcher's Britain.[11]

Successive Conservative budgets in the 1984 to 1988 period certainly spoke of deficit-reduction aspirations including the above noted Nielson Task Force but to no real overall avail politically or in practice.[12] In part this was also due to the fact that the all consuming real focus in the latter half of Mulroney's first term was the free trade negotiations with the U.S., the management of the free trade debate nationally, and the eventual gearing-up to fight the 1988 election which was quickly dubbed the free trade election. Without doubt the main political achievement of the Mulroney first term was the signing of the Canada-U.S. Free Trade Agreement. Free trade agreements are not fundamentally about public spending but as we will see further below, they can effect and in fact regulate certain kinds of spending in the form of subsidies.

The second Mulroney period from 1988 to 1992 did not change the overall failure to reduce the federal deficit. It did however lead to two important changes on the tax side of the fiscal equation. Following the lead of both Thatcher and Reagan, the personal tax system was changed in a major way by reducing the number and level of marginal tax rates at different income levels. This both simplified the personal tax system but also made it less progressive and less capable overall of redistributing income. Some increased progressivity did occur, however, due to the elimination of inflation indexing below 3 per cent.[13] The second Mulroney change was the introduction of the Goods and Services Tax (GST). This also partly followed developments elsewhere particularly in response to the growing view among economists that it is better overall to tax what people take out of the economy when they purchase goods and services than what they put into the economy (their labour and entrepreneurial inventiveness).[14] The GST was also adopted because of the need to replace a highly perverse Manufacturer's Sales Tax, especially given the start-up of the Free Trade Agreement with the U.S. which had no such sales tax. The GST had two main effects: one, fairly immediate and political; the other, more medium term and financial. It was initially extremely unpopular and seen as a tax grab, which hurt the Tories eventually in the 1993 election. But it also eventually contributed, along with other tax impacts as the economy grew, to the increased revenues and eventual budgetary surpluses in the later 1990s under the Chrétien-Martin Liberals.

The other priorities and preoccupations of the Mulroney Conservatives were its early 1990s Green Plan[15] and the eventual failed constitutional initiatives on the Meech Lake Accord and the Charlottetown Agreement. While these key constitutional developments are well beyond the fiscal focus of this chapter, they did contain within them the seeds of three "spending" issues with constitutional overtones, that are alive and well (see more below); namely, the desire in some political quarters to reduce and control the "spending power" of the federal government in areas of provincial jurisdiction, the various claims of the need to solve the fiscal imbalance in federal-provincial revenue-spending capacities, and the aspirations of Aboriginal communities for self-government and fiscal capacity.[16]

The Chrétien-Martin Era (1993 to 2005): Taming the Deficit and the Era of Budgetary Surpluses

The Chrétien-Martin era has a dual meaning. From 1993 to 2003 Jean Chrétien was Prime Minister who won three consecutive majority governments and Paul Martin was his finance minister for most of that decade, a rarity in Canadian political history.[17] The second sense of the term is that then Martin succeeded Chrétien as prime minister but in a short-lived minority government context until Martin's defeat in the January 2006 election. The Chrétien-Martin team through the 1993 Liberal Red Book election agenda and its subsequent first actions in power took dead aim at the deficit mainly by launching the 1993–1996 Program Review process but also by reneging on its own election promise to get rid of the Mulroney GST.

Program Review (see more below) was cast as a rational review of government programs on a cross-governmental basis but its intent was unambiguous, namely to cut public spending in a major way, about 20 per cent overall (in transfers to other governments, and defence spending). In some program realms even deeper cuts were made in a somewhat more rational analytical way. For the total cuts to add up to the right totals, this meant some cuts in social spending (including health care) mainly, as noted above, through cuts in federal-provincial established programs funding.

It is worth noting that during the previous Mulroney era, social spending, despite the fear of cuts planted or suggested by Liberal and NDP opponents, were not significantly reduced overall.[18] This was in part precisely because the Mulroney Conservatives did not want to be seen or cast as being anti-social policy. During the first Chrétien government from 1993 to 1997, the Liberals were able to do both in part because they faced across the aisle of the House of Commons a decimated Progressive Conservative Party, a weakened NDP presence, and a strengthened fiscally conservative Reform Party that strongly favored such cuts and social policy retrenchment. But the cuts occurred as well because the Chrétien-Martin partnership at the centre of the Liberal Party and Cabinet was determined to take such action in the larger public interest in the sense that the required level of cuts could not be reached without social policy cuts.

Once federal surpluses emerged after three years of fiscal pain, the Chrétien-Martin fiscal agenda focused on overall economic growth and low inflation achieved through continuous surpluses on top of more transparent provision for contingency funds (see further discussion below) to meet crises and unexpected needs. The dispersal of the surplus was typically presented as a notional 50/50 strategy, with 50 per cent going to the reduction of the cumulative national debt and tax reductions; and 50 per cent to new spending initiatives. Unusually, near the top of their spending initiatives, was a massive eventual $13 billion increase in funding research and development activity and innovation, mainly through support for Canada's universities; unusual, because such spending was aimed more at elites in Canadian society than the proverbial average voter.[19]

When Paul Martin himself became prime minister in 2004 after a bitter internal battle with Chrétien, the penchant for surpluses continued. But Martin's view of the public purse was also mightily influenced by his desire to right the wrongs of having had to make, under his watch, social policy cuts in the mid-1990s.[20] Thus he immediately reached a long-term federal-provincial social programs and health care funding deal (especially the latter) both to restore cuts and to stabilize spending in these areas.[21] In a linked but different area of social justice, he obtained agreement via the Kelowna Accord to increase spending related to Aboriginal Peoples, a significant commitment that later did not survive when the Harper Conservatives won power in 2006.

The Harper Conservatives (2006 to present): The End of the Surplus and the Return of Deficits

The latest period covered is that of the Harper Conservatives under their two minority governments from 2006 to 2008, and at present.[22] The Harper Conservatives were critical of the size of Liberal surpluses, arguing that these were themselves evidence of excessive taxation. They maintained surpluses in their first two budgets but in the January 2009 post election and post global banking crisis budget they have reintroduced deficits in a major way.

On taking office in January 2006, the Harper Conservatives moved in a confident and sure-handed manner to implement their initial five-point agenda: the Accountability Act, very much centred on righting previous Liberal era areas of financial excess and corruption; a one per cent cut in the GST (followed later by a further 1 per cent cut in 2008); a child care plan (an allowance and spaces initiative); a tougher approach to crime and punishment; and, a patient wait times guarantee in health care. The Accountability Act was the Tories lead off promise and was their response to the main issue that saw them win power, the Liberal's corruption record centered on federal spending on the Québec-centered Sponsorship program. Each of the next three priorities was a part of the Tory effort to reach out to the hard pressed suburban middle classes. However, the cut in the GST was opposed by many economists as precisely the wrong kind of tax to cut. It was bound to and intended to reduce the federal surplus and return money to taxpayers.

Harper's budgetary stance has also been influenced by his so-called "open federalism" approach. Under open federalism, the federal government respects provincial areas of policy jurisdiction but also strongly defends, and indeed focuses, on federal realms such as national defence, law and order, northern sovereignty, vigorous foreign and trade policy, and overall national economic development, including support of measures that will produce a more open internal market. These core instincts have of course had to be mellowed and adapted to the realities of actually having to govern. Thus open federalism still leaves room for strong federal involvement in areas such as education and related R&D support, infrastructure development and a related but more tentative cities agenda.

Harper's initial electoral and policy strategy in his first three years in office also stressed that he would solve the federal-provincial fiscal imbalance problem, an issue that Québec governments had raised for several years.[23] Coupled with a Conservative preference for a much more decentralized federation, the fiscal imbalance issue found resonance in Québec even though the actual issue of fiscal imbalance is dubious in many respects in that provinces, as self-governing jurisdictions, are free to fix their own imbalances between taxing and spending if they chose to do so. These policies were discussed by Harper in Québec, much more than in the rest of Canada, and when a new deal was reached in 2007, it was clearly the Québec aspects of the deal that mattered most in terms of Conservative policy and electoral strategy. In the end, the strategy did not deliver the Conservatives the bounty of numerous new Québec seats in the 2008 election that they had sought, although other policies contributed to this result more directly that its response to fiscal imbalance.

In terms of overall federal public spending the Harper Tories committed themselves to levels of spending over the next five years, which were virtually identical to those of the previous Martin Liberal government. And this was before the spring 2007 spending splurge once the Tories discovered that they too presided over a handsome budgetary surplus and could play the largesse and distributive spending game, despite their ardent criticism of the Liberals for this kind of fiscal indiscipline.

Early Harper budgets delivered lower taxes for all Canadians partly through highly targeted but politically noticeable small tax breaks on textbooks for students, tools for apprentices in skilled trades, and for users of public transit. Again the needs of the beleaguered average Canadian and the "swing voter in the swing constituencies" of an already strategized "next" election were a key part of the calculus of Conservative agenda-setting. Taxes were also reduced for small businesses and overall regarding corporate taxation. In the 2007 budget alone, were 29 separate tax reductions. Federal spending was then projected to increase by $10 billion to $233 billion in 2007–2008, including a 5.7 per cent increase in program spending. A small surplus of $3.3 billion was planned almost all of which will go to debt reduction.

As Harper savoured his 14 October 2008 re-election with a strengthened minority government but without his much desired majority government, he and his Minister of Finance already knew that his surpluses were likely gone in the face of the then-occurring banking and stock market crash and crisis, already lowered and meagre economic growth, and a looming recession, nationally and globally. Future deficits were firmly back on the agenda.[24] But the Harper performance after the October 2008 election was among the most incompetent ever seen in modern Canadian politics. Its 27 November 2008 budget update statement ignored the looming global crisis, planned for a small surplus, announced cuts in public spending rather than a needed stimulus, and in a stunningly vindictive way, announced it would eliminate public funding for political parties, and ban strikes by federal government workers for two years.²⁵ Within a few days the opposition parties announced that a Liberal-NDP coalition government was ready to govern with the support of the Bloc Québecois. Harper was then forced to seek a prorogation of a newly elected Parliament to avoid losing a vote of confidence in the House of Commons, and the Liberals had a new a credible leader in the person of Michael Ignatieff. The core premises of the economic update had to be abandoned as Finance Minister Jim Flaherty prepared his and Harper's January 27th budget.

MEZZO-BUDGETARY DESIGN AND EXPERIMENTATION

The macro summary account above tells quite a general but important overall budgetary story but it needs to be complemented by a brief look at other more particular mezzo-level examples of budgetary design and experimentation. Aided by table 1, we highlight 13 selected examples of evolving budgetary change, success and failure that have been examined in *HOS* analyses and which show how governments over the last thirty years have sought and often struggled to cope with the power and management of the public purse in the face of both incremental and also great and often turbulent change.

Envelopes and the Policy-Expenditure Management System (PEMS)

The PEMS approach was established in 1979 by the short-lived Clark Conservative government and then continued by the Trudeau Liberals and operated for four years before being downgraded by the short-livened Turner Liberal government and then abolished by the Mulroney Conservatives in 1984.²⁶ The essence of the system was to create budgetary envelopes of new money that would be directly managed by ministers in the main cabinet committees. The intent was to get ministers to make more integrated decisions regarding policy and budgets. The system before (and after) PEMS had been the classic separation of these two tasks, with policy decisions being made/approved by ministers and then by the relevant cabinet committee but with budgetary decisions made later by the Treasury Board and also by Finance and the prime minister (regarding how and where to allocate the limited amount of new money).

Under PEMS, the cabinet committees were given an envelope of funds. Ministers in these committees then had to bid for the available funds and in effect queue-up and participate in a kind of auction. Accordingly, ministers were both spenders and guardians over this limited pool of new money. The PEMS system probably did create among ministers a greater day-to-day sense of the need to match their policy plans with their money and program efficacy needs in direct competition with their cabinet colleagues. But the system

Table 1
Selected Examples of Budgetary Design and Experimentation: 1980–2009

Example	Core Features	Impacts/Implications
Envelopes and the Policy-Expenditure Management System (PEMS)	– Trudeau era reform to better link policy and expenditure choices within Cabinet committee processes	– resulted in need for complex "auctions" among ministers in main committees; eventually abandoned in 1984 in part because it created too much conflict among ministers who had to be both spenders and guardians rather than just spenders as in the pre-1980 and post 1984 systems when the Department of Finance and the Treasury Board were the acknowledged and preferred guardians.
Program Review	– 1993–1996 Chrétien-Martin era process for cutting public spending in comprehensive manner to reduce federal deficit; – device for getting at, reviewing, and cutting the A-Base of public spending which is arguably at least 90 to 95 per cent of the public purse compared to the smaller amount of new money;	– produced the 20 per cent plus cuts in the federal expenditure budget; – also resulted in some cancellation of and/or redesign of particular programs and departmental mandates, structures and names; – contributed to loss of policy capacity in some departments as planning units easy to cut politically
Tax Credits: When Taxing Becomes Spending	– Use of tax regime in 1980s and 1990s to provide refundable tax credits (spending) to targeted citizens (e.g. child tax credits) or firms (the SR&ED tax credit).	– Tax credits on the social spending side (e.g. child tax credit) allow greater redistribution to low income Canadians, including those who do not have enough income to pay taxes; – Tax credits on economic (SR&ED for business R&D) delivered targeted benefit to smaller mainly Canadian firms engaged in R&D but not yet in profit position.
Costing Political Party Electoral Platforms and Promises	Begin's with Liberal's 1993 Red Book to show to electorate what the costs of promises are and what they total.	– resulted in somewhat more responsible platforms compared to earlier "wish list" platforms. – media and others also then reported "score card" style on the costed election agenda platform items.

Earmarked Funds Accountability and Sustainability: Pensions and Employment Insurance	– Liberal Changes in 1998 to ensure that Canada Pension Plan is funded as investment through arms-length independent agency. – Conservatives creation in 2008 of the Canada Employment Insurance Financing Board	– previous CPP funding had been tax based pay as you go with provinces having access to funds; – new system was investment-based with pension funds invested in stocks by independent body; – employment insurance reform to create a legislated structure to ensure that EI premiums are dedicated exclusively to the EI program.
Federal-Provincial-Urban/local Fiscal Imbalance	Long term fiscal federalism issue related to real or alleged imbalance of federal versus provincial governments to fund their constitutional responsibilities	– Often raised as issue in various ways; – federal government has richest overall tax base; – Harper Conservative promise and later agreement to solve fiscal imbalance, especially vis a vis Québec – Issue also raised regarding weak fiscal capacities of cities given limited nature of their property tax base in the face of growing demands on an urban-centred Canada, such as for infrastructure.
Trade Policy as Expenditure Regulation: Reigning-in on subsidies	Beginning in Mulroney era new rules and dispute processes (external trade and internal trade) for reducing subsidies by determining whether they constitute an illegal barrier to trade under trade regimes(WTO, NAFTA, and Internal Trade agreement)	– Subsidies by government's (via spending or taxation) could be countervailed through trade law if proven before trade dispute panel that found it to be trade distorting; – governments forced to carefully design or redesign supports for industry that would be more general and economy wide and hence not deemed to be a subsidy.
Measures to Foster a Culture of Reallocation: Continuous Expenditure Review	Chrétien-Martin and Harper era processes for ensuring on regular annual basis that some low priority spending is cut in the name of: expenditure restraint; the shift of spending to other priorities; or the better management of programs.	– Can be considered in some senses as a "mini-version" of program review though much less threatening to departments; – reduces somewhat the assumption that spending will always continue; – but still involves very small amounts of money in any annual reallocation round; – Harper Conservatives have begun a process whereby all expenditures will be reviewed over a four year cycle, about 25 per cent each year.

Table 1
Selected Examples of Budgetary Design and Experimentation: 1980–2009 (*Continued*)

Example	Core Features	Impacts/Implications
Contingency Funds	Chrétien-Martin era practice of specific announced earmarking of an annual "fund" or percentage of the federal budget (e.g. 1 per cent) for unforeseen emergencies or contingencies.	– Earmarked contingency funds seen as actions conducive to prudent transparent budgeting; – Always a question about how big is big enough to handle a contingency such as SARS or the 2008 banking crisis. – Harper Conservatives did not continue this practice.
Regulating the federal "spending power"	Long term post World War II issue concerning the federal government's claimed and practiced right to spend money in the national interest on areas of provincial jurisdiction.	– became a key part of the Meech Lake and Charlottetown agreement debates; – Harper Conservatives have committed themselves to reducing and regulating the federal spending power in the name of open federalism.
Spending Versus "Investment": Still No Capital Budget	Efforts in budgetary discourse to characterize some spending as "investment" in physical, human and natural capital. Also greater use of "endowment" funds lodged in foundations such as the Canada Foundation for Innovation.	– some kinds of spending are easily cast as distributive politics and largesse sprinkled out by governments to curry favor and therefore seen as wasteful or short term in nature; – pressure to distinguish spending that is more long term and investment-like in nature – But in practice governments do not have a real capital budget (for assets that depreciate and need renewal across multiple years/decades; e.g. infrastructure; education; ecosystems).
Budgeting and Debt Reduction: Intergenerational Fiscal Politics	Genuine debate and argument in 1980s and 1990s that debt reduction is undertaken in the name of ensuring that the next generation and "voters" not yet born, will not be burdened by excess spending or self-serving spending of the current dominant generation.	– Big Deficit era from 1980 to 1997 saw the debt reduction intergenerational argument emerge more explicitly; – Issue also emerges in discussion of populous and rich "baby boomer" demographic generation growing old and having to be supported by the taxes of a less populous post-boomer generation. – the question of "investment" spending noted above also resonates in terms on intergenerational issues and obligations;

Budget Watchers and Budgetary Forecasting	Changing range and number of professional competitive "budget watching" institutions.	– The Department of Finance and Bank of Canada and their economists were the dominant analytical power base in 1980; – At present, there are competitive multiple analytical sources of analysis, forecasting and commentary (banks; international agencies; think tanks; financial rating agencies; and academic centers and teams such as those that produce How Ottawa Spends); – Federal forecasts are typically some kind of selected average of private forecasts; – In 2008, the Harper Conservatives created an independent Parliamentary budget officer; – Parliamentary budget and estimates scrutiny is still considered to be quite weak, especially in situations of majority government; – Accidental or contrived arts that lead to budget-time overestimating of deficits (in 1980s and early 1990s) or underestimating surpluses (in 1997–2008 period) so as to look good later when deficits were not as big or surpluses were even greater.

also generated continuous conflict among ministers. Under this system it was no longer the case that the Treasury Board and Department of Finance played the role of the budgetary "bad guys" (they were mainly men!). Ministers themselves had to be good guys and girls one day and bad the next as they sought their share of new money in the fiscal pie. By 1984 both the Liberals and then the Mulroney Tories decided that this kind of direct inter-ministerial conflict was not worth the candle.

Policy and expenditure management integration still remains an unsolved puzzle in many ways. There are under present systems many proposals that have cabinet policy approval but may never get budget approval or enough budgetary resources to do the job properly. But ministers and outside interest groups may be happy just to get some kind of approval, knowing that if they do not get everything or indeed anything, they can always go back to the fiscal trough next year or in several subsequent next years.

Program Review

As deficits grew in the 1980s, reformers knew that budgetary systems not only had to cut spending in a serious way but also to have a mechanism to get at the A-base of federal spending, the cumulative structure of programs created across the decades by successive governments that constituted arguably about 90 to 95 per cent of the federal public purse. One approach advocated was so-called "zero-based" budgeting where advocates argued that all spending should be re-evaluated every year and all should potentially be the object of cancellation and reallocation. This proved to be an utterly unrealistic goal in basic raw political terms, again due to the likelihood of too much internal conflict, a fact first born out by the work of the previously mentioned Nielson Task Force.

The Chrétien-Martin era Program Review that occurred in the 1993 to 1996 period was a one-off major exercise in political will and power to reduce the huge federal deficit and to examine and cut the base of public spending.[27] The review resulted in the 20 per cent plus cuts in federal spending already referred to in our account above of the Chrétien-Martin era. Departments were involved in some aspects of what to cut with some opting to cut program spending but to preserve staffing capacity, and others doing the reverse, or myriad combinations of the two. Revenue-raising through charging fees for some activities also grew.

The review process also contributed to the redesign of particular programs, as well as departmental mandates and structure. It also resulted in some considerable loss of policy and planning capacity in the federal government, in part because such units were politically easy to cut because they had no or little outside political support when serious cuts were on the table.

The Program Review process was judged a political success in the sense that it did help reduce the deficit in a major way but it was also a brutal and often effective process internally in that it was not across the board and PCO and not just Finance managed the process. It was also highly conflictual among interest groups and thus most governments have since been averse to repeating the exercise. As we see further below, however, there are always concerns about the composition of the base of public spending and how to foster a continuous culture of reallocation.

Tax Credits: When Taxing Becomes Spending

Budgetary and fiscal reforms in Canada and elsewhere in the 1980s and 1990s included the greater explicit use of tax credits to redistribute income directly to targeted groups or categories of Canadians via the tax system through direct payments from the tax collection agency (Revenue Canada, later the Canada Revenue Agency). Their greater use is also directly tied to the fact that since 1977 at least 30 per cent of tax filers paid no net income tax. Under tax credits, Canadians could apply for such refundable credit payments at the revenue agency even if they did not have sufficient income to pay taxes and submit their own regular tax return. In short, they could enjoy the privacy of the tax or revenue system process rather than the more invasive processes of a welfare benefit agency process and the latter's means-test procedures.

By the 1980s, the overall social welfare system had evolved into a mixture on the direct spending side of both universal and targeted programs. But the level of actual successful targeting to populations in need was less and less effective. Social groups themselves began to look at ways in which the tax system could be used to deliver targeted benefits and to lobby governments accordingly.[28]

Similar principles were also invoked in areas of business and industrial support on the economic side of the policy equation. As the innovation economy loomed larger in policy discourse and practice, federal policy makers in the 1990s had to devise new ways to get R&D and science and technology incentives in the hands of corporations in Canada.[29] If companies were big multinationals, the Canadian tax system already had tax deductions that served this purpose. But if companies were small (mainly Canadian companies), were engaged in R&D, but did not yet earn profits and pay corporation taxes that allowed them to benefit from "deductions", then refundable tax credits became the fiscal instrument of choice. But in this case the revenue agencies had to hire and develop R&D expertise in order to be able to judge the validity of applications and of the specific expenses being claimed. The tax credits were also to be about "scientific research and experimental research" (SR&ED) the actual title of the program. Thus the program had to be sector-neutral, among industries, and did not become sector specific through the lobbying of sectoral interest groups who thought that "SR&ED" would be different for their sector than for others. There were also dangers that such more particularized definitions would soon render the scheme as a subsidy (see more below) and hence be subject to possible countervailing action by other countries under various free trade agreements.

Costing Political Party Electoral Platforms and Promises

Pressure mounted in the midst of high deficits in the 1980s for Canada's political parties to be more electorally responsible and accountable for their own policy platforms and promises. Party agendas at election time were typically long wish-lists of initiatives with no sense conveyed of general costs or specific costs to taxpayers.

This changed in 1993 when the Liberals produced its Red Book proposals prior to the 1993 election that led to the victory of the Chrétien Liberal Party.[30] Individual items were costed and the range of priorities was kept to a more minimalist list. Thus, a more responsible approach was in evidence but by no means a perfect one. For example, the Liberals had indicated that they would abolish the GST but quickly changed their mind once in power.

The Red Book model also meant that for the next two or three years, the media and other commentators were able to develop a grading or scorecard reporting of the extent to which the agenda was being adopted and also about its costing efficacy.

The Harper Conservatives arguably took this model even further by essentially focusing, as we have seen above, on five core priorities, and making this their political mantra for the 2006 to 2008 period.

Earmarked Funds Accountability and Sustainability: Pensions and Employment Insurance

Public finances always involve complex issues of trust in the funding of programs that are unambiguously long term in nature.[31] A key success story in budgetary trust and innovation was the establishment in 1998 of the Canada Pension Plan (CPP) Investment Board.[32] Created as a Crown Corporation by the Chrétien government and participating provincial governments, its mandate was to invest CPP savings in capital markets. In the 2008 federal Budget, the Harper Conservatives adopted a similar quasi-independent Crown Corporation to manage employment insurance funds.[33]

Concerns had arisen in the mid 1990s about the sustainability of the CPP which was taxpayer funded on a pay as you go basis. Provincial governments under the old system also had full access to CPP funds at preferential interest rates. The old system raised important issues of trust in the ability of current and future governments to maintain a viable pension system.

The essence of the new system introduced by Finance Minister Paul Martin was to move from a pay-as-you-go system to one of partial funding (with higher initial taxpayer contribution rates). The CPP reserve fund was to be invested in a portfolio of market securities to get higher returns. These investments would be controlled and managed by an independent and transparent Investment Board. Provincial governments would henceforth only access to a portion of the reserve at market rates of interest.

As a restructured accountability and investment instrument, the Canada Pension Plan Investment Board quickly produced a much more sustainable system for the national state pension plan. Like any investment fund, it has had varied rates of return on its equity investment but overall the CPP fund has grown much more rapidly than it would have as a pay as you go system. It has established greater trust in a crucial long term issue of public finances that is, like the public debt, intergenerational (see further analysis below) in its very nature.

In 2008, the Harper Conservatives adopted a similar arm's length approach to employment insurance funds. It established a Crown Corporation, the Canada Employment Insurance Financing Board, to provide a legislated basis that would ensure that EI premiums paid by Canadians are dedicated exclusively to the EI program and not to other purposes as had been done in the past.

Federal-Provincial-Territorial-Aboriginal-Urban/local Fiscal Imbalance

Fiscal imbalance in a complex, evolving federation like Canada is a long term issue that takes on many forms.[34] Typically, issues of fiscal capacity and intergovernmental relations centre on real or suggested imbalances in the basic capacities of the federal government and the provinces to fund their constitutional responsibilities. More recently in the history of the Canadian federation, the imbalance question has also been raised with regard to the imbalances in the capacity of territorial and Aboriginal governments as active, responsible governments as well as with the capacity of city and local governments to meet their responsibilities as creatures of the provinces. HOS authors over the years have made notable contributions to studying and assessing most aspects of this expanding field of fiscal federalism and multi-level governance in Canada.

As already indicated in our discussion above of the Harper era, federal-provincial fiscal imbalance was in particular the argument advanced by the Québec Government and by nationalist forces in Québec generally. In their bid to win favor in Québec, the Harper Conservatives promised to address and "solve" the fiscal imbalance. They delivered on this promise but the extent to which the Harper Government can claim it is solved is highly problematical.

The federal government undoubtedly has a richer tax base in comparison with the provinces, Alberta's oil revenues making that province the only possible exception. But the provinces do have the power to tax and spend on their own, and so the question always arises that if some provinces make choices involving higher levels of spending, then they can also tax their own citizens to pay for them. Québec in particular had incurred higher spending and also higher deficits and then made the case for fiscal imbalance. As a province, it was not particularly interested in more federal transfers per se but rather more tax room through the federal government vacating or reducing its levels of taxation in favor of the provinces.

The provinces for their part were also facing a further version of this issue, namely imbalances in the tax capacities of their cities and local governments. Dependent almost entirely on property tax revenues, the cities in particular were arguing that they too needed a new deal from their rich parents, their respective province. Their national lobby groups lobbied the federal government in the last decade, with some success in the Paul Martin Liberal Government in particular, for city agenda funds overall and infrastructure funds in particular.[35]

While there are certainly aspects of the proverbial shell game in the politics of fiscal imbalance there is also, as Gilles Paquet has argued, a very real "failure of governance" if it cannot be addressed periodically in a more considered conceptual way in response to the changing nature of social and economic problems and opportunities.[36]

Trade Policy as Expenditure Regulation: Reining-in on Subsidies

Trade policy issues in the free trade era from the mid-1980s on have certainly been explored in HOS as crucial federal agenda issues, particularly in the Mulroney era when trade was at or near the top of the agenda both regarding the Canada-U.S Free Trade Agreement (CUFTA), the WTO agreement, the follow-up North American Free Trade Agreement (NAFTA) and the mid-1990s Conservative- led Agreement on Internal Trade.

Ordinarily, trade issues are several steps removed from federal spending and fiscal matters but trade policy did serve[37] as a regulatory mechanism to discipline and reign-in on government subsidies. In earlier eras of industrial and regional policy, Canada, as had other countries, spent fairly liberally on initiatives to foster industrial and regional development. But this kind of subsidization (through spending or tax breaks) became a focal point of free trade agreements.

Under various agreements, subsidies by governments could be countervailed through trade law and dispute panel processes if they were proven to be trade distorting in specific defined ways. As a result, the federal government had to end some subsidies that it knew would not meet the new trade criteria, alter and redesign others, and generally watch its subsidy practices much more closely. It also had to watch the actual or potential subsidy practices of other countries, especially those of the U.S., Canada's biggest export market by far. The more those industrial incentives were designed to be sectoral or firm specific (e.g. supporting national or provincial "champions") the higher the probability that they would be countervailable subsidies under trade law. The more those incentives were general and economy-wide, the more they would not be deemed a subsidy.

Measures to Foster a Culture of Reallocation: Continuous Expenditure Review

As indicated in the discussion above of program review, governments have sought ways on an ongoing basis to review public expenditure, particularly the A-base of spending. But the task of continuous reviewing and of creating a culture of budgetary reallocation, as attempted by the Chrétien, Martin and Harper governments, has led to only modest success.[38]

Expenditure review can be considered a partial or mini-version of the 1993–1996 program. It is of course a much less threatening process than the program review exercise was for departments and their program clientele in part because when it was attempted in the latter Chrétien period and under Paul Martin as prime minister, it was occurring in a time of fiscal surpluses and economic plenty. Such processes reduce somewhat the assumption that spending will always continue. But it still has to date involved small amounts of money in any annual review round. As Joanne Kelly's HOS analysis stressed, three distinct budgetary objectives have been involved: fiscal restraint, reprioritization, and the encouragement of better public expenditure management but no review model has been able to achieve these goals equally well.[39]

The newest version of expenditure review under the Harper Conservatives involves a commitment to review all spending over a four-year cycle.[40] This may well make it a more comprehensive process although maintaining political discipline during a now second round of minority government may make this especially difficult. Another wrinkle to the Conservative's approach is that their more comprehensive review process may be behind their decision to not have a formal contingency budget as discussed further below.

Contingency Funds

The federal government always has some kind of capacity for contingency funding in that if emergencies happen, it can seek supplementary estimates. During the Chrétien-Martin era, however, earmarked contingency funds became a key part of formal budgetary announcements. Such more transparent funds were presented as actions to ensure more prudent budgeting.

Estimated as a percentage of the federal budget (1 or 2 per cent) or simply on the basis of recent years practice, there is always the practical question as to whether the contingency proves to be adequate enough to cover the actual costs of an emergency such as SARS or the BSE (mad cow) crises, let alone something like the 2008–09 banking crisis and recession.

There are also questions about what happens to the contingency fund if all of it is not needed. Does it get sprinkled near the end of the fiscal year on last minute political distributive disbursements or is it kept for future contingency use or put into future surpluses. The Harper Conservatives suspicions caused them to not establish a contingency fund (or at least none appears in the 2008 Budget). This was perhaps because of the above noted four year full expenditure review process noted above.

Regulating the Federal "Spending Power"

The debate over the federal spending power cuts across all of the past 30 years and indeed across the decades since the development of the post-World War II welfare state. The "spending power" refers to the federal government's claimed and practiced right to spend money in the national interest on areas of exclusive provincial jurisdiction. It cannot legislate in those areas but it can transfer funds to Canadians through spending. It can also cut back on such spending as happened during the severe federal budget cuts of the mid-1990s. Québec in particular, but also other provinces, has objected to this practice as being both unconstitutional and an unwarranted intervention in provincial fields.

The spending power issue became one of the key issues in the Mulroney era when it formed a part of the ill-fated Meech Lake Accord and the Charlottetown Agreement, both of which went down to political defeat, the latter through a referendum. The Liberal Party federally has regarded the spending power as a powerful pan-Canadian unifying and centralist force. Many Canadians also favorably viewed programs funded in this way by federal money in concert with money from the provinces (many of the programs being conditional grant forms of spending). Ottawa's spending power also became an issue in the Chrétien years, with a policy response of sorts in 1999, in the form of the Social Union Framework Agreement, which placed a largely symbolic, non-enforceable limit on the use of the federal spending power in launching new shared cost programs in provincial fields of responsibility.

As we have seen above in our discussion of the current Harper era, the federal Conservatives have promised to reduce and regulate the spending power in the name of "open federalism." It remains a critical part of the Conservatives' hopes to make further gains in Québec and to construct a much more decentralized form of federalism. Despite this promise, the Conservatives have not given up using the spending power themselves in areas such as higher education and urban infrastructure, not to mention its version of day care recast as a revived form of family allowance on a per child basis.

Spending Versus "Investment": Still No Capital Budget

Governments are always vulnerable to some extent to the charge that they are buying votes or engaging in political/wasteful distributive spending. Cabinet ministers like to spend and like to announce and take credit for such spending as often as can be arranged through media and communications strategies. Because of greater criticism of spending of this kind, budgetary discourse in Budget speeches and debate has shifted somewhat so as to characterize some kinds of spending as "investment" in medium and longer term forms of physical, human, and, more recently "natural" or environmental capital. Governments have also used the concept of endowment funding to arms-length foundations such as the Canada Foundation for Innovation.

Federal spending on infrastructure (buildings, roads, bridges, and internet networks) is increasingly crafted in this way. So are federal expenditures on health care, education, and research and development. In practice, however, governments do not have a real capital budget for long term assets that depreciate and need renewal across multiple years and decades. Money is not put away for these capital investment-type decisions the way it is in the private sector. It is more difficult for the federal government to devise a capital budget, but no federal government has tried very hard either. The proper funding of real investment assets remains a serious weakness in fiscal decision making architecture and debate.

Budgeting and Debt Reduction: Intergenerational Fiscal Politics

As we have seen, deficits (managing and avoiding them) have been a crucial part of the fiscal story captured in *HOS* assessments over the past 30 years. Deeply embedded in budgeting is an even greater philosophical and ethical concern about cumulative national debt. This concern is anchored in intergenerational fiscal politics.

Genuine debate and argument arose during this period about the need to reduce the national debt to ensure that the next generation and "voters" not yet born, are not burdened by excess spending or the self-serving spending of the dominant current generation. The Conservative Party and the earlier Reform and Canadian Alliance parties led this debate but it also found favour in other political parties to some extent as well.

Once federal surpluses emerged in 1997, both the Chrétien-Martin and the Harper regimes were committed to debt reduction as a part of their allocative strategies. As a result, the national debt, as indicated in Appendix 1, has been reduced considerably in the last decade.

Intergenerational budgetary issues also have arisen in discussions of the populous and relatively wealthy baby boomer generation now growing old and exercising grey power but whose needs and desires have to be supported by the taxes of a less populous and more indebted post-boomer generation. Some of the previous section's discussion of "investment" spending also resonates in these terms as intergenerational spending and burden-sharing.

Budget Watchers and Budgetary Forecasting

Last, but not least, in this survey of budgetary design and change is the important issue of budget-watchers and the arts of budgetary forecasting. By the former, I mean simply the array of government, private sector and academic institutions, which engage formally and publicly in the analysis of the federal budget. By the latter, I refer to controversies, which emerge over budgetary forecasting including the tactical or unintended arts of over and underestimating federal deficits and surpluses.

In the early 1980s it would not be inaccurate to say that the Department of Finance and the Bank of Canada were the dominant, almost monopolistic fiscal and macro economic analytical power basis. Bodies such as the Auditor General of Canada and, also until the early 1990s, the federal Economic Council of Canada were budget watchers but with narrowly defined mandates, the former on value for money auditing on Parliament's behalf, and the latter on medium term economic issues and selected budgetary realms which it chose to study.

The situation regarding budget watchers has changed considerably since and very much for the better. At present, there are simply more competitive multiple analytical sources of analysis, forecasting and commentary which are more active, public and aggressive in offering fiscal advice and in assessing fiscal performance. These include banks, financial rating agencies, international agencies such as the OECD and IMF, think tanks (with a range of political perspectives) and academic centers and teams (such as those that produce *How Ottawa Spends*).

The common practice now is for federal forecasts of key economic and budgetary factors and assumptions to be based on some kind of average of private sector and selected think tank forecasts so as to advance the legitimacy of the forecasts. To be sure, areas remain where political arts, accidental or contrived, are criticized. These included opposition party criticism of budget-time overestimating of deficits (in 1980s and early 1990s) or underestimating surpluses (in 1997–2008 period) so as to look good later when deficits were not as big or surpluses were even greater. It is difficult to know if the practice is tactically contrived or not but governments are routinely criticized if opposition parties think that the government is somehow manipulating particular forecast elements to suit its own political purposes.

In 2008, the Harper Conservatives also created an independent Parliamentary budget officer whose early reports have probably turned out to be more independent than they had expected from their new creation.[41] Parliament is, of course, also a budget watcher, both in its debates on the Budget Speech and on its comment and criticism of the annual autumn economic statement of the minister of Finance. The potential for Parliamentary budgetary and estimates scrutiny has been improved somewhat by new systems of reports on departmental spending plans and priorities but overall it is still quite weak and often very partisan in nature, especially during minority government situations as at present.[42]

The more pluralistic budgetary watchdog situation needs perhaps a final cautionary note about the state of the earlier dominant player, the Department of Finance. The above noted debacle over the 27 November 2008 fiscal update statement suggests that the Department of Finance has lost some of its core credibility as the Prime Minister and his political office (PMO) has taken a more active role in budget making. Prime Ministers and ministers of finance (and the latter's department) are always partners to some significant and necessary extent in budgeting but, given the dubious content and tone of the budget update of 2008, the Department of Finance ceded far too much ground.

CONCLUSIONS

This chapter has provided a review of evolving federal budgetary policies and developments as revealed in 30 years of *How Ottawa Spends* (*HOS*) as an annual commentary on Canadian fiscal dynamics, politics and policy. As we have seen, when the publication began in 1980, there were far fewer independent public budgetary watchdogs in the Canadian political-economic system than there are now. Now there are many more voices of commentary but few of these offer the full political-economic breadth of *How Ottawa Spends*, its explorations of detailed policy fields and budgetary realms and its authors' placing of these issues in an appropriate historical context.

The summary review above of macro budgetary policy and outcomes across the past four prime ministerial realms since 1980, reveals both clear patterns of change, failure and relative success, but also continuities across the periods of political party incumbency. Burgeoning deficits were an initial Trudeau Liberal policy creation but the failure to deal with the deficits continued under the Mulroney Conservatives. The Chrétien-Martin Liberals tackled the overriding deficit and ushered in the 10–year era of healthy budgetary surpluses. Both the Chrétien-Martin Liberals and the Harper Conservatives helped reduce the cumulative public debts that Canadians owed and which if not addressed would been a greater burden on future generations. With the exception of the mid to late 1990s, the trajectory of public spending increases across the 30 year period shows one of steady growth by both Liberal and Conservative governments, including social spending.

As we have seen, the 30-year story regarding overriding macro economic policy theories is more subtle but still important. The demise of Keynesian macro economic policy was already evident as the final Trudeau years of the early 1980s played out. Monetarism and a greater focus on low inflation and on securing a manageable non-inflationary rate of unemployment emerged in the Mulroney years. Once surpluses became the norm in the late 1990s, any return to deficits was viewed as the ultimate fiscal political-economic sin. However, following the banking/financial crash of 2008–2009 neo-Keynesian views are reemerging in political and economic discourse as well as in policy and fiscal actions in Canada and abroad.

Our survey of mezzo-level budgetary reform and institutional experimentations shows, not surprisingly, a much more varied picture of success, failure, and indeterminate results. Thus, mid-1980s experiments with a more rational Policy-Expenditure Management System proved to be too conflictual for day-to-day relations among ministers who would rather spend than directly control their colleagues. Program review in the mid 1990s has been judged a success but subsequent efforts to induce a culture of continuous budgetary reallocation have been problematical at best. The logic is sensible but the politics, internally and vis-à-vis outside political interests, is difficult to manage and sustain.

The federal spending and fiscal system overall still grapples very imperfectly with how to factor in and take into account the intergenerational needs and longer term impacts of taxing and spending decisions and policy needs in particular policy fields. The brief discussion above of an array of features, changes and experiments ranging from investment logics and non-existent capital budgets; earmarked arms-length funds/bodies; contingency funds; and even the federal spending power in fiscal federalism are all part of a seemingly never ending set of challenges in the political economy of the public purse.

APPENDIX 1:
1980 TO 2007 DATA ON FEDERAL DEFICITS/SURPLUS, NATIONAL DEBT AND SPENDING

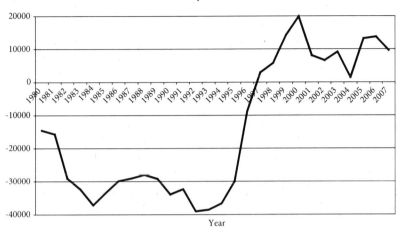

Deficit/Surplus in Millions

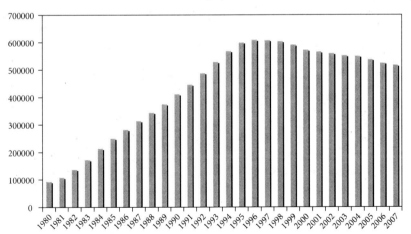

National Debt (net) in Millions

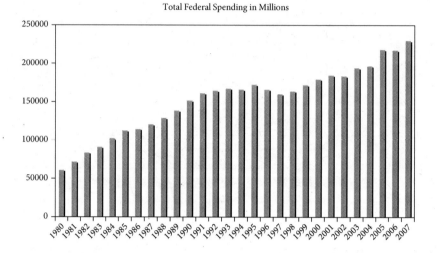

Total Federal Spending in Millions

NOTES

1 Special thanks are due to Allan Maslove, Michael Prince, David Good, Peter Aucoin, and Geoffrey Hale for extremely useful and helpful comments on an earlier draft of this chapter.
2 See Bruce Doern, Allan Maslove, and Michael J. Prince, *Budgeting in Canada: Politics, Economics and Management* (Carleton University Press, 1988), chapter 1. Mezzo-level refers to middle-level changes in budgetary approaches linked to but separate from both macro budgeting and micro-budgets within departments or agencies. For other more recent in-depth analysis of budgetary reforms and political dynamics, see David Good, *The Politics of Public Money* (University of Toronto Press, 2007) and Geoffrey Hale, *The Politics of Taxation* (Broadview Press, 2001).
3 See the first edition, Bruce Doern, ed. *Spending Tax Dollars: Federal Expenditures 1980–1981* (School of Public Administration, Carleton University, 1980), chapter 1.
4 William T. Stanbury and Jane Fulton, "Suasion as a Governing Instrument," in Allan Maslove, ed. *How Ottawa Spends 1984: The New Agenda* (Methuen, 1984), 282–324.
5 See Bruce Doern, Allan Maslove and Michael J. Prince, *Budgeting in Canada: Politics, Economics and Management* (Carleton University Press, 1988).
6 See Bruce Doern, "Liberal Priorities 1982: The Limits of Scheming Virtuously," in Bruce Doern, ed. *How Ottawa Spends Your Tax Dollars: National Policy and Economic Development 1982* (James Lorimer Publishers, 1982) 1–36.
7 David Good, *The Politics of Public Money*, 253–4.
8 Allan Maslove, "Tax Expenditures, Tax Credits and Equity," in Bruce Doern, ed. *How Ottawa Spends Your Tax Dollars: Federal Priorities 1981* (James Lorimer Publishers, 1981) 232–54.

9   See Allan M. Maslove, ed. *How Ottawa Spends 1984: The New Agenda* (James Lorimer Publishers 1984), Chapter 1, and Michael J. Prince, ed. *How Ottawa Spends 1987–1988: Restraining the State* (Methuen, 1987), chapter 1, and Katherine Graham, ed. *How Ottawa Spends 1990–1991: Tracking the Second Agenda* (Carleton University Press, 1990)

10 Donald J. Savoie, "ACOA: Something Old, Something New, Something Borrowed, Something Blue," in Katherine Graham, ed. *How Ottawa Spends 1989–1990: The Buck Stops Where?* (Carleton University Press, 1989) 107–130.

11 V. Seymour Wilson, "What Legacy? The Nielson Task Force Program Review," in Katherine Graham, ed. *How Ottawa Spends 1988–1989: The Conservatives Heading Into the Stretch* (Carleton University Press, 1988) 23–48.

12 Michael J. Prince, ed. *How Ottawa Spends 1987–1988: Restraining the State* (Methuen, 1987), Chapter 1, and David Good, The Politics of Public Money, 261–3.

13 Geoffrey Hale, *The Politics of Taxation* (Broadview Press, 2001), 266.

14 Allan Maslove, "The Goods and Services Tax: Lessons From Tax Reform," in Katherine Graham, ed. *How Ottawa Spends 1990–1991: Tracking the Second Agenda* (Carleton University Press, 1990) 27–48.

15 See Glen Toner, "The Green Plan: From Great Expectations to Eco-Backtracking…to Revitalization?," in Susan Phillips, ed. *How Ottawa Spends 1994–1995: Making Change* (Carleton University Press, 1994) 229–60.

16 See Alain-G. Gagnon, "Everything Old is New Again: Canada, Québec and Constitutional Impasse," in Frances Abele, ed. *How Ottawa Spends 1991–1992: The Politics of Fragmentation* (Carleton University Press, 1991) 63–106; and David C. Hawkes and Marina Devine, "Meech Lake and Elijah Harper: Native-State Relations in the 1990s," in Frances Abele, ed. *How Ottawa Spends 1991–1992: The Politics of Fragmentation* (Carleton University Press, 1991) 33–62.

17 See Susan D. Phillips, ed. *How Ottawa Spends 1994–1995: Making Change* (Carleton University Press, 1994), chapter 1, and Leslie A. Pal, ed, *How Ottawa Spends 1998–1999: Ballancing Act-The Post Deficit Mandate* (Oxford University Press, 1998), chapter 1.

18 See Michael J. Prince and James J. Rice, "Governing through Shifting Social Policy Regimes: Brian Mulroney and Canada's Welfare State," in Raymond Blake, ed. *Transforming the Nation: Canada and Brian Mulroney* (McGill-Queen's University Press, 2007), 164–77.

19 See Geoffrey Hale, "Managing the Fiscal Dividend: the Politics of Selective Activism," in Leslie A. Pal, ed. *How Ottawa Spends 2000–2001: Past Imperfect, Future Tense* (Oxford University Press, 2000) 59–94; and Allan Tupper, "The Chrétien Governments and Higher Education: A Quiet Revolution in Canadian Public Policy," in Bruce Doern, ed. *How Ottawa Spends 2003–2004: Regime Change and Policy Shift* (Oxford University Press, 2003) 105–17; and Bruce Doern and Chris Stoney, eds. *Research and Innovation Policy: Changing Federal-University Relations* (University of Toronto Press, 2009, in press), chapter 1.

20 See Bruce Doern, ed. *How Ottawa Spends 2004–2005: Mandate Change in the Paul Martin Era* (McGill-Queen's University Press, 2004), chapter 1; and James J. Rice and

Michael J. Prince, "Martin's Moment: The Social Policy Agenda of a New Prime Minister," in Doern, ed. *How Ottawa Spends 2004–2005*, 111–30.

21 See Gerald W. Boychuk, "How Ottawa Gambles: Rolling the Dice in Health Care Reform," in Bruce Doern, ed., *How Ottawa Spends 2005–2006: Managing the Minority* (McGill-Queen's University Press, 2005) 41–58.

22 See chapter 1 of this edition of *HOS*, and Bruce Doern, ed. *How Ottawa Spends 2007–2008: The Harper Conservatives-Climate of Change* (McGill-Queen's University Press, 2007), chapter 1.

23 See Peter Graefe and Rachel Laforest, "La Grande Seduction: Wooing Québec," in Bruce Doern, ed. *How Ottawa Spends 2007–2008: The Harper Conservatives-Climate of Change* (McGill-Queen's University Press, 2007), 46–62.

24 See Office of the Parliamentary Budget Officer, *Economic and Fiscal Assessment* (Office of the Parliamentary Budget Officer), 20 November 2008.

25 Department of Finance, *Protecting Canada's Future: Economic and Fiscal Statement* (Department of Finance), 27 November 2008.

26 See Sanford F. Borins, "Ottawa's Expenditure 'Envelopes': Workable Rationality at Last?," in Bruce Doern, ed. *How Ottawa Spends Your Tax Dollars: National Policy and Economic Development 1982* (James Lorimer Publishers, 1982) 63–86; Richard Van Loon, "Ottawa's Expenditure Process: Four Systems in Search of Coordination," in Bruce Doern, ed. *How Ottawa Spends: The Liberals, The Opposition and Federal Priorities* (James Lorimer Publishers, 1983) 93–120; and Doern, Maslove, and Prince, *Budgeting in Canada*, chapter 6.

27 See Gene Swimmer, ed. *How Ottawa Spends 1996–1997: Life Under the Knife* (Carleton University Press, 1996)

28 See James J. Rice, "Restitching the Safety Net: Altering the National Social Security System," in Michael J. Prince, ed. *How Ottawa Spends 1987–1988: Restraining the State* (Methuen, 1987), 211–36.

29 See Bruce Doern, *Institutional Aspects of R&D Tax Incentives: The SR&ED Tax Credit* (Industry Canada, 1995)

30 See Allan Maslove and Kevin Moore, "From Red Books to Blue Books: Repairing Ottawa's Fiscal House," in Gene Swimmer, ed. *How Ottawa Spends 1997–1998 – Seeing Red: A Liberal Report Card* (Carleton University Press, 1997), 23–50.

31 See Eric M. Patashnik, "Ideas, Inheritances, and the Dynamics of Budgetary Change," *Governance*, 12, no. 2 (April 1999), 147–74.

32 Michael J. Prince, "Taking Stock: Governance Practices and Portfolio Performance of the Canada Pension Plan Investment Board," in Bruce Doern, ed. *How Ottawa Spends 2003–2004:Regime Change and Policy Shift* (Oxford University Press, 2003), 134–54.

33 Canada, *The Budget in Brief 2008: Responsible Leadership* (Department of Finance), 6.

34 See Gilles Paquet, "Fiscal Imbalance as Government Failure," in Bruce Doern, ed. *How Ottawa Spends 2004–2005: Mandate Change in the Paul Martin Era* (McGill-Queen's University Press, 2004), 25–45; and Frances Abele and Michael J. Prince,

"A Little Imagination Required: How Ottawa Funds Territorial and Northern Aboriginal Governments," in Allan Maslove, ed. *How Ottawa Spends 2008–2009* (McGill-Queen's University Press), 82–109.
35 See Neil Bradford, "Global Flows and Local Places: The Cities Agenda," in Bruce Doern, ed. *How Ottawa Spends 2004–2005: Mandate Change in the Paul Martin Era* (McGill-Queen's University Press, 2004), 70–88.
36 Paquet, "Fiscal Imbalance"; Abele and Prince, "A Little Imagination Required."
37 See Brian Tomlin and Bruce Doern, "The Free Trade Sequel: Canada-United States Subsidy Negotiations," in Frances Abele, ed. *How Ottawa Spends 1991–1992: The Politics of Fragmentation* (Carleton University Press, 1991), 157–82.
38 See Joanne Kelly, "The Pursuit of an Elusive Ideal: Spending Review and Reallocation Under the Chrétien Government," in Bruce Doern ed. *How Ottawa Spends 2003–2004: Regime Change and Policy Shift*, Oxford University Press, 2003), 118–33, and Evert Lindquist, "How Ottawa Reviews Spending: Moving Beyond Adhocracy?," in Bruce Doern, ed. *How Ottawa Spends 2006–2007: In From the Cold – The Tory Rise and the Liberal Demise* (McGill-Queen's University Press, 2006), 185–207.
39 Kelly, "The Pursuit of an Elusive Ideal," 130–1. For a similar, more historical analysis of the shifting functions of public budgeting, see Michael J. Prince, "Budgetary Trilogies: The Phases of Budget Reform in Canada," in Christopher Dunn, ed. *The Handbook of Canadian Public Administration* (Toronto: Oxford University Press, 2002), 400–12.
40 Canada, *The Budget in Brief 2008: Responsible Leadership* (Department of Finance), 6.
41 See for example, Office of the Parliamentary Budget Officer, *Economic and Fiscal Assessment* (Office of the Parliamentary Budget Officer), 20 November 2008.
42 See John Chenier, Michael Dewing and Jack Stillborn, "Does Parliament Care? Parliamentary Committees and the Estimates," in Bruce Doern, ed. *How Ottawa Spends 2005–2006: Managing the Minority* (McGill-Queen's University Press, 2005), 200–24.

PART ONE

Issues of Structure and Process

3 How Ottawa Assesses Department/Agency Performance: Treasury Board's Management Accountability Framework

EVERT LINDQUIST

INTRODUCTION[1]

In casual conversation, mention of the Treasury Board's Management Accountability Framework (MAF) often leads to strong reactions, ranging from a mix of exasperation, sighs, and cynicism in some quarters, but also, interestingly, a sense of pride, conviction, and momentum in others. Some of the negative reactions are predictable allergic reflexes among many officials and observers who treat the latest management acronym like a dangerous microbe: something to be analyzed, discounted, and quarantined or expelled not long after it has been received. Others have more principled objections based on methodology or its value given the non-trivial costs of collecting, aggregating, and analyzing data, and then debating and reporting on the performance of departments. However, not only has MAF been around for five years, becoming more elaborate and public – "like a snowball gathering mass as it rolls down a hill" in the words of one official – it has gained international attention and become a critical focus and process of the Treasury Board Secretariat, a distinctive and central part of its identity.

The Treasury Board Secretariat's Management Accountability Framework system is an attempt to assemble quantitative and non-quantitative data as indicators (at one point 41 indicators and 134 measures) to gauge the performance of departments and agencies in ten broad areas of management: governance and strategic direction; values and ethics; people; policy and programs; citizen-focused service; risk management; stewardship; accountability; results and performance; and learning, innovation, and change management. MAF reports from TBS seek to provide an overall picture and assessment of the quality of management and key systems of departments and agencies. Its guiding framework is a high-level model of the attributes of a "well-performing" public sector organization, but MAF increasingly has the look and feel of a quality assurance and risk management assessment system.[2] The MAF assessments ultimately inform, along with other information, the performance reviews of deputy ministers and agency heads by the Committee of Senior Officials. They are eventually publicly posted on the TBS web site.

The Management Accountability Framework is often seen as one of the results of the post-2006 *Federal Accountability Act* environment but it was introduced in early 2003 as an effort to gather up, carry forward, articulate and ground the ideas of the Modern Comptrollership and Results for Canadians initiatives of the late 1990s and early 2000s. Moreover, it can be traced back to the early 1990s on the Shared Management Agenda launched by then Treasury Board Secretary, Ian Clark, even if it was less robust and public. Indeed, the current MAF regime is the outcome of a longer search and struggle by the Treasury Board Secretariat to monitor and challenge departments and agencies in areas other than the budget and specific Treasury Board policies, a process that took on particular resonance in the new accountability and control environment. It is also a telling case study on how long it takes to move from rhetoric to capabilities, data, and procedures in a complex organizational system like the Government of Canada.

This chapter reflects on these developments. It is not a systematic study of the validity of the Management Accountability Framework, its methodology, indicators, and effect on departments and agencies or on the compensation of executives – an external evaluation commissioned by TBS will take on this task. Rather, this chapter seeks to provide background and perspective on MAF's emergence and how it has generally evolved over the last five years. The first section provides an overview of the origins, precursors, and general architecture of MAF. The second section describes in more detail the specifics and reporting on MAF, while the third section provides observations on reporting based on a review of MAF assessments from the 2005 and 2006 cycles for the Canada School of Public Service, Canadian Heritage, Environment Canada, Western Economic Development Canada, and Treasury Board of Canada Secretariat (the 2007 assessments had not yet been released at the time of writing). The fourth section steps back to identify or reflect on several issues associated with the MAF regime. The paper concludes with observations on the implications of MAF for TBS, managing reform more generally in the Canadian Public Service, and the directions that a renewed MAF might move.

MAF: ANTECEDENTS AND DESIGN CONSIDERATIONS

The advent of the Management Accountability Framework is often associated with the 2006 *Federal Accountability Act*, a response and arguably an over-reaction to instances of mismanagement of public programs and funding such as the Sponsorship affair, the implementation of the federal gun registry, the activities of the Privacy Commissioner, and others in the early 2000s. However, it is best seen as a small phoenix rising from the embers of previous initiatives, given life by some entrepreneurial and committed public servants, and, in a fundamentally different climate in the mid-2000s, quickly gathering momentum, critical mass, and meaning. What follows is a high-level sketch of the origins, antecedents, and expectations of the Management Accountability Framework as well as markers for success.

The Management Accountability Framework was announced in 2003 by the Treasury Board of Canada. It was connected to and grew out of the government-wide Modern Comptrollership Initiative (MCI), which was nearing the end of its second three-year phase. Indeed, to evaluate what MAF ultimately evolved into, as well as its implications for the Treasury Board Secretariat and government more generally, we must have an appreciation of the aspirations behind MCI, a response to the recommendations of the Independent Review Panel on the Modernization of Comptrollership in the Government of Canada, which was set in motion by Peter Harder in 1996, then Secretary to the Treasury Board of Canada, as part of post-Program Review positioning of TBS (the Clerk had also set in motion the Deputy Minister Task Forces on several challenges confronting the Public Service of Canada).

The report of the Independent Review Panel was wide-ranging, but its most important feature for our purposes was its vision:

The Panel believes modern comptrollership is about ensuring that: management decision making has the benefit of rigorous, complete and integrated financial and non-financial, historical and prospective performance information as well appropriate advice, analysis and interpretation of this information; the oversight, accountability and public reporting responsibilities of elected officials are supported by rigorous, complete and integrated financial and nonfinancial performance information; a mature risk management environment is created and sustained; control systems are appropriate to management needs and risks; [and] ethics, ethical practices and values (beyond a focus on legal compliance) are in place.[3]

Although the lengthy report discusses many different perspectives on comptrollership, as well as the roles and responsibilities of various actors in the system, it was surprisingly short on specifics about what a new regime would look like, as well as concrete steps for moving forward. But the vision it articulated is useful for assessing what today's MAF is and isn't. The vision for the Government of Canada could be interpreted as having simply put forth an audit or control model of government, but it was broader and more ambitious than that: not only was it calling for high-quality information for financial management, control and accountability, it was arguing for a system of quality assurance for ministers and executives alike, and providing better information for decision making. Indeed, the availability, quality, and intelligent use of information were core themes, ones that would persist in the years to come.

Though not always proceeding under "comptrollership", there have since been multiple initiatives in TBS over the last decade to build new processes and capabilities as well as vertically and horizontally integrated information systems, linking not only financial data on programs and organizations, but also strategic objectives, results, performance indicators, and issue areas. One, of course, was the Modern Comptrollership Initiative (MCI), but others included quality management principles, business planning,[4] reform of the estimates, the Treasury Board's designation as a "management board", the Results for Canadians vision,[5] moving the Planning, Reporting and Activity Structure (PRAS) towards a hierarchical, activity-based architecture linking estimates to results areas, and improvements to Expenditure Management Information Systems (EMIS), the expenditure data management system for tracking booked and new initiatives. Perhaps the least well-known initiative, but one introducing ideas that would eventually shape much of the form and content of the high-level MAF schematic, emerged out of TBS' Quality Services Initiative in 1997 and sought to articulate a list of "quality" criteria with the National Quality Institute for developing effective public sector organizations.[6]

Following receipt of the Independent Review Panel's report, and consistent with its recommendations, the Treasury Board announced in 1998 the first three-year phase of the Modern Comptrollership Initiative. This involved working with thirteen pilot departments and two agencies to build awareness, identify capabilities and gaps, develop benchmarks and priorities, and arrive at standards and practices for control, performance information, risk management, procurement, asset and real property management, etc. The second phase, another three-year initiative announced in mid-2001, expanded the reach of the initiative to include 88 departments and agencies, include the full array of Treasury Board policies affecting these entities, and aimed to ensure greater support from TBS with more centers of expertise.[7] As this second phase was winding down TBS started thinking about whether to move into a third phase (a "sustaining" phase as originally envisioned by the Independent Review Panel), wind down the MCI, or start something new.

Here it is useful to recall not only the breadth of Treasury Board oversight and interests, but also the number of initiatives that had been set in motion since the mid-1990s. These included, but were not limited to, citizen-centred service delivery, Government On-Line, modern comptrollership, business planning, various financial management initiatives such as adopting full accrual accounting, improved reporting to Parliament, program integrity, human resource modernization, promoting values and ethics, risk management, rationalizing Treasury Board policies, etc. Further complicating matters was the fact that "meta-initiatives" like Modern Comptrollership and *Results for Canadians* encompassed, or were said to inspire, more specific initiatives. The number and overlap among the initiatives was confusing – we could reach back further in time, at a finer grain, and identify many more – and it was difficult to ascertain where one began and another ended. This confusion came on top of the difficulty of coordinating policies, information requests, approvals, and advice to specific departments and agencies from the different parts of TBS and the Public Service Human Resources Management Agency of Canada (now the Canada Public Service Agency).

TBS strategists, of course, were well aware of this situation and worried about launching another initiative. Indeed, it was widely perceived that TBS had lost credibility and standing in comparison to the Department of Finance and Privy Council Office, in part because flexibilities granted to departments and agencies over budget and human resource management meant it had less veto and design influence on programs. There was an ongoing search to streamline submissions and rationalize its "policy suite." By the mid-1990s, it was not a central player in priority-setting and resource allocation and had considerable difficulty assembling information on government-wide initiatives. Governments only episodically undertook program reviews, and, when they did, it was an open question as to whether TBS would be given lead responsibility for coordinating them.[8] Moreover, by the early 2000s, the pressure on the government and TBS to improve the quality of management and control systems of departments and agencies, as well as the centre of government, greatly increased as a result of controversies over the HRDC grants and contributions program, the Sponsorship program, and implementing the firearm registry.[9]

For these reasons the progenitors of the Management Accountability Framework regime sought to develop a comprehensive system that would attempt to gauge and report on the quality of management of departments and agencies, and encourage improvement every year. Learning from the Modern Comptrollership and other initiatives, its designers understood that it would be critical to offer coherence to departments and agencies, as well as other users of the information, given the plethora of initiatives and expectations emanating from the centre – hence the early emphasis on developing a comprehensive "framework." Moreover, the initiative could not work unless there were sufficient incentives to collect and share data, and unless TBS could identify credible measures of performance. Building such a system would be a multi-year effort, again starting with a smaller set of departments and agencies, and a limited number of indicators.

For officials with some institutional memory, there were lessons to be learned from the early 1990s when Ian Clark, as secretary to the Treasury Board, introduced the Shared Management Agenda (SMA), underpinned by Departmental Management Assessments (DMAs). In the midst of great flux in management initiatives in the late 1980s and very early 1990s flowing from the Increased Ministerial Authority and Accountability initiative, Public Service 2000, the shift to operating budgets, special operating agencies, employment equity, and ongoing expenditure cuts – to name only a few – Clark sought to engage deputy ministers in a more collaborative manner. This included using advisory councils and undertaking department "management assessments" based on information drawn from across TBS and the Office of the Comptroller General and their respective policy domains (then TBS included what would eventually become the Canada Public Service Agency). This information was assembled and distilled by an analyst in the Management Initiatives group with modest support, and used as a basis for a short two or three page note to inform bilateral meetings between the secretary and deputy ministers and agency heads to identify mutual management priorities. The DMAs were also used by the Committee of Senior Officials in the performance review of these top executives.[10]

The SMA/DMA process was side-swiped by the June 1993 restructuring of the federal public service, the 1994 Program Review, and the departure of Clark to the International Monetary Fund. This experience, however distant, informed the design of MAF, whose progenitors sought a more robust and sustainable process (the same could be said of business planning a few years later[11]). It also serves as a useful comparison since MAF would rely on more systematic collection of data, allow for more challenge on TBS assessments, explicitly inform evaluations of deputy ministers, get posted for public consumption, and require substantially greater time and resources to operate.

THE MAF REGIME: ORIGINS, CYCLE, ASSESSMENTS

To the extent that MAF has received attention beyond Treasury Board of Canada press releases and call letters, debate has focused on the reporting burden it has created as part of a larger concern about the "web of rules" and the growing list of accountabilities that always seem to fall on deputy ministers and agency heads. But this presumes that MAF was something "done" to these leaders and their organizations, another burdensome and useless reporting requirement, and not something on which they were consulted and may have shaped, and perhaps found useful for tracking progress and choosing where to make investments of scare leadership time to promote organizational development. It also does not take into account the extent to which TBS relies on information from departments and agencies as the basis for the assessments. This section seeks to describe how MAF was designed and rolled out over time. It offers an overview of the reporting cycle and of the style of public reporting.

Developing MAF: From MCI to MAF in a Fertile Environment

As early as 2002, staff responsible for the Comptrollership initiative were acutely aware that the second three-year phase was winding down, and began to consider what the legacy would be, or an equivalent to the third phase originally envisioned by the Independent Review Panel, where consolidation, cultural change, and improvements would occur. There was a view that Modern Comptrollership as a "brand" had run its course, but there was still much work to be done, and, for this to happen, there had to be deputy minister engagement. Moreover, there would not nearly be the same level of funding, so a creative approach was in order.

Several other factors were at play. First, there were advocates for a renewed initiative on comptrollership, emphasizing financial management and related systems. Second, other TBS executives and staff in the Strategic Policy and Planning Division were keen to broaden the comptrollership agenda to include a more holistic view of management based on notions of quality management principles and organizational excellence, and actively sought out alternative comprehensive models for public sector organizations.[12] Third, still others worried about the litany of management improvement initiatives – and MCI was about to join the junk heap of acronyms – and whether anyone could possibly keep track, let alone ensure that they had traction in departments and agencies. Fourth, there persisted great concern inside and outside TBS about the range of Treasury Board policies, and its inability to see departments and agencies holistically; TBS had fragmented perspectives because of myriad policy-driven organizational stovepipes.[13]

The initiative gathered steam with the arrival of Jim Judd as secretary, an experienced deputy minister, who was losing patience with management initiatives and sought more clarity for departments and agencies. He challenged his staff to develop something that would address the "questions that keep deputy ministers up at night" and that would offer coherence, clearer expectations, and be useful to deputy ministers (see Table 1).[14] This inspired staff to develop a list of questions and a ten-part framework that covered the waterfront of management of departments. After positive reactions from the secretary, the TBS Executive Committee, the clerk, and the Coordinating Committee of Deputy Ministers (CCDM) in late 2002 and early 2003, consultations were held in Spring 2003 with actors around the system and outside, including deputy ministers, the Committee of Senior Officials, Treasury Board Secretariat Advisory Council, the Public Policy Forum, the Standing Committee on Government Operations and Estimates, Office of the Auditor General, and several experts and academics.

The result was the Management Accountability Framework and "the chart," comprised of ten elements (see figure 1). Four "outside" elements

Table 1
Ten Expectations for Deputy Ministers as Questions[15]

As Deputy Minister, do I...
• Exemplify Public Service values and ethics?
• Enforce organizational coherence and alignment to outcomes?
• Require and use performance information?
• Foster organizational confidence in the face of inevitable change?
• Secure adequate analytic capacity?
• Define the corporate context for managing risk?
• Develop the workforce/workplace needed by the department and Public Service of Canada?
• Establish a comprehensive and comprehensible system of internal controls?
• Consider the citizen's perspective first?
• Manage accountabilities systematically?

provided the strategic context, underpinnings and directions for "good management" and included: strategic governance and strategic direction, public service values, focusing on results and performance, and capacity for learning, innovation and change. The six "inside" elements included policy and programs, citizen-focused service, people, risk, stewardship, and accountability. This framework could be used at several levels: general framework with expectations in each of the broad areas; identification of specific management indicators or what eventually would be called "areas of management"; and, finally, specific measures or lines of evidence (which ranged from process, practices and codes, outputs, and outcomes) to show the extent of progress in those more specific areas.

The irony here, of course, is that while MAF was designed and tailored for leaders, it was not about evaluating leadership *per se*. Rather, the focus was on the capabilities, values, perspectives, and systems that leaders ought to cultivate for their organizations in light of external demands and government priorities. One goal was to encourage policy-oriented or less managerially-focused deputy ministers to take a comprehensive look at their department's capabilities and needs, and, as leaders, identify priorities for action. The framework would put these choices in perspective and provide a checklist of additional management issues to take up in the future.

Interest in MAF grew in 2003 as a result of high-profile instances of mismanagement in the Canadian government, the struggle for the leadership of the Liberal government, and efforts to regain public credibility in managing government and its operations. There was considerable incentive for the government to promote integrity, more strategic review of programs, and more vigilance of the quality of management of government departments and agencies. The expectations associated with MAF were quickly connected to the renewed *Guide for Deputy Ministers* and the development of other TBS documents.[16]

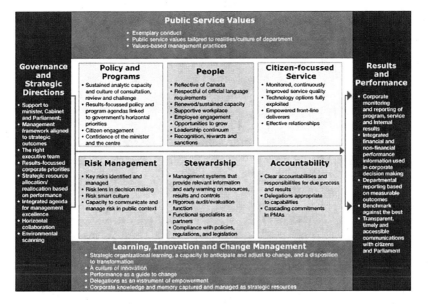

Figure 1
The Management Accountability Framework

MAF began its life in a consultative and emergent manner, in part because it was meant as a tool *for* deputy ministers and their executive teams. While the ten expectations and indicators (later re-dubbed as "areas of management") were intended to be relatively durable, the more specific measures were "likely to evolve as conditions, priorities and government-wide targets change." TBS might rate the performance of departments and agencies in specific areas, but it could not set targets; that could only be done following negotiations between a deputy minister and the Secretary.[17] The first round of MAF for 2003–04 not only included TBS assessments but also self-assessment by 27 departments and agencies using the framework and the vetting of sixty measures proposed by TBS (27 were endorsed).

MAF soon expanded its scope and found itself riding a wave of interest. The number of participating departments and agencies doubled to 50 in Round II, and then to 100 in Round III. One third of the smaller agencies are reviewed each year, so that the rolling total of MAF assessments is close to sixty each year. Early on departments and agencies were critical of the information and indicators utilized by TBS staff. During the 2005–06 the Round III MAF assessments grew to embrace 41 areas of management, drawing on 134 lines of evidence, a startling increase. TBS pared back the number of measures in the next round, but the assessments were then considered sufficiently robust to inform the performance reviews of deputy ministers and agency heads,[18] and there was mounting demand for public release of the MAF assessments. There was interest at the centre of government about what MAF could say about the overall state of management across government in different management areas, system-wide issues, and directions for investments. This could be done by showing what proportion of departments and agencies fell into different quartiles.

TBS circulated a template for the first two rounds, and soon developed a relational database for MAF, which linked current to previous assessments. This was carried an important step further in Round IV (2006–07) when the database was broadened to link to data and reports held elsewhere by TBS including internal audits, evaluations, reports from the Office of the Auditor General, etc. Round V was facilitated by a new platform in the form of the TBS MAF Web Portal. Organized around different elements of MAF, it allowed departments and agency leads to upload files to TBS to inform assessments, to ask questions and receive updates from TBS counterparts, to comment on assessments, and to minimize the amount of e-mail swirling in the system. The portal had the potential to be "open" year-round, but, to economize on time and create focus for TB analysts and department counterparts alike, it was thought best to foster a rhythm to the year and have the portal live for select periods.

Overview of the MAF Process

The cycle begins in late August with deputy ministers notified by the MAF Directorate of the plans for the next round and seeking the names of the department or agency contact who TBS will deal with. At this time the TBS "leads" in different areas settle on the final requirements for MAF reporting. This is followed with call letters and other information in September from TBS to explain what areas of management and lines of evidence will be required for the next round, and what changes are in order.[19] The MAF web portal is activated in early October, the primary vehicle for most transactions between TBS and departments in this process.

The number of areas of management over the first five rounds were 27, 31 41, 32, and 21, respectively. There was a high of 134 lines of evidence in Round III in support of the 41 areas, but in response to internal and external feedback, the number was lowered to 70 in Round V.[20] Table 2 below provides a recent list of the areas of management.

Departments and agencies are asked to submit their information to the MAF Directorate by November 1st, giving them over two months to reply; this also provides time for TBS to train new staff, deepen their understanding on requirements in particular areas, or to encourage them to make adjustments based on feedback from departments and agencies on the previous round. Previously, TBS would post in early January the first draft of its comprehensive report and summary, giving departments and agencies three weeks to reply. Factoring in

Table 2
Areas of Management (Indicators)

1. Values and Ethics	12. Information Management
2. Corporate Performance Framework	13. Information Technology
3. Corporate Management Structure	14. Asset Management
4. Extra-Organizational Contribution	15. Project Management
5. Quality of Analysis	16. Procurement
6. Evaluation	17. Financial Management and Control
7. Performance Reporting to Parliament	18. Internal Audit
8. Managing Organizational Change	19. Security and Business Continuity
9. Risk Management	20. Citizen-Focused Service
10. Workplace	21. Alignment of Accountability Instruments
11. Workforce	

comments and other information, TBS then would post the second draft of its comprehensive assessment by February 28th for additional comment.

Staff from the respective policy centres first review the documentation or lines of evidence from departments. These reviews are, in turn, vetted by the program sector analysts, more senior staff in the sectors, and then the area-of-management leads. With the receipt of the second set of comments from departments and agencies, the area-of-management leads work with program sector analysts, and more senior staff, to sift through the materials, check for consistency in ratings in areas across departments, and make final determinations. Each department is given commentary and a rating in each area of management on a four-level scale (see below).

From October to early March analysts deal with departments through the web portal (although there are some black-out periods to allow for concentration on both sides), and from January through March, the Program Sector assistant secretaries are available to consult with department counterparts. In late March the program analysts prepare the context page for each report (see below), which goes through another internal vetting process with the Policy Centre and Program assistant secretaries. In early April, deputy ministers receive the streamlined report and a comprehensive version if desired, followed by bilateral meetings in the weeks that follow. The late spring months are used for post-mortems and planning for the next round.

In the end, the MAF Assessments are TBS documents, representing the informed view of executives and analysts based on information received and comparisons with practices and indicators from other departments and agencies. TBS may adjust perspectives in response to additional information supplied by departments and agencies, but the process has never been cast as a negotiation. One executive noted that TBS staff would "not give credit for effort, only accomplishment." As is the case with reports from the auditor general, some departments and agencies write responses to the final MAF reports and post them on their web sites.

This brief account suggests that a significant number of TBS staff assist in preparing MAF assessments. There is a dedicated unit for this purpose: in November 2008 there were 9 full-time staff working in MAF Development and Implementation group.[21] It has been said that program analysts spend about a third of their time working on MAF-related transactions, and the time of Program Sector assistant secretaries, the Priorities and Planning Sector which houses the MAF directorate, and other parts of TBS, OCG and CPSA which supply information, should also get factored in. None of this includes the time and effort of staff in the departments and agencies across the government.

What Are the Assessments Like?

The 2005 (Round III) and 2006 (Round IV) assessments were posted on the TBS web site respectively in May 2007 and March 2008. The Round V assessments had not yet been released by early February 2009, with slippage attributed to the October 14th, 2008 federal election and the subsequent proroguing of Parliament. I did not have the time, nor was there sufficient space here, to undertake a comprehensive and detailed review of all MAF assessments. However, I reviewed the 2005 and 2006 assessments for the Canada School of Public Service, the Department of Canadian Heritage, Environment Canada, Western Economic Diversification Canada, and the Treasury Board of Canada Secretariat in order to get some diversity in terms of their scale and experience with MAF. Rather than provide an account of the assessments for each department, I offer an overview of the nature of the documents and the messages they seem to send. It is important to bear in mind that the 2005 indicators were far more extensive than in subsequent years, but I have included the list at the end of this chapter to give the reader a sense of the type and range of information that can be drawn on (see Appendix).

MAF assessments are substantial documents: typically each 2005 departmental or agency assessment was over 20 pages in length once pulled off the TBS web site, and the 2006 assessments were well over 30 pages each. In many ways they read like the detailed report card on a child in grade school that most parents never receive, with substantial comments on the child's strengths and weaknesses in different areas, with reference to observations and other evidence used to make the assessment. Each report begins with a summary that provides highlights on the positive and negative elements contained in the assessment, with some effort to provide context based on previous assessments and other challenges, such as new mandates or restructuring. Some acknowledge progress made on priorities identified in the previous year. The assessments do not provide a summary of the key program responsibilities or resources for the department. Commentary is provided in each of the "elements" or "areas of management," with specific comments keyed to the lines of evidence relied on. Although the specific evidence is not itemized (presumably this sits in the MAF Portal server), there are frequent references to specific initiatives and results from which the conclusions are drawn.

An interesting feature of the assessments is how often indicators of progress include initiatives, agreements, delegations, codes, orientations, courses, training, committees, advisory boards, horizontal collaboration, and measurement and reporting systems. On the other hand, many indicators are based on surveys, timeliness and quality of TB submissions (as well as responsiveness to TB comments), Public Accounts plates, and Question Period cards, whether the Management, Resources, and Results Structure (MRRS) and Program Activity Architecture (PAA) development and reporting is complete and performance indicators supplied, the linkage of Reports on Plans and Priorities (RPPs) and Departmental Performance Reports (RPPs), the completion of various TB reporting requirement, demographic information, and results from the Public Service Employee Survey or other surveys conducted by departments. There are interesting assessments of policy frameworks and capabilities. Particular attention is paid to financial and information systems, internal audit, evaluation, procurement, contract management, transfer payments, risk and legal management, and asset management – a key question revolves around whether a department works within budget and existing authorities, implements projects in a timely way, and integrates business planning with HR planning. There is finer-grained detail supplied about performance. However, more often than not, this evidence is not shared – the MAF assessors seem more interested in whether departments have a system to collect, access, and share such information, and whether key policies have been shared with appropriate staff. Passing references are made to certain initiatives or files where gaps in information or difficulties were experienced. Many observations focus on how the departments progress on implementing government-wide initiatives.

Careful reading of the documents shows that the assessors have a keen sense of the trajectory of the department (turning around, consolidating, growing, etc.) in the form of observations dispersed throughout the assessments, but the assessments do not contain a detailed situation analysis of the state and challenges confronting the organization at the beginning of the period under assessment. Often the assessment suggests actions that the department could take to remedy a gap or improve further, and often flags what plans the department has articulated or initiatives it has set in motion, but there is little comment on their quality or potential. In some areas the department is not rated (that is, systematically reviewed and compared with other departments) because a new area of management and/or line of evidence has been identified by TBS, but evidence can be supplied by departments and agencies if they so choose. If departments want to reply or contextualize the MAF assessment, they post a "management response" on their home web site (which are similar in tone to responses to audits by the auditor general), which are sometimes linked below the assessments on the MAF web site.

Table 3
MAF Rating Scale

Attention Required	Opportunity for Improvement	Acceptable	Strong
Little corporate attention. Gathers little information regarding its conditions. Little effort to understand vulnerability. Little done about key issues.	Aware of its deficiencies and taking steps to redress. Plans/activities underway and accountabilities may be assigned. Corporate engagement not yet sustained.	Robust corporate engagement. Sound management structure in place. Compliant with TB policies. Demonstrated accountability.	Continuous learning and improvement to achieve highest standards. Sets best practices. Derives greatest value from its management. Is a leader and an example to others.

Adapted from "Management Accountability (MAF)," PPX Presentation, May 2008, p.10

Generally, there seemed to be more consistency in format across the 2006 assessments, which had more substantial and front-end summaries that provided context and more parsimoniously reported on data and key findings. There was often more information available on how departments comparatively rated across the system in different areas. It did not appear that any of the departments quickly moved up the assessment scales in one year, so the "grading" appeared consistent and firm. No matter how well a department is performing, the assessments give deputy ministers and their executive teams a lot to think about, and plenty of scope and ideas for further improvement. There are similarities to undertaking performance reviews of scholars in university departments, where all could be productive and performing reasonably well in the face of demands, but the notion of what is "acceptable" shifts because all colleagues could be productive and improving, thus setting the collective bar higher over time. Another comparison might be with 360-degree evaluations of leaders: there are always gaps between personalities, the strategic priorities animating specific assignments, and the culture and capabilities of specific organizations. Indeed, different gaps loom larger given the mandate and responsibilities of different departments and agencies (e.g., asset management is critically important for the Department of Canadian Heritage).

One deputy minister suggested that his colleagues felt that the MAF framework was intuitive, provided a framework and tool for reviewing their leadership and setting priorities and, presumably, engaging their executive teams.[22] There can be no doubt that, however daunting and comprehensive the MAF assessments, they should have that effect on deputy ministers and executive teams. However, the assessments do not evince any sense of whether TBS expectations about the prospects for progress in any area of management (let alone across all areas) are reasonable, particularly given the resources and other challenges a department has – at base, the assessments provide a clear-eyed view of where the organization stands. Moreover, TBS has found a means for engaging departments and agencies on an "organization-to-organization" basis – not by exercising the challenge function associated with the budget process, but by assessing organizational capabilities and performance.[23]

THE MAF REGIME: SOME ISSUES TO CONSIDER

The progenitors and advocates of MAF have always been aware of the trade-offs in designing and implementing the assessment system, and presumed that it would evolve significantly over time. Below we consider several issues associated with MAF, which are best posed as a series of questions: What is MAF seeking to achieve? Do MAF assessment ratings and scores seem more concrete than they actually are? Do the MAF assessments assess the quality of leadership of deputy ministers? Are the benefits of undertaking MAF assessments worth the costs, and do we understand these properly? Are MAF advocates realistic about the influence of assessment findings in other decision-making processes?

What are the "operative" goals for MAF?

Organization theory tells us to look beyond the official or espoused goals of systems, and to identify the "operative" goals to see what really animates them.[24] In the case of MAF it has long been recognized that learning and oversight are both desirable goals, but less appreciated are the goals of fostering change and maintaining appearances in a difficult environment.

- *Learning vs. oversight?* Early on, TBS strategists identified a key tension between different broad means for promoting better managerial performance – a tension to this day. In 2006, a TBS executive suggested there were two approaches. One was the broadening the horizons of leaders and fostering dialogue on organizational development in departments. In this view, promoting reflection and change with a "code of excellence" approach might lead to franker exchange, more executive engagement, and shared agendas between departments/agencies and TBS, but less comparability and accessibility. Indeed, TBS would prefer that the MAF document be seen less as a reporting requirement and instead become "owned" by deputy ministers and department executive teams.[25] The other goal was oversight, which would have more "requirements" in the form of monitoring, reporting, and ratings. The more public and aggressive the monitoring, the more likely departments would see MAF as an "instrument of oversight." Improving oversight would require investing in more and better measures to increase confidence in the findings, but this might reduce genuine executive engagement. By 2006, the executive suggested that TBS had opted for a balanced approach,[26] but a year later another TBS official suggested it was "evolving into an oversight tool in support of Treasury Board Ministers."[27] Clark and Swain suggest the cost of moving too far in this direction is that many deputy ministers will create sufficient capability to credibly feed reporting requirements, but effectively "quarantine" it from strategic dialogue and decision-making in departments focused on dealing with pressing challenges.[28]

- *Change or appearances?* Both the learning and oversight orientations seek to foster change in the management of departments and agencies. However, there are real concerns that MAF has focused on paper-pushing, informed largely by information supplied by departments and agencies. In this view, TBS expends relatively little effort gauging the actual quality of practice "in" departments and agencies, and does not provide sufficient expertise and support to help departments and agencies for dealing to close gaps and change. This implies that MAF could be used a tool to evaluate the depth of expertise and knowledge of TBS and cognate central agencies in each assessment area in the form of centres of expertise. Indeed, if TBS has not developed the capability to advise and assist with concrete change in departments and agencies across the waterfront of management, and MAF reporting relies heavily on information from departments (as opposed to site visits and audits), then essentially we have a paper-based process that "looks" like it fosters learning and change when it may not do much of either. As one colleague observed, "there is reason to be concerned for delineating the appearance of reporting, oversight and assessment and accountability and an actually fulsome effort",[29] and another wrote that "without audit capabilities, this approach runs the risk of becoming a massive paper exercise."[30] While not an explicit goal, the celebration and choice of MAF methodology combine can be seen as providing the *appearance* of a substantial accountability system. Organization theorists might suggest that MAF functions as an elaborate rationalized myth and ceremony, one that does not materially change what transpires inside departments and agencies, but does convince governments and the public that meaningful oversight is occurring.[31]

MAF has become a poster child for accountability and a tool for oversight, but because of its reliance on information from the very entities it seeks to monitor (see below), and uneven ability to provide advice and support on change, there seems a gap between appearances and reality. Presuming that more accountability is desirable, this may require a significant investment in centre-of-excellence capabilities and oversight methodologies.

Validity, measurement, scoring

Undertaking a proper assessment of the validity of MAF methodology could be the subject of a separate paper, and would require full access to internal documents specifying the rationale for the indicators chosen for each, as well as the precise manner in which measurements or judgments were made.[32] Such a study would also delve into whether and how "scoring" proceeds on the basis of the findings. None of this information is available on the TBS web site, and thus it is difficult to evaluate the basis on which assessments are made, except at the most general level. What follows are some observations based on a review of public information.[33]

- *Reporting vs. effectiveness.* Although there are some examples of independent measures from the employee survey, workforce profiles, and compliance with submissions, etc., a significant proportion of the "lines of evidence" for areas of management rely on the existence of official positions to lead or coordinate a function, the presence of strategic/risk management plans or policies on file, whether events or training have taken place, etc. *However, such indicators do not constitute evidence about whether filled positions, completed plans and policies, or interventions had an impact on the quality of decisions and practice, and the competence and culture of departments and agencies* – the presumption is that if those boxes are ticked, the better the quality of management and systems, and the more likely higher quality management practice occurs. However, as one reviewer of this paper noted, the results may simply indicate that departments and agencies are better at "taking the test" and no improvement of management can be presumed.
- *Qualitative analysis and judgment.* Many lines of evidence are comprised of qualitative interpretation of the quality of documents, advice, frameworks, etc., and thus rely heavily on judgment of analysts, executives, and leads responsible for certain lines of evidence. Qualitative analysis, of course, is entirely legitimate and often the only way to assess some management functions, but it should be systematic and described in parallel to quantitative indicators.
- *Scoring and aggregation.* The effort to achieve more consistency in assessment across departments is laudable, but MAF's public reporting does not indicate, for example, how many departments and agencies in aggregate fall into each category of the rating scale (strong, acceptable, opportunity for improvement, attention required) for each assessment area. While MAF has not emulated the UK's league table approach for internal purposes, and there is no evidence of such figures appearing on the TBS web site, one hears that departments are given numeric scores across the areas of management based on the rating scales. These are summarized to show areas of relative strength and weakness, and, in turn, are aggregated into an overall score (if TBS does not do this, an enterprising analyst inside or outside government would do it anyhow). This would make the MAF assessments seem more concrete and robust than warranted, particularly given the

complex contexts in which departments perform. It presumes equal confidence in the lines of evidence for each area of management and that each area of assessment should be equally weighted. Given that MAF assessment introductions note how many areas have led to improved or decreased ratings, one could imagine word would spread around the system about which department was "most improved" or the opposite.[34]

- *Confidence vs. parsimony.* Streamlining the number of lines of evidence can be problematic, given that more may be required to confidently assess the quality of management in certain areas. One can surmise interesting internal debate at such times: for all the laudable effort to pull together and integrate information and perspectives on departments from TBS and other central agencies, bureaus are advocates for progress in their respective administrative policy domains. So, the decisions to reduce the number of indicators for any area of management could be seen as taking a less complete and thorough approach, thereby downgrading the "worth" and robustness of measuring in that management area, and decreasing the validity of the assessments by central and departmental officials alike.

Like the grading of graduate student papers, it is difficult for TBS to assess the state of departmental management performance in complex circumstances and with many managerial dimensions to consider. In addition to the challenge of choosing credible lines of evidence, there is the challenge of economically summarizing the results of judgments to facilitate comparison and learning across entities and time.

MAF assessments and leadership

MAF has striven to encourage thinking about, and leadership in, management, and to gauge progress. However, it is challenging to assess and measure leadership in complex public organizations, and any effort to do so leads to worry about how judgments about performance are made, and whether they capture the essence of good leadership.

- *Partial input into performance review.* Some who worry about MAF methodology are concerned that there might be too tight a relationship between the TBS "MAF scorecards" and the COSO evaluations of deputy ministers. Others are chagrined about judgments made by staff without senior executive experience and conveying them with a scorecard system. Still others point to the incongruence between MAF results and the awarding of bonuses to deputy ministers. But the MAF reports are one of many inputs into these broader assessments – COSO also weighs feedback from ministers and the prime minister (most ministers, however, worry very little about the organizational readiness of departments and agencies – they want action and as few errors as possible!), deputy minister colleagues, and, of course, factor in the strategic priorities given to deputy ministers by the prime minister and the state of the department or agency they inherited. Clark and Swain have argued for COSO "the matters that count when performance is assessed, bonuses recommended, and promotions arranged are the real, deep, permanent matters of character, judgment, toughness, energy, and quality of mind" and "managerial performance will be rightly judged on how real management issues have been handled."[35]

- *A focus on organizational leadership?* When MAF was designed, "leadership" was not intended to be the object of measurement, but "leadership is implicit in all the management expectations."[36] Rather, as noted earlier, MAF sought to motivate and inform good leadership by deputy ministers in moving departments forward, while striking balances among competing priorities, skillfully responding to ministers, and handling emerging situations. Arguably, then, assessing leadership qualities and performance falls into the domain of the COSO process, not MAF. But it is worth acknowledging that the COSO review has its limitations, too – it is not a complete review of organizational leadership capabilities, particularly from the vantage point of managing the real-time challenges of departments and agencies and effecting longer-term change. For this purpose different assessment methodologies and instruments would have to be utilized, and MAF clearly falls short in this regard. However, one official noted that MAF "sets a minimal and more consistent level of expectations," even if they are not always clear.[37]

- *Leadership as balancing priorities.* A virtue and drawback of the comprehensive view of well-performing and well-led organizations inherent in MAF is the notion that leaders should aspire to better performance in all areas of management. The reality is that every deputy minister must manage to certain political "asks" at a given point in time, and every department has its strengths and weaknesses. It is well-known in the leadership literature that good leadership is situational, requires a strategic orientation, and necessarily involves balancing or making choices among competing priorities.[38] Underneath the criticism of the MAF assessments is the sense that, despite all the lines of evidence, the assessments fail to provide a holistic view of departments and agencies, the environment in which they need to operate, a realistic sense of what the possibilities for change and success are – in short, the makings of a strategic perspective on management performance and change.[39]

These perspectives suggest, then, that while encouraging "leadership in management" has been a prime motivation behind MAF, it is difficult to assess, and depends on the vantage point of assessors. There is a need to set out expectations but it is difficult to gauge real-time performance and strategic choices.

MAF as a systems check

The current MAF assessments are best understood as paper-based snapshots of systems quality and capabilities in departments and agencies. With this narrower definition of the MAF enterprise, what are its virtues and limitations?

- *Virtues.* Few would dispute that the MAF is a useful way to conceive of the scope of management requisites and challenges. MAF has the virtue of shedding light on the huge domain of accountability requirements for deputy ministers and agency heads, particularly as they settle in their roles as accounting officers. The MAF assessments aggregate in one place most management expectations on deputy ministers, except for those involving managing "up" the system, and used properly, can provide context for any single accountability and reporting requirement. They create remarkable and daunting pictures of the many demands on deputy ministers, particularly as they respond to new expectations from governments and central agencies alike. These assessments – along with audits, evaluation, and other studies – feed into a broader risk management profile of departments.
- *Limitations.* We must recognize what MAF assessments do *not* do: capture the challenges deputy ministers must wrestle with, particularly when juxtaposed against the challenge of serving ministers and the prime minister, nor do they provide assessments of the quality of specific programs (unless a department or agency is small). The assessments can provide an indirect sense of how well a department can or might be able to manage a program, but is not a substitute for proper program evaluation, even though MAF assessments do gauge the strength of a department's evaluation function. Interestingly, despite the methodology and measurement issues noted above, TBS has suggested that successive rounds of MAF assessments have shown improvements in the quality of management[40] – perhaps another realization of the adage that "what gets measured, gets managed." An alternative view is that departments and agencies may be better at preparing MAF submissions.

MAF has evolved into an oversight and accountability system, but a particular one that relies on certain methodologies and operates more like a quality assurance system, at a remove. If the Treasury Board seeks to make MAF more robust and credible, this will require a new approach, which will likely be more intrusive.

Costs and benefits of managing MAF

An abiding question has been the cost of the MAF regime. A TBS executive noted in 2006, when the number of MAF indicators were at their greatest, that the "workload is enormous."[41] This, of course, has to be considered and weighed against the benefits.

- *Costs are significant.* One way to focus our attention on the implications of MAF is to consider its annualized costs. As a starter, let's consider a very conservative and "back-of-the-envelope" estimate: 10 FTE's in the MAF directorate and its parent unit; 60 FTEs associated with the program sectors and policy centres of TBS and related central agencies (20 per cent of time of around 300 full-time staff); 350 FTEs in departments and agencies (say 6 FTEs on average for the 55–60 departments and agencies covered by MAF each year, recognizing the larger departments devote more resources than smaller agencies). This leads to a conservative estimate of 420 FTEs and an annual cost of $42 million (priced at $100,000 per FTE) to run MAF. There are many officials who would argue that this grossly underestimates the cost of staff time in central agencies, departments, and agencies. While this estimate does not include the information technology and management requirements, the costs may be lower than it might seem since MAF relies on data and information already in the system, provided as part of a much larger system of accountability and reporting.[42]
- *Public reporting and turnover.* There has been ongoing work to improve the quality of lines evidence and to ensure greater consistency in the ratings across departments and agencies. All of this leads to more transactions, more leads, more sign-offs up the line, and generally greater coordinating effort inside the central agencies. Perhaps the most critical driver has been the advent of public reporting of MAF assessments, which according to one official has increased "exponentially" the number of checks and clearances within TBS and involved communications specialists from TBS and departments. So, even with fewer lines of evidence since Round III, the workload to produce them has increased significantly. Another condition concerns the regular turnover of TBS staff: new analysts and managers must be trained up so that they are sufficiently knowledgeable about the process, various policies, and departments and agencies they liaise with. On the other hand, the MAF assessments and database would provide a useful aggregation of information for new managers and analysts who can ramp up quickly on important history and the strengths and weaknesses of particular departments and agencies.
- *Opportunity costs.* In addition to direct costs, many observers worry about how the MAF regime, with its emphasis on oversight and providing proof of progress, fits with the many other Parliamentary and central-agency reporting requirements now expected of departments and agencies. Given the costs involved, top public service executives might ask whether the resources poured into MAF assessments could be deployed to other processes – such as strategic reviews, program evaluation, and internal audit – also dedicated to improving programs and management. One could go a step further and ask whether MAF contributes to the broader reporting burden associated with the "web of rules,"[43] even if MAF may roll up much reporting done for other purposes.

- *Some benefits to consider.* Accountability and public reporting, of course, are one of the requirements of public service institutions in Westminster democratic systems. We can safely assume that most ministers, members of Parliament, and citizens will never review a MAF assessment, but we might agree that it is important that our public organizations act *as if* they might be held to account for the quality of the management of their departments. This is a non-trivial expectation and benefit, even if we might agree there could be different approaches to assessment and reporting. For TBS, the development and implementation of MAF (whatever staff inside think about the specific methodology in place), along with other initiatives, has been instrumental in rebuilding its reputation, providing input into COSO reviews of deputy ministers, and facilitating the cross-department learning and sharing of information. Moreover, there may be spillover and yields from knowledge gained through MAF into other arenas and processes: analysts may be better trained and have broader understanding of client departments, more TBS staff may develop a shared understanding of departments and agencies (particularly when non-routine transactions require integrated analysis), more information may be on tap, and MAF assessments and the supporting information through the portal would shorten the learning cycle of new analysts and managers.

The costs of managing the MAF regime are significant, but I believe that most officials and observers would agree that having effective monitoring and oversight with respect to management capabilities is essential in a modern public service in a democratic system. They would also agree that TBS had to start somewhere. The challenge is whether and how to invest in the system in order to make it as effective and credible as possible.

Realism about integration

The original vision emanating from the Independent Review Panel, and more recent communications from TBS, suggests that MAF results should inform EMS, EMIS, MRRS, strategic and program reviews, and a strengthened evaluation capability.[44] In this view MAF assessments, by focusing on the state of general organizational capabilities, would inform decisions pertaining to the renewal of programs, developing new programs, and re-allocation. This seems a stretch, since EMS emphasizes budget information and MRRS is focused more on the connection of strategic objectives and results of program of organizations with voted appropriations. A MAF assessment might provide context (or at least impressions may have been formed in the minds of several individuals involved in making recommendations and decisions), and broad conclusions might be referred to in advisory notes, but MAF assessments would not likely be appended. The conclusions on specific capabilities might influence whether TBS conditions are attached to the release of funds and securing other approvals.

Much more could be said about the use, methodology, presentation, and impact of MAF assessments. What constitutes the most significant issues, and whether, for what purpose, and how well MAF furthers the quality of management and informs decision-making, will depend significantly on where one stands: the deputy minister of different kinds of line departments or agencies, a central agency head, a Treasury Board program analyst or line-of-evidence lead, department MAF point-of-contact, minister, etc. As will be noted in the conclusion, while MAF has been an important step forward for Treasury Board, TBS, and the Government of Canada, there is certainly scope for improvement and further evolution of the regime. We also have to have appropriate expectations about the use and impact of such information in a complex, public sector governance environment.

CONCLUSION: MAF, TBS, AND PUBLIC MANAGEMENT REFORM

This has been a high-level reflection on the evolution of the Management Accountability Framework – it deserves a book-length treatment, carefully reflecting on the precision of indicators and the quality of data, considering the actual impact of MAF reporting on the thinking of department/agency leaders and their executive teams, and developing a sense of the influence of MAF assessments when COSO evaluates deputy-level performance. We have to bear in mind that process *is* often more important than outcomes when it comes to generating information and knowledge, and that seeking a one-to-one result for information use is not only misleading but hard to gauge – most information use occurs in indirect and often serendipitous ways.[45] Evaluating MAF without a good sense of the larger field of play can lead to impoverished conclusions.

The Management Accountability Framework does seem to be an important step forward, even if it will not preclude new initiatives or the reannouncement or re-packaging of old ones. It is a useful way to take stock of initiatives and assess the progress of agencies and departments holistically; by doing so, it forces the Treasury Board, and perhaps governments, to consider what deputy ministers are in aggregate expected to balance and manage to. MAF was forged in difficult circumstances, with the Chrétien and the Martin governments under enormous pressure to demonstrate commitment to control, values and ethics, management improvement, and accountability, and with departments and agencies frustrated, not to mention central agencies, at the complexity of management policies and increased reporting requirements. These pressures, expectations, and many other forms of reporting only increased with the arrival of the Harper government and the adoption of the *Federal Accountability Act* in late 2006. Difficult circumstances can provide political impetus for management change and also lead to innovation, particularly when designers seek to strike new balances, and this seems to be the case with MAF.

TBS certainly believes it has developed something distinctive and worthy of note –indeed, one executive observed that "Our MAF graphic has become a veritable Brand" to an international audience over two years ago.[46] Despite the halo, TBS leaders and staff have always been aware of MAF's emergent and evolutionary qualities, as well as its costs and the frustrations in many quarters, but nevertheless proceeded with an interesting combination of resolve and flexibility. Among its other roles and responsibilities, TBS has created a significant new niche with MAF, including a constituency for the process and its products. MAF is best understood as a quality assurance system rather than a review of leadership or program effectiveness. Indeed, having more credible assessments of the management of departments and agencies was long overdue, and it has led TBS to work in new ways and realize the potential of information held by departments and central agencies. Many of the most important consumers in the system – deputy ministers and agency heads, as well as central deputy colleagues – seem to have a zone of comfort with MAF (or perhaps they need to appear so in the current governance environment!), putting the process in perspective given the long lead times, the loosely-coupled nature of reporting and use over time,[47] and as a means for engaging staff and central agencies. Whatever the flaws and drawbacks of the MAF regime, organization theorists would say that TBS has achieved a modest degree of "domain consensus" in this area.

That MAF reporting might serve multiple uses is intriguing, even if it seems to promise too much. Yes, the TBS assessments could continue to inform dialogue with departments and the evaluation of deputy minister performance; they *could* assist deputy ministers engaging ministers (but how many would be interested?); and they could be aggregated and allow TBS to provide government-wide assessments of strengths and weaknesses in different management domains, to complement the messages from the clerk and the Public Service Commission on the state of public service. However, such uses – real or imagined – will only be as good as the information on which they are based and the standards against which they are judged. While reporting and fostering learning across departments and agencies will lead to progress, the next phase will require securing more direct evidence of management improvement as well as external points of reference (already considered by TBS), which suggests benchmarking with similar organizations in other jurisdictions or perhaps other sectors. Securing this additional information would have its costs, but it is the next frontier for assessment and reporting.

MAF was initiated with an acute sense of how long it takes to effect change in large-scale public service institutions. Many of the ideas and aspirations animating MAF, of course, were not new: it has been over a decade since the report of the Independent Review Panel on the Modernization of Comptrollership was completed, which in turn had gathered up many ideas and initiatives from the previous decade. It has also taken a decade or more for TBS to choose its ground, find its footing, and build capability associated with new strategic directions: it was easy to announce that the Treasury Board was a "management board" in 1997, but successive governments, Secretaries, and staff had to experiment and discover what that term really meant. Arguably, in addition to its budget and management policy responsibilities, the emerging information capabilities in TBS have allowed it to become more of a "knowledge board," tapping into data, reporting and insight already in the system and using it towards new purposes.[48] To do so, TBS has built "off-line" capabilities in the form of the MAF group and developed more robust ways to share information with departments and across the central agency units that have insight and data on department and agency systems. The style of change has involved less in the way of big announcements, and more in terms of its focus on getting started within spheres of authority and competence, and actively learning from experience. And, the timing was right: as the population ecologists would argue, TBS and MAF were "selected" by the governing and "hyper-accountability" environment that fueled interest in their reporting strategy, supplied resources, and built further momentum.[49]

Many officials and observers believe that MAF is costly, unwieldy, does not have much impact, and diverts scare resources from other functions such as deepening knowledge of programs and strategic review. My own view – and, interestingly, sometimes shared by officials in line departments and agencies – is that having credible oversight, challenge, and support capabilities from the centre is critical for furthering better management in public service institutions. Indeed, an essential question should be asked: *what would it say about the Government of Canada and TBS if little to no systematic effort was made to measure and report on the quality and performance of management systems, and the capabilities of departments and agencies?* Elected representatives and citizens, while not likely to ever read a MAF assessment posted by TBS, would be surprised and even shocked to learn that such assessments were not undertaken by central agencies, however imperfect. Common ground may be found by finding ways to ensure that such reporting and oversight systems are as credible, meaningful and as cost-effective as possible, and that either central agencies and/or vanguard departments can assist lagging organizations.

In late 2008, the secretary to the Treasury Board, Wayne Wouters, commissioned an independent evaluation of the first years of MAF by PricewaterhouseCoopers and Interis Consulting Inc. Its purpose is to provide "a comprehensive assessment of MAF performance, analysis of key issues including governance, methodology of assessments, reliability and accuracy of assessments, reporting requirements, systems, processes, treatment of entities, and alignment to the Government of Canada's planning cycle and initiatives (e.g. Strategic Review, audit), including international benchmarking and comparisons, as appropriate...[and] recommendations on any proposed changes to MAF, as well as a roadmap and implementation plan for proposed key activities that can be implemented in the short and longer term."[50] Possibilities include exploring whether there might be a role for third-party assessors.[51] The evaluation's stunning scope reflects an acute appreciation of the considerable resources currently dedicated to MAF and the need to bridge gaps between promise and practice. To inform and learn from the evaluation, a DM Steering Committee was established in early 2009, along with an Inter-departmental MAF Network comprised of representatives from departments and agencies.

Where might all this go? The government could wind down MAF, perhaps in the name of reducing the "web of rules," but the optics of reducing apparent oversight of management in departments and agencies makes this unlikely. A simple step might involve *not* posting the detailed MAF assessments on the TBS web site, thereby reducing the amount of communications-related and levels of clearance which take time and likely add little value. This would reduce costs, perhaps lead to the sharing of more candid reporting, and create more room for dialogue. Another possibility is to deepen MAF by developing a two-tiered approach, a combination of regular systems checks and an intermittent audit cycle, the latter relying on case studies and site visits, either by TBS-led or external assessor teams, to evaluate how well departments and agencies responded to particular challenges using plans and systems (a variant on this might involve reserving such deeper reviews once a deputy minister has occupied a position for two years). The Treasury Board might consider developing a system of peer review of departments and agencies by top leaders from similar organizations in other jurisdictions, similar to the approach used by universities for academic units. Finally, MAF could be used in reverse by TBS and cognate central agencies to self-assess how well they ascertain management readiness and performance in departments and agencies, and also their ability to provide assistance and support by means of centres of excellence and the coordination of other expertise in the system. These ideas, of course, are not mutually exclusive.

The costs and validity of indicators for measuring capability and performance, of course, should be revisited regularly and balanced against benefits, and ways should be found to further shorten the reporting cycle and make it somewhat more transparent. It may also be prudent to commission an epistemological and methodological review of MAF by a team of applied academics – along with the evaluation in progress – to more fully assess its presumptions, methodology, and measurement strategy, and to identify options for a more robust approach, one that focuses on leadership as well as the performance of departments in management areas. It will take time to develop the regime envisioned here, but the project of a renewed and refocused MAF regime – like TBS's commitment to achieving vertically and horizontally integrated expenditure information systems, undertaking strategic reviews, and strengthening the program evaluation function – deserves ongoing support and should be insinuated into the routines of government.

APPENDIX
MAF ELEMENTS AND INDICATORS – 2005

PUBLIC SERVICE VALUES

Through their actions, departmental leaders continually reinforce the importance of public service values and ethics in the delivery of results to Canadians (e.g. democratic, professional, ethical and people values).

Leadership
Leadership recognized internally and externally as demonstrating strong ethics and values behaviour, as evidenced by:
- Leadership communication with employees about expected ethical behaviour and public service values;
- Selection, evaluation, promotion and discharge of leaders based on their conduct with respect to PS values and ethics.

Organizational Culture
Organizational culture reflecting public service values and ethics, as evidenced by:
- Feedback from employees on fairness, respect, satisfaction and engagement;
- Departmental benchmark results and implemented improvements
- Trends in management and program irregularities, regularly reported on and reviewed by management.

Guidelines and Recourse
V&E policies, guidelines, standards, recourse and disclosure mechanisms in place and understood by all employees, as evidenced by:
- Customized codes of conduct, including standards of behaviour, consequences and rewards for exemplary behaviour;
- Effective communication, learning and orientation strategies for the Code of Public Service Values, for customized organizational codes and guidelines and for public service values and ethics in general;
  - Appropriate, accessible avenues for employee advice, reports of wrongdoing and resolution of conflicts.

GOVERNANCE AND STRATEGIC DIRECTIONS

The essential conditions – internal coherence, corporate discipline and alignment to outcomes – are in place for providing effective strategic direction, support to the minister and Parliament, and the delivery of results.

Governance Legitimacy
A legal framework of powers, duties and functions related to the institution (or its Minister) reflective and enabling of its objectives, as evidenced by:
- Programs and activities authorized by and in compliance with the law (e.g. constitutive legislation, the Financial Administration Act, the Charter of Rights and Freedoms, and other applicable statutes or regulations);
- A corporate process to identify areas where legal authority may be lacking or issues of lawfulness, including:
  - a requirement that an assessment of the adequacy of legal authority and lawfulness for new programs and activities be incorporated into the decision-making process when these programs and activities are developed;
  - a process and work plan to review whether current programs and activities are authorized.

Governance Structure
A stable Management, Resources And Results Structure (MRRS) as the foundation for results-based management as evidenced by:
- Clearly defined, measurable strategic outcomes that reflect the organization's corporate mandate and vision;
- Clear results outcome statements that are linked to corporate/government-wide priorities;
- PAA sufficiently populated with results and financial information;
- Defined governance structure outlining the decision-making, mechanisms, responsibilities, and accountabilities of the department.

Effective Planning Function
An effective planning function, as evidenced by:
- Approved organizational strategy to integrate business and strategic planning, human resources planning, resource management, and performance monitoring;
- Established process and calendar for corporate planning and decision making;
- Operational plans and performance agreements aligned with and linked to strategic plans.

Horizontal Initiatives
Commitment and contribution to the results-based management of horizontal initiatives, as evidenced by:
- Leadership where appropriate;

- Active participation; and
- Responsibilities for horizontal initiatives reflected (including leadership) in performance agreements.

Portfolio Management
An effective portfolio management structure and process in place, as evidenced by:
- Clear direction, leadership and communications;
- Information exchange, sharing of common/best practices;
- Structured consultations on: priority-setting and decision-making, resource allocation and budgeting, policy development and planning
- Committee processes and an organized governance structure;
- Integrative operational mechanisms and shared services;
- Graduated portfolio-based approval processes;
- Integrated mandate and common objectives.

RESULTS AND PERFORMANCE

Relevant information on results (internal, service and program) is gathered and used to make departmental decisions, and public reporting is balanced, transparent, and easy to understand.

Evaluation Function
An effective evaluation function, as evidenced by:
- Capacity of the evaluation function;
- The deputy head as chair of an active evaluation (and audit) committee(s);
- Risk-based evaluation plans;
- Management action plans to address evaluation findings/recommendations;
- Evaluation reports submitted to TBS and posted in a timely fashion (3 months);
- Performance information regularly audited or evaluated;
- Audit and Evaluation or other executive committee review of performance information.

Financial Reporting
Accounting and reporting of financial activities consistent with Government policies, directives and standards, as evidenced by:
- Timely and accurate financial reporting including accuracy of public accounts plates and improvements on the quality and timeliness of departmental financial statements;
- Quality of Central Financial Management and Reporting System (CRMRS) trial balance submissions, including materiality and number of errors and timeliness of corrections;
- Quality presentation and accounting for specified purpose accounts.

Information and Decision-Making
Access to and use of integrated information for corporate decision-making, as evidenced by:
- Integrated information from financial, human resources, payroll, and asset and real property management systems in support of senior management decision making and related to the achievement of strategic objectives; and
- Regular DM and senior management challenge of proposed investment decisions on the basis of integrated information from various sources, linked to strategic objectives.

Performance Reporting
Planning and reporting systems to support executive decision-making as evidenced by:
- RPPS/DPRS reflective of information contained in MRRS;
- DPRS linked to RPPS;
- Electronic, meaningful real-time data linking resources and results.

LEARNING, INNOVATION AND CHANGE MANAGEMENT

The department manages through continuous innovation and transformation, promotes organizational learning, values corporate knowledge, and learns from its performance.

Innovation and Change Management
Anticipation and management of significant organizational change, as evidenced by:
- Change management strategies at the corporate and "initiative" levels;
- Change management function, assignment of responsibilities and support to change management practices.

Organizational Learning
An organization that learns from its results, as evidenced by:
- An organizational learning strategy incorporating regularly reviewed learning objectives, opportunities and requirements;
- A strategy to determine organizational knowledge needs, and to capture, manage and apply organizational knowledge to shape action and improve results.

POLICY AND PROGRAMS

Departmental research and analytic capacity is developed and sustained to assure high quality policy options, program design and advice to ministers.

Policy Framework
A solid policy framework, as evidenced by:
- Consistency with the departmental mandate;
- Alignment with the government-wide policy agenda;
- Appropriate horizontal linkages to the policy frameworks of other departments;
- Clarity to central agencies and other departments; and,
- Utility in managing competing demands and allocating scarce resources.

Strategic Policy Capacity
A solid strategic policy function and analytic capacity, as evidenced by:
- Ability to anticipate challenges and respond in a strategic rather than a reactive manner;
- Organizational model to harness distributed policy capacity;
- Strong and sustainable community of analysts;
- Policy development process grounded in fact-based analysis with reliable modeling and due regard to implementation and operational matters;
- Outcomes-focused policy and program development informed by past performance;
- Stakeholder engagement to effectively inform policy making without creating expectations that unduly constrain government decision-making.

RISK MANAGEMENT

The executive team clearly defines the corporate context and practices for managing organizational and strategic risks proactively.

Legal Risk Management
Adequate management of legal risk, as evidenced by:
- Ongoing/regular scanning of programs for legal risks, in a manner commensurate with the nature of the department's activities and mandate;
- Senior management engagement in LRM, including the active review, avoidance, mitigation and management of legal risks;
- Effective sharing of information on legal risks, including with Department of Justice and central agencies (in large part to create a whole of government perspective);
- Contingency planning to respond to risks that have materialized.

Risk
Risk as an active factor in decision-making processes, as evidenced by:
- Evergreen executive committee assessment of corporate risks and the status of risk management (Corporate Risk Profile);

- An integrated risk management function (organizational focus) linked to corporate decision making;
- Protocols, processes and tools to ensure the consistent application of risk management principles throughout departmental decision making and delivery; and,
- Continuous organizational learning about risk management and lessons learned from risks successfully identified and mitigated or not.

PEOPLE

The department has the people, work environment and focus on building capacity and leadership to assure its success and a confident future for the Public Service of Canada.

Workplace
A workplace that is fair, enabling and healthy and safe in order to provide best possible services to Canadians as evidenced by:
- Fair employment and workplace practices and effective labour relations;
- Clear direction, collaboration, respect and support for employees' linguistic rights, diversity and personal circumstances in order to enable them to fulfill their mandate;
- Healthy and safe physical and psychological environment.

Workforce
A workforce that is productive, principled, sustainable and adaptable, as evidenced by:
- The size, mix of skills and diversity of backgrounds to competently perform its duties.
- Reflective of Canada's population, respectful of Canada's official languages and performs its duties guided by the values and ethics of the Public Service.
- Renewable and affordable over time.
- Versatile, innovative and engages in continuous learning.

Employment Equity
Embracing Change objectives for visible minorities met, and workforce availability targets met for designated groups, as evidenced by:
- Demonstrated results in meeting Embracing Change targets for:
  - recruitment
  - promotions
  - EX appointments
- Specific initiatives planned or underway to meet targets of WFA for:
  - Women
  - Persons with disabilities

- Aboriginal persons
- Visible minorities

HR Planning
A well-developed HR planning process integrated with business planning, as evidenced by:
- HR planning aligned with the organization's strategic outcomes and integrated with business planning.
- HR planning that incorporates future needs, effective recruitment and retention, succession planning, learning and diversity.

Official Languages, Language of Work
Legislation and policy on Official Languages in the workplace respected, as evidenced by:
- Composition of the workforce reflecting the presence of both official language communities of Canada.
- Incumbents of positions with bilingual requirements meeting those requirements.
- Use of the official language of their choice by employees in bilingual regions.
- Availability of communications, tools and products in both official languages in bilingual regions.
- Availability of training in both official languages.

Performance Review
An effective performance assessment process, as evidenced by:
- Performance agreements that:
  - Have specific outcomes and are results-based
  - Clearly identify expectations in line with Clerk's priorities
  - Require sound financial and human resource management
- Rigorous performance assessment process (e.g. quality and distribution of performance pay) and HR follow up.

Readiness for PSMA Implementation
New legislation and delegations of authority, policies and procedures in place, as evidenced by:
- Collaborative labour relations;
- Training, tool kits, guides and other supports available for managers and HR professionals;
- Current and future needs identified leading to their use in clear staffing criteria ;
- Internal policies, procedures and monitoring to ensure consistent and fair implementation of new act.

STEWARDSHIP

The departmental control regime (assets, money, people, services, etc.) is integrated and effective, and its underlying principles are clear to all staff.

Capital Assets
Effective investment planning in capital assets, as evidenced by:
- Adequate information on condition and use of capital assets in support of investment planning;
- A long-term plan that integrates all capital asset classes (real property, materiel and IM/IT); and
- A clear linkage between asset and program delivery.

Financial Analysis
Solid financial analysis, as evidenced by:
- Frequent and accurate year-end forecasts and variance reporting (most especially at mid-year) showing the organization's true financial status;
- Analyses of high-risk areas in relation to reference levels by program activity and major funding approvals (real and projected) including anticipated funding pressures and re-profiling trends; and,
- A reasonable history of carry-forwards and lapses.

Information and IT Management
An IM/IT vision and strategy supportive of the organization's business strategy and government-wide directions, as evidenced by:
- A governance structure that includes program representation and is effective in priority setting of IM/IT investments and resources;
- IM/IT enabled projects that have effective governance and are executed well;
- Strategy and approved plans that reflect a GOC Enterprise approach to common IT services;
- Implementation of Management of Government Information (MGI) Policy strategy, based on an IM capacity assessment; and,
- Integrated privacy and security measures.

Internal Audit Function
An effective internal audit function, as evidenced by :
- An appropriate infrastructure to effectively discharge its internal audit responsibilities as outlined in the Internal Audit Policy (governance structure and appropriate level of resources);
- A completed risk-based audit plan; and
- All reports including progress reports are submitted to TBS for follow-up activities.

Management of Transfer Payments
Effective Transfer Payment Program management in place, as evidenced by:
- Timely renewal of transfer payment programs;
- Departmental internal audit plans include provision for the review of internal management policies, practices and controls of transfer payment programs;
- Regular audit of transfer payment programs and timely follow-up.

Materiel Management
An appropriate materiel management framework in place as evidenced by:
- Clear accountabilities consistent with organizational capacity; and
- Reliable life-cycle cost and performance information that supports decision-making.

Procurement and Contract Management
Risk-based approach to procurement and contracting management, as evidenced by:
- Clear delegations of authority are tied to knowledge and capacity;
- Demonstrated compliance with delegated contracting authorities and conditions identified by Treasury Board policy; and,
- Explicit oversight, monitoring and on-going review of procurement and contracting function and processes (e.g. Contracts Review Committee, quality of contracting data, timely completion of contracts over $10,000 disclosure information, implementation of audit recommendations where applicable, etc);
- Methods for procuring demonstrating the most cost-effective end-to-end process.

Project Management
Risk-based project management approach as evidenced by:
- An integrated, achievable up-to-date long-term capital plan or planning document in place that is being implemented (linked to the organization's key priorities);
- Explicit project management accountability framework, that addresses decision-making and oversight and effective monitoring and ongoing review;
- Properly resourced projects (e.g. project management capacity, appropriately trained officials);
- Demonstrated compliance with delegated project approval requirements and conditions identified by Treasury Board.

Quality of TB submissions
Quality TB submissions, as evidenced by:
- Draft submissions regularly vetted through common departmental quality control to ensure consistency, clarity and conciseness;

- Accurate, substantiated and comprehensive financial components; and
- Frequency with which TB conditions are imposed.

Real Property
An implemented real property management framework to meet its obligations under TB Real Property policies, as evidenced by:
- An organizational structure which includes clear accountabilities and appropriate delegations;
- Integrated support systems; and
- An information management framework to provide complete and accurate inventory data.

TB conditions
Organizational compliance with conditions imposed by TB, as evidenced by:
- Timeliness of compliance;
- Adequate engagement with TBS; and
- Appropriate reporting.

CITIZEN-FOCUSSED SERVICE

Services are citizen-centred, policies and programs are developed from the "outside in", and partnerships are encouraged and effectively managed.

External Service Delivery Strategy
Client centred external service delivery strategy that drives efficiencies, respects client privacy rights and reflects an enterprise view of government services and that results in effective external service delivery, as evidenced by:
- Review of key public-facing services to achieve measurable improvements in responsiveness to client needs, effectiveness and value for money; partnerships with other programs, organizations or jurisdictions to achieve more client-centric or cost-effective service delivery or to align program rules and regulations (e.g., MOUs/service level agreements in place when partnerships established);
- Measurement of the cost-effectiveness of delivery by channel and migration of clients to lower cost channels where appropriate; and
- Measurement of client satisfaction in a transparent way (e.g.., reporting to clients and Parliament) using the Common Measurement Tool, and use of the results to guide continued improvement in client satisfaction.

Government-wide Services
Internal service delivery supportive of enterprise-wide (Government of Canada-wide) approach (e.g. shared and common services and infrastructure in IT, HR, Finance, Materiel), as evidenced by:

- Commitments met on using Secure Channel services (timing and transaction volumes);
- Active participation in enterprise-wide initiatives and adoption of Shared service and systems.

Official Languages for External Service Delivery
External communications in both official languages, as evidenced by:
- Availability of communications, tools and products in both official languages, for external services to clients.

Service Delivery and User Fees
Compliance with service delivery and user fee requirements, as evidenced by:
- Performance information for all user fees to which the Act applies; it is based on the DPR (or an alternative report employed by the department) and observations of departmental compliance with the User Fees Act relative to the disclosure of service standards.

ACCOUNTABILITY

Accountabilities for results are clearly assigned and consistent with resources, and delegations are appropriate to capabilities.

Authorities and Delegations
Compliance with approved financial authorities and delegations, as evidenced by:
- Issues identified through departmental contacts, Internal Audit reports, OAG reports, by Program Sectors, and through review of media reports or other relevant sources of information.

NOTES

1 This paper benefited greatly from the knowledge, perspectives, insight, and challenge from close to twenty individuals in the academic, government, and consulting sectors. None are responsible for the views, interpretations, and errors it contains. These include Mark Jarvis, Johanne Ascoli, Harry Swain, Jim McDavid, and David Good (University of Victoria); Ian Clark (University of Toronto); and Allan Maslove and Robert Shepherd (Carleton University). I want to acknowledge, but cannot name, several consultants and public servants in central agencies and departments who provided useful comments, including at the Treasury Board Secretariat, where debate over such issues often exceeds the range of debate outside its walls. Finally, I want to personally salute the amazing contributions of G. Bruce Doern, whose academic leadership led to the *How Ottawa Spends* series, scores of other books and collections, an

incredible corpus of writing on federal government organizations in Canada and elsewhere, two generations of new scholars, and his role in the institutionalization of a flagship centre of scholarship and learning in the field of public administration and public policy at Carleton University.

2 For previous studies that point to potential elements of a management framework, see James C. McDavid and D. Brian Marson (eds.), *The Well-Performing Government Organization* (Toronto: Institute of Public Administration of Canada, 1991); Ole Ingstrup and Paul Crookall, *The Three Pillars of Management: Secrets of Sustained Success* (Montreal and Kingston: McGill-Queen's University Press, 1998); and Kenneth Kernaghan, Brian Marson, and Sandford Borins, *The New Public Organization* (Toronto: The Institute of Public Administration of Canada, 2000).

3 Independent Review Panel on the Modernization of Comptrollership in the Government of Canada, *Report on the Independent Review Panel on the Modernization of Comptrollership in the Government of Canada* (1997), 19–20; Evan H. Potter, "Treasury Board as Management Board: The Re-invention of a Central Agency," in Leslie A. Pal (ed.), *How Ottawa Spends 2000–2001* (Toronto: Oxford University Press), 95–130.

4 Evert Lindquist, "Business Planning Comes to Ottawa: Critical Issues and Future Directions," in Peter Aucoin and Donald Savoie (eds.), *Strategic Management in the Public Sector: Lessons from Program Review* (Ottawa: Canadian Centre for Management Development, 1998), 143–68, and "Expenditure Management in the Millennium: Vision and Strategy for Integrated Business Planning," a discussion paper prepared for the Treasury Board of Canada Secretariat (19 February 1998).

5 Canada, *Results for Canadians: A Management Framework for the Government of Canada* (Ottawa: Treasury Board of Canada Secretariat, 2000).

6 The encompassing NQI framework broached leadership, planning, citizen/client focus, people focus, process management, supplier/partner focus, and organizational performance, and emphasized continuous improvement and a fact-based approach to decision-making. See "Canadian Quality Criteria for the Public Sector - National Quality Institute" (June 1998). Web site: http://www.tbs-sct.gc.ca/pubs_pol/opepubs/otherpubs/cqcps1-eng.asp. See also Government Review and Quality Services Division, Financial & Information Management Branch, "Potential synergy between review and quality management" (April 5, 1995). Web site: http://www.tbs-sct.gc.ca/pubs_pol/dcgpubs/TB_H4/dwnld/quality-qualite-eng.rtf.

7 Jean Dupuis, "Modern Comptrollership and the Management Accountability Framework," Library of Parliament Report PRB 06-23E (3 April 2006), 6–7; Treasury Board of Canada Secretariat, "Treasury Board Announces a Government-Wide Approach to Modern Comptrollership," *Press Release* (1 June 2001); and Treasury Board Secretariat, *Modern Comptrollership Initiative: A Progress Report on Government-Wide Implementation* (March 2003). The first two phases cost $39 million over six years.

8 Joanne Kelly and Evert Lindquist in John Wanna, Lotte Jensen, and Jouke de Vries (eds.), *Controlling Public Expenditure: The Changing Roles of Central Budget Agencies – Better Guardians?* (Cheltenham, UK: Edward Elgar, 2003), 85–105; Joanne Kelley, "Pursuit of an Elusive Ideal: Review and Allocation under the Chrétien Government,"

in G. Bruce Doern (ed.), *How Ottawa Spends 2003–2004: Regime Change and Policy Shift* (Toronto: Oxford University Press, 2003), 118–33; Evert A. Lindquist, "How Ottawa Reviews Spending: Moving Beyond Adhocracy?," in G. Bruce Doern (ed.), *How Ottawa Spends 2006–2007: In from the Cold, the Tory Rise and the Liberal Demise* (Montreal: McGill-Queen's University Press, 2006), 185–207; and David A. Good, *The Politics of Public Money: Spenders, Guardians, Priority Setters, and Financial Watchdogs Inside the Canadian Government* (Toronto: University of Toronto Press, 2007).

9 Treasury Board of Canada Secretariat, *Meeting the Expectations of Canadians: Review of the Responsibilities and Accountabilities of Ministers and Senior Officials* – Report to Parliament (Ottawa: The President of the Treasury Board of Canada, 2005); and Government of Canada, *Management in the Government of Canada: A Commitment to Continuous Change* (Ottawa: The President of the Treasury Board of Canada, 2005).

10 Ian D. Clark, "Restraint, renewal, and the Treasury Board Secretariat," *Canadian Public Administration* 37, no.2 (1994), 222. As TBS visiting fellow in the early 1990s I sat next to the official responsible for assembling this information. My view was that TBS, by reducing all the information collected into short notes for limited and discrete use by the Secretary missed an opportunity to show (to TBS and outsiders alike) that it had a multi-dimensional and comprehensive perspective on departments and agencies.

11 Evert A. Lindquist, "Business Planning Comes to Ottawa: Critical Issues and Future Directions," in Peter Aucoin and Donald Savoie (eds.), *Strategic Management in the Public Sector: Lessons from Program Review* (Ottawa: Canadian Centre for Management Development, 1998), 143–68.

12 TBS staff tapped into work on fostering excellence in public sector organizations and encouraged more to be brought forward. See Treasury Board Secretariat, "Public Sector Organizational Excellence Symposium," Report, 5–6 July 2001. Ivan Blake brought his experience with results, performance, and comptrollership, and worked with Ralph Heintzman and Brian Marson on the project, bring their perspectives on values and ethics, service improvement and citizen-centred service delivery, learning organization, evidence-based decisions, organizational excellence, etc. For reflections on how the principles and programs of the National Quality Institute linked to MAF, see John Perry and Dan Corbett, "The Treasury Board Secretariat 'Management Accountability Framework' and NQI's 'Progressive Excellence Program,'" National Quality Institute (20 August 2003). Web site: http://www.nqi.ca/articles/article_details.aspx?ID=394.

13 See Robert Fonberg, "Measuring Management: The Canadian Experience," Treasury Board of Canada Secretariat Presentation Notes to National School of Government Conference on "21st Century Public Services - Putting People First," London, United Kingdom (6 June 2006), for some of these points. Web site: http://www.nationalschool.gov.uk/news_events/psrc2006/downloads/presentation_robert_fonberg.pdf.

14 Ivan Blake, "Presentation on the Management Accountability Framework," (Transcript), Canada School of Public Service Armchair Dialogue (c.2004). Web site: http://www.tbs-sct.gc.ca/maf-crg/documents/video-video/transcript-transcription-eng.asp

15 Adapted from Virginie Ethier, "Management Accountability Framework (MAF): Overview," presentation to the Planning and Performance Exchange, Ottawa (15 May

2007), 5. Web site: http://www.ppx.ca/Symposium/2007_symArchive/Presentations07/DayOne_ChallengesE.pdf.
16 See Canada, *Guidance for Deputy Ministers* (Ottawa: Privy Council Office, 2003). Web site: http://www.pco-bcp.gc.ca/index.asp?lang=eng&page=information&sub=publications&doc=gdm-gsm/doc_e.htm.
17 Blake, "Presentation on the Management Accountability Framework." This took up the idea of bilateral dialogue, a hallmark of the Shared Management Agenda, despite the aspiration of a government-wide initiative.
18 Robert Fonberg, "Measuring Management," 7.
19 In Round VI, for example, a few requirements were deepened, others were lightened, or previously well-performing departments in certain management areas were given the opportunity to attest to nothing having changed from the previous year. Management Accountability Framework Directorate, "MAF VI Methodology Changes 2008–2009," no date.
20 Alister Smith, "Roles of Treasury Board and Others in Reforms of Budget and Management Systems: Canadian Experience," 22 October 2007.
21 The Government Employee Directory Services (GEDS) listed eighteen at this time in the MAF directorate, but the listing was out of date.
22 Fonberg, "Measuring Management," 6.
23 In the mid-1990s I came to believe that TBS insufficiently exercised the "challenge function" in the budget process. My view was that TBS should move beyond having the program analysts represent the budget requests of departments and agencies, and instead institute organization-to-organization meetings with executive teams. TBS would gather comprehensive evidence on the programs, management, and effectiveness of specific departments and agencies, whose representatives, in turn, could challenge TBS on its evidence, and the coherence and effectives of its policies and resourcing on department management and program operations – a mutual challenge and accountability session. A dedicated capability outside the program sectors would obtain information from program analysts and others responsible for non-budget related policies, and to serve as a single-window to each department and agency. These ideas had little traction but are one standard for judging MAF. See Evert Lindquist, "On the Cutting Edge: Program Review, Government Restructuring, and the Treasury Board of Canada," in Gene Swimmer (ed.), *How Ottawa Spends 1996–97: Living Under the Knife* (Ottawa: Carleton University Press, 1996), 205–52.
24 Charles Perrow, "The Analysis of Goals in Complex Organizations," *American Sociological Review*, 26 (1961), 854–66.
25 There were similar aspirations for the business planning documents required by the Treasury Board in the late 1990s. Lindquist, "Business Planning Comes to Ottawa."
26 Fonberg, "Measuring Management," 12–13.
27 Ethier, "Management Accountability Framework (MAF): Overview."
28 Ian D. Clark and Harry Swain, "Distinguishing the real from the surreal in management reform: suggestions for beleaguered administrators in the government of Canada," *Canadian Public Administration* 48, no.4 (Winter 2005), 453–76.

29 Confidential correspondence with author, 6 February 2009.
30 Confidential correspondence with author, 8 February 2009.
31 Meyer, J.W. and B. Rowan, "Institutionalized Organizations: Formal Structure as Myth and Ceremony," *American Journal of Sociology* 83 (September 1977), 340–63.
32 See US Government Accountability Office, *Program Evaluation: OMB's PART Reviews Increased Agencies' Attention to Improving Evidence of Program Results, Report to the Chairman, Subcommittee on Government Management, Finance, and Accountability, Committee on Government Reform, House of Representatives* (Washington, D.C.: October 2005). PART refers to Program Rating Assessment Tool administered by the Office of Management and Budget. See http://www.whitehouse.gov/omb/part/. Thanks to Jim McDavid for bring this to my attention.
33 This includes the 2005 and 2006 MAF assessments from the five departments noted earlier, and, from the Treasury Board Secretariat web site, "Management Accountability Framework: Areas of Management and Lines of Evidence to be Assessed in Round V," accessed at http://www.tbs-sct.gc.ca/maf-crg/indicators-indicateurs/2007/elements-elements-eng.pdf, and "MAF VI Methodology Changes 2008–2009" (Management Accountability Framework Directorate), accessed at http://www.tbs-sct.gc.ca/maf-crg/indicators-indicateurs/2008/elements-elements-eng.pdf.
34 An important question of reliability arises when a department moves significantly (i.e., up two or more levels in the rating scale) in one or more categories. This suggests that either the quality of data submitted to TBS was not of sufficient quality in the previous year (and that should lead to questions about how the quality of data is monitored), the information TBS relied on was wanting, and/or the interpretation by TBS shifted. Leaving aside questions about the validity of evidence for given areas of management, there is obviously considerable incentive for departments to submit better rather than worse information.
35 Clark and Swain, 473 and 472, respectively.
36 Confidential personal correspondence to author, 5 February 2009.
37 Confidential personal correspondence, 8 February 2009.
38 Robert E. Quinn, *Beyond Rational Management: Mastering the Paradoxes and Competing Demands of High Performance* (San Francisco: Jossey-Bass, 1988), and, for example, more recently, Kim S. Cameron and Robert E. Quinn, *Diagnosing and Changing Organizational Culture: Based on the Competing Values Framework*, Revised Edition (San Francisco: Jossey-Bass, 2006).
39 Harry Swain notes: "The ten basic areas that MAF purports to measure are all very nice, but not one of them has to do with how effectively or excellently the department carries out its mandate ... A good MAF would start with the question of what the program/department/agency was supposed to deliver and paint the picture of its management against the environment in which it must operate." Correspondence to the author, 6 February 2009.
40 Ivan Blake, "Program and Management Performance: An Integrated Canadian Approach," presentation to an Asia-Pacific Economic Cooperation Workshop on

"Government Performance and Results Management, Taipei, Chinese Taipei (26–28 March 2008), 17. Web site: http://aimp.apec.org/Documents/2008/EC/WKSP2/08_ec_wksp2_009.pdf.

41 Fonberg, "Measuring Management," 8.
42 Peter Aucoin and Mark D. Jarvis, *Modernizing Government Accountability* (Otttawa: Canada School of Public Service, 2005).
43 Canada, Independent Review Panel on Grants and Contributions, *From Red Tape to Clear Results: Report of the Independent Review Panel on Grants and Contributions Programs* (Ottawa: Treasury Board of Canada Secretariat, December 2006). Web site: http://www.brp-gde.ca/pdf/Report_on_Grant_and_Contribution_Programs.pdf.
44 For a comprehensive view of the budget process, see Good, *The Politics of Public Money*.
45 See James G. March and Guje Sevon, "Gossip, Information, and Decision-Making in Organizations" in James G. March (ed.), *Decisions and Organizations* (London: Basil Blackwell, 1988), 429–42.
46 Fonberg, "Measuring Management," 4.
47 Evert Lindquist, "There's More to Policy Than Alignment: (Or) Cultivating Capacity, Brokering Insight, and Fostering Appropriate Expectations in Results-Driven and Loosely-Coupled Governance Environments," Research Paper, Canadian Policy Research Networks, forthcoming 2009.
48 In addition to the new Expenditure Management System (EMS) and the Management, Resources, and Results Structure (MRRS), Ivan Blake reports (but this has been flagged by other officials) that "EMIS [Expenditure Management Information System] enables TBS to: align all spending to government-wide outcomes; track performance of all programs; identify related spending anywhere in government; and report on government-wide performance." From Blake, "Program and Management Performance," 10. For links to EMIS and MRRS, see http://www.tbs-sct.gc.ca/emis-sigd/index-eng.asp.
49 See Michael T. Hannan and John Freeman, "The Population Ecology of Organizations," *American Journal of Sociology* 82, no.5 (March 1976), 79–105, and W. Graham Astley, "The Two Ecologies: Population and Community Perspectives on Organizational Evolution," *Administrative Science Quarterly* 30, no.2 (June 1985), 224–41.
50 Secretary of the Treasury Board, "Invitation – MAF 5–Year Review Steering Committee" (5 January 2009).
51 Public Works and Government Services Canada, "Request for Proposal (RFP) for the Provision of Internal Audit Services for the Treasury Board of Canada, Secretariat, Priorities and Planning Sector" (24 October 2008).

4 Design Challenges for the Strategic State: Bricolage and Sabotage

RUTH HUBBARD
AND GILLES PAQUET

"The idea of design involves inquiry into systems that do not yet exist."
A. G. L. Romme

INTRODUCTION

Much reengineering of the state is bound to occur as the welfare state is retrofitted and gradually replaced by a strategic state that is less focused on protection and redistribution and much more on productivity and innovation. This has led to the emergence of a multitude of new organization forms that are not, strictly speaking, patterned on the traditional hierarchical departmental model. This has, in turn, created new challenges in the design of organizations that can ensure a requisite mix of reliability, accountability, nimbleness, exploration capability, innovation, and creativity. Yet, organization design capability is poorly instituted in the Canadian system.

Organizational design is most often inherited from tradition and history, or is the result of improvisation by the last batch of imperial newcomers, eager to inflict their footprint on the organization they have just recently joined. As a result, there is often not a good fit between the design, the mission and the context of the organization: neither the faceless forces of history nor the hastily drafted back-of-envelope organization charts ensure good design.[1]

So, concern about design surfaces, but the response is rarely adequate: the skimpiest of contours are sketched (as amateurishly as the last time the concern emerged) and the ensuing job of fleshing out the details is delegated to junior executives as part of what is called an implementation strategy. It is hardly surprising that what ensues is not of great significance: little more than tinkering with organization charts.

The major source of the problem is that this sort of architectural work requires a wholly different way of thinking. It is not (and cannot be) guided by the single-minded sort of logic that dominates science (the search for general knowledge and the subsequent test of its validity), but by an inquiry into systems that do not yet exist. The logic, in this latter case, is that of disclosing and crafting a new "world", with the sole purpose of ascertaining if it works, and to ensure that it does.[2]

In the first section, we provide a conceptual framework, and we identify the particular challenges created by the emergence of a world in which nobody is in charge. In the second section, we sketch the many dimensions of the organizational design process. In the third section, we use this approach to examine two pathologies of governance recently observed on the federal scene in Canada: a case of *passive sabotage* (where fixation on an old and inadequate design in the face of new challenges has proved disastrous – nuclear safety) and a case of *active sabotage* (i.e., deliberate use of design to ensure failure – Service Canada). In conclusion, we suggest ways in which the organizational design function might be bolstered at the federal level in Canada, but we also underline the fact that this kind of function needs to be instituted as well within the federation, and that such mechanisms should be helpful not only in improving effective governance but also in exposing the ugly face of sabotage early enough to prevent the worst outcomes.

DESIGNING A LIVING ORGANIZATION

Organization and Organization Design

An organization may be X-rayed as a mix of *people* (stakeholders of all sorts with their skills, talents, and responsibilities), *architecture* (relationships of all sorts defined by the organization charts and the like), *routines* (process, policies and procedures), and *culture* (shared values, beliefs, language, norms and mindsets).[3]

At any particular time, these components (PARC) are assembled within organizations in various ways – bound together by ligatures making them into a more or less coherent whole. A shock disturbing any of these components (whether it originates within or without the organization, whether it modifies a physical or a symbolic dimension) triggers some re-alignment in all the other dimensions. So the organization continually evolves: more so and faster when the environment is turbulent.

Organizations are therefore assemblages that are constantly undermined (over-ground and underground) as a result of new circumstances, of the action of new or transformed stakeholders, new emerging relationships, new procedures, or changes in the material or symbolic order. The role of the organization designer is to intervene in real time in an existing assemblage to improve this four-dimensional configuration of the organization in a manner that generates better dynamic performance and resilience. This sort of intervention has to take into account the turbulence and evolution of the environment in which the organization operates, but also the limitations of such tweaking given imperfect knowledge and the profound uncertainty about what it will generate in terms of unintended consequences.

The core task of organizational design is to disclose new worlds. For organizations are worlds: they are a totality of interrelated pieces of *equipment* to carry out a specific task (such hammering in a nail); tasks that are undertaken for some *purposes* (like building a house); and the activities involved bestow those accomplishing them with *identities* (like being a carpenter).[4] This is the sense in which one speaks of the world of medicine, business or academe.

However, there is more to organizations than the interconnection of equipment, purposes and identities. In talking about these new worlds, Spinosa et al use the word *style* to refer to the ways in which all the practices are coordinated and fit together in an organization. Style is what coordinates action, what makes certain kinds of activities and things matter.

In their study, Spinosa et al show how economic, social and political entrepreneurs are those who spot disharmonies between what seems to be the *rules* in good currency and what would appear to be the sort of *practice* likely to be effective. They detect anomalies. Those anomalies create puzzles. The reaction to puzzles by inattentive observers is often to ignore them, and pursue the on-going tasks. Entrepreneurs recognize instead that the anomalies are creating mysteries, and that what is called for are *ways of understanding mysteries*, the search for "guidelines for solving a mystery by organized exploration of possibilities."[5]

Tackling such an exploratory task can only be done by trial and error. This is the world of prototyping, of experimentation, of serious play, of organization design. Innovative and entrepreneurial persons in all areas (economic, political, social) become organization designers and redefine the style of their organization.[6]

A significant handicap in this sort of endeavor is that this type of world-disclosing activity or inquiry – based on empathy (for one designs always for somebody else), on holistic problem-solving (looking for what works *in toto*), and prototyping (not waiting until one has the best solution, but starting with anything promising, prototype it, get feedback, play with it, and learn in that way) – Tim Brown quoted in Martin 2004:11) – is not what higher education is organized to foster, and, as a result, the skills required are not necessarily cultivated and widely available.[7]

Successful design work in a world where nobody is in charge

One of the most important changes of kind that has occurred over the last while in the institutional order that defines the rules of the game in our democratic societies is the drift from a world where some person or group could (legitimately or not) claim to be in charge, to a world where complexity, turbulence and surprises are so important that it cannot be argued persuasively that anybody is in charge.[8]

This has significantly increased the complexity of the design work necessary to keep the institutional order up to the challenges generated by such a turbulent environment. It has been argued that what is required is: (1) a new vocabulary because critical description is crucial at the diagnostic phase; (2) a new form of knowledge, a new type of exploratory activity and a new process of experimentalism-based creative thinking; and (3) a new type of competencies to do this work.

Moreover it requires (4) windows of opportunity to "tinker" with the organization with a modicum of chances of success (i.e., at a time and in a way that prevents these efforts from being neutralized by the dynamic conservatism of those who benefit from the existing order). This often calls for exceptional circumstances. Otherwise the pressures of those confronted with real and substantial losses in the short term will trump the timid actions of those hoping for uncertain future benefits from a new order.

However, this process will lead to nothing substantial unless one has been able to develop (5) a mental tool box of levers capable of guiding the work of crafting new organizations, and useable in such design work. But, because organization design is akin to creating a new world, none of the above will suffice unless the design process (6) truly discloses a coherent world (a body) and contributes to impart it with a style (a soul) that provides it with a sextant – focal points that underpin its being able to sustain effective coordination and change.

Given these conditions for successful design, it is hardly surprising that such work is eschewed, and that so many organizations are so poorly designed. It is much easier for governors and managers to focus their attention on less daunting tasks.

A SKETCH OF THE DESIGN PROCESS

The design process is difficult and elusive, very much like the pragmatic inquiry of professionals in their practice. But it must be anchored, at the very least in a loose protocol if it is to serve as a launching pad for effective exploration.

The What: The Simons-type Model as a Possible Template

Robert Simons (2005) has proposed a template based on four basic questions that one might reformulate in the following way:

- Customer/Stakeholder definition
  what are the best possible assemblages of meaningful primary stakeholders that would represent fully the range of effective partners, clients, etc. making up the broad unit structure?

- Performance variables
  what are the most effective diagnostic control systems (the various mechanisms likely to best monitor the organization and to suggest ways to excite them)?
- Creative tension resolution
  what are the best mechanisms to resolve the creative tensions between the frames of mind of the different layers and rings of partners in the organization and likely to catalyze interactive networks?
- Commitment to others
  what are the mechanisms of shared responsibilities and commitment to others that will ensure some coherence for the organization and the requisite mix of reliability and innovation?

The answers to these questions are meant to help define the four basic dimensions of the Simons framework:

- the span of control (who should decide?),
- the span of accountability (tradeoffs in performance measures when it comes to rendering of accounts),
- the span of influence (the full nature of the interactions and the degree of mobilization they entail), and
- the span of support (the full range of shared responsibilities).

Simons suggests that proper alignment for the organization requires that the spans of control (hard) and support (soft) – on the supply side of resources – be adequate to meet the obligations imposed by the spans of accountability (hard) and influence (soft) – on the demand side of resources.

The How: Experimentalism and Serious Play in a Dynamic World

At the source of the process leading to the constant adaptation of the organization design when nobody is in charge, is the dual capacity of allowing (1) as many stakeholders as possible who detect an anomaly to initiate remedial action, and (2) such action to proceed experimentally even though the remedial action is not perfect on the basis of a strong belief that mass collaboration will help improve it and thereby find a faster way to the next best (always temporary) solution.

This calls for (1) a drift toward open source governance (i.e., a form of governance that enables each partner, as much as possible, to have access to the "code" and to "tinker" freely with the way the system works within certain well-accepted constraints)[9] ; and (2) a priority to "serious play" (i.e., a premium on experimentation with imperfect prototypes one might be able to improve by retooling, restructuring and reframing innovatively and productively).[10]

By partitioning the overall terrain into issues domains and communities of meaning or communities of fate (i.e., assemblages of people united in their common concern for shared problems or a shared passion for a topic or set of issues), it is possible to identify a large number of sub-games – each requiring a specific treatment. Each issue-domain (health, education, environment, etc.) and even some sub-issue domains (like mental health), being multifaceted and somewhat different must be dealt with on an *ad hoc* basis (in the way a sculptor facing blocks of stone of different texture must deal with each block differently) with a view to allowing the design of its own stewardship to emerge.

This open system takes into account the people with a substantial stake in the issue domain, the resources available and the culture in place, and allows experiments to shape the required mix of principles and norms, of rules and decision-making procedures likely to promote the preferred mix of efficiency, resilience and learning. A template likely to be of use everywhere may not be available yet, but it does not mean that a workable one cannot be elicited *hic et nunc*.

However, it is not sufficient to ensure open access, one must also ensure that the appropriate motivations are nurtured so that all meaningful stakeholders are willing and able to engage in "serious play" (i.e., become truly producers of governance through tinkering with the governance apparatus within certain limits). This in turn requires that a modicum of mass collaboration and trust prevail,[11] and calls for a reconfiguration of governance taking the communities of meaning seriously. Such an approach may not only suggest that very different arrangements are likely to emerge from place to place, but would underline the importance of regarding any such arrangement as essentially temporary: the ground is in motion and diversity is likely to acquire new faces, so different patterns of organization designs are likely to emerge. Consequently, good governance would require that any formal or binding arrangement be revisited, played with, and adjusted to take into account the evolving diversity of circumstances. It would open the door to the design of more complex and innovative arrangements likely to deal more effectively with deep diversity.[12]

Prototyping would appear to be the main activity underpinning serious play:

- identifying some top requirements as quickly as possible,
- putting in place a quick-and-dirty provisional medium of co-development,
- allowing as many interested parties to get involved as partners in improving the arrangement,
- encouraging iterative prototyping, and
- encouraging all, through playing with prototypes, to get a better understanding of the problems, of their priorities, and of themselves.[13]

The purpose of the exercise is to create a dialogue (creative interaction) between people and prototypes. This may be more important than creating dialogue between people alone. It is predicated on a culture of active participation that would need to be nurtured. The sort of democratization of design that ensues, and the sort of playfulness and adventure that is required for "serious play" with prototypes, are essential for the process to succeed, and they apply equally well to narrow or broad organizational concerns.

The Wherewithal: Tripartite Bricolage

In the beginning is the anomaly noted by a stakeholder that points to an aspect of the performance of the organization that would appear to be much below legitimate expectations. This calls for *bricolage* (i.e., tinkering with the ways the organization operates, or with certain of its structural features, or with the definition of the purposes of the organization – re-tooling, restructuring or reframing will be the labels used for such *bricolage*).

As Donald Schon explained, any social system (and organizations are social systems) contains technology, structure and theory: "the structure is the set of roles and relations among individual members. The theory consists of the views held within the social system about its purposes, its operations, its environment and its future. Both reflect, and in turn influence, the prevailing technology of the system. These dimensions all hang together so that any change in one produces change in the others."[14]

Obviously the law of least effort entices stakeholders to tinker with technology and operations first, for it is likely to be easier (e.g. generate least resistance, take less time, and involve fewer people) than if one were to fiddle with the structure or to question the purpose of the organization. Yet often, most efforts to correct anomalies often quickly become a mix of the three sorts of *bricolage*.

Continuous trial and error lead to experimentation with different prototypes that embody different degrees of retooling, restructuring and reframing. Indeed, minor retooling often triggers a cascade of effects that end up, over time, with major reframing. However there is no guarantee. In other cases, blockages at one of these levels may be powerful enough to derail the whole process of repairs that has been triggered by the original anomalies, and organizational decline may ensue.

Finally, the nature of the anomalies and the severity of their impact may trigger different approaches to the required repairs. The inertia of the organization and the degree of cognitive dissonance may well mean inattention to the early warning signals, and significant denial of difficulties even in the face of very poor performance. This often makes minor bricolage less likely, and allows organizational decline to proceed unhampered until some threshold is reached when action is finally seen as mandatory. In such cases, instant major overhaul is often the only option.

In a mega-system like the state apparatus of a modern industrialized socio-economy, the potential for inattention to anomalies and neglect of repairs is very high especially if there is no agency charged with the responsibility of oversight of the adequacy of the organizational infrastructure, of detection of anomalies requiring repairs, and of the conduct of repairs when needed.

In the Canadian federal government, following a 2007 restructuring of the Privy Council Office (PCO), the "machinery of government" apparatus is described as follows: "(it) provides advice and supports the prime minister on matters related to the prime minister's prerogative and responsibilities as the overall manager of Canada's system of Cabinet government ... supply(ing) advice on matters relating to:

- The structure, organization and functioning of government;
- The organization of Cabinet and its committees;
- Ministerial mandates and responsibilities;
- Transitions from government to government;
- Ethics and accountability issues (consistent with Westminster-style government); and
- The role of the Crown, the governor general and Government House, as well as issues related to honours policy[15]

Part of the responsibilities of a deputy secretary, it is grouped with legislation and house planning as well as formal legal advice to the prime minister and others in the PCO portfolio. It does not seem to give priority to monitoring the state of the organizational infrastructure in a continuous and particularly careful way, and appears prone to be inattentive to any anomaly that does not generate a crisis.

To the sort of inattention or neglect that this seems to imply, one must add the possibility of active resistance of officials (in private, public and social organizations) to any profound change, and even more so when what is involved constitutes nothing less than "a challenge to the psychological comfort of the powerful."[16]

The massive redesign of many organizations and institutions as a result the drift from Big G government to small g governance (from the welfare state to the strategic state) in some cases (like Canada) has generated forceful resistance within the technocracy (often emboldened by an ambivalent citizenry not eager to lose state protection) to new deals that would call for a lower valence for the state, more inter-sector partnerships, and more mass collaboration – all initiatives that have been seen as reducing the power of the powerful including, especially, the upper levels of the bureaucracy in place, and implying a greater personal responsibility for the citizenry. In a context inhabited by neglect of organizational design issues, badly equipped capacity-wise to deal aptly and seriously with such issues, and plagued with powerful defensive technocracies, superficial tinkering with organization charts is often administratively expedient even though it is hardly a recipe for wise design.

When crises boil over, technological pathologies and a few minor structural defects are corrected, but when the cultures of organizations are indicted (when what is involved is nothing less than a need to rethink and reframe the notion of the business the organization is in, the theory of what the organization is about), the forces of inertia, self-interest, or fear often succeed in stopping any profound transformation. By a sleight of hand that amounts to nothing more than a modification of some superficial rules of the game or a slight exercise of musical chairs for the officials in the top ranks of the sick organization, the pretense that the problem has been resolved quickly gets accredited.

Even when particular committees of inquiry or mandate review forums draw attention to the need for more fundamental transformation at the level of theory and organizational culture, those matters are readily dismissed as fuzzy and too elusive to be tractable, and there is little will either within the organization or at the oversight or monitoring agency level to insist on those foundational dimensions being dealt with on the pretense that such endeavors are too complex, take too much time, and are rarely successful. Such rationalizations force these foundational issues off the table.[17]

As a result, most initiatives that are carried out under the general rubric of organizational design are merely tinkering with innocuous technological features (as open annual meetings and the like) or superficial structural features or organization charts without ever attempting to resolve the admittedly more difficult and obviously more important problem of the reconciliation of the different frames of reference and of the trans-substantiation of the organizational culture or theory of what the organization is about. The rationale is that it is easier to start with easy moves, but it is hardly persuasive when this entails never going beyond that stage.

Indeed, one of the most important occluded factors in the study of organizational design is the capacity for sabotage by groups with a vested interest in the status quo. These occluded forces are often so important that some wise transformation experts, like Albert Hirschman, have suggested that no reform is likely to succeed unless it comes as a total surprise, and act as a thunderbolt. This may be unduly pessimistic. Much can probably be done, despite the countervailing forces, but only if the saboteurs are exposed (be they passive or active) and if corrosive critical thinking is allowed to openly question their rearguard action as sabotage.

The best way to illustrate the significance of organization design may be to expose some failures that can be ascribed either to deliberate design sabotage or to a nonchalant attitude that allowed poor organizational design to survive. Such active or passive sabotage can easily do much damage, especially when there is no one monitoring the scene, when the forces of denial are powerful, and when there is little in place that might serve as fail-safe mechanisms.

THE ALL-TOO-EASY WORLD OF SABOTAGE

The design process sketched in the last sections suggests the basic elements of effective design and redesign. Such an ideal continuing dynamic adjustment is rarely observed in the real world. There are always weaknesses that survive at different pressure points in the process.

One can identify four major sources of design failures:

1 the six preconditions not being in place
2 the Simons conditions being unmet: the what
3 poor social learning through prototyping and serious play failing: the how
4 the failure of going beyond the superficial in the tripartite *bricolage*: the wherewithal

The first major source explains why organizational design is not well done in general. It can only be repaired by a fundamental change in the mindset and a massive investment (intellectual and financial) in this type of work. While it must be held responsible for much of poor or whimsical design everywhere, it is difficult to ascribe particular failures to this general disease.

Nothing but full recognition of the centrality of this long-term function, and its being embedded formally in the institutional architecture will ensure that the work is done. In the absence of such embeddedness, it may be said that there will be no continuous monitoring and evaluation of organizational design, and that it is hardly surprising that the what, the how and the wherewithal of good organizational design is not what it should be.

The other three sources are more proximate, one might say. They point to particular actions that might have prevented observed failures or might have triggered them.

In the rest of this section, we briefly describe the background, the issue and observed blockages in two recent files, and we point to significant design failures and equally important inaction when repairs were in order. In each case, the Simons conditions were not met, social learning was stunted, and critical reflections about the philosophy of the organization did not occur.

Two vignettes

CANADIAN NUCLEAR SAFETY COMMISSION

Background. The independent Atomic Energy Control Board (AECB) was established in 1946 to control and supervise the development, application and peaceful uses of nuclear energy in Canada, as well as to participate in an international measure of control. From the beginning, the AECB was given regulatory powers aimed at encouraging and facilitating research and investigations as well as developing, controlling, supervising and licensing the production, application and use of atomic energy. The possibility existed from the beginning for a company to be established. Atomic Energy of Canada Limited (AECL) was established in 1952 with no mandate specified for it in legislation.[18]

Canada quickly became a world leader in this sector – creating multipurpose research reactors from scratch, and enabling the first Cobalt-60 treatment for cancer in the world in Victoria, B.C. in 1961; together with AECL, Ontario Hydro and General Electric, a commercial power generator (CANDU) was brought forth in 1962.

Nevertheless, the passage of time has changed the landscape. In the twenty years between 1974 and 1994, several reviews took place including one by Parliament, two ministerial reviews and other studies.[19] The 1994 Auditor General's Report enumerated key changes that had transformed the context since the AECB's inception – federal regulatory reform, cost recovery (with the consequence that regulatees wanted more say), more age-related failures of reactors, increasing citizen concerns over the environment, environmental assessment requirements, etc. – noting that stricter procedures were being required and that judicial review of regulatory inspections and enforcement was increasingly being invoked.[20]

A refurbished regulatory apparatus was put in place – the Canadian Nuclear Safety Commission (CNSC) through legislation that received Royal Assent in 1997, and came into effect in 2000. The new apparatus was designed to split regulatory powers from concerns about research and development as well as marketing, and provided for a much more detailed and prescriptive approach to regulating. The CNSC was directed by the authorizing legislation to regulate "the use of nuclear energy and materials to protect (to a reasonable level and in a manner consistent with Canada's international obligations) health, safety and the environment ... (as well as) to respect Canada's international commitments on the peaceful use of nuclear power."[21] This was (and is) to be done through regulations that must be vetted by the Governor in Council. The CNSC has the authority to exempt any activity, person, class of person or quantity of nuclear substance, temporarily or permanently, from the application of the governing legislation, in accordance with regulations. The CNSC also conducts legislated environmental assessments, and implements non-proliferation provisions of nuclear cooperation agreements between Canada and its nuclear trading partners, and Canada bilateral agreements with the International Atomic Energy Agency (IAEA) on nuclear safeguards verification.

The CNSC is a "court of record,"[22] whose president may establish panels of commission members and decides if they should act as the commission (except with respect to regulations and by-law making), but has no voting privileges except in case of a tie. It operates with 800 employees and a budget of $90M.[23]

The minister of Natural Resources Canada has the authority to issue binding directives to CNSC "on broad policy matters with respect to the objects of the Commission."[24] In effect, CNSC is part of the minister's portfolio. Nevertheless, because it is an independent quasi-judicial administrative tribunal, the responsible minister and any other minister (e.g., one whose responsibilities are affected by it) are expected to follow centrally issued advice in dealings with it. That advice states "(t)he nature of the relationship between a Minister and an administrative tribunal with independent decision-making or quasi-judicial functions is a particularly sensitive issue. ... Ministers and Secretaries of State shall not intervene, or appear to intervene, on behalf of any person or entity, with quasi-judicial tribunals, on any matter before them that requires a decision in their quasi-judicial capacity, unless authorized by law."[25]

The change in the nuclear industry has broadened and deepened since the auditor general's 1994 Report. On one hand, it has become an increasingly sensitive industry worldwide for several reasons including those related to aging facilities as well as fears related to security, health and the environment. Aging nuclear power generating facilities are raising questions of replacement choices and decommissioning costs. Security fears related to proliferation together with the rise of state and non-state terrorism, as well as growing health and environmental concerns including waste management, are also increasing in importance as time passes. (For example, some strongly safety-minded experts call for a design of a nuclear reactor that ensures the probability of an accident causing harm to a member of the public who is outside a nuclear facility is less that one in a million in one year. In 1990, with various upgrades, an accident at a key AECL research reactor for world medical isotope production that was built in 1957 was conjectured by critics as likely to be in the range of one in 10,000.[26] It is of course, significantly higher today.)

On the other hand, peaceful uses continue to grow in nature and scope: the world has begun to take a hard look at its dependency on oil and to look at nuclear energy as an alternative; medical applications of nuclear technology blossom, and agricultural applications emerge.

AECL was created to further peaceful uses of nuclear energy based on heavy-water technology. Significantly subsidized (with estimates in the billions) but operationally profitable and commercially oriented, it remains deeply embedded in Canada's nuclear research efforts. It has stimulated and launched successful commercial ventures in both medical and power generation worldwide, currently accounting for the production of raw material for half of the world's medical isotopes.

Nevertheless, with its reliance on longstanding heavy-water technology, AECL is argued by some to be destined to become lightweight player. Ottawa-based corporation MDS-Nordion is a dominant player in nuclear medicine and relies to a large degree on AECL as a major supplier.

By the very nature of its business, AECL is one of CNSC's important regulatees. Several federal ministers together with their policy departments have a significant interest in this industry, including those concerned with the environment, health, international affairs, and national security as well as the two that are currently represented on AECL's Board of Directors (Industry Canada, and Natural Resources Canada) by their deputy ministers.

Issues. Recent difficulties involving an extended shutdown of a 50-year old AECL research reactor that produces more than half of the world's medical isotope spiraled, over a few weeks (from the initial reactor shut down in mid November 2007 to its restart in mid-December 2007), into an international crisis in which a hasty legislative override of CSNC was used to authorize the restart of the reactor.

The president of CNSC was removed from her post (but kept on as a member of the Commission), accused by the prime minister of needlessly endangering the lives of Canadians, and the minister responsible for Natural Resources Canada asked her in a letter to provide reasons why she should not be fired.[27] In response, she sued the federal government over what she saw as an unfair dismissal,[28] and resigned in September 2008. The chairman of AECL's Board of Directors resigned in December 2007, after just over a year in the job.

The longer-term consequences of this shutdown crisis for Canada, for AECL and for MDS Nordion may well turn out to be significant. Canada's leading medical journal put it this way "why is something as important as the world's medical isotope supply dependent on a half-century old reactor? Will coordination with Europe be improved to guard against future shortages? How long will it be before the United States starts making its own isotopes?"[29] The difficulties have been exacerbated by a recent announcement by AECL of the abandonment, for costs reasons, of its decade long plan to replace the reactor with two modern ones dedicated to medical isotope production.

The inability of AECL to meet its longstanding commitment to its important customer MDS Nordion (to successfully bring modern replacement reactors on stream) as well as the inability of CNSC and AECL (until recently) to reach agreement on a process for some kind of pre-project design review of the latter's new flagship project (an advanced CANDU reactor) could only translate into a significant disadvantage for AECL in its marketing efforts to domestic and foreign governments, as well as for its marketability – should the government wish to pursue the full or partial privatization of AECL.

Blockages. While there would appear to exist some levers in the law to deal with unexpected situations when CNSC and AECL might not be in agreement (such as the possibility for the Natural Resources minister of providing binding directives, and Governor in Council vetting of regulations proposed by the CNSC), it is not at all clear that these mechanisms are adequate to deal smoothly with broader public interest tradeoffs. The aim of the underpinning legislation is, inter alia, to limit the risks to national security, the health and safety of persons and the environment that go with the development, production and use of nuclear energy and substances to a reasonable degree, and in a way consistent with international obligations.

While the wording may allow for a little flexibility of interpretation, the former President of CNSC – who held the post from 2001 to very early 2008 – signaled that as she saw it, the agency's regulatory regime was "the most modern in the world, separating health and safety from economic and political interests."[30] For her, the authors were told, protection of domestic markets (something Canada's competitors seem to find a way to do) was irrelevant.

At the same time, the admonition to ministers and secretaries of state to treat quasi-judicial bodies sensitively and specifically to refrain from intervening or being seen to intervene on behalf of an entity on any matter that requires a decision in their quasi-judicial capacity, appears to preclude any minister with a legitimate policy interest from doing or being seen to do anything to push for creative approaches being applied by the CNSC. Similar admonitions would apply to policy deputy ministers; those who are also board members for AECL might feel doubly hamstrung. Even the clerk of the Privy Council might be anxious to avoid any perception of inappropriate interference.

The main levers for dealing with necessary discussions and tradeoffs in the public interest by the different stakeholders are therefore ineffective because the barriers erected to safeguard CNSC's independence prevent them from being used in a timely-enough fashion if an unexpected crisis arises. This leaves CNSC's governance *de facto* to itself thereby placing over-reliance, some might say, on the perspectives of a few individuals without sufficient built-in checks and balances (i.e. embedded loops for social learning) to ensure that other points of view are given adequate attention.

The joint CNSC / AECL "lessons learned" exercise – carried out by the Talisman International LLC as a result of the fiasco – reported in June 2008. Given a narrow mandate, Talisman concluded that "the overarching root cause of the ... extended outage in late 2007 was due to a CNSC and AECL set of processes which were "expert based" not "process based". The prevalent culture of informality was considered a significant and fundamental flaw in both organizations' methods of operation, and contributed to a series of misunderstandings regarding reactor plant safety system upgrade status, AECL licensing commitments, and CSNC regulatory requirements and license conditions...(i)n summary the Talisman team believes that improved communications, clear license conditions, and a mutual understanding of plant status and outstanding licensing and inspection issues, along with improved inspector training and enforcement and in-house legal staff, would help prevent the misunderstandings which led to the extended outage in late 2007)."[31]

SERVICE CANADA

Background. In 1989, the then Clerk of Privy Council (Paul Tellier) was the driving force behind PS2000 – the first administrative review at the federal level in Canada to designate "quality of service to the public" as an overarching goal of public management.[32]

In 1993, connectivity to the Internet moved to center stage at Industry Canada as a Director General, in charge of a relatively obscure function, was able to get backing for an approach that evolved into a major "branding" effort that, by 1999, was announced in the Speech from the Throne as an objective "to be known as ... (the government that was) most connected to citizens."[33] To reach this objective of being most connected to citizens and businesses, the government proposed the GOL initiative (Government on Line) GOL (1999–2006)) as a project that was ultimately allocated $880M in new money over 6 years, and that was built around two principles: grouping information and services around client's needs and priorities, and partnering within the federal government as well as with other governments to cluster services in order to better serve the public[34]. At the same time as the GOL initiative was launched, a 3-year Service Canada pilot project was brought forth, including the two existing channels of communication (the Canada web site and a 1-800 line).

As well Service Canada involved a federally driven integrated front door for information and services (SII (1999–2006)) comprised of Service Canada Access Centres located in different federal departments and agencies, co-located in federal and provincial places, or located in municipal organizations, and in non-governmental agencies.[35] By 2004–2005 the network operated at 76 locations.

In 1997, the then Clerk of Privy Council (Jocelyne Bourgon) – who saw service to the public as a key goal for federal public sector/service reform – gave full support to the recommendation of a federal-provincial-municipal public service managers conference that had expressed a strong interest in learning about the main drivers of service quality improvement, and launched the Citizens First survey of 1998 – an initiative that was celebrated as "leading edge"[36] in the service quality community.

The 3-year Service Canada pilot project was extended in 2002 with a view to developing a single window strategy based on a three-way partnership of Treasury Board Secretariat (policy and coordination), Communications Canada (website & 1-800), and HRDC – which had its own federal social services delivery network – that was given responsibility to manage the integrated front door Service Canada network for the system as a whole. A committee of DGs was charged with the coordination work. This committee reported to a DM level committee and each DM in turn reported to his or her minister.

By 2004–2005, HRDC's own network had become 320 (in person) Human Resources Centres – operated a little differently across the country as needed – plus mail services. HRDC had been split into two departments and both networks were located in one part of the former department, while telephone and Internet services were located in the other. In 2005, the government announced in its budget that one of the two new departments was to become the foundation of the new government of Canada network.

In this way, the three objectives – citizen-centered service delivery, e-Government, and on-going service delivery of a range of federal social programs by one department came together organizationally in 2005 when Service Canada was launched as a stand-alone entity combining delivery networks (i.e., SII plus social services). The deputy head was also named associate DM for one of the "policy" departments that had been part of the "old" HRDC, and became responsible for providing corporate services for the two "policy" departments (HRSD and HRDC) as well as for itself.

Service Canada, the new (integrated) backbone, opened its doors in September 2005. In its first annual report in 2005–2006, Service Canada described its mandate this way: "To improve services for Canadians by working with partners to provide access to the full range of government services and benefits that Canadians want and need in person, by telephone, Internet or mail."[37] The spirit of entrepreneurialism and serious play that had been engendered by spinning Service Canada off into a separate entity was clear in its words that year. It was also clear in its actions that included the introduction of a performance scorecard, establishing an office for client satisfaction, entering partnerships with other governments (e.g. registration of births in Ontario), having its executives spend four days a year at the front line, and using service offerings themselves to see how they work.[38]

In early 2006, Service Canada was moved back closer to the two policy departments (which were merged back into one that is called HRSDC). The deputy head of Service Canada was required to report to the departmental DM and, as a result, its corporate services were no longer shared with *separate* entities, but shared within the same departmental (i.e. HRSDC) "skin". Reports on its plans and accomplishments (including the 2005–2006 Annual Report) became part of HRSDC's reports.

In June 2008, Service Canada's website described what it does this way: "Service Canada is about improving the delivery of government services … offer(ing) … single window access to a wide range of Government of Canada programs and services for citizens."[39]

Issues. Since 2000, the global company Accenture has been issuing highly regarded annual reports on the progress of 22 national governments (including Canada) in their journey toward citizen-centered service delivery. Their four-pillar model (citizen-centered, cross-government, multi-channel, proactively

Table 1

Stage / Factor	1– Establishing eGoverment	2 – Using eGovernment	3 – Embracing the four pillars	4 – Building the trust
Goals	• Number of services on line	• High percentage of citizens and business uptake	• Services cross-channel and cross-government – one stop / end-to-end	• Citizens trust their government implicitly
Key challenges	• Internet capability	• Citizen outreach • Citizen uptake	• Cross-government collaboration • Service integration	• Content of services
Service implications	• Service availability	• Service delivery	• Service Value	• Service Trust

Extracted from Accenture 2006: 6 and slightly modified

communicated service) sets out goals, key challenges, and service implications in four stages (see table 1).

Canada scored very well from the beginning (2000) with the combination of GOL and SII. In particular, Canada's vision of streamlined service delivery (for individuals and for businesses collaboratively across jurisdictions, and later for federal corporate services) was seen as one of the most far-reaching and inspirational in the world (Accenture 2007: 87), and Canada has been lauded for "being ahead of the curve for years" (Accenture 2006: 45).

In fact, by the 2006 Report, Canada (along with the US) was ranked as one of the two trendsetters based on its performance [40] (46).

Accenture observed in its 2007 Report, however, that Canada was nudged out of its first place ranking by Singapore (by a little) mostly because of how citizens perceive their performance in terms of service availability, delivery, value and trust. It reported that "citizens are clearly seeing a gap between the government's promise and its practice … in terms of … "citizens voice" alone, Canada ranked 9th out of 22 countries … (and) less than half of the respondents believe service has improved compared to three years ago, a greater number think it has stayed the same or in fact, gotten worse "(Accenture 2007: 87). In fact Canada is now listed as a country in danger of losing momentum (87).

Blockages. Virtually from Service Canada's inception as a stand-alone entity, problems began to emerge with the main policy departments (formerly HRDC) both with respect to the policy-service delivery linkage as well as with the shared corporate services. "Service delivery" is an issue domain in its own right that requires policy choices and decisions to be made. By its very nature it cuts across other issue domains (e.g. labour market or aging) both within and across jurisdictions, and as such, demands integration at the political level. Yet, it is still treated as just one of a raft of management issues, and it is without either a designated spokesperson at the cabinet table or one who can hold Service Canada properly to account within the government of the day for progress towards the public pan-Canadian goal of service to the citizens *and* service integration, taking into account the expectations generated by earlier pronouncements.

The very entrepreneurialism of Service Canada as a separate organization was directed to improving services to Canadians. This citizen-focused service delivery goal encompassing all levels of government could not but be strongly constrained (and be bound to lose out) to the goal of federal service delivery integration and efficiency, when Service Canada was required to share corporate services, in effect, with an important federal department (or two in its "split" mode) that was meant to be only one of its partners.

This shared corporate services partnership, involving very unequal players in terms both of "clout" and of "size", could only lead to the commitment to federal government program delivery improvement *trumping* the much broader objective of providing the best possible access to the full range of government services that Canadians want and need.

Without political direction as a counterweight, the earliest opportunity to tame Service Canada and bury it back into HRSDC (and to redefine its role much more narrowly as to serve only the federal government) seems to have been too attractive to senior central bureaucrats to let pass by.

Design failures

These two files would warrant a much more detailed treatment than that which is possible in the context of a short chapter. Moreover, much in these files is still not available for external scrutiny. So we are forced to provide nothing more than a short statement about organization design flaws, and a tentative identification of what would appear to be the main sources of the problems.

THE CANADIAN NUCLEAR SAFETY COMMISSION CASE
The fundamental issue in this case is the failure to have seen *ab ovo* the need to devise (and put in place) satisfactory and workable ways to (1) debate, discuss and integrate different legitimate perspectives (expert versus policy, security versus social and economic dimensions), (2) to do so smoothly (in a different but timely manner, as the context changes) and (3) to have satisfactory fail-safe mechanisms in place in case of stalemate.

It is our view that the organizational failure was quite predictable, and that the process was *passively sabotaged* by a gross neglect of the scrutiny required by the precautionary principle at the time of designing the new regulatory framework for CNSC. The Simons conditions were not met, and, as a result, the social learning engine was prevented from going into action, and the tripartite *bricolage* proved impossible.

The Simons equation was clearly out of balance. The spans of control and support on the supply side proved unable to meet the requirements of accountability and influence on the demand side. An unduly restrictive mandate that *precluded* consideration of social and economic impacts meant that the weight was entirely on security-focused control without due consideration of the commitments to others. Although there is a real need for safeguarding (and being seen to safeguard) a regulatory agency from undue political interference, this does not obviate the need to take into account the full the range of stakeholders who are best able to serve partners and clients in considering organizational design. In this case, the range was obviously truncated so that some (e.g. those dealing with legitimate citizen/client concerns related to R & D, economic growth and Canada's reputation in the hunt for alternate power generation) were excluded. Moreover there was no margin of maneuverability as a result of the unduly narrow definition of performance, and of the absence of any viable conflict resolution mechanism with the demand side.

A modicum of prudence and design competence would have led to a refusal of such an overly prescriptive mandate for the CNSC, of such a fundamentalist focus on security as an absolute, of the exclusion of social and economic considerations altogether in final decisions, and of the consequent insularization of the CNSC from its life world context.

Tradeoffs must be made between legitimate public policy objectives such as risk to environment (and even health) versus risks to the country's ability and legitimacy to contribute to a field be it with research and development or selling and using its own high quality products at home and abroad for worthy causes.

In an advanced democracy like Canada's, these kinds of tradeoffs need to be brought to the cabinet table – something that was *de facto* not possible. The unduly narrow definition of stakeholders and of acceptable performance variables was a major flaw leaving too much to the diktats of experts.

Another element dictated by a modicum of prudence and design competence would have been the provision for forums where differences of opinions might be legitimately discussed. In this case, the quasi-taboo attached to any effort to make other viewpoints available to the CNSC constitutes a major design flaw. And the Talisman recommendation about improving communication does not address this fundamental problem.

Finally the legal setting has provided no fail-safe mechanism in case of irresolvable differences of opinion except ministerial or parliamentary directives that can only kick in when there is a full-blown crisis – not only an apprehended crisis. A less flawed design would have not only provided for legitimate forums for discussions, but also for processes of conflict resolution.

These flaws were an important source of the fiasco of 2007 and prevented any possible social learning, and closed the door to any possible *bricolage* (retooling, restructuring or reframing). Unless the legal framework is amended, the on-going necessary conversations (temporarily made possible by the post parliamentary decision *glasnost*) may not be capable of being carried out except in a paralegal way without a true *perestroika*. As a result, little or no innovation can be anticipated.

The potential for informal exchanges at a time when informality has been damned as the main source of the problem by Talisman (even in a narrow way) is very limited. It is more likely that CNSC experts with strong views, reinforced by an international body (IAEA) – that is worried exclusively about global proliferation, security, environmental and health concerns and sees Canada's CNSC as a "poster child" – will be unmoved by any argument echoing a different perspective.

THE SERVICE CANADA CASE

The fundamental issue in this case is the power struggle between those in the technocracy who put a priority on serving the citizen well and those who see their job as improving the functioning of the federal government taken by itself (and not incidentally, the functioning of the federal bureaucracy). In this case, the latter group clearly saw Service Canada as undermining the basis of the federal government and its bureaucracy by working collaboratively with other governments, and thereby opening the door to possibilities that the new packages of services might come to be seen as better delivered by other levels of government. The specter of subsidiarity was seen as almost around the corner. Especially in the world of human resources and social development where the federal authority is widely contested, any weakening of the base of federal operations could be seen by the federal technocracy as a threat. As a result, serving the federal machine came to trump serving the citizen well.

As opposed to the CNSC case where neglect of the importance of good organizational design led to passively sabotaging a very important and complex regulatory process, the case of Service Canada looks like one of *active sabotage*. The redirection of the Service Canada initiative away from its original mandate in 1999 appears to be a deliberate effort to tame and neuter an initiative that was, in the process of better serving the citizen, seen as disserving the federal bureaucracy.

The consequence of failure in this case is not a life-threatening crisis likely to trigger some overt corrective action, but something much more insidious. The consequence may well be the slow abandonment (at least at the federal level) of international leadership around citizen-centered service delivery (even though the drum-beating rhetoric about it may continue), the resurgence of the sort of mindless and insensitive "rationalizations" of the sort that has led to the closing of post offices and the disappearance of the federal presence and service wickets locally, or to the centralization of taxation offices that has drastically eliminated any possibility of face to face interaction with tax collectors regionally. Increased distance between federal bureaucrats and citizens can only increase the level of cynicism about government's ability to serve them well. With it, one may speculate on the increase in the exasperation of elected public officials at the federal level with the ability of the public service (as its main administrative partner) to do its job well.

In this case, the failure has little to do with neglect or error, but it has a lot to do with organizational behavior in a bureaucracy and the principal-agent problem.

Important tradeoffs are made at the cabinet table – in this case between (a) improving service to individual citizens and businesses (over a broad range of activities) through collaboration among governments and sectors, and (b) improving service to them by one government and/or one or two key federal departments and agencies – as they are made in the case of major procurement decisions that have domestic and foreign policy implications.

Asking the minister responsible for those one or two federal departments to tradeoff the benefits for his units against the benefits of the Canadian citizens from a much larger initiative is bound to pose problems and is probably unreasonable. This is the reason why Australia has created a ministerial post to ensure that the interests of the broader initiative would be defended at the cabinet level and that appropriate accountability for such broader initiative would be in place. Pushing the tradeoff down to the level uppermost bureaucracy (i.e., the DM of one department of which Service Canada had become one part in 2005), as happened in the second stage of the evolution described above, made the situation even more unworkable.

Having no way to have the tradeoffs made at the cabinet table allows those bureaucrats with their own objectives (such as, at their worst, bigger budgets, more prestige, more discretionary resources to indulge in amenities of all sorts, etc.) to advance their own version of what the priority should be: in this case, the self-serving objective of the federal government infrastructure *trumped* the interests of the Canadian citizens and businesses

It has been shown in the past that even a super-bureau like the Bank of Canada might be led to pursue objectives that did not appear to be the same as those of the government or those that the best interests of the citizenry may dictate.[41]

Bureaus have a capacity to pursue their own objectives independent of the government to some degree. Our hypothesis is that such may be the case in the Service Canada events. Prestige-survival-power might be said to have trumped the "public interest" as the citizen would see it. The fact that, in so doing, the bureaucracy has also been led to punish success, adds to the gravity of the indictment.[42]

More important perhaps is the reasonable conjecture that the Service Canada experience may not be unique. How many creative and successful federal initiatives to better serve Canadian citizens are scuttled in the name of the prestige-survival of the federal technocracy? How would we know? The question is all the more important that cases that might be construed as active sabotage are infinitely more costly and reprehensible than the trivial abuses of a head of agency circumnavigating to his destinations in the most roundabout way just to fatten his personal air miles account, yet the former actions are infinitely less visible in the absence of any oversight of organizational design than the petty abuses likely to be picked up by internal auditors.

One may therefore infer from the information available that the derailed design came to be clearly out of line with what the Simons conditions would suggest, that prototyping, serious play and experimentation were clearly sabotaged and social learning consequently stunted, and that tinkering with organization charts came to be used as a decoy to hide a deliberate effort to modify the philosophy of Service Canada away from its original vocation of serving Canadian citizens at large better, to the immensely more reduced task of serving the integration of services of the Canadian federal government.

As to the question of what sort of organizational design might have succeeded in preventing such slippage, there is no simple and absolute answer. One may easily envisage a variety of schemes (independent agency, department, but also horizontal political mechanisms to bring clusters of ministers together, etc.) that would have ensured that the original direction would have been maintained. Therefore a separate minister is not the only thinkable solution. The experience of various other countries has shown that a wide range of mechanisms may accomplish this sort of task.[43]

CONCLUSION

It is difficult to underestimate the toxic effect of organizational design failures (whether they are the result of passive or active sabotage) and as a result, it is difficult to overestimate the benefits that might flow from a greater attention to organization design in the private, public and social sectors.

Yet this trail has not been as fully explored as it should have been, and much of what one might call *pathologies of governance* must be properly ascribed to these flaws. Such a possibility is all the more probable because of the fact that cumulative social learning on this front has turned out to be less effective that it should be. Design inquiry is so often left to practitioners and management consultants, that, as a result, "the body of design knowledge appears to be fragmented and dispersed" – much more so than in other bodies of knowledge.[44] The time may be ripe for a revolution! As Chalmers Johnson[45] would put it, "multiple dysfunctions plus elite intransigence cause revolution."

The question is: what should the revolution entail?

It might take three forms.

First, what is required is a better and fuller appreciation of the organization design function, and the development of the required competencies to ensure that *ex ante* proper advice is sought and obtained about the sort of architecture required for effective performance. This applies both at the level of individual organization (e.g., department or agency) and centrally (e.g., the federal government as a whole).

It is mindless to ask intelligent and well-trained personnel to operate in organizational settings that can only lead them to be predictably irrational and therefore to render the organization dysfunctional.

Second, what is required is an oversight function *in real time* to monitor organizational performance. This sort of *veille organisationnelle* and organizational vigilance (again both at the individual organization and "central" levels) should be as important as the sort of monitoring that is in good currency for human and financial resources. It should not be an audit function that would best be performed *ex post* and might fall into the bailiwick of the Office of the Auditor General, but an activity designed to detect as soon as possible any sign of malfunctioning, it being understood that organization design is always somewhat experimental. Moreover this *veille* should be of central import in social learning by highlighting successes that might deserve more attention and might lead to imitation elsewhere, by detecting early warning signals of problems so as to be able to draw attention to repairs before a crisis occurs, and by questioning organizational redesign that would appear to make no sense or worse still, be toxic.

Third, what is required is that the Office of the Auditor General instead of being allowed to creep into policy matters be directed to pay more attention to organizational matters. This might lead to *ex post* in depth evaluation of major organizational disasters like the assignment of massive operational tasks to agencies having little or no operational experience and capability as seems to have happened in the gun registry file.

These three initiatives are also listed by order of priority, with the autopsy phase obviously being given a lesser priority in a world that emphasizes the importance of social learning.

These macroscopic changes cannot however replace the need to ensure that greater attention is paid in all departments and agencies to matters of organizational design and organizational performance. Nor can it replace the need to ensure, at the local level, that the requisite failsafe mechanisms are in place to ensure that blockages and sabotages are not allowed to prevail.

Anticipating in advance that something awful may ensue from a flawed design is marvelous when one can, but it cannot suffice, because, capacity for anticipation is as problematic as capacity to design perfect apparatuses right from the start. One must accept the inevitability of prototyping and experimenting on this front, and work at ensuring that learning loops are going to be as short and fast as possible. Indeed, even this may be too optimistic. One may have to be satisfied to prevent harm.

Promoting good things and working at reducing bad things may look the same on the surface, but, at the operational level, they are quite different: "scrutinizing the harms themselves, and discovering their dynamics and dependencies, leads to the possibility of sabotage. Cleverly conceived acts of sabotage, exploiting identified vulnerabilities of the object under attack, can be not only effective, but extremely resource-efficient too."[46]

Preventing harms, experimenting, learning as fast as one can along the way would appear to be the best we can hope for. This is the only way to harness complexity. The word "harness" is quite apt here: it conveys "a perspective that is not explanatory but active – seeking to improve but without being able to fully control."[47] In the world of organization design, it may be the only way to go.

NOTES

1 Gilles Paquet, 2007. "Organization Design as Governance's Achilles' Heel," www.governância.com 1 (3), 1–11.
2 A. Georges L. Romme, 2003. "Making a Difference: Organization as Design," *Organization Science* 14 (5) 558.
3 John Roberts, 2004. *The Modern Firm* (Oxford: Oxford University Press)
4 C. Spinosa, F. Flores, F., H.L. Dreyfus, 1997. Disclosing New Worlds (Cambridge: The MIT Press) 17.
5 Roger Martin, 2004. "The Design of Business," *Rotman Management*, Winter, 7.
6 Charles Sabel, 2004. "Beyond Principal-Agent Governance: Experimentalist Organizations, Learning and Accountability," in E. Engelen and M. Sie Dhian Ho (eds) *De Staat van de Democratie*. Democratie *Voorbij de Staat*. WRR Verkenning 3. (Amsterdam: Amsterdam University Press), 173–95; Michael Schrage, 2000. *Serious Play* (Boston: Harvard Business School Press).
7 Gilles Paquet, 2006. "Savoirs, savoir-faire, savoir-être: In Praise of Professional Wroughting and Wrighting. A Think-piece for Campus 2020 – An Inquiry into the Future of British Columbia's post-secondary education system" (available at http://www.campus2020.ca/EN/think_pieces/)
8 Harlan Cleveland, 2002. *Nobody in Charge* (San Francisco : Jossey-Bass); Ruth Hubbard, Gilles Paquet 2007. *Gomery's Blinders and Canadian Federalism*. (Ottawa: The University of Ottawa Press).
9 Charles Sabel, 2001. "A Quiet Revolution of Democratic Governance: Towards Democratic Experimentalism" in *Governance in the 21st Century* (Paris: OECD), 121–48
10 Michael Schrage, 2000. *Serious Play* (Boston: Harvard Business School Press).

11. Don Tapscott, Anthony D. Williams, 2006. *Wikinomics* (New York: Portfolio).
12. Gilles Paquet, 2008. *Deep Cultural Diversity: A Governance Challenge* (Ottawa: The University of Ottawa Press).
13. Michael Schrage, *Serious Play*, 199ff.
14. Donald A. Schön, 1971. *Beyond the Stable State* (New York: Random House), 33
15. Available at www.pco-bcp.gc.ca/index.asp?lang=eng&page=information&sub =publications&doc=Role/role2007_e.htm; accessed 17 August 2008
16. James O'Tole, 1996, *Leading Change* (New York: Ballentyne Books), 238
17. Gilles Paquet, 2004. Pathologies de gouvernance (Montréal: Liber); Gilles Paquet et al, 2006. "The National Capital Commission: Charting a New Course. Report of the NCC Mandate Review Panel"; Gilles Paquet, 2007. "Background paper prepared for the Task Force on Governance and Cultural Change in the RCMP."
18. Auditor General of Canada Report: Special Examination Report, Office of the Auditor General, 5 September 2007.
19. Auditor General of Canada Report, 1994, ch 15:7
20. Ibid.
21. "Canadian Nuclear Safety Commission: An Overview," available at http://www.nuclearsafety.gc.ca/eng/respurce/publications/CNSC_0748/CNSC_0748.cfm; accessed 15 April 2008
22. Nuclear Safety and Control Act (powers)
23. CNSC 2008–2009 Report on Priorities and Plans
24. Nuclear Safety and Control Act 1997, c. 9 19. (1)
25. A Guide for Minister and Secretaries of State 2007: 14, 68
26. Available at www.thestar.com/print/Article/33604; accessed 11 June 2008
27. www.nationalpost.com/news/canada/story.html?id=228794; accessed 15 April 2008
28. *Ottawa Citizen*, 19 May 2008, "Nuclear Safety Watchdog Names New President," Tobin Dalrymple
29. www.cmaj.ca/cgi/content/full/178/5/536; accessed 11 June 2008
30. www.tbs-cst.gc.ca/dpr-rmr/2006–2007/inst/csn01–eng.asp; accessed 12 June 2008
31. "Atomic Energy of Canada Limited National Research Universal Reactor Safety Systems Upgrade and the Canadian Nuclear Safety Commission's Licensing and Oversight Process," A Lessons Learned Report by Talisman International, LLC June 2008 (available on the websites of AECL and the CNSC)
32. Brian O'Neal, 1994, "Reorganizing Government: New Approaches to Public Service Reform," http://dsp-psd.tpsgc.gc.ca/Collection-R/LoPBdP/bp375–e.htm; accessed 28 August 2008
33. Speech from the Throne to Open the Thirty Sixth Parliament of Canada, 1999, available at www.pco-bcp.gc.ca; accessed 22 July 2008
34. unpan1.un.org/intradoc/groups/public/documents/UNPAN/UNPAN023528.pdf accessed 8 June 2008. The federal investments were for: on-line service improvements (130 most-used services in 34 departments and agencies); strategic infrastructure (privacy protection including a secure channel); service improvements (service

quality and standards as well as obligatory measurement and improvements); communication and measurement; and public servants' readiness to make the highest and best use of these new channels.

35 (www.tbs-sct.gc.ca/rma/eppi-ibdrp/hrdb-rhbd/archive/sc-sc/descry[ption_e.asp (date modified 31 January 2006); accessed 3 June 2008

36 Accenture 2006: 48

37 Service Canada Annual Report 2005–2006: 8

38 Ibid. 26–28

39 www.servicecanada.gc.ca/en/about/index.shtml; accessed 3 June 2008

40 Although "still working on connecting vision to implementation in Service Canada" (: 46).

41 K. Acheson, J.F. Chant, "Bureaucratic Theory and the Choice of Central Bank Goals: The Case of the Bank of Canada," Journal of Money, Credit and banking 5 (2) (1973), 637–55. An earlier case (and a more juicy one) is exposed in H.S. Gordon. The Economists versus the Bank of Canada. Toronto: The Ryerson Press, 1961. The personal costs borne by Gordon as a result of his drive to expose Coyne`s misdemeanor is a cautionary tale. His original letter was signed by 29 economists and the short book he wrote soon after demonstrated very effectively that there had been deception on the part of the Governor of the Bank of Canada. But after this event, Gordon was marginalized and shunned by the federal bureaucracy. His part-time career as a mediator in public service affairs was brought to a halt, and he was explicitly ignored by a royal commission later struck on monetary affairs (even though he was one of the best known Canadian experts in this area). He was later to depart from Canada to pursue a most successful career in the United States. This cautionary tale illustrates the perils of exposing deception and misinformation generated by the officialdom in the public sector in Canada.

42 R. Hubbard, G. Paquet 2008, "Cat's Eyes: Intelligent Work versus Perverse Incentives," www.optimumonline.ca 38 (3).

43 J. Roy and J. Langford, *Integrating Service Delivery across Levels of Government: Case Studies of Canada and Other Countries* (Washington: IBM Center for the Business of Government), 2008.

44 A. Georges L. Romme, op.cit. 569.

45 C. Johnson, *Revolution and the Social System* (Stanford: Hoover Institution, 1964), 22.

46 M.K. Sparrow, *The Character of Harms* (Cambridge: Cambridge University Press, 2008), 27.

47 R. Axelrod, M.D. Cohen, *Harnessing Complexity* (New York: The Free Press, 2000), xvi.

5 Evaluating the Rationale of the New Federal *Lobbying Act*: Making Lobbying Transparent or Regulating the Industry?

ROBERT SHEPHERD

INTRODUCTION[1]

"We must clean up corruption and lift up the veils of secrecy that have allowed it to flourish. We must replace the culture of entitlement with a culture of accountability."

Stephen Harper, November 2005.[2]

In 2005, while in opposition, Stephen Harper promised that if his party formed the government, a light would be shone on corruption, perceived or real, and that he would pave the way for a more transparent democracy in order to clean up the apparent lack of accountability and poor performance that defined, in his view, the workings of the federal government.[3] He pointed to then Prime Minister Paul Martin and his ties to the Earnscliffe Strategy Group, an Ottawa-based lobbying and research firm, suggesting "that a contract the company received from the Ministry of Finance when Paul Martin was in charge was unfairly awarded."[4] Also highlighted was the now infamous "sponsorship scandal" where accusations abounded about lobbyists passing brown envelopes and making secret deals to win much coveted federal money to encourage Québecers to remain part of Canada. There was also the matter of the murky relationship between Brian Mulroney and Karlheinz Schreiber whereby it remains unclear as to what was paid to whom for as yet undefined services.

In Canada, as elsewhere, lobbying is not generally regarded as an honourable profession.[5] Indeed, this fact has posed some complex challenges for mediating the relationships of advocates and other intermediaries and their governments in a way seen to be legitimate by citizens.

The *Lobbyist Registration Act* was proposed by former Prime Minister Brian Mulroney in September 1985, presented to Parliament in June 1987, received Royal Assent in September 1988, and came into force on 30 September 1989. In all, the Act has been amended with varying degrees of impact in 1995, 2003, 2005, and 2006 with the passing of the *Federal Accountability Act* (FedAA), Bill C-2. The latest law came into force on 2 July 2008. The FedAA amended the *Lobbyists' Registration Act* (LRA) and, as part of those amendments, renamed it the *Lobbying Act*.

Although lobbying legislation has been enacted in Canada since 1989, its objectives and orientation have changed over time. Changes to the Act have tended to focus on matters of information disclosure, and buffeting existing laws on influence-peddling, conflict of interest and post-employment. The key objective of the original LRA was to make transparent the activities of lobbyists by requiring information on their communications with public office holders. However, over time there has been a notable shift from a concern for transparency with respect to the activities of lobbyists to one with a commitment to regulating lobbying and lobbyists.

The 2006 changes to the Act were influenced in large part by Ottawa's obsession with accountability, performance and rule-making but also by a fashionable mistrust of lobbyists, especially the "hired guns" of the industry. Its preferred approach to resolving ethical shortcomings, including lobbying, has been to add more rules and to regulate behaviours.[6] The consequence of this shift for federal lobbying laws, in my view, has been a departure from a principled approach that adhered to broadly based objectives to a more comprehensive rules-based administration of codified requirements.[7] It is this shift in orientation that is the subject of this piece. The main question is: what are some of the likely outcomes and impacts of an increasingly regulatory based approach on public office holders and the lobbying industry? Although there may have been incremental shifts in the purposes of the Act prior to 2006, the FedAA solidified nascent preferences for regulation as the principal governance tool.

The paper is organized into three main parts. The first section describes the basic principles underlying most lobby legislation around the world and the manner in which these are typically interpreted. The next section describes the basic tenets of the Canadian Act that accord with these principles including its approach and significant reforms since it was first enacted in 1989. In particular, it tracks the changes to the legislation and the reasons for several of them. There are many moving parts to this legislation which means that much effort is required to capture some of the nuances. This description is necessary in order to situate the reader in the current reform debates. The last section provides a description and assessment of the latest reforms to the Act. The paper concludes with the view that although the FedAA solidified the rules-based approach, it also paves the way for more regulation as demands for enforcement increase. This trajectory of reform could potentially take the *Lobbying Act* in a direction that is untenable and unwarranted.

APPROACH

An evaluative approach is used to assess the *Lobbying Act* in light of the latest reforms emanating from the *Federal Accountability Act 2006*. Specifically, the paper focuses on whether these reforms are consistent with the Act's objectives as set out in its Preamble using some basic policy evaluation questions: i) Do the reforms reinforce or undermine the intent and spirit of the objectives?; ii) Do the reforms address key concerns or problems identified by those affected and is the response appropriate?; and, iii) What are the likely impacts of the reforms on those being affected by the Act? The questions are applied to the key elements of the legislation: definition and scope of lobbying; disclosure requirements including registration administration; accountability (e.g., Code of Conduct); and enforcement.

The broad objectives of the Act are set out in its Preamble:

- Free and open access to government is an important matter of public interest;
- Lobbying public office holders is a legitimate activity;
- It is desirable that public office holders and the public be able to know who is engaged in lobbying activities;
- The system for the registration of paid lobbyists should not impede free and open access to government.[8]

Given that the *Lobbying Act* has only been in force a short time, the observations and assessments are likely to be cursory at best. However, as indicated, this legislation is not new nor is Canada inexperienced with such legislation. As such, some reasoned suppositions can be made about likely impacts. To assist in this regard, a total of twenty-two in-depth interviews were conducted with federal and provincial officials (14), not-for-profit officials (3) and, industry participants (5), between June and September 2008.[9] Although twenty-two interviews are not likely to afford a comprehensive assessment, the respondents selected are very experienced with this legislation and understand its nuances. Federal officials included representatives from the previous Office of the Registrar of Lobbyists and the Treasury Board Secretariat, provincial officials included commissioners and senior officials from selected provincial lobbying offices, industry respondents included partners in large government relations firms and lobbying representative bodies and, not-for-profit respondents included senior officials from advocacy groups and charitable organizations.[10]

PRINCIPLES UNDERLYING LOBBYING LEGISLATION

Ensuring Transparency in Government

A principal purpose of lobbying legislation is to ensure transparency in the making of government decisions in response to potential popular concerns that lobbying gives special access or, at least, advantage to vested interests with the perceived result that these may override the general wishes of the public in such decision-making.[11] As such, the democratic purpose of transparency is to expose the policy and decision-making processes of government to public view in order to enable decision-makers and the public to know who is lobbying whom for what so that suitable precautions may be taken to protect the public good, however defined. From a procedural perspective, transparency may be regarded as a process for reassuring the public that decisions are being made openly and honestly. Procedural concerns of transparency are concerned with processes and procedures for identifying lobbyists, their methods of access to government, and possibly how they are paid. This usually involves the creation of a registry and a series of rules for its proper management including timely access by the public.

Ensuring Integrity and Accountability in Government

Integrity is a key principle of lobbying legislation but differs in kind from transparency. It refers to a subjective assessment on the part of citizens that government is acting in their best interest and is not a vehicle for vested interests that can afford to pay for their wants. In this view of integrity, lobby legislation is concerned with promoting equal and reasoned constraints regarding access to government, ethical standards for acting in public life, and limiting undue influence.

Accountability in government with respect to lobbying legislation is closely connected to integrity but is usually expressed in procedural terms. Accountability means providing an appropriate means to check that the expectations of government are being met with respect to the performance of individuals and organizations subject to the legislation. In simple terms this means having policies, processes and procedures in place that such individuals and organizations must follow that demonstrate they are living up to their responsibilities under the legislation. Processes are instituted to provide assurance that such performance is monitored. Based on this performance, enforcement mechanisms are triggered that support compliance if the Act's obligations are not respected.

Integrity and accountability can be expressed in provisions such as disclosure rules that shed a light on lobbying activities. This generally means that a registry is created which tracks the interactions of lobbyists with government officials. However, the registry is dependent on the provision of required information and that those subject to the legislation comply with those requirements. Closely tied with disclosure rules is the creation and adoption of codes of conduct to regulate the behaviour of public officials and lobbyists. However, most lobby legislation does not have a code as part of their lobby package – Canada, federally, is part of a minority of countries in this respect. Such codes are attached to registration statutes and are enforced by a public official, usually a registrar or commissioner. They provide the registrar or commissioner with limited authorities to monitor compliance with the legislation and to investigate lobbying behaviour and, through parliamentary reporting, draw attention to breaches of the code. Again, the scope of such codes and the authorities they afford vary but most are aimed at supporting compliance through rules or public shaming such as reports to the legislature.

Ensuring Effectiveness and Efficacy in Legislative Arrangements

Efficacy and effectiveness also guide lobby legislation in the sense that these assist to set boundaries on communication. With respect to effectiveness, setting *effective* controls on lobbying must be balanced with a democratic desire to ensure information between citizens and their governments is unimpeded. As such, setting boundaries involves determining who is captured by the legislation and who is not such as government officials from other levels of government, and the range of lobbying activities to be addressed. Effectiveness of legislation is generally concerned with the rigour of reporting requirements and the extent to which there is compliance. Effectiveness is usually gauged according to at least four key measures: a) legislation is perceived to support broader public policy objectives such as promoting transparency and integrity in government; b) the rules governing lobbyists are consistent with the political values of the country; c) legislation is consistent with the ethical regime of the country and is a supporting element of its practice; and, d) that the legislative requirements allow public officials to realistically carry out their duties without overburdening them.[12] Enforcement is expressed in terms of investigatory and/or verification powers although most jurisdictions do not afford investigatory powers or the ability to impose penalties – again, Canada is unique in this respect.[13] The balance that must be maintained, and this is key, is that those subject to the legislation must regard such codes are enforceable and that their end purpose is considered legitimate in the sense of serving higher principles such as transparency and integrity. In other words, there must be an understanding that the Act serves a useful purpose and that this purpose does not impair higher principles.

Applying the Principles – Key Questions

There are important questions to consider when preparing cohesive lobbying legislation:

- Who is to be regulated? That is, who's in and who's out?
- What information ought to be required for disclosure?
- Should lobbyists' conduct be regulated? If so, how?
- How can compliance with the legislative requirement be attained?
- How can the integrity of lobby legislation be ensured?

Depending upon the answers to these questions, the following elements of lobby legislation are required. Note that these questions act as a guideline and that the question of whether existing legislation meets the implicit standards implied by these is dependent on the perceptions but also the impacts felt by those directly affected by the legislation.

- A clear, unambiguous definition of the regulatory target;
- Disclosure requirements that are meaningful and attainable;
- Procedures for securing compliance are effective and realistic; and,
- The integrity of the regulatory process is maintained by an appropriate administrative framework.[14]

CANADA'S EXPERIENCE WITH LOBBYING LEGISLATION, 1989–2005

Mulroney introduced the *Lobbyists' Registration Act*, Bill C-82, as a result of pressure from backbench MPs who were deeply troubled about the growing influence of vested interests in the 1960s and 1970s.[15] In addition, a number of ministers and MPs in Mulroney's government were uncomfortable at the time with a series of events[16] they felt left the impression among voters that their government was untrustworthy and lacked integrity.[17] The bill set out to define who would be covered by the Act but stopped short of defining "lobbying" or "lobbyist," the requirement to register, the establishment of a registry, and distinguishing between consultant lobbyists and those who worked for corporations and non-profit organizations. It is important to note that although the Act is considered modest by today's standard, its implementation was noteworthy at a time when public perceptions about lobbying and government were capturing public attention in a negative way.

Exploring the Key Elements of Canada's Lobbying Laws

The essential elements of lobbying legislation include: 1) a basic definition of lobbying that sets coverage or scope; 2) determining disclosure; and, 3) compliance and accountability under the Act for lobbyists and government officials. Each of these elements is described in turn as they evolved over time up to the 2005/2006 amendments.

LEGISLATIVE SCOPE AND OBJECTIVES: UNDERSTANDING THE PURPOSE OF THE LAW

Lobbying legislation generally applies to at least two main bodies of policy actors: government officials and legislators, and lobbyists. The purpose of the *Lobbyists Registration Act* (LRA) was to provide for the public registration of individuals who were *paid* to communicate, written or oral, with defined "public office holders" with regard to federal laws, policies, programs and obtaining government contracts or procurement: this is most notably referred to as "lobbying."[18] This definition was introduced in 2003 given that the 1989 definition of "communicating with the intent to influence" was too problematic to ensure compliance. This definition has not been altered significantly with the introduction of the new *Lobbying Act 2008*. "Public office holders" were "defined as all persons occupying an elected or appointed position in the federal government, including members of the House of Commons and the Senate and their staff, officers and employees of federal departments and agencies, and members of the Canadian Forces and the Royal Canadian Mounted Police.[19]

Defining "lobbyist" is more challenging. The original classification of lobbyists under the 1989 version of the Act separated lobbyists into two categories: "professional lobbyists" and "in-house lobbyists." This categorization was amended in 1995 from two categories to three and it is this typology that remains today: consultant lobbyists; in-house lobbyists (corporations); and, in-house lobbyists (organizations). Consultant lobbyists are individuals who lobby for payment on behalf of a client. These are the "hired guns" and could be government relations consultants, lawyers, accountants or other similar professions. In-house lobbyists for corporations are employees of private sector corporations who carry out commercial activities for financial gain, and where lobbying is a significant part of their activities. In-house lobbyists in organizations are employees of not-for-profit organizations such as advocacy groups, industry and professional associations, charitable organizations, and universities.

In general terms, separating the in-house lobbyist category appeared to make sense at least when examined from the perspective of intentions behind lobbying activities. Parliamentarians have been concerned about who is lobbying them on behalf of another and who is being paid regardless of the source of the lobbying activity in order to understand pressures being brought to bear on their decisions. Parliamentarians also wanted to understand the nature of lobbying from companies and their influence on government decisions, regulations or policy such as procurement that may have an impact on their competition, and other matters. Likewise, Parliamentarians have complained that the representations of "special interests" have not been fully captured under any mechanism. However, it is recognized that such representations have "been legitimized and for the most part, institutionalized as part of the way in which our country is governed."[20] Such legislation is needed to at least monitor the *source* of the representations.

DISCLOSURE REQUIREMENTS:
ENSURING INTEGRITY AND ACCOUNTABILITY

Disclosure requirements are those demands that require lobbyists to provide information about mainly who is lobbying whom and for what reasons and that this information is sufficient to satisfy government decision-makers that the activities of lobbyists are open and transparent. Ideally, disclosure requirements would enlighten decision-makers on the intent of the lobbying activity, identify the beneficiaries of lobbying, and identify those governmental officials and offices that are the main target of lobbying activity. This information allows parliamentarians especially, to weigh the appeals and wants of lobbyists against, presumably, the needs and wants of citizens.[21] Although such information goes a long way to ensuring transparency, it is rarely considered adequate. There are always demands to ask for more especially to learn of competing lobbying interests, the extent to which these are credible and, to determine whether such information is critical in order to protect government integrity – no small task. The challenge, of course, is to balance the demand for information with a manageable registration system that does not overwhelm administrators and users of the system. The tests of such balance include a regular revisiting of information requirements through legislative amendments to determine whether they are consistent with the goals of the legislation, the demands are realistic for both government officials and lobbyists, and that information is easily and efficiently accessible.[22]

The 1989 Act made only modest requests for information including that consultant lobbyists were required to give their name and the name of those being lobbied as well the name of their organization. Little information was required regarding the subject matter of the engagement. In-house lobbyists were only required to provide their names and the name and address of the corporation or organization employing them. Although transparency was considered important, it was not the only consideration of the first Act. The Act's original intent was mainly to provide parliamentarians with information as to who was lobbying them and some basic data about the various topics of interest in order to make informed decisions based on the relevant concerns of interested parties.[23] Transparency was interpreted to mean that, "the registration of paid lobbyists shall help remove the shroud of mystery from this important activity. A publicly available record of paid lobbyists, their clients and other information called for would go some distance to demonstrate the government's commitment to transparency and integrity in its relations with the public."[24]

The specific issue of transparency to the public would not be discussed until the 1995 amendments when, interestingly, two parliamentary committees were struck around the time of the federal election: Holtmann under the Progressive Conservative Party in 1993; and, the Zed Committee under the Liberal Party in 1994. The Holtmann Committee was struck in November 1992 and held hearings in early 1993 and delivered its report in June. During the 1993 election, all political parties agreed to follow up on the Holtmann Report and in June 1994, a sub-committee of the House Standing Committee on Industry appointed Paul Zed to study and report on amendments emanating mainly from the Holtmann hearings. Bill C-43 was presented in the fall of 1994, passed in 1995 and came into force on 31 January 1996. Both the Holtmann and Zed committees agreed that attention was needed to tighten the disclosure requirements. However, they also focused on questions relating to the scope of activities covered by the Act, the investigatory powers of the Registrar, the independence of the branch administering the Act, and the need to encourage professional standards among lobbyists. In essence, the wheels had been set in motion, albeit below the surface at the time, to moving the law away from simply collecting information to assuming a more interventionist role in the industry in order to make lobbying engagements more transparent to parliamentarians and the public.

Disclosure requirements were amended significantly around two concerns: that the requirements remain simple; and, that more information should be sought while maintaining open access to government. Both committees understood that there must be a solid rationale for demanding information but they also understood the concerns of parliamentarians who maintained that they really only knew as much as lobbyists were willing to disclose to the registrar, a key point of concern especially given public discussions around influence peddling surrounding the Airbus deals – a key driver at the time for greater regulation of lobbying activities.[25]

In overall terms, the Holtmann Committee made recommendations that would expand the information requirements of lobbyists calling for more detail on the subject matter of lobbying engagements and the identification of departments approached. The Zed Committee was more cautious in this regard. For example, each committee differed in their approach on how to address the disclosure requirements of grassroots campaigns (i.e., generating public pressure on legislators). Whereas the Holtmann Committee suggested that registering professional lobbying efforts aimed at the grassroots (which exceeded a threshold amount of funding), the Zed Committee argued that only the techniques should be registered that would be used to influence government decisions. The latter was far less revealing in terms of making transparent the activities of paid lobbyists.[26] In other words, the debates at the time centred around the degree of information required to satisfy demands that lobbying activities were being not only monitored, but controlled in some way. Questions abounded about the need for information and the appropriate incentives to cooperate with governmental demands for that information, and to carry out their lobbying activities with the federal government in an accepted way.

Discussions were already underway in the early 1990s about the purpose and approach of lobbying legislation and the accompanying disclosure requirements. As these requirements were increasing, so too were the responsibilities of the registrar, and it is this fact that highlighted questions related to the accountability and enforcement provisions of the Act and the authorities to be assigned to the registrar. The 1995 disclosure requirements can be summarized as follows:

- The name or description of the specific legislative proposals, bills, regulations, policies, programs, grants, contributions or contracts sought;
- The names of the federal departments or other governmental institutions lobbied;
- The source and amount of any government funding;
- The communications techniques used including grassroots lobbying;
- Organizations and corporations were also required to provide a general description of their institutional activities (organizations) or the nature of their business (corporations).[27]

The most notable of these amendments were, firstly, that all categories of lobbyists would now have to explicitly disclose who they were lobbying in order to identify key pressure points in government – a clarification of the 1989 version.[28] Second, disclosure must be made of government funding in order to identify those areas under pressure from various interests. Third, information regarding lobbying techniques was required.[29] Finally, and most notably, corporation and organization lobbyists would now have to name their senior officers under the Act as opposed to simply individual lobbyists in order to disclose who is behind, supporting and benefiting from the lobbying activities. This meant that the senior officer was in some ways held responsible for the lobbying activities of their organization which was a major shift in the law's approach. No longer could organizations distance themselves from improper lobbying activities – a key step along the way to regulation.

In addition, the reporting obligations differed markedly for in-house corporate and organization lobbyists. Corporations would only be required to register the most *senior paid officer* for activities that amount to a total of what was interpreted to be 20 percent or more of *combined* employee efforts whereas associations must name *all* employees if lobbying activities amount to 20 percent or more of *one* full-time employee. This difference in reporting would have ramifications in 2006.

The next set of amendments to disclosure requirements were made in 2005 but were not nearly as substantial.[30] Two shortcomings were addressed. First, all categories of lobbyist would be required to renew their registrations semi-annually rather than annually. It was argued that this would allow for a more up-to-date registry including better ability to track lobbying engagements over time. Second, with respect to requirements for officials, former public office holders would now be required to disclose their former offices if they were subject to register under the Act. The result of these combined reforms was a significant increase in registrations after a long period of low registrations especially for in-house association lobbyists, so that by April 2007, the registrar of Lobbyists reported the registration of 1,889 corporate lobbyists and 2,545 association lobbyists.[31]

Arguably, the most significant change to the disclosure requirements up to this point was the wording change that replaced the phrase "in an attempt to influence" with "communicate."[32] One of the key events that had a major impact on this change was clearly the "Sponsorship Scandal" whereby it was pointed out by some commentators including the auditor general in her 2003 report that "only a handful of people had participated in decision making" around the program and that insufficient attention had been paid as to who was influencing government with respect to the awarding of contracts.[33] It had become clear even before the release of this audit report that prosecuting on the basis of influence was improbable but that the Act should "not attempt to regulate how lobbyists lobby."[34] There remained some reticence to regulate some aspect of lobbyists' conduct short of providing some guidelines in a code of conduct on principles to follow when carrying out their activities. It was recognized that the challenge with respect to building disclosure requirements was to identify what information is necessary and sufficient but also in identifying precisely why it is required – the "evil" that disclosure is combating.[35]

ACCOUNTABILITY, ENFORCEMENT, AND ADMINISTRATION OF THE ACT

Administration of the *Lobbyists Registration Act* includes the relationship of the registrar (now commissioner) to the Public Service and Parliament, the increased allocation of resources to administer the Act including the monitoring of a code of conduct, and enforcement of the Code and disclosure requirements. The most significant amendment to the Act in 1995 was the addition of a code of conduct. In my view, this led to a number of important changes in orientation of the Act which had implications for its management. In essence, the addition of a code of conduct marked the shift to a regulatory approach given that Parliament not only wanted information on the activities of lobbyists but also to compel lobbyists to adhere to a standard of behaviour when dealing with federal political and bureaucratic officials and enforced through a system of fines and penalties upon a conviction by a court.

It was presumed that given the powers of the registrar and the resources dedicated to the office that this would result in the efficient management of the Registry and consistent and timely public access to information. The ability of the registrar to meet his/her obligations has been raised at various points in the evolution of the Act as a contentious point because it speaks directly to the question as to how much regulatory responsibility ought to be vested in the office especially regarding enforcing the disclosure and code of conduct requirements and his/her ability to deal with those who might evade the Act's requirements intentionally or not. It is difficult to avoid the question as to how much authority ought to be granted the registrar or commissioner with respect to some defined scope for enforcement of the Act.

Reporting Relationship of the Registrar: Ensuring Integrity. Understanding the reporting relationship of the registrar is important because it speaks to how the Act will be implemented. If the registrar is too closely connected to political interests, then questions of legitimacy are raised. The argument is that with independence, a registrar or commissioner is afforded an arms-length and independent voice free from political interference, whatever this may be. However, given recent events surrounding the independence of Kevin Page, Parliamentary budget officer, it is suspect as to how much political interference can reasonably be avoided if political masters want to make their wishes apparent.

Under the 1989 version of the Act, the registrar of Lobbyists was a junior executive resident within the Department of Consumer and Corporate Affairs and eventually Industry Canada in a new organization called the Office of the Ethics Counsellor. A staff of four was assigned to the office with a total budget of $467,000 to be used for collecting basic business card information. Allocation of resources changed little between 1989 and 2004.[36] The status of the Act and the Registrar was revisited in 1995 under the Chrétien government as part of his "ethics package" of reforms when he created the position of ethics counsellor, a Governor-in-Council appointment, whose responsibility it was to develop a *Code of Conduct* for lobbyists in consultation with the policy community and for monitoring its implementation as well as that of the *Conflict of Interest Code*.[37] As per Bill C-43, the ethics counsellor was required to report to the prime minister on matters relating to managing the Registry required by the *Lobbyists Registration Act*, but also on matters relating to the *Conflict of Interest Code*. The reporting relationship was widely criticized at the time for being tied too closely to the preferences of the prime minister.[38] The key point here is that with greater prominence afforded the Ethics Counsellor, thought would have to be given to the Office's authorities and the limits of that authority. In other words, there was thought given to the purpose of the Office: to manage a registry and/or enforce the codes. Discussions were increasingly about authorities and enforcement assigned to the counsellor and less about questions of transparency.

In 2004, amendments to the Act afforded the Registrar responsibility for managing both the Registry and the *Code of Conduct*. For the first time, a senior public servant at the rank of assistant deputy minister (ADM) was designated Registrar of Lobbyists within Industry Canada although the ADM had other duties. In 2005, a Registrar was designated by the Treasury Board as a full-time appointment with additional resources in order to accommodate increased management responsibilities resulting from the expanded disclosure requirements. In February 2006, the prime minister announced that the office would report through the Treasury Board portfolio as a stand-alone office and the Registrar would assume the authority of a deputy head.[39] Questions arose at the time as to whether more independence was required and the authorities to be assigned in order to avoid any potential for intimidation by senior officers and politicians.[40]

Codes of Conduct: Securing Accountability. Codes of conduct are becoming increasingly an accepted feature of lobby legislation. These are generally of three types. The least coercive of these types are professional codes that are created and adopted by lobbyists in specific jurisdictions. These usually involve the setting of basic expectations of professional conduct and set an expectation of training to members in order to live up to such expectations. The challenge, however, is that unlike medical, law, engineering and other professions, there is no formal expectation of membership and there is no ability to regulate members as a result. As such, most codes of this type have been largely ineffective. In Canada, the Government Relations Institute of Canada (GRIC) adopted such a code in 1995 and has been considered less than enthusiastic in regulating the behaviour of its members.

The second type of code refers to employment and post-employment and the rules governing the conduct of members of legislatures and senior public servants. Such codes regulate the employment of former members of legislatures and their offices, and public officials by stipulating a "cooling off" period and disclosure requirements for communicating with current office holders. Although lobbyists are not subject to such rules, the consequences of ignoring them can be severe potentially in the sense that public exposure of a perceived breach can limit future work for the lobbyist. Consequences for public office holders are far less clear but are generally minimal to none. Canada's post-employment code to this point stipulated a cooling off period of one year for public office holders.[41]

The third type of code is an imposed code regulating the conduct of lobbyists that sets out conditions of access to legislatures and government offices and is usually linked to legislation. In Canada, the *Code of Conduct* for Lobbyists came into force on 1 March 1997. Its purpose is "to assure the Canadian public that lobbying is carried out ethically and according to the highest standards [and to]enhance public confidence and trust in the integrity, objectivity and impartiality of government decision making."[42] The Code identifies three major principles: transparency, confidentiality and conflict of interest. With respect to transparency, for example, lobbyists are required to provide full and accurate information to public office holders, they must disclose the identity of the people and organizations they are representing, and the overall purpose of their representations.[43] Under the 1995 amendments, the Act afforded limited authority and powers to the Registrar to enforce the Code, other than following up on complaints and submitting evidence to the RCMP regarding potential Code violations.

Enforcement of the Act and the Code: Ensuring Effectiveness. Enforcement of lobby legislation has generally relied on a set of tools in varying degrees of severity. From least severe (for some decision-makers) is public shaming through reports to Parliament or other legislative body, to fines or penalties, to imprisonment. In Canada, as elsewhere, such enforcement mechanisms have been ineffective deterrents against non-compliance. Equally noteworthy, the processes for enforcing such legislation have also been shown to be ineffective in terms of applying penalties. As such, there are always calls by critics to increase enforcement powers of officials while at the same time ensuring that the burden of such legislation does not restrict access to government.

The 1989 version of the Act provided little by way of enforcement although it did specify fines and prison terms for filing false information. However, this became a higher priority in 1995 when two important aspects of the Act were included pertaining to enforcement. First, section 14(1) holds that, on summary conviction, a person who knowingly contravenes any part of the Act (other than subsection 10.3(1) concerning compliance with the Code of Conduct) shall be liable to a fine of up to $25,000. Likewise, section 14(2) applies to individuals who, on summary conviction, are found to have filed misleading or false statements and documents, are subject to a fine of up to $25,000, imprisonment for up to six months, or both. Where a conviction of this type has been arrived at through indictment, the penalty increases to $100,000 and imprisonment for up to two years. The limitation on these penalties is spelled out in section 14(3) whereby proceedings by way of summary conviction related to offences in section 14 must be instituted no later than two years after the subject matter of the proceedings arose.[44] The responsibilities of the Registrar also extended to managing the Registry. In this regard, a significant reform at the time with implications for the most current round of changes was an expansion of the Registrar's powers to include the ability to seek clarification of information filed with the registry and to conduct random audits of the information on file – at present, an underutilized tool.[45]

The second aspect of enforcement concerns violations of the *Code of Conduct*. Section 10.3(1) requires that individuals who are required to file a return must comply with the Code. Likewise, section 10.4(1) states that the

Registrar must investigate if he/she believes that a breach of the Code has occurred.[46] If the Registrar should find that a breach of the Code has occurred, these findings with supporting evidence must be filed as a report to Parliament. The powers to enforce the Code are quite limited especially given that the authority to prosecute rests ultimately with the Attorney General. The pressing problem with respect to the Code, and the registration requirements under the Act, is that lobbyists may purposely avoid observing the Act or simply may not know that the Act applies to them. Compliance with the Act may not depend on penalties but on awareness that it is in their best interest to do so. That is, the cost of a penalty may not be as severe as the cost to one's reputation. The process for determining a breach of the Act or the Code may involve internal observations by the Registrar/Commissioner which may lead to an administrative review or it could be sparked by external complaints of a breach. The RCMP is responsible for following up on the reviews and laying charges. As of March 2008, 34 administrative reviews were underway. However, no penalties or charges have been laid under the Act or the Code – a lacklustre record. Despite this fact, however, the federal government was becoming increasingly committed to regulating the conduct of lobbyists.

THE LATEST ROUND OF REFORMS: MORE RULES OR MINEFIELDS?

Shifts in Approach to Ethics

Not unlike the Airbus scandal that rocked the Mulroney government in the 1980s which lead to calls for the creation of lobbying legislation, political scandal was also the impetus behind changes to the *Lobbyists Registration Act* following the Gomery Inquiry into the federal government's Sponsorship Program and advertising activities. Justice Gomery had highlighted the alleged illicit activities of lobbyists and the fact they were not registering under the Act as a key contributor to events.[47] As a result of the hearings, Prime Minister Paul Martin had initiated changes to the Act in anticipation of the final report. In addition, former Registrar, Michael Nelson had requested additional resources to address a potential increase in workload. The budget of the office was increased from roughly $500,000 annually to $3.5 million in 2006/07 so that more staff could be dedicated to managing the Registry and investigate breaches of the Code of Conduct. Although in-house corporate lobbyist registrations increased by 847 percent by the end of the 2005/2006 reporting period, it is likely the increase could be attributed to the heightened caution taken by corporations resulting from the Gomery Inquiry hearings.[48]

In addition to the increase in registrations, four investigation reports into breaches of the Code by Neelam Makhija, an unregistered lobbyist, had been tabled in Parliament by March 2007.[49] However, based on a judicial review in March 2008 with the Federal Court, the decision was to quash these reports on the grounds that, "the Registrar did not have the jurisdiction to investigate him under the *Lobbyists' Code of Conduct*."[50] This decision was appealed later in 2008 resulting in a decision that the Registrar did in fact have the jurisdiction to investigate on the grounds that "if Mr. Makhija was required to file the prescribed form because he agreed to undertake lobbying activities, he was, by the same token, required to comply with the Code."[51] This case was an important test of the Registrar's authorities because the ruling, in essence, upheld the Registrar's approach to use the *Code of Conduct* to regulate lobbying activities and lobbyists. Had the Federal Court upheld the lower court ruling, Parliament would have been forced to address the question as to whether the *Lobbying Act* should regulate lobbying and provide the Commissioner with explicit authorities to do so. In my view, because the Court upheld the Registrar's approach in these cases, only serves to support the view that the Act is a regulatory tool or that it can be used as a regulatory tool.

There was little question that the Sponsorship Program was a major factor for the Conservative election victory in January 2006 and the Gomery Inquiry's serious findings of corruption and financial mismanagement aimed squarely at the Liberal Party.[52] The introduction of the *Federal Accountability Act* (Bill C-2) was intended to address major breaches of trust the Harper Conservatives believed were at the centre of Liberal corruption. However, and most importantly, the Act represented a major shift in emphasis from one essentially rooted in a values or deontological approach to one that has become increasingly rules-based, premised in large part on the American predisposition to codification.[53] This shift has meant that Ottawa's ethics program has become less cohesive in terms of pointing to an overall set of guiding principles and structured more around ethical silos focused on rules for particular activities including lobbying. As such, it is difficult to assess the lobbying regulations in terms of improving the overall ethics of government but some comments can be made about the extent to which the current amendments may detract from previous approaches and some likely effects on those covered by the Act.

The FedAA set its sights on the *Lobbyists Registration Act* and the issue of non-compliance which was a major concern of Justice Gomery.[54] In addition, the government argued that the information disclosed to Parliament was insufficient which when combined with perceived non-compliance the Act was inadequate to the task of identifying the activities of lobbyists and whether these were being conducted in a way that was consistent with the Code of Conduct. The FedAA was intended to provide the Commissioner with enhanced investigatory powers in order to look into breaches. Most notably, the Conservatives wanted to ensure the public of the integrity of government and that access to the corridors of power was not limited to a chosen few.[55]

131   Evaluating the Rationale of the New Federal *Lobbying Act*

Amendments to the Act and Their Assessment

Each of the following changes arising from the *Federal Accountability Act 2006* will be examined in turn:

- To rename the *Lobbyists Registration Act*, the "Lobbying Act" (LA), presumably because it will seek to regulate the activities of lobbyists, rather than simply monitor them by means of a registry system;
- To replace the Office of the Registrar of Lobbyists with an independent Office of the Commissioner of Lobbying;
- To grant the new Commissioner of Lobbying increased investigation and reporting powers and some enforcement measures;
- To prohibit any contingency fee arrangements by lobbyists;
- To impose a five-year lobbying ban on designated public office holders;
- To impose greater disclosure requirements on lobbyists, particularly in relation to dealings with designated public office holders;
- To increase the monetary penalties for offences under the Act; and
- To provide longer limitation periods for the commencement of summary conviction proceedings under the law.[56]

RENAMING THE ACT

Although renaming the Act, *Lobbying Act*, appears at first glance to be a relatively minor change, in fact, it is symbolic of the shift to a more codified approach to ethics in much the same way as similar legislation including the *Conflict of Interest Act*. The *Lobbying Act* is more appropriate in terms of its intentions and objectives: the Act reinforces previous amendments to "regulate" the *activity* of lobbying as opposed to simply collecting and monitoring information provided to a registry. This change was not lost on most of the respondents (15 of 22) who commented that the combination of increased investigatory powers and the addition of new disclosure requirements meant that lobbyists themselves would be monitored more closely. According to two government relations consultants, "the Lobbying Act is a highly restrictive law whose regulations reflect the spirit of the Act. Details matter."[57]

INDEPENDENCE OF THE COMMISSIONER

Clause 68 of the FedAA established the commissioner of Lobbying as an officer of Parliament. It is a 7–year Governor-in Council (GIC) appointment and under sections 4.1(1) and 4.1(2) of the *Lobbying Act*, both houses of Parliament must give their support for his/her appointment and removal. The commissioner is responsible not only for ensuring compliance with the Act, but also to promote its understanding and acceptance among lobbyists, their clients and public office holders. The rationale for an independent commissioner with regulatory responsibilities has long been debated, the most clearly articulated of which is that such an officer should be free from political pressure in order to carry out his/her responsibilities effectively but it is not entirely clear as to the nature of political pressure likely to be exerted.[58]

In theory, a clear mandate, sufficient authority and resources, effective tools for compliance and enforcement, and enough time to carry out the prescribed responsibilities must be afforded the commissioner in order to ensure *effective* administration of the Act. Given these conditions, respondents were split on the merits of an independent Commissioner. Indeed, respondents were more concerned about the practical authorities and the advantages to be gained from an independent officer of Parliament. In other words, most respondents considered the creation of an independent commissioner less important than the actual value to be gained by such independence with respect to the *day-to-day* administration of the Act.

In this regard, when asked about whether they thought the mandate of the commissioner was clear, several respondents (17 of 22) indicated that although the Act appears explicit on this point under section 4.2, for example, there was confusion about Parliament's expectations of the role in practical terms. They argued that it was not clear whether the priority of the commissioner of Lobbying was to regulate lobbying and lobbyists under the *Lobbyists' Code of Conduct* or whether the commissioner was to manage the Registry for purposes of ensuring transparency to Parliament regarding the activities of lobbyists. In their view, administering the Code assumes the role of "enforcer" while the other supports a democratic purpose of ensuring transparency. Although respondents believe the roles could be compatible, they said the resources and authority commensurate with each function do not point in an obvious way to either. To be precise, the commissioner serves a regulatory function when administering the disclosure requirements and safeguards the ethical or deontological aspect of the Act when enforcing the *Lobbyists' Code of Conduct* – that is, administrator and policeman.

Either way, the question posed by these respondents was what advantages are gained through independent administration of the Act with respect to serving either role of administrator or enforcer. When examining the commissioner's responsibilities from the perspective of lobbyists, respondents concluded that the independence granted the previous Registrar appeared sufficient to the task. That is, lobbyists were expected to abide by the Act and the Code regardless of the relationship of the commissioner to Parliament. They said that independence appears to serve very little purpose especially when combined with the limited practical authorities of the commissioner to sanction under the Act or the Code. Aside from a major investigation by the commissioner on the scale of a *Sponsorship Scandal* that would likely grip the interest of citizens, the commissioner is virtually powerless to curb any routine matters of bad behaviour under the Act or the Code without the "hassle" of triggering the criminal investigation powers of the RCMP. The only area highlighted for concern with respect to this aspect of the relationship related to the ethical conduct of lobbyists and the financing of political parties. However, the advantages offered by lobbyists in terms of gifts and favours are covered through other legislation and codes including ethical codes for parliamentarians through such offices as the Conflict of Interest and Ethics Commissioner.

The relationship, however, was viewed differently when examined from the perspective of public office holders and their obligations under the Act. In this respect, their principal obligations are, firstly, to make certain that records are available specifying arranged meetings with lobbyists and that these are accurate should the commissioner wish to check the information submitted by lobbyists. Second, and most importantly, public office holders are expected to abide by the post-employment requirements of the Act. It is on this element that independence assumes more prominence especially with respect to adjudicating section 10.11 of the *Lobbying Act* and who may be exempted from this provision under section 10.11(2) respecting applications for exemption. On this point, respondents were clearer about the rationale for an independent commissioner recognizing that an impartial officer is required to adjudicate applications for exemptions in order to avoid the appearance of being in a position of conflict of interest with the sitting government of the day. However, it was also recognized that this function likely serves a "political" interest when parliamentary officers and staff apply for such exemptions. For respondents, an impartial Registrar could as easily fill the role as much as an independent commissioner. The troublesome point may be who is appointed to the role of commissioner and their likely ties to a particular political party – a risk created by the GIC mechanism, not resolved by it. For respondents, an independent commissioner was more a matter of political interest rather than serving a rational management interest.

AMENDED DISCLOSURE REQUIREMENTS
AND POST-EMPLOYMENT BAN

Disclosure requirements were amended for both newly defined public office holders and lobbyists. In addition, the post-employment ban was extended for public office holders. Each of these is discussed in turn.

The Perspective of Designated Public Office Holders. As indicated in the Regulatory Impact Analysis Statement (RIAS) that accompanied the *Designated Public Office Holder Regulations* comprising part of the new regulations that came into force on 2 July 2008, "the Lobbying Act creates a new statutory category ... to refer to officials responsible for high-level decision-making in government. This term is defined in the Act (subsection 2(1)) to include ministers, ministers of state, and ministerial staff, as well as deputy ministers and chief executives of departments and agencies and officials in those organizations at the ranks of associate deputy minister and assistant deputy minister."[59] The purpose for creating this category is "to ensure that senior-level public office holders do not use advantages and personal connections derived from their government positions for lobbying purposes, by making these officials subject to a five-year prohibition on lobbying the federal government after leaving office."[60]

Section 9(1) of the Act provides that the commissioner may request information from designated public office holders that confirms the accuracy and completeness of information provided by lobbyists in their returns to the Registry. Section 9(2) affords the commissioner the authority to report to Parliament on the "failure by a present or former designated public office holder to respond relative to information sent... or the provision... of an unsatisfactory response." Although designated public office holders are not obligated to maintain records of their meetings with lobbyists, there are incentives for doing so.

With respect to the application of the five-year ban, designated public office holders may make application to the commissioner under 10.11(3) of the Act if they believe the ban does not apply to them. The decision for the commissioner is whether he/she believes the designated public office holder is exempt. Clearly, the commissioner can potentially be placed in the awkward position of adjudicating exemption requests for high profile applicants especially those received from former political office holders. There is the potential that the commissioner may be thrown into the realm of politics should such exemptions become a matter of public sensitivity. However, there have been few exemptions requests to date to test political sensitivity.

Respondents raised two main concerns regarding disclosure requirements related to public office holders. First, public servants were particularly concerned about the creation of a new category of public servants under the Act and the imposition of the extended post-employment ban. Second, public servants and non-government officials were equally worried about maintaining records of meetings with lobbyists and the implications of verification should the records of lobbyists not correspond with those of public officials.

With respect to the creation of a separate category of public official, federal government respondents (8 of 14) indicated that the net cast by the *Lobbying Act* may be too wide but in some respects they said it could have been cast even wider to include officials at the director-general rank who have equivalent duties to that of an ADM and frequently meet with lobbyists. For them, the argument was that many of these officials under the definition, aside from being a confusing catch-all, may never meet a lobbyist in their career but are subject to the post-employment ban regardless. According to one federal official, "the collateral damage caused by the DPOH category is not necessary – we've gone overboard with transparency to such an extent that one has to really consider whether taking on any senior government position is worth the hassle of all of these rules." For them, the "nuisance factor" created by such definitions has yet to reveal itself but there are signs already that senior government officials are taking a second look at whether it is "worth" assuming these positions if one has aspirations for working with the federal government once they leave their position.

In addition to the definitional problems associated with the DPOH category, federal and provincial respondents (14 of 14) thought without exception that the 5–year ban was excessive. Although they recognized that the ban was "effective" in the sense that it addresses abuse, a shorter ban was thought to be "adequate" to the task. Again, in their view, the ban was regarded as a rule that is "over the top" especially when one considers that most provincial post-employment rules require a two year ban on average. In addition to these concerns, it is reasonable to suggest that this ban is likely to have negative consequences for ministers wishing to staff their offices or the prime minister wishing to appoint senior officials to boards, commissions, tribunals or even to be the Commissioner of Lobbying.

With respect to the second concern regarding the responsibility of DPOHs to verify communications with lobbyists, federal government respondents (8 of 14) were concerned about two matters. First, they were worried that their names would be posted on the Registry regarding lobbyist's undertakings. For them, this was a matter of legitimacy. Several federal officials argued that the mere existence of the *Lobbying Act* indicates that lobbyists, by definition, are an unsavoury lot and that a perverse effect of this requirement is that such postings potentially taint their name. Incidentally, lobbyists recognized this effect and expressed consternation that public office holders would question lobbying as being a legitimate activity. Second, federal public officials were nervous about being in compliance with the lobbying law when meeting with lobbyists. They wondered whether it was incumbent on them to verify whether lobbyists were "registered" before agreeing to meet with them. This raises a very troubling question: has it become the case that public office holders who meet with lobbyists now constitute an unnecessary management risk? Again, what does this say about open access to government and the idea that lobbying is a legitimate activity? An argument can be made that a perverse effect of the legislation is that rather than attract attention of even a meeting, arranged or not, it is better to close the doors altogether, which raises larger concerns related to democratic government.

THE PERSPECTIVE OF LOBBYISTS

The most significant changes to the disclosure requirements were made respecting the various categories of lobbyist. These are summarized as follows:

- Lobbyists must submit an initial return that includes all types of communication with public office holders. The new requirement is that lobbyists

file monthly returns if they carry out oral and arranged communications with designated public office holders. Oral and arranged communications include pre-arranged telephone calls and meetings.
- Oral and arranged communications *initiated* by DPOHs related to the development of policy, programs or legislation is exempt from the reporting requirements. However, oral and arranged communications relating to contracts or engagements where there is financial benefit must be reported regardless of whether the engagement was initiated by a DPOH.
- All types of lobbyist must disclose the name, title and department of each DPOH with whom they have communicated, the date of the communication and the subject matter.
- Consultant lobbyists: this category of lobbyist must file a report to the commissioner within 10 days of entering into an undertaking and must notify the commissioner of the completion or termination of the undertaking. With respect to the monthly report, the lobbyist must file within 15 days at the end of each month when within that month, lobbying activity occurred that was directed at a DPOH. Finally, under section 5(4.2), if the lobbyist has filed a monthly report stating no undertakings, the lobbyist must file again within five months of that monthly report verifying no additional undertakings.
- In-house lobbyists, corporations: The same monthly filing obligations apply except that corporations are also only required to register the most *senior paid officer* for activities that amount to a total of 20 per cent or more of *combined* employee efforts. Returns must be filed within two months of the commencement of an undertaking. Any changes to this return must be filed within 30 days. Senior officers and employees are reported on separate lists.
- In-house lobbyists, associations: The same monthly filing obligations apply except that associations must name *all* employees if lobbying activities amount to 20 per cent or more of *one* full-time employee. Registration requirements are identical to corporate lobbyists except all lobbyists are reported on one list (implications to be discussed).

Respondents commented about three principal matters regarding these disclosure rules for lobbyists: the disclosure rules and their influence on lobbying activities; disclosure rules relative to the post-employment ban; and, effectiveness of the *Lobbyists' Code of Conduct*.

Perhaps the principal concern of respondents (20 of 22) related to the rules surrounding disclosure. Public officials and non-government representatives alike expressed trepidation about not only the breadth of the rules but also what they might mean regarding the principles set out in the Preamble to the Act. By taking a simple glance at the rules above, it is difficult not to come to the conclusion that some confusion may be experienced by both governmental and non-governmental actors who "might" be subject to the Act. Perhaps the most significant concern expressed by lobbyists was that the rules could suggest an obligation on the part of the lobbyist "to be safer than sorry" and register their activities despite a determination that what they are doing may not constitute lobbying under the Act or that a registration is not required (e.g., meeting was not arranged, or undertaking had no financial benefit). Under these scenarios, if a DPOH has recorded a meeting as a lobbyist undertaking and a lobbyist has not registered it, an investigation could be launched. In addition, public officials could choose to be cautious and require that all meetings with lobbyists be registered before any meeting takes place despite the possibility that the lobbyist may be compliant with the Act. Recall that it is the lobbyist's responsibility to be compliant, the only obligation on the part of the public official is to be assured that the lobbyist is compliant. Equally important, however, is that a registration is only required *if* the communication is arranged by the lobbyist. It does not speak to those communications initiated by DPOHs. Certainly, this opens the possibility that non-transparent lobbying remains possible – an incredibly large loophole in the provisions.

One clearly gets the message from these possibilities that disclosure is not straightforward and that all parties understand there is a risk of being non-compliant. Several implications are evident from the perspective of lobbyists. First, lobbyists continue to fight the perception that lobbying is a negative activity regardless of type of lobbying. For example, one would hardly suggest that lobbying for cleaner air and water or against child poverty is negative yet the halo effect of lobbyists as corrupt may persist. Second, the expanded disclosure rules might cause a "chill" on the ability of lobbyists to arrange meetings or communicate with public officials because such officials fear being in non-compliance. Finally, and certainly this is not exhaustive of other implications, such rules may impede access to government not because the rules may be too strict but because public officials may not wish to be implicated by them and so will avoid meeting with lobbyists altogether. At the very least, there is the possibility that lobbying will be driven down the hierarchy so that DPOHs are not captured by the rules. In other words, someone in the office not covered by the Act can meet with the lobbyist. This was as much a concern to lobbyists as public office holders. Although public office holders ought to be able to consult the public without impediment, the question raised by respondents was why such consultations initiated by DPOHs cannot be transparent.

The last point made by lobbyists was concern about the disclosure rules as they apply to the post-employment ban for DPOHs. As noted, corporations are required to register the most *senior paid officer* for activities that amount to a total of 20 per cent or more of *combined* employee efforts whereas in-house lobbyists for associations must name *all* employees if lobbying activities amount to 20 per cent or more of *one* full-time employee, noting that the senior official in both cases may not be performing any lobbying. The concern is that a DPOH who wishes to work for a charitable organization and lobbying amounts to 20 per cent or more of one person's time, *all* employees who lobby would be subject to registration regardless of proportion of their time. However, if a DPOH wishes to work for a corporation, and as long as one's lobbying duties do not account for more than 20 per cent of time, he/she is not subject to the Act's post-employment rules.[61] In effect, therefore, the law is skewed in favour of corporations. Not surprisingly, volunteer organizations are frustrated that they will not have the ability to recruit DPOHs whose job would be to communicate with government. Some respondents were hard-pressed to control their cynicism suggesting that the Conservative government is ensuring that their senior officials are able to land jobs in the corporate sector without being subject to the ban.

Several respondents (10 of 22), mainly federal officials, lobbyists and advocacy representatives, commented on the effectiveness of the *Code of Conduct* for ensuring integrity in government. Whereas these officials believe that a code of conduct is necessary in deontological terms to maintain ethical undertakings with government officials, almost all of these respondents said that it is suspect as to whether most lobbyists are aware of it. In this respect, there has been little promotion of the Code by the federal government and spotty promotion, at best, by industry associations. Again, whereas members of industry associations may have been introduced to the Code and its requirements, the fact is that only a small percentage of lobbyists are part of such associations. Federal officials explained that neglect of promoting the Code only reinforces negative perceptions that the integrity of government may not be as important as professed.

Some of these same respondents also explained that the federal government has shown itself to be predisposed to setting rules on disclosure and other matters rather than promoting good behaviour on the part of lobbyists and also public officials. As such, they indicated that in practical terms the Code has little teeth as the commissioner has few ways to monitor it except through complaints from public office holders or lobbyists themselves. On this point, the ability to sanction requires a great deal of effort and resources which effectively translates into the necessity on the part of the commissioner to prioritize investigations and pursue those complaints that have the greatest chances of a conviction. The combination of these factors regarding the effectiveness of the Code can only sustain negative perceptions on lobbying and lobbyists. For these respondents, the efforts of the commissioner should be spent on encouraging ethical lobbying and lobbyists rather than enforcing rules that attempt to catch lobbyists in bad behaviour. Equally important, however, it means that public officials also have to abide by these same principles in order to build a public service with integrity. As noted by one public official, "a code of conduct is about changing the way we do things, for the better – one does this by encouraging positive behaviour, not bringing attention to negative behaviours."

INCREASED INVESTIGATION POWERS AND SANCTIONS

With respect to "increased investigatory powers," the more appropriate wording here would be "expanded" investigatory powers. Under the previous *Lobbyists Registration Act*, the Registrar had no authority to investigate breaches of the Act (meaning those elements related to managing the disclosure requirements). The ability to investigate referred to breaches of the Code of Conduct. Section 10.4(1) of the *Lobbying Act*, provides the commissioner with the authority to "conduct an investigation if he or she has reason to believe, including on the basis of information received from a member of the Senate or the House of Commons, that an investigation is necessary to ensure compliance with the Code or this Act, as applicable."[62] This authority includes the power to summon witnesses and compel the production of documents, akin to that of a superior court. Should the commissioner find during an investigation that a breach of the Act or the Code has occurred, section 10.4(7) requires the commissioner to "advise a peace officer having jurisdiction to investigate the alleged offence and immediately suspend the commissioner's investigation." Finally, should the commissioner find that a breach of the Act or the Code has occurred; section 10.5(1) of the Lobbying Act requires the commissioner to "prepare a report of the investigation… and submit it to the Speaker of the Senate and the Speaker of the House of Commons."

With respect to sanctions respecting disclosure, the amended section 14(1) of the *Lobbying Act* makes it a new offence to "fail to file a return" as opposed to simply being in contravention of the Act as per the previous LRA and, it is a new offence to knowingly make a false or misleading statement in response to the commissioner's request for information as per section 9.1(1). It continues to be an offence to knowingly file a false or misleading statement. Fines imposed for contravening these sections were increased from $25,000 to $50,000. Where proceedings are by way of indictment, the fine is increased to from $100,000 to $200,000. With respect to a Code of Conduct violation, the fine is increased from $25,000 to $50,000. The Senate Committee examining the Act had recommended that an obstruction of justice clause be added to the commissioner's authorities. However, the House of Commons rejected the recommendation. In addition to penalties, the limitation period for investigating infractions of the Act was extended from two years to ten years. Finally, the commissioner is empowered to sanction those *convicted* under the Act by prohibiting the offending party of lobbying for a period of up to two years.

Several respondents made comments regarding the powers to conduct investigations and levy sanctions and penalties under the Act (15 of 22). Almost all of these respondents said that the commissioner's authorities were impractical arguing that short of a major breach that attracts public attention, the commissioner's powers to sanction are minimal. They argued that in practical terms, the commissioner is able to check the accuracy of information provided to the registry and investigate a failure to file a registration but cannot actually dispense penalties if there are inconsistencies without working through the RCMP. Likewise, the commissioner may respond to complaints of breaches of the *Lobbyists' Code of Conduct* but cannot actually apply sanctions in case of a breach, again without the assistance of the RCMP. One respondent summed up the commissioner's powers this way, "One can look through the window and determine whether anything is wrong but without clear and undisputed evidence, he/she must leave the scene, call the police and convince them that a crime is being committed. If the police think the crime is important enough, they might, just might, send an officer to look over the scene and even that does not guarantee a conviction."

Some federal officials argued that this was an appropriate demarcation – investigate wrongdoing but prosecution is the responsibility of a peace officer. The challenge, however, is that prosecution is almost entirely dependent on the RCMP to follow up on the commissioner's findings and conduct a criminal investigation. This may be optimistic given that the RCMP has shown that breaches of lobby legislation are a low priority. Conversely, other federal and provincial officials made the point that publicity surrounding an investigation may be enough of a deterrent for lobbyists to behave. However, section 10.4(1.1) affords the commissioner the authority to conduct or cease an investigation under specified conditions. The previous Registrar interpreted this clause to mean that all investigations will continue to be conducted in private, meaning that publicity is removed as a deterrent to bad behaviour except if and when an investigation report is made public through a formal criminal investigation.[63]

Interestingly, non-government officials (8 of 22) said that they would prefer to have a commissioner with clear authority to enforce both the Act and the Code especially if the federal government's preference is to move toward a regulatory framework. In their view, this "look but do not touch" mandate, or half-way measures, dilutes the ability of the office to ensure those subject to the Act take it seriously. More importantly, respondents said that "lobbyists are already learning that there is less than 50/50 chance they will be caught for not filing a registration. Even if we are caught and have not registered, the commissioner is virtually powerless to secure a conviction." Although public shaming was regarded as a potentially effective deterrent for violating the Act, the fact is that without a conviction, reporting infractions to Parliament is not possible.

According to most respondents (18 of 22), in order for the commissioner to be effective in the administration of the Act, he/she should have a system of monetary penalties. For them, such a system would ensure a more consistent mandate, on the one hand, with consistent authorities to both investigate infractions of the Act or Code, and the ability to dispense justice immediately – again, in keeping with a regulatory mandate. In this regard, reporting to Parliament would depend less on a full criminal investigation and more on internal policing powers. They maintain that if the commissioner's mandate is to "regulate" with appropriate sanctioning authority, the incidences of contravening the Act would diminish exponentially.

PROHIBITION OF CONTINGENCY FEES

Section 10.1(1) of the *Lobbying Act* makes it clear that individuals covered by the Act "shall not receive a payment that is in whole or in part contingent on the outcome of any matter ... on the individual's success in arranging a meeting." In addition, public officials are prohibited from making such arrangements or making payments. This prohibition clarifies the conflict between Treasury Board's policy prohibiting contingency fees in relation to procurement or granting of funds from federal sources[64] and is consistent with an amended section 5(2)(g) of the *Lobbying Act* prohibiting payment on a contingency basis.

All respondents agreed that the banning of contingency fees serves a legitimate public policy purpose: it increases transparency with respect to who is receiving financial benefit from public funds. Many provincial commissioners agreed with the ban also on the grounds that it ensures integrity in government spending. The ban responds to various complaints in this regard including arrangements David Dingwall made with the Technology Partnerships Canada Program (TPC) between May 2000 and March 2003 regarding the securing of a contract for BioNiche Lifesciences Inc. Although he was in compliance with the LRA at the time, Democracy Watch, in particular, argued that Mr. Dingwall was in contravention of the Lobbyists Code of Conduct.[65]

CONCLUSIONS: WHAT DOES IT ALL MEAN?

It would be banal to suggest that Canada's federal lobbying law is moving toward a complex web of rules and requirements.[66] The challenge with respect to moving in such a direction is that it is difficult to aim any ethics program without having some deontological or ideal conception of what positive attributes we individually or collectively wish to engender. The shift to greater reliance on rules that exemplify positive behaviours means that one is hard-pressed to grasp exactly what impact we are making that resembles our ideal. The best that one can say is that we are compliant with the rules but there is little doubt that this alone would in no way suggest we are encouraging the behaviours we want. The collective exasperation on the part of the people who participated in this study was that as long as we are all trying to be compliant, we are not really focusing on what is important: are we making a cultural difference that suggests that we are all better people building better public organizations? Are lobbyists more transparent about their activities as a result of this law?

It is too early to know whether the law is making any real difference in the conduct of lobbyists but it does hold some hope that it will have some degree of impact on the culture of federal organizations. If there is one thing that can be concluded from this study, it is that very few people are pleased with this legislation, and that may be regarded as positive for many of the respondents. As Kernaghan notes, rarely are codified options for the management of ethics effective on their own.[67] Indeed, a major conclusion of this study is that as deficiencies are discovered in our lobbying laws, the natural inclination has been to add more rules or requirements to address these. The problem, of course, is that as one adds more rules, there may be unintended or perverse consequences for inculcating the very ideals one is trying to support. For example, lobbyists are right to be concerned that any lobbying legislation does not place their profession in a bad light especially given that a strong argument can be made that the majority of lobbyists conduct themselves ethically, let alone within the rules of the Act. An unfortunate result, however, is that public office holders, for their part, have been more worried about being in strict compliance with the rules for each undertaking rather than inculcating transparent communications as a matter of organizational practice – an unfortunate by-product of a rules-based approach.

The other side of this argument is that alongside a deontological imperative, there ought to be some means of ensuring compliance with the law and sanctioning offenders. On this point, the *Lobbying Act* as a response for greater regulation of lobbying is weak to the task. The Commissioner has no means of monitoring and enforcing the *Lobbyists' Code of Conduct*. In fact, under the current law, it is highly inconceivable that any convictions can or will be made against offenders. Likewise, the Act provides minimal tools for the commissioner to sanction offenders regarding the disclosure rules. In either the case of the Code or the Act, the commissioner may only use a hammer when a fly swatter would suffice if given the tools to do the swatting. One may go so far as to say that this was the intention: let's demonstrate we are serious about lobbying offences and ramp up the penalties knowing full well that no penalties are ever likely to be levied – regulate but do not actually regulate.

When respondents were asked whether the reforms to the legislation accord with the Act's preambular principles, the answer was perhaps, but not likely. This is an appropriate response because the legislation only provides the basic elements for an ethical framework. It contains rules of disclosure, a deontological roadmap for lobbyists, and rules for lobbyists to be transparent about their activities. The problem, it seems, is that its logic is premised on building a better rulebook for regulating appropriate lobbying activities as opposed to encouraging ethical behaviour in the conduct of those activities.

In this latter respect, all agreed that the commissioner has the profound opportunity to educate and encourage positive ethical behaviour for lobbyists and public office holders which for them would likely yield far better results. The question is whether the current Parliament will encourage the commissioner in this direction or continue on the current course and demand that he/she assume the role of a weak beat cop carrying a heavy baton that cannot possibly be wielded in any practical way.

NOTES

1 I wish to acknowledge everyone who agreed to an interview as part of this paper particularly those from the Treasury Board Secretariat, Office of the Commissioner of Lobbying, various federal departments and agencies, a number of provincial offices responsible for lobbying legislation, not-for-profit organizations and advocacy groups, and members of lobbying firms and their representative bodies. Although I am not at liberty to name all of these individuals, I am sincerely thankful for the time and energy each offered me to get at the right questions in a meaningful way. This paper was certainly enriched by their experience, knowledge, insight, and perspectives. In addition, I would like to thank in a heartfelt way Dr. Paul Pross (Dalhousie) and former Registrar of the Office of the Registrar of Lobbyists, Mr. Michael Nelson, for reviewing this paper and offering their valuable insights and perspectives. Finally, I want to personally acknowledge the contributions of Dr. Allan Maslove (Carleton) for his tireless patience listening to my ups and downs throughout this process and his attention to detail in reviewing and editing this paper. For purposes of full disclosure, my spouse, Karen Shepherd, is interim commissioner of Lobbying. It should be noted that she was not interviewed, nor were her comments solicited during the research, preparation or review of this chapter, which was written before her appointment. The author prepared this paper given prior experience with the legislation and publicaly available information.
2 CTV.ca. "Harper unveils Conservative 'Accountability Act,'" available at http://www.ctv.ca/servlet/ArticleNews/story/CTVNews/20051104/conservatives_accountabilityplatform_20051104/20051104?hub=TopStories, 5 November 2005.
3 See Gary Orren, "Fall from Grace: The Public's Loss of Faith in Government," in Joseph S. Nye Jr., Philip D. Zelikow and David C. King, eds., *Why People Don't Trust Government* (Cambridge: Harvard University Press, 1997), 77–108. See also Michael Bliss, *Right Honourable Men: The Descent of Canadian Politics from Macdonald to Mulroney* (Toronto: Harper-Collins, 1994), xiii. Bliss maintains that the "descent" "has been a devolution of power from political elites towards the people, who in turn expect higher standards of performance from their leaders." One of his underlying themes is that the public is repatriating their institutions from elites who have been seen to wield power for themselves.
4 CBC News, "Paul Martin and the Lobbyists," available at http://www.cbc.ca/canadavotes/politicalhistory/paulmartinlobbyists.html, January 2006.

5 I am thinking here of Madison's notable indictment of "factions" in Federalist Papers #10, and Rousseau's thought that no obstacle ought to stand between the citizen and their legislatures. See Alexander Hamilton, James Madison and John Jay, *The Federalist Papers* (Toronto: Bantam Books, 1982), 42–9; Léon Dion, *Société et Politique: La Vie des groupes*, Vol. 1 (Québec: Presses de l'Université Laval, 1971), 207. I define "regulation" as involving the "setting of rules of behaviour backed up directly by sanctions (penalties) of the state." See G. Bruce Doern and Richard W. Phidd, eds., *Canadian Public Policy: Ideas, Structure, Process*, 2nd eds (Scarborough: Nelson, 1992), 97.
6 John Langford and Allan Tupper, "How Ottawa Does Business: Ethics as a Government Program," in G. Bruce Doern, ed., *How Ottawa Spends 2006–2007: In From the Cold, The Tory Rise and the Liberal Demise* (Montreal and Kingston: Queen's University Press, 2006), 126–8.
7 See Paul Pross, "Law and Innovation: The Incremental Development of Canadian Lobby Regulation," unpublished manuscript, March 2008. Pross makes the argument that Canada's lobby legislation has been largely evolutionary and that it has taken on a particularly regulatory approach since the mid-1990s.
8 Department of Justice Canada, *Lobbying Act*. (Ottawa: Department of Justice, 2008), consolidated version (1985, c.44, 4th Supplement). Referred to from this point forward as the *Lobbying Act* or the "Act."
9 Note that 3 interviews comprised more than one respondent. I have counted each of these as single interviews for purposes of quantifying responses.
10 The respondents spoke to me on the proviso that their names would not be made public. As such, only significant perspectives are raised. However, where appropriate, minority positions are highlighted but these will be identified as such.
11 Such concerns were raised, for example, at the OECD Ministerial meeting on "Strengthening Trust in Government: What Role for Government in the 21st Century?" Held in Paris, June 2007.
12 See: OECD, "Comparative Review: Building Blocks for Enhancing Transparency and Accountability in Lobbying," in *Lobbyists, Governments and Public Trust: Building a Legislative Framework for Enhancing Transparency and Accountability in Lobbying* (OECD: August 2008), 40.
13 In Canada, the federal government has afforded limited investigations powers to the Commissioner to enforce the Code. In most jurisdictions, such powers are vested with police authorities. The Commissioner of Lobbying in Québec can impose penalties for breaches of their Code of Conduct.
14 Ibid., 41. Note these are expressions of principles that support the objective of ensuring transparency, integrity and accountability in lobbying legislation.
15 Debate about the introduction of lobbying legislation had been recurrent in Canada since the 1960s when over time, 19 private members' bills had been introduced by the Liberals, Progressive Conservatives, and NDP. Mulroney had indicated in his 1985 statement that the time had come to "monitor lobbying activity and to control the lobbying process by providing a reliable and accurate source of information on the activities of lobbyists." This prompted the preparation of a discussion paper which was used as the impetus for hearings on the subject. See Consumer and Corporate Affairs Canada,

Lobbying and the Registration of Paid Lobbyists (Ottawa: Supply and Services, 1985). For a full description of the incremental development of this legislation, see Paul Pross, "The Rise of the Lobbying Issue in Canada: The Business Card Bill," in Grant Jordan, ed., *The Commercial Lobbyists* (Aberdeen: Aberdeen University Press, 1991), 76–95.

16 A well-known case at the time was that of fisherman Ulf Snarby who wanted a fishing license and secured Government Consultants International (GCI) to set up a meeting with then fisheries minister, John Fraser, in late 1984. According to Stevie Cameron, Fraser was "outraged to find that Snarby [had]paid to have the meeting set up." In addition, the apparent ties between former Newfoundland Premier Frank Moores and GCI raised eyebrows at the Prime Ministers' Office (PMO) when it was alleged there was a conflict of interest when Moores, as a board member with Air Canada, parlayed a deal with Wardair and Nordair to purchase several Airbus aircraft. See Stevie Cameron, "Like Magic," *Report on Business Magazine*, February 1988, 56.

17 John Sawatsky, *The Insiders: Government, Business and the Lobbyists* (Toronto: McClelland and Stewart, 1987), 1–11. Mulroney was deeply troubled about the perception of "insiders" or lobbyists with unrestricted access to his ministers and his office.

18 Canada, *Lobbyists Registration Act 1985*, c.44 (4th Supp.), s. 5(1) and 7(1). Note that the original definition in the 1989 version of the Act defined lobbying as "communicating with the intent to influence a public office holder, for payment" with respect to various matters covered in the Act. Clearly, determining "intent" is full of pitfalls. This aspect of the definition was dropped in 2003 to read simply "communicating." The trigger for registration is compensation.

19 More specifically "DPOHs" include at the level of the public service, deputy ministers and deputy heads (or other equivalent title), associate deputy ministers (or comparable rank), assistant deputy ministers (or comparable rank) and other positions designated by regulation (e.g., chief of the Defence Staff and other senior military personnel, senior advisors to the Privy Council appointed by governor in Council, deputy minister of Intergovernmental Relations (PCO), comptroller general of Canada and other senior officers appointed under the Public Service Employment Act. See Canada, "The Lobbying Act and You: Information for Designated Public Office Holders," (Ottawa: Office of the Commissioner of Lobbying, 2008).

20 House of Commons. *Minutes of Proceedings and Evidence of the Standing Committee on Consumer and Corporate Affairs and Government Operations*, Issue 61, June 1993, 1. The issue contained the Holtmann Report entitled, *A Blueprint for Transparency: Review of the Lobbyist Registration Act*.

21 House of Commons. *Minutes of Proceedings and Evidence of the Sub-Committee on Bill C-43, An Act to Amend the Lobbyists Registration Act and to Make Related Amendments to other Acts of the Standing Committee on Industry*, 20:18.

22 OECD, "Comparative Review: Building Blocks for Enhancing Transparency and Accountability in Lobbying," 64.

23 Based on interviews conducted as part of an unpublished paper regarding Bill C-82. Robert Shepherd and Christine Chudczak, "The Registration of Lobbyists: Ghostbusting in the Canadian Political System?" University of Ottawa, 15 April 1988. See also: Pross, "Law and Innovation," 8. Pross argues that committee members were

persuaded to follow the American practice at the time which focused on monitoring lobbying activity rather than regulating it.

24 Department of Consumer and Corporate Affairs, *Lobbying and the Registration of Paid Lobbyists* (Ottawa: Supply and Services, 1985), 4.

25 Paul Pross, "The Lobbyist Registration Act: Its Application and Effectiveness," in Commission of Inquiry into the Sponsorship Program & Advertising Activities, *Restoring Accountability: Research Studies Volume 2* (Ottawa: PWGSC, 2006), 171. The most notable attack on the Mulroney government was Stevie Cameron, *On the Take: Crime, Corruption and Greed in the Mulroney Years* (Toronto: MacFarlane, Walter and Ross, 1994).

26 Ibid., 169. There were other major differences in approach but this is a major example.

27 Michael Nelson, "Canada's Federal Lobbying Legislation: Evolution and Operation of the Lobbyists Registration Act," in Organization for Economic Cooperation and Development, *Lobbyists, Governments and Public Trust: Building a Legislative Framework for Enhancing Transparency and Accountability in Lobbying* (OECD: August 2008), 96–7.

28 House of Commons. *Sub-Committee on Bill C-43,* 20:30. Under the Act, lobbyists tended to identify the departments they were lobbying under disclosing the "subject area." See *Canada Gazette*, Part I, 10 June 1989.

29 House of Commons, *A Blueprint for Transparency: Review of the Lobbyists' Registration Act*, 16. Emphasis added. The issue of financial disclosure is complex. The most notable argument for financial disclosure is to provide reasonable assurance that the Code is being followed. This is different from simply seeking transparency on "techniques" in order to demonstrate the breadth and degree of pressure being brought to bear on government(s). Significant resources would be required in order to monitor such campaigns versus simply posting individual engagements that may not be simple to connect to other lobbying engagements.

30 See Pross, "Law and Innovation," 14.

31 Office of the Registrar of Lobbyists, "Presentation to the OECD Symposium on Lobbying: Enhancing Transparency and Accountability," (Ottawa: Office of the Registrar of Lobbyists, 8 June 2007), 12. Also note, the review period was extended from six months to two years.

32 Canada, *Lobbyist Registration Act* 1985, c.44 (4th Supp.), s. 5.(1)(a), 7.(1)(a).

33 Office of the Auditor General of Canada, *Report of the Auditor General of Canada 2003*, "Chapter 3: The Sponsorship Program" (Ottawa: PWGSC, November 2003), ss. 3.24 – 3.29. See also Pross, "The Lobbyist Registration Act: Its Application and Effectiveness," 199 and fn 85. In Pross' article to the Gomery Inquiry, he points out that the Registrar at the time reported on difficulties with managing within the wording of the Act in terms of its administration.

34 Office of the Auditor General of Canada, Report of the Auditor General of Canada 2003, "Ch. 2: Accountability and Ethics in Government" (Ottawa: PWGSC, November 2003), 2.74.

35 See Howard Wilson, "Lobbying: Key Policy Issues," OECD Public Governance Committee, 4 January 2005, 12–13.

36 Nelson, "Canada's Federal Lobbying Legislation," 109.
37 House of Commons, *Sub-Committee on Bill C-43*, 20:52.
38 Several media articles were written on this subject at the time including, for example: Tom Korski, "Media Turn Critical Eye on Ethics Commissioner," *Hill Times*, 13 June 2005; Jennifer Saltman, "Opposition Parties Unite to Condemn Ethics Post," Capital News Online, 18 October 2002. In this latter piece, significant changes were called for including, "We want him to report directly to Parliament. We don't want the ethics counsellor to be seen as a lapdog of the prime minister, which is what he is now."
39 Nelson, "Canada's Federal Lobbying Legislation," 108.
40 Such concerns are not new. For example, Democracy Watch launched a formal complaint with the Ontario Superior Court of Justice arguing that, "Nelson is subject to the direction and control of the Minister of Industry. In his position of Registrar of Lobbyists, he serves at pleasure, pursuant to an appointment by the Minister of Industry." Although this refers to the office as a branch within Industry Canada, the arguments have tended to remain the same. See Ontario Superior Court of Justice, "Democracy Watch vs. the Attorney General of Canada," Notice of Application, 23 December 2005, available at: www.dwatch.ca/camp/Ethics_Court_Application.pdf
41 Canada, "Conflict of Interest and Post-Employment Code for Public Office Holders," (Ottawa: Privy Council Office, 2006), section 28.
42 Nelson, "Canada's Federal Lobbying Legislation," 95.
43 Office of the Commissioner of Lobbyists of Canada, "Lobbyists' Code of Conduct," available at: http://www.ocl-cal.gc.ca/epic/site/lobbyist-lobbyiste1.nsf/en/nx00019e.html
44 Canada, *Lobbyists Registration Act 1985*, c.44 (4th Supp.), s. 14(1),(2),(3).
45 Ibid., 20:46.
46 Note that if the Registrar's investigation reveals that the Act has been contravened, the investigation of the Code must be suspended until the breach of the Act has been investigated and concluded by other authorities.
47 Commission of Inquiry into the Sponsorship Program and Advertising Activities, "Public Hearing," Vol. 10 (Ottawa: PWGSC,2005), 20192–20194.
48 Nelson, "Canada's Federal Lobbying Legislation," 100.
49 See Office of the Commissioner of Lobbyists, *Registrar of Lobbyists: Annual Report 2006–2007* (Ottawa: Office of the Commissioner of Lobbyists, 2007), 27.
50 Office of the Commissioner of Lobbyists, *Registrar of Lobbyists: Annual Report 2007–2008* (Ottawa: Office of the Commissioner of Lobbyists, 2008), 30. The case referred to is that of Neelam Makhija who was found to be in breach of four major elements of the *Lobbyists Code of Conduct*. The Registrar of Lobbyists appealed the court's decision in March 2008 as the decision would likely have a significant impact on the Registrar's (now Commissioner's) ability to investigate Code violations by unregistered lobbyists.
51 *Attorney General of Canada vs. Neelam Makhija*, 2008 FCA 402, [9]at 4.
52 G. Bruce Doern, "The Harper Conservative Agenda: True Blue or Liberal Lite?," in G. Bruce Doern, ed., *How Ottawa Spends 2006–2007: In From the Cold, The Tory Rise and the Liberal Demise* (Montreal and Kingston: Queen's University Press, 2006), 5.

53 Langford and Tupper, "How Ottawa Does Business," 131–2.
54 Commission of Inquiry into the Sponsorship Program and Advertising Activities, *Restoring Accountability: Recommendations* (Ottawa: PWGSC, 2006), Chapter 9, 171–4.
55 See Canada, "Accountability Act and Action Plan: Toughening the Lobbyists Registration Act," April 2006, available at: http://www.faa-lfi.gc.ca/docs/ap-pa/ap-pa05-eng.asp
56 Library of Parliament, "Legislative Summaries: Bill C-2: The Federal Accountability Act," Document: LS-522E (Ottawa: Library of Parliament, 18 December 2006), 26.
57 Government Relations Institute of Canada, "The Law of Lobbying the Government of Canada: An Update," Presentation by Colin MacDonald (Borden, Ladner, Gervais) and Cyrus Reporter (Fraser, Milner Casgrain), (Ottawa: GRIC, 13 May 2008), slide 27.
58 OECD, "Comparative Review: Building Blocks for Enhancing Transparency and Accountability in Lobbying," 27 and 81.
59 *Canada Gazette*, "Designated Public Office Holder Regulations," Vol. 142, No. 9, April 2008. See Regulatory Impact Analysis Statement.
60 *Ibid*. See Regulatory Impact Analysis Statement.
61 Note that for in-house corporate lobbyists, two lists are required for registration. The first list names all senior officers for which lobbying amounts to more than 20 per cent, and a second list for those whose duties amount to less than 20 per cent of their time.
62 Canada, *Lobbyist Registration Act* 1985, c.44 (4th Supp.), s. 10.4(1).
63 Library of Parliament, "Legislative Summaries: Bill C-2: The Federal Accountability Act," 28.
64 See Treasury Board Secretariat, "Contracting Policy," Appendix M: Lobbyists and Contracting, 8 September 1997. "Contractors who do business with the government must not retain a lobbyist whom they pay on a contingency basis. This means that lobbyists must not be paid a fee or compensation related to the value of the contract. If lobbyists are retained in connection with a proposed or actual contract with the Crown, they should be paid on a fee for services or retainer basis." At: www.tbs-sct.gc.ca/pol/doc-eng.aspx?id=12027&section=text#M
65 Democracy Watch, "News Release: Past Lobbying Regulation System Failed To Catch Illegal Lobbying And System Is Still Fatally Flawed (Ottawa: Democracy Watch, 28 November 2005), available at: www.dwatch.ca/camp/RelsNov2805.html
66 Langford and Tupper, "How Ottawa Does Business," 116–17.
67 See Kenneth Kernaghan, "Promoting Public Service Ethics: The Codification Option," in Richard A. Chapman, ed., *Ethics in Public Service* (Ottawa: Carleton University Press, 1993), 18–20.

PART TWO

Selected Policy Fields

6 Could the Senate Be Right? Should CIDA Be Abolished?

CHRIS BROWN AND
EDWARD T. JACKSON

INTRODUCTION

In February 2007 the Senate Standing Committee on Foreign Affairs and International Trade released a report on Canadian foreign policy toward Africa. Titled "Overcoming 40 Years of Failure: A New Road Map for Sub-Saharan Africa," the report contained a scathing indictment of development failure in post-Independence Africa. Although laying much of the blame on poor governance in Africa itself, the report also condemned the many failings of development assistance over the years. In particular, the Canadian International Development Agency (CIDA) came in for withering criticism for its "failure...over the past 38 year to make an effective foreign aid difference." Flowing from this analysis, the headline-grabbing recommendation in the report was that "the Government of Canada should conduct an immediate review of the future of the Canadian International Development Agency (CIDA) to determine whether the agency should be abolished or whether it should be improved with a statutory mandate."[1]

This chapter examines the performance of CIDA. We ask whether the Senate committee is correct. Is CIDA's performance so poor that radical measures, up to and including abolishing the agency, are required? We argue that any discussion of CIDA must be placed within the context of the changing global architecture of development assistance and the on-going international debate about aid effectiveness. Seen within this context, and notwithstanding the many difficulties involved in measuring aid effectiveness, it is clear that CIDA's performance has indeed been poor. This poor performance, we argue, is due to long-standing and well-documented policy failures. This chapter examines these policy failures by considering CIDA from four different perspectives: i) CIDA within the international development community, ii) CIDA in the Canadian political process, iii) CIDA in the federal civil service and iv) CIDA in the post 9/11 world. Overall, while we certainly do not think it is time to abolish Canadian development assistance, we do agree with the Senate committee that it may be time to consider abolishing CIDA in its present form. Whether abolished and reconstituted, or simply reformed, it is clear that CIDA must change for it to play the constructive leadership role on the international stage that Canadians so clearly desire. For this to happen, however, there must be strong leadership at the political level, leadership that unfortunately has not been forthcoming from the current Conservative government.

THE CHANGING GLOBAL ARCHITECTURE OF DEVELOPMENT ASSISTANCE

Canada has been providing development assistance since Louis St. Laurent agreed to our participation in the Colombo Plan in the early 1950s. The halcyon days for Canadian aid were the 1960s, when Lester B. Pearson helped stake out an international leadership role for Canada. Pearson himself headed the 1969 UN expert commission which established the widely accepted target for donor countries of 0.7 per cent of Gross National Income (GNI) for overseas development assistance (ODA). It was during this period that CIDA was created as a separate agency under the terms of the Foreign Affairs and International Trade Act of 1968.

Now 40 years old, CIDA operates in an international environment that is radically changed from Pearson's day. The obvious and well-known transformations in global politics relate to the end of the Cold War, the emergence of the United States of America as the world's only superpower, and the launch of the so-called "War on Terror" following the attacks of 11 September 2001. Each of these global transformations has had their impact on Canadian development assistance, as will be discussed below with respect to 9/11. Perhaps less obvious and less well-known have been transformations in the global architecture of development assistance, transformations which have completely changed the context within which Canada provides aid. Both the demand side and the supply side of the development assistance equation have been completely transformed since CIDA was founded.[2]

On the demand side, many former aid recipient countries have "graduated" and no longer require development assistance. Fully 4.1 billion of the world's 5.2 billion people now live in countries ranked by the United Nations as middle-income or better. Some of these countries, most importantly China and India, are former recipients that have now become important aid donors themselves. This still leaves, of course, the "bottom billion" of people world-wide who live in low-income countries needing aid, most of them in sub-Saharan Africa. According to Amar Bhattacharya, the Director of the Group of 24, a group of developing countries coordinating action on international monetary affairs and development, this means we now live in a new "bi-modal" world. Whereas in Pearson's time, 80 per cent of the world's countries were potential aid recipients and only 20 per cent were potential donors, today the situation is reversed: for 80 per cent of countries around the world aid is largely irrelevant, while for the other 20 per cent it remains as important as ever. Indeed, in many of the countries where the bottom billion live, there is increasing aid dependence.[3]

On the supply side, the changes have been equally profound. From a relatively small Western club represented by the Development Assistance Committee (DAC) of the Organization of Economic Cooperation and Development (OECD), the community of bilateral aid donors has grown both in number and diversity. Within the DAC, Japan has now become the world's second largest donor, after the United States. Outside the DAC, China, India, Venezuela, many Arab countries, and a scattering of other countries around the world are now giving development assistance. Just as importantly, the number and diversity of multilateral donors has also multiplied; at last count there were 234 multilateral agencies involved in the aid business. Complementing the proliferation of multilateral agencies has been the increasing number of International Non-Governmental Organizations (INGOs) working in the development field. The biggest of these are very large; World Vision, for instance, the world's largest developmental INGO, has an annual aid budget bigger than Australia, Belgium and Switzerland combined. Perhaps the biggest change, however, has been in the rise of private aid donors. The paradigmatic example here is the Bill and Melinda Gates Foundation, which in a few short years has risen to become one of the world's most influential donors, especially in the health care sector and in the fight against HIV/AIDS. The Gates Foundation alone gives more aid than Ireland. Altogether, total giving by INGOs and private donors now approach total official giving through bilateral and multilateral channels.

What are the implications of the changing global architecture of development assistance for CIDA? Most obviously, they suggest that the days of a generalist organization, with operations in a wide range of sectors in countries throughout the world are over. There are far too many other aid channels, and the need is far too concentrated in a relatively small number of countries, for a medium-sized donor such as Canada to spread its assistance widely across sectors and countries and still expect to achieve a real impact. Yet this is precisely what CIDA does. According to Adam Chapnick, there is a "culture of generalism" that pervades the Canadian development-assistance community, while CIDA "has led the developed world in the breadth of the dispersion of its aid program, providing assistance to nearly every developing state."[4] The data certainly support this assertion. According to its most recent statistical report, in the 2005/06 financial year CIDA had bilateral country programs in 100 states around the world, while a total of 136 states received Canadian ODA of one type or another (the difference between the two measures is accounted for by regional programs, the Canada Fund for Local Initiatives, the Canada Partnership Branch and multilateral aid, all operated within CIDA, and ODA expenditures by other government departments). On the narrower measure, 75.7 per cent of CIDA's country program expenditure of $972 million was concentrated in the top 20 states. On the broader measure, 54 per cent of Canada's ODA of $3,272 million was concentrated in the top 30 states.[5]

Another way of looking at the same data is to ask how important a donor CIDA is in the countries where it operates. Overall, Canada is, at best, a medium-sized player. In 2007, of the 22 members of the DAC, Canada's ODA ranked 9th in terms of total volume and 15th in terms of the percentage of aid to Gross National Income;[6] Canada's contribution amounted to about 3 per cent of total bilateral aid dispersed by members of the DAC.[7] Considering how widely this aid is dispersed, it is therefore not surprising to discover that Canada is a major donor almost nowhere. Among the 30 leading recipients of Canadian ODA, Canada was the third largest donor in only two countries, Indonesia and Haiti; everywhere else it was a less important actor, usually significantly so. Only in Haiti did Canada's development assistance amount to more than 10per cent of the recipient country's ODA.[8] Attempting to operate everywhere and in every sector, CIDA risks making an impact nowhere.

HOW EFFECTIVE IS CIDA?

The question of impact raises the issue of aid effectiveness. Perhaps surprisingly, for many years very few questions were asked in the official development community about the effectiveness of aid, though in recent years there has been increasing attention paid to the issue. Notwithstanding the recent attention to the issue of aid effectiveness, the data necessary for a systematic quantitative assessment of CIDA's overall impact are simply not available. Those more qualitative assessments that have been carried out, however, are uniformly negative in their judgment of CIDA's overall impact.

The whole issue of aid effectiveness has acquired increasing salience in the public mind with the publication in 2006 of *The White Man's Burden* by William Easterly and in 2007 of *The Bottom Billion* by Paul Collier. Easterly and Collier, both of whom are former senior executives at the World Bank, disagree on many things, including the best way forward for development assistance, but they agree on one central proposition: most development assistance over the last 40 years has been ineffective. They also agree on one further point: measuring aid effectiveness is difficult at best. Roger C. Riddell provides the most comprehensive discussion of the difficulties involved. According to Riddell, there are six main challenges in measuring aid effectiveness, three of them old and three of them new.[9] The three challenges are poor data, the attribution problem and the lack of counterfactuals. Statistical data are poor in many developing countries, while most projects continue to operate without good base-line data or on-going monitoring. The attribution problem arises because development is a multi-dimensional process, with many other factors beside aid entering into the equation. How is it possible to separate out the discrete impact of aid? (As an aside, it is relevant to point out that the Senate report criticizing CIDA falls prey to the attribution problem. The report notes that Africa's share of global GNP has fallen steadily over the last forty years, and then leaps to the conclusion that CIDA is partially to blame. Of course, Canadian aid accounts for only a miniscule proportion of financial flows into Africa over the last forty years, so it is impossible to infer from data on African GNP how effective CIDA is as an aid organization.) The counterfactual problem relates to the difficulty of comparing the impact of aid with what would have happened had no aid been provided. Finding, developing or constructing such counterfactuals is virtually impossible.

The three new challenges in measuring aid effectiveness are the shift to new aid modalities, the shift in attention away from outputs to outcomes, and the shift in aid provision to new sectors. New aid modalities, especially sectoral strategies and budget support mechanisms, make it increasingly difficult for an individual agency to assess what its own impact has been, especially when it is a relatively small player in a large donor consortium. Furthermore, it has always been easier to measure outputs (was the school built?) than outcomes (did the quality of education improve?). Formerly, output measures were often sufficient; today's debate on aid effectiveness is correctly focused on outcome measures. Finally, development assistance today has expanded from traditional sectors, such as education and health, to include newer ones such as governance and capacity building. In these newer sectors, outcomes are often intrinsically more difficult to define and measure.

Given all the difficulties, Riddell is understandably cautious in his own assessment of aid effectiveness. In his view, most evaluations are done *ex post*, i.e. they ask how effective the chosen aid project, program or policy was. There are almost no *ex ante* evaluations, which ask whether the correct project, program or policy was chosen in the first place. Of those evaluations that do exist, the large majority examine individual projects. Perhaps unsurprisingly, most of these studies find that the project was effective, at least in the sense that the project achieved its broad objectives; such evaluations rarely have the time, resources or mandate to conduct *ex ante* analysis, or to ask about counterfactuals. Fewer evaluations exist at the sectoral level, and fewer still at the country level. These assessments tend to be more mixed, with those evaluations of the overall effectiveness of aid that do exist usually being quite negative.[10]

The general picture that Riddell paints is certainly replicated in the literature on the effectiveness of CIDA. While evaluations of specific CIDA projects are often positive, general assessments of CIDA as an aid organization are almost uniformly negative. CIDA in fact routinely carries out project evaluations, which typically find that the project in question met its objectives. Unfortunately, these types of evaluations are all too often used as mechanisms of control and justification, rather than as tools for learning and disseminating findings.[11] More importantly, successful individual projects do not necessarily add up to a positive overall developmental impact. Recent academic assessments of CIDA as an agency have echoed the Senate committee report, arguing that it has failed to "develop an effective aid program,"[12] that CIDA remains "relatively weak politically and in its policy-making capacity and influence,"[13] and that there is nothing in current policy that will "have a transformative effect, let alone a significant positive impact on either Canada's development aid program or CIDA's international standing."[14] Perhaps the most telling report was authored in 2005 by Robert Greenhill, who immediately thereafter became President of CIDA for three years. Greenhill, who was then working at the International Development Research Centre (IDRC), interviewed 40 world leaders and asked them about their perceptions of Canada's role in the world. As regards development assistance, their perception was that Canada had gone from being a "leader" to a "laggard". As one foreign leader put it, "In the 70s and 80s, Canada belonged to like-minded countries making a difference in development. Canada was truly one of the leaders. Canada has totally lost that in the past 15 years."[15]

Why are external assessments of CIDA so uniformly negative, even while internal evaluations of specific projects are usually positive? In fact, as Riddell suggests, the data for a comprehensive assessment of the effectiveness of CIDA, or any other aid agency, simply do not exist. Lacking comprehensive data on agency outcomes and therefore developmental impacts, all that can really be assessed are inputs and policy processes. In both these regards, CIDA's record compares poorly with other development assistance agencies around the world.

As mentioned above, the international input target is that donor countries should devote at least 0.7 per cent of GNI to development assistance. There are cogent reasons to question the utility of a target expressed in these terms: why should development assistance be pegged to donors' capacity to give rather than recipients' needs? Nonetheless, this remains the standard measure for assessing commitment to development assistance; it is a measure on which Canada does poorly. Notwithstanding the commitment in the 2007 budget to double aid from 2001/02 levels by 2010/11, Canada remains 15th among the 22 DAC countries, with only 0.28 per cent of GNI devoted to overseas development assistance in 2007. Canada's ODA would have to increase by about $2 billion annually, to a figure almost 50 per cent above the current total, in order to reach the DAC average of 0.45 per cent of GNI devoted to aid.[16] On another common input measure, percentage of tied aid, Canada does even more poorly. According to OECD data, in 2005, 43 per cent of Canadian aid was tied, as against the average among Western donors of 8 per cent.[17] Recently, Canada has committed to untying all its aid by 2012/13; it remains to be seen whether this target will be achieved.

At the level of inputs, therefore, Canada is a poor performer. It trails most other OECD countries in terms of ODA as a percentage of GNI and in terms of the percentage of tied aid. Beyond the input questions of how much aid Canada gives, and how much of it is tied, there is a series of long-standing and well-documented policy failures that reduce CIDA's effectiveness. The next four sections of this chapter look at the causes and consequences of these policy failures by considering CIDA from four different perspectives.

CIDA WITHIN THE INTERNATIONAL DEVELOPMENT COMMUNITY

One major point of reference for CIDA policy is the international development community. Through the DAC and other donor coordination mechanisms, CIDA keeps up to date with current thinking and best policy practices. As many commentators have noted, however, the international development community itself is notoriously subject to policy shifts in response to changing academic and ideological fashions or, as Benu Schneider of the UN Department of Economic and Social Affairs puts it, to "herding behavior."[18] Unfortunately, CIDA is more prone than most agencies to this sort of behaviour. As David Morrison argues, "like other donors, but with more alacrity than most, CIDA has associated itself with new fashions and policy thrusts."[19] Two current examples are CIDA's commitment to PBAs and to the Paris Declaration.

Program-Based Approaches, or PBAs, emerged out of discussions in the DAC in the mid-1990s on a "New Policy Agenda" for development assistance. Reacting to criticisms of the structural adjustment policies of the time, donors sought new aid modalities that were market-based, but at the same time were sensitive to political and social contexts in recipient countries. These discussions led to the World Bank's 1999 Comprehensive Development Framework and the creation of PBAs. PBAs include Poverty Reduction Strategy Papers (PRSPs), Sector-Wide Approaches (SWAPs) and Multi-Donor Budget Support (MDBS), among others. The principles underlying these instruments include the pooling and coordination of contributions from multiple donors, the use of recipient government budget systems, and country ownership of the spending agenda by the government's receiving aid. The PBA paradigm rejected traditional, stand-alone project funding by individual donors as too fragmented, too idiosyncratic and too micro-level in their impacts. There was considerable merit to this assessment, of course. Starting with the presidency of Len Good in the early 2000s, and running through the term of his successor, Robert Greenhill, the champions of PBAs inside CIDA were rewarded with greater prominence and responsibility, and new tools and training taught managers and officers how to implement these instruments. By the latter part of the decade, a majority of Canada's bilateral aid to very poor countries, particularly in Africa, was being channeled through PBAs. By then, PBAs had taken on the character of common sense, almost of a "religion," that was seldom questioned, at least publicly.

Closely linked to PBAs is the Paris Declaration on Aid Effectiveness. Adopted in Paris on 2 March, 2005, the Declaration represents a commitment by donors and recipients alike to improve the effectiveness of aid delivery. It is based on many of the same principles as PBAs. In particular, it calls for recipient country ownership, alignment of donor support with country strategies, harmonization of donor activities, management for results, and mutual accountability between donors and recipients.[20] The "Paris Process" has involved a series of consultative conferences on aid delivery, culminating in a High Level Forum in Accra, Ghana, in September 2008. At this Forum, an Agenda for Action was adopted stressing four key points for action: improve predictability of donor support through 3–5 year forward plans, deliver aid through recipient country systems rather than donor systems, switch to conditions for spending donor funds based on recipient countries' own development objectives, and untie aid.[21]

Laudable as the goals of PBAs and the Paris Declaration are, they have been subjected to strong criticism. PBAs represent a new dynamic in the donor-recipient relationship, one which is heavily weighted in favour of donors. Whereas in earlier times recipient countries negotiated one-on-one with bilateral donors over specific projects, they now find themselves confronted with a consortium representing all the donors involved in a given sector. Very poor countries are badly overmatched by the organization, momentum and leverage of donor groupings, leaving them with little choice but to accept the policies and programs promoted by donors. The result is that "country ownership" comes to mean little more than that recipient governments are willing to defend PBAs against domestic and international critics. As Paolo de Renzio, Lindsay Whitfield, and Isaline Bergamaschi of the Global Economic Governance Programme at Oxford University argue, the donors define ownership as "commitment", whereas genuine ownership entails "control". Their study of aid relationships in eight African countries finds that African governments have actually *lost* ownership of aid to the donors. They report that a "first finding from our research is that while many aid agency officials start out with a commitment to ownership defined as control over policies, as soon as there is some disagreement over policy choices they tend to fall back on a definition of ownership as commitment to their preferred policies."[22] The result is that PRSPs remain "donor documents", largely outside the real political process of recipient countries.

Beyond the key concern with the lack of genuine country ownership, there are several other common criticisms of PBAs. First, to date at least, the PBA strategy has been entirely statist, excluding civil society from participating in the implementation of poverty reduction programs. To be sure, states need to be strengthened, especially in regions of conflict, but so do non-governmental organizations and community-based groups in order for development to be optimized. Second, PBAs have a mixed record, at best, on gender equality. In fact, the gender dimension has too often been ignored by the Finance Ministries that negotiate PRSPs, SWAPs and MDBS arrangements with donor consortia. Finally, PBAs in practice seem not to have advanced human rights in any substantive way, and have, in practice, been impervious – or served as distractions and deflectors – in relation to donor concerns about rights abuses.

The entire Paris Process has been subjected to many of the same criticisms as PBAs. Critics point out that the process is focused solely on the delivery of aid, thus ignoring more fundamental questions about the content of aid programs. Furthermore, there is an inherent tension between the goals of harmonization and mutual accountability on the one hand, and country ownership on the other. That is to say, as donors harmonize their policy interventions through donor consortia and demand accountability through these consortia, it becomes increasingly difficult for recipient countries to control the content and implementation of their own development programs. The result is old-fashioned conditionality and micro-management of recipient country development programs by donor consortia, all in the name of greater country ownership.[23]

CIDA's leadership has enthusiastically embraced and remains fully committed to PBAs and the Paris Declaration, even while some CIDA personnel and their external partners have remained privately skeptical, if not directly opposed. At a North-South Institute conference on aid held in Ottawa in June 2008, out-going CIDA President Robert Greenhill vigorously defended PBAs and the Paris Process, denying that there was any tension between country ownership and either harmonization or accountability.[24] It is clear, however, that there are serious concerns. As discussed above, there are important questions about the actual impact of PBAs and of the Paris Process, especially about the degree of recipient country ownership. Beyond that, there is the question of CIDA's own contribution. Collectivities of donors are usually dominated by the largest and strongest agencies, typically the World Bank and DFID, the UK's aid agency. Small donors like Canada, in practice, exert little influence except perhaps in small sectoral niches, and even then only within the framework set by the major donor powers. In effect, by entering into multi-donor sectoral support mechanisms, usually as a relatively junior partner, CIDA effectively concedes any distinctive policy role for itself. As Stephen Brown points out, there is a contradiction between CIDA's stated desire to become the "world's best development agency" and its slavish adherence to the international donor consensus.[25] You cannot simultaneously be a leader and a follower. By being such a committed follower of the ever changing donor consensus, CIDA has given up any pretense to a distinctively Canadian approach to development assistance.

CIDA IN THE CANADIAN POLITICAL PROCESS

Why has CIDA failed to develop and sustain a long-term philosophy of development assistance? Part of the explanation can be found by looking at CIDA's place within the Canadian political process. Public support for development assistance in Canada is a mile wide but an inch deep. As a consequence, CIDA lacks a strong domestic political support base, making it especially vulnerable to changing political pressures. The result in recent years has been serious budget cuts and a failure to define and sustain a geographic focus. The current Conservative government was elected on a platform emphasizing domestic issues; there is very little indication that it has the interest or the desire to address the problems CIDA faces.

As a preliminary point, it is important to distinguish between international and domestic influences on CIDA. As discussed above, the international development community is the decisive influence with respect to *aid modalities* – what type of aid CIDA will give, through what type of aid delivery mechanisms. When it comes to questions concerning the *scale and direction of aid*, however, the decisive influence is domestic. That is to say, questions about how much aid Canada will give, and who that aid will be given to, are decided within the Canadian political process, not as a result of pressures emanating from the international donor community.

When examining CIDA's place within the Canadian political process, the first thing to note is the ambiguous position of development assistance in Canadian public opinion. In general, the Canadian public perceives Canada as a generous and enlightened country that has an international mission as a peace-keeper and problem-solver. With respect to development assistance, we perceive ourselves as humanitarians who have much to offer the world. It is not surprising to discover, therefore, that there are very high overall levels of public support for development assistance, and indeed for increases in our aid budget. A 2002 poll commissioned by CIDA, for instance, found that 57 per cent of Canadians favoured increasing our ODA, while a 2005 Ipsos-Reid poll found that 70 per cent of Canadians agreed that part of the government's budget surplus should be devoted to increased aid.[26] The significance of such strong public support is diminished somewhat when it is realized that Canadians are largely uninformed about how our aid budget is actually spent. Most respondents assume, for instance, that Canadian aid is wholly altruistic, whereas in fact Canada has one of the highest percentages of tied aid among Western donors. The real weakness of public support for development assistance, however, is revealed when poll respondents are asked to prioritize aid in comparison to domestic policy objectives. The very same respondents who say we should increase foreign aid also consistently place it second behind any major named domestic policy priority. Canadians want to see increases in foreign aid, just not at the expense of anything that affects them directly. As Jean-Sébastien Rioux concludes after reviewing the polling data, "for better or for worse, ODA is often perceived by the public as a luxury, to be spent when other priorities, such as education and health, have been adequately financed."[27]

In one important sense, the public perception that ODA is a luxury is correct. Unlike much of the rest of the federal budget, which is legislatively mandated and therefore difficult to change dramatically on an annual basis, over 80 per cent of the CIDA budget consists of discretionary grants. Combined with the shallow public support for development assistance, this means that the CIDA budget is uniquely vulnerable to budget-cutting pressures in hard times. Certainly, this was the experience during the 1990s, when Finance Minister Paul Martin led the Liberal assault on the government's budget deficit. Almost all government agencies felt the pinch of Martin's budget-slashing, but some suffered more than others. According to figures compiled by the North-South Institute, CIDA suffered most of all. In the decade from the 1988/89 to the 1997/98 budgets, overall federal government expenditure declined 5 per cent in real terms; CIDA sustained the largest drop of any government agency with a 33 per cent cut to its budget. This led to a decline in Canadian ODA from 0.49 per cent of GNI in 1991 to 0.30 per cent of GNI in 1997, the level at which it has remained ever since.[28] To put the budget figures in context, the second largest drop was experienced by the Department of National Defence, whose budget fell by 22 per cent in real terms. Former Chief of Defence Staff Rick Hillier powerfully argued that these were "days of darkness" for DND, and launched a very public national campaign for increases in DND's funding. It is instructive to note that the current Conservative government, reacting at least in part to Hillier's public relations offensive, has begun to restore the DND budget. No similar public figure has come forward to lament any days of darkness at CIDA, even though the budgetary pain was worse at CIDA than at DND.

Why does CIDA have no high profile political champion? Part of the answer, of course, is that it lacks a strong domestic constituency, such as DND enjoys among current and former military personnel and, in particular, the defence industry. It is a truism of the international relations literature that foreigners do not vote in domestic elections, so foreign affairs will always have a weak domestic political constituency. Diaspora communities in Canada's multicultural mosaic can and do sometimes take an interest in development assistance, but their attention has tended to focus on immigration and other matters of more direct personal concern to them. The natural domestic political constituency for CIDA is in fact the many Canadian-based NGOs working in international development. At last count, there were over 400 such NGOs, working in 79 countries around the world.[29] As it turns out, however, these NGOs have a complex and contradictory relationship with CIDA. On the one hand, they are heavily financially dependent on CIDA. Individual agencies vary greatly, but on average 47 per cent of their income comes in the form of grants from CIDA. CIDA, for its part, channels 12 per cent of its budget through NGOs, a sign that it sees them as an important vehicle for delivering Canadian aid.[30] On the other hand, dependence often breeds resentment. CIDA proclaims its commitment to partnership and consultation with the NGOs, but from the point of view of many NGOs the partnership is not real and the consultation is all one-way. They have to listen to CIDA, but CIDA does not listen to them. The result is that, rather than being its strongest advocates, the NGOs are often CIDA's greatest critics. It is striking, for instance, that at the time the Senate committee report came out proposing that CIDA be abolished, very few people in the NGO community leapt to its defence.

The estrangement between CIDA and NGOs has been worsened by CIDA's embrace of PBAs, discussed above. Over the last several years we have witnessed the decline of the Canadian Partnership Branch (CPB) within CIDA. While the Agency's bilateral program was always "richer" and more powerful than other branches, CPB was the interlocutor with a voluble, activist constituency: Canadian NGOs and their southern partners. As the statist PBA paradigm and the new "aid effectiveness" agenda gained currency, the role of civil society was systematically marginalized at every level – global, national and local – in developed and developing countries alike. For its part, CPB was not able to frame its mandate within the PBA paradigm, and its leadership steadily lost influence within CIDA. Externally, Canadian NGOs were destabilized by the new paradigm, fighting to hold their ground and not able, until very recently, to promote a new vision of their role in the development process. All of this meant that the constituency that has been, historically, the most important driver of public opinion and political support for Canada's development assistance program has been effectively sidelined for much of the last decade.

Lacking a strong domestic political support base, CIDA is weakly positioned to promote any long-term development philosophy that runs counter to the short-term interests of its political masters. This is most apparent in CIDA's on-going struggle to define and sustain a geographic and sectoral focus for its work. There is virtual unanimity in the scholarly and policy community that one way for CIDA to improve its performance would be for it to focus on a limited number of recipient countries and sectors, where it could be a major player and could develop long-term relationships and expertise. There has been talk about focusing in this way at least since 1987, when the Standing Committee on External Affairs and International Trade advocated a focus on the poorest of the poor.[31] In 2002, CIDA tried to move decisively in this direction by proposing to focus its work in only nine countries and four policy sectors. This proved to be politically unacceptable, so in the Liberal's 2005 International Policy Statement this commitment was expanded to include 25 countries and five sectors plus one cross-cutting theme. As John Cameron shows in a detailed analysis of the data, in practice this degree of focus has yielded no change at all from the existing distribution of Canadian aid.[32]

The political difficulty of defining a clear focus becomes most apparent, however, when one considers the changing position of Africa in CIDA's list of priorities. In July 2001, the Organization of African Unity (now the African Union) set out an ambitious agenda for good governance and development in Africa with its New Partnership for Africa's Development (NEPAD). Liberal Prime Minister Jean Chrétien was among the developed world's leaders who responded most enthusiastically to NEPAD. He invited a number of African leaders to the June 2002 Kananaskis G8 Summit, and made partnership with Africa a major focus of the Summit and of Canadian foreign policy. Coming out of the Summit, Canada promised to double aid to Africa from 2003/04 levels within five years. In addition, it also declared that 14 of the 25 countries where Canada would focus its aid would be in Africa. If anything, Chrétien's successor, Paul Martin, was even more committed to Africa, even going so far as to invite Irish rock star Bono to speak about aid to Africa at the convention that made him Liberal leader and Prime Minister. After Stephen Harper and the Conservatives came to power in 2006, however, things changed. The Harper Conservatives did reiterate the pledge to double aid to Africa, but the government's intended geographic focus for CIDA is clearly elsewhere. Many of CIDA's efforts are now concentrated on Afghanistan, discussed below. Beyond that, however, and in line with its broader hemispheric policy, the current government has encouraged CIDA to focus more of its attention on Latin America and the Caribbean. As Prime Minister Harper said in June 2007, "re-engagement in our hemisphere is a critical international priority for our Government. Canada is committed to playing a bigger role in the Americas and to doing so for the long term."[33] The Conservatives see the Americas as more directly connected to Canada's national interests, and they hope for synergy between CIDA programming in the Americas and their proposed free trade agreements in the hemisphere.[34] The new focus has yet to be reflected in changing programs and budgets, but as one sign of the changing times it is perhaps appropriate to note that CIDA's home page, accessed in mid October 2008, contained no less than five features related to the Americas, and none at all about Africa.[35] The much vaunted African focus of only a few years ago is apparently already fading away and being replaced with a new emphasis on the Americas.

Overall, the question of geographic focus reflects the weak political position of CIDA. The Harper Conservatives were elected with a platform concentrated on domestic policy issues and a caucus containing very few members with foreign-policy experience. Their general distrust of government, domestic focus and free-market orientation made them instinctively suspicious of CIDA, a government agency assisting foreigners through state action. In power, and with the obvious exception of Afghanistan, the Conservatives have not shown any great interest in CIDA. When it has suited them, however, they have not hesitated to declare their intention to reorient CIDA towards the Americas, notwithstanding prior policy decisions to focus on Africa.

CIDA IN THE FEDERAL CIVIL SERVICE

Not only is CIDA politically weak, it is also a weak and marginalized player within the federal civil service. A series of short-term and relatively weak Ministers have not been able to protect CIDA from the budget cuts discussed above or to help it stake out a strong and independent policy line. At the same time, CIDA has been subjected to new thinking in management orthodoxy, even when these new ideas have not been appropriate to its unique role as a provider of overseas development assistance.

One of the most trenchant criticisms that Robert Greenhill made of CIDA in his 2005 report was that it lacked strong ministerial leadership. As he noted, CIDA had ten different ministers between 1989 and 2005.[36] The result was a vicious circle of inexperience and ineffectiveness reinforcing each other. Because they were new in their post, ministers did not have the time to establish the domestic and international networks that would allow them to be effective in their post. Because CIDA was perceived to be increasingly ineffective, senior ministers with clout in Cabinet did not want the post, so only inexperienced junior ministers were prepared to take it on. The great irony of Greenhill's own tenure as president of CIDA from 2005 to 2008, of course, is that he had three different ministers in three years, none of whom were considered Cabinet heavyweights.[37] As Greenhill himself argues, without Ministerial credibility and effectiveness, it was impossible for CIDA to resist the budget cutting of the 1990s; this crisis of funding, combined with an absence of sustained political leadership, meant that it lost its leadership role among international development agencies.[38]

Even as it has gone through a succession of different ministers, CIDA has been subject to almost continuous policy and administrative reviews. There have been two major policy reviews in the last six years, with a third currently underway. First, the 2002 CIDA document, *Strengthening Aid Effectiveness*, recommended a strengthened field presence, a greater policy role, more focus and untying aid. Second, the Liberal government's 2005 *International Policy Statement* identified five strategies for development assistance: streamlining aid, enhancing partnerships, renewing public engagement, focusing on Africa, and doubling aid.[39] The current policy review takes place in the context of the passage in May 2008 of Bill C-293, the so-called "Better Aid Bill." This Bill mandates that CIDA's annual budget shall be used to reduce poverty, in a manner that is consistent with the Paris Declaration, sustainable development, democracy promotion and human rights.[40] While taking these objectives into account, the policy review will likely shift CIDA's geographic focus toward Latin America and the Caribbean. As this history suggests, the problem at CIDA is not a shortage of good policy suggestions, but rather a failure to sustain over the long term a single clear policy focus.

Constantly changing ministers and continuous policy reviews create bureaucratic paralysis, as officials wait for the latest policy directives from above. On top of this, it is arguable that bureaucratic paralysis has been worsened as a consequence of administrative reform at CIDA, and the wider political pressures for increased accountability in the federal public service. In recent years, the entire federal civil service has been reformed in line with the ideas of the New Public Management (NPM). A world wide public sector reform movement, NPM argues that public bureaucracies can become more accountable, efficient and cost-effective by borrowing ideas from the private sector. In particular, it argues that public sector managers need to become more entrepreneurial and market-oriented, that large bureaucracies should be split up into potentially competing cost-centres, and that recipients of public sector services should be conceptualized as customers rather than clients. The emphasis is all upon efficiency, with every action scrutinized in terms of its contribution to defined agency outcomes.

Laudable as the goals of the NPM may be, when imposed upon CIDA they have frequently had a counter-productive effect, promoting accountancy, not accountability.[41] Part of the problem is simply the short-term and process-oriented focus of the reforms, as compared to the necessarily long-term and substantive perspective of development. The demand placed upon CIDA is for measurement of performance indicators in the current reporting cycle; when development outcomes may take years or even decades to become apparent, it is understandable that the Agency ends up focusing on more easily measurable indicators such as dispersal of funds. The more pernicious problem arises, however, as a result of the multiple lines of accountability within a development agency. The rhetoric of the Paris Declaration is all about recipient country ownership and hence "downward" accountability to host country governments and partners. As discussed above, there is strong reason to doubt the actual extent of country ownership and downward accountability. The public sector reforms are a major part of the problem, since they are premised on "upward" accountability to CIDA headquarters. CIDA's reporting frameworks are rarely integrated with recipient country reporting systems, so all too often the result is parallel reporting systems within a given project or program.

These tendencies have been worsened by the Accountability Act and other accountability procedures instituted in the wake of the sponsorship scandal. As a result of these measures, CIDA's internal reporting and due-diligence systems have been torqued by the Agency's newly empowered contracts administrators, bogging down all stakeholders, both inside and outside CIDA, in an unnecessary overburden of paper and time. This serves no-one's interest, least of all the Canadian taxpayer – or, indeed, the orphan with AIDS in southern Africa or the destitute street woman of Bangladesh. Reputedly, it takes now takes the Agency 43 months to plan, design, contract and launch a new bilateral intervention. Overall, the New Public Management reforms and the political pressures for greater accountability have promoted a culture within CIDA that emphasizes short-term process-oriented thinking and accountability defined in strictly financial terms, as opposed to the sort of long-term developmental focus that is required.

CIDA IN THE POST-9/11 WORLD

As noted above, the major exception to the Conservative government's indifference to CIDA is Afghanistan. From no program at all in 2001, Afghanistan has quickly become the number one recipient of CIDA country program aid. As the Manley report highlighted, however, aid to Afghanistan is far from achieving its objectives; indeed, the security situation seems to be deteriorating in that country. Furthermore, there are serious questions that need to be asked about whether the securitization of aid is distorting CIDA's developmental mission.

If the Conservatives appear indifferent to, or ambivalent about, much of what CIDA does, there is no doubting their strong commitment to the war in Afghanistan and CIDA's role in it. Even though the Canadian commitment to Afghanistan was first made under the previous Liberal government, Prime Minister Stephen Harper has made it abundantly clear that his government is fully committed to the mission. Furthermore, it has always been equally clear that CIDA has a major role to play in Afghanistan. This role arises from the "3D" concept: defence, diplomacy, and development as an integrated response to insurgency. The 3D concept rests on the recognition that it is normally not possible to achieve a purely military victory over a guerrilla insurgency. There is an unavoidable political dimension to the struggle that involves winning the hearts and minds of local populations. Purely military measures against the insurgents must therefore be accompanied by diplomatic efforts to address genuine political grievances and win over wavering support, and by development efforts to rebuild shattered infrastructure and get the economy going again. In theory, a virtuous circle is thereby created, with military measures creating the space for successful diplomacy and development, and diplomatic and developmental initiatives building the public support necessary for further military success.

In Afghanistan, the logic of the 3D approach has led to a major role for CIDA. According to the data from its most recent statistical report, in 2005/06 Afghanistan received $94.8 million in country program aid from CIDA, or 9.8 per cent of CIDA's total aid expenditures, making it the leading recipient of CIDA aid.[42] More recent data show that total Canadian ODA to Afghanistan for the five years up to 2006/07 amounted to $741 million, with total commitments to 2011 reaching $1.2 billion. This is by far Canada's largest contemporary long-term aid commitment. All this money is intended to "build the capacity, legitimacy and popular support of Afghan government and non-governmental institutions."[43] In particular, these funds are being used to repair and construct roads, irrigation schemes and other infrastructure; to provide micro-finance to small businesses; to build schools and promote rural development; and to support community development councils.

The Manley Report, released in January 2008 and formally known as the *Independent Panel on Canada's Future Role in Afghanistan*, is highly critical of CIDA's contribution to Canada's mission in Afghanistan. It observes that, due to CIDA administrative constraints, over 85 per cent of Canadian aid is delivered through multilateral and other channels not controlled by Canada. It charges that, because of security concerns, CIDA staff rarely leave Kabul and therefore have not developed the knowledge or networks necessary to design effective programs. Based on these and other observations, it therefore concludes "that Canada's civilian programs have not achieved the scale or depth of engagement necessary to make a significant impact."[44] Other observers are even more critical of Western aid, including that from CIDA. In March 2008 the Agency Coordinating Body for Afghan Relief (ACBAR), a coalition of over 100 NGOs working in Afghanistan, released an assessment of the effectiveness of Western aid in Afghanistan. It found that 40 per cent of aid goes back to donor countries in the form of corporate profits and consultant salaries; that due to a lack of coordination and communication the Afghan government does not know where one-third of all aid since 2001 has been spent; that over half of aid to Afghanistan is tied; and that over two-thirds of aid bypasses the Afghan government.[45] Drawing on these and other observations, it therefore concluded that "thus far aid has been insufficient and in many cases wasteful and ineffective."

Given the continued deterioration of the security situation in Afghanistan, what is to be done to improve aid effectiveness there? The Manley Report argues that "Canada's contribution to the reconstruction and development of Afghanistan should be revamped giving higher priority than at present to direct, bilateral project assistance that addresses the immediate, practical needs of the Afghan people, especially in Kandahar province, as well as longer-term capacity building." In particular, the Report calls for Canada to undertake a "signature project", perhaps a hospital or the construction of an irrigation scheme that will have a large immediate impact, and thus raise Canada's profile. There are several reasons to believe that such a signature project would be a mistake. For one thing, as the ACBAR report argues, "too many projects are designed to deliver rapid, visible results, rather than to achieve sustainable poverty reduction or capacity building objectives."[46] Gratifying as a Canadian-built signature project may be for voters back home, the bitter experience of decades of development assistance is that such projects all too easily become white elephants unless they are fully integrated within the host country's administrative and financial systems, such that it is able provide the staff and recurrent funds necessary to keep it going after the donor leaves. For another thing, of course, any such signature project, especially in Kandahar province, risks becoming a magnet for insurgent attacks.

Thankfully, there is no indication to date that CIDA intends to implement this particular recommendation of the Manley Report. Nonetheless, the broader questions remain about CIDA's role in Afghanistan. In particular, how well do defence and development really mix? As regards Afghanistan, as the Manley Report argues, there is very little evidence to date to indicate that development aid has limited the insurgency. Indeed, the ACBAR report suggests that some aid may in fact promote the insurgency, due to the perverse incentives that the regional distribution of aid in Afghanistan creates. Furthermore, as the security situation deteriorates, it becomes increasingly difficult to deliver aid at all. Such concerns point to broader questions about the impact of the securitization of aid on CIDA. Although some of the money for Afghanistan is new money that would not otherwise have gone to CIDA, much of it is diverted from other uses. More fundamentally, the Afghanistan mission represents a significant diversion of CIDA's management time and organizational focus from its broader developmental mission. Notwithstanding the "3D" rhetoric, Canada's Afghanistan mission has been a war-fighting enterprise, with an aid component running alongside it. So significant is this aid to Afghanistan that CIDA has in effect set up a whole new branch to deal with it: the Afghanistan Task Force. Perhaps unavoidably, Afghanistan occupies a great deal of political and bureaucratic attention. Outside the Afghanistan Task Force, senior managers at CIDA are frequently left, in essence, to fend for themselves. Overall, the Afghanistan mission has had a troubling impact on CIDA. Much as security and development are undeniably connected, this is not what CIDA is equipped to do. As Erin Simpson persuasively argues, "development discourse, development resources, and the public support for development have been hijacked by an agenda that, in reality, has little to do with development."[47]

CONCLUSION: THE PRIORITY OF POLITICS

Was the Senate committee therefore right? Should CIDA be abolished? What emerges from the discussion above is a picture of an agency that has lost its way. Canadian ODA is dispersed across too many countries and too many sectors, and too much of it is tied. Total ODA as a percentage of GNI is low compared to other OECD countries. CIDA slavishly follows the latest donor fad, at the expense of developing any long-term development philosophy of its own. Public sector reforms and post-sponsorship scandal demands for greater accountability have encouraged a mindset within CIDA that focuses on short-term financial accounting, rather than long-term developmental thinking. And the mission in Afghanistan has diverted resources while arguably distorting the developmental mission of CIDA.

None of these criticisms are new; they have been advanced with increasing urgency over the years by a wide range of commentators. The path to greater effectiveness in Canadian development assistance has been spelled out before as well. Indeed, many of the key recommendations have even been embraced by CIDA itself, in rhetoric if not in reality. In brief, much of the consensus in the literature argues that what Canada needs is a *development* agency, with a strong sectoral and geographic *focus*, sustaining *long-term* commitments with its partners, operating in a *decentralized* manner, following an *independent* policy line, and receiving adequate *resources*.

A development agency is one that makes development assistance its sole *raison d'être*. If Canada wants to promote its exports overseas, or provide short-term emergency relief following humanitarian disasters, or help rebuild failed states in war zones, it should do so; these are all valid foreign policy objectives. They are also objectives which, while obviously connected in one way or another to development assistance, are distinct from it. Indeed, when combined with development assistance, they can undermine it. Tying aid in order to boost Canadian exports makes development assistance inefficient; responding to the latest short-term disaster distracts attention from long-term goals; linking aid to the war on terror politicizes it and distorts it. If Canada wants to pursue these other valid foreign policy objectives it should establish separate agencies to do so; its development assistance agency cannot be effective unless it is squarely and exclusively focused on long-term development assistance.

In the new global architecture of aid, it is impossible to be all things to all people. A generalist orientation, such as CIDA still maintains, is simply no longer viable. In order to be effective, Canadian development assistance must have much greater geographic and sectoral focus. Deciding upon and sustaining a tight geographic and sectoral focus is not easy; especially in multicultural Canada there is a domestic constituency for programming in virtually every country in the world. Yet, for development assistance to be effective, focus is absolutely vital.

A major reason to focus is that it facilitates a long-term commitment to a given country or sector. CIDA has had its greatest successes where it has managed to remain engaged in a particular country or sector over a period of time measured in decades. These sorts of long-term commitments achieve two purposes. They allow a development assistance agency to build up institutional expertise in the country or sector, and they help create and sustain a network of overseas partners with whom the development agency can work.

A corollary of focus and long-term commitment is a decentralized management structure. At present, CIDA is notoriously centralized, with few staff and even less resources or authority in its country bureaus. Yet development success depends upon detailed country knowledge. Only country experts in the field, with authority and resources to respond creatively to local needs, can create the sorts of innovative programming tailor-made to country requirements that will lead to development success.

The successful development assistance agency needs to pursue an independent policy line. The international donor consensus provides an important point of reference for development policy, but sustaining a long-term commitment in a relatively limited number of sectors and countries requires the courage to stick with a particular programming philosophy in the face of the ever-changing fashions of the development industry.

Finally, without adequate resources, nothing else matters. Canada's own Lester Pearson set the international target of 0.7 per cent of GNI for overseas development assistance. Several countries, most notably the Scandinavians, have already exceeded this target, while many others have committed to reaching it in the near future. Making a significant contribution to global development requires contributing significant resources to development assistance.

Can CIDA be transformed into such a development agency? The evidence from elsewhere suggests that it is possible. There is wide agreement in the literature that the United Kingdom's Department for International Development, DfID, was transformed under Tony Blair from a laggard to a leader.[48] Elements of its successful transformation included a clear focus on long-term poverty relief even at the expense of the UK's short-term commercial interests, a strong concentration on the poorest of the poor undiluted by conflicting priorities, and an internal agency culture that embraced discussion and debate about long-term development goals. But the key to the transformation of DfID was political leadership. Tony Blair made development assistance a priority of his administration. He appointed a powerful Minister, Clare Short, to the development assistance portfolio, and he kept her there for most of his time in power. Only with a lead from the prime minister, and a powerful minister in Cabinet, was the British development assistance agency successfully transformed.

Can a similar transformation occur in Canada, or should we simply abolish CIDA and start over as the Senate committee suggests? There are at least four options for the future of Canadian development assistance that are under informal discussion in the broader development community.

1 Transform the existing CIDA: The first option is to transform the existing structure and systems of CIDA in the same way that DfID was transformed.

There are two major problems with this approach. For one thing, just as in the British case, it would require strong Ministerial leadership. CIDA's political leadership has lacked continuity, vision and professionalism, lurching ideologically between the Liberals and Conservatives in a series of minority governments. For another thing, as discussed above, a number of "transformation" initiatives have already been attempted at CIDA over the past decade, resulting in very little substantive change. The current structure and system have so far proven resistant to serious reform, and are likely to do so going forward.

2. Give the aid file to DFAIT: A second option often canvassed is to hand the entire aid file over to the Department of Foreign Affairs and International Trade (DFAIT). This would simplify some matters, and might even result in cost-savings in Canadian embassies around the world as well as at headquarters. The fundamental problem with this option, however, lies in the fact that the Foreign Affairs Department is run by career diplomats, not specialists in international development. In fact, there is a demonstrable lack of respect for and understanding of development knowledge in the culture and practices of DFAIT. The second serious drawback of this option is the potential for even greater political interference by the minister of Foreign Affairs in decisions on aid strategy and spending.

3. Distribute CIDA's functions among existing organizations: A third option is to distribute the various functions and programs currently run by CIDA among several existing organizations: bilateral programs could be given to DFAIT, research and partnership programs to the International Development Research Centre (IDRC), human rights programs to the International Centre for Human Rights and Democratic Development (informally called Rights and Democracy) and environmental programs to the International Institute for Sustainable Development. While this option has some merit, it also means that there would be no single agency to coordinate aid policy across these various organizations. DFAIT would likely attempt to do so, thus raising the problems associated with option two above. Another downside of the "distribution" option is that it would almost certainly heighten competition and conflict among these four agencies.

4. Create a special operating agency (SOA): If not outright abolition, this was the option preferred by the Senate committee. The report argued that, if "it is to be retained, CIDA should be given a statutory mandate incorporating clear objectives against which the performance of the agency can be monitored by the Parliament of Canada."[49] IDRC has benefited from being a crown corporation, being less subject to political influence and more able to internally tailor its structure, systems, policies and programs to achieve its mandate. One especially valuable feature of IDRC's approach has been the presence of accomplished experts from the South on its board of directors. While a special operating agency would be obliged, rightly, to be transparent and accountable to the government, and would naturally be

guided by Treasury Board policies in this effort, the SOA would itself decide precisely how to implement accountability, evaluation and reporting systems that would be appropriate to its mission and its capacity.

Overall, our assessment is that the best option is, in fact, the option the Senate committee advocated: the creation of a special operating agency. In a technical and legal sense, this is a very feasible course of action. The main challenge is how to build political support to make it actually happen. It would help if CIDA had a president who was capable of doing for CIDA what Rick Hillier did for DND. The new president of CIDA as of 1 July 2008 is Margaret Biggs, a senior government bureaucrat with an impressive track record and good ties to the prime minister and central agencies through her previous job as a deputy secretary to Cabinet. Perhaps she will be able to mobilize public support behind a renewed Canadian development assistance program. But the really decisive leadership will have to come from the political level, starting with the prime minister himself. Unfortunately, there is nothing to indicate that Prime Minister Harper takes a great interest in development assistance, beyond its contribution to the Afghanistan mission and its possible tie-in to hemispheric trade deals in the Americas. It is, however, an interesting question as to whether the recently emboldened opposition parties could decide to work together on this issue and force the prime minister to lead a transformation of Canadian development assistance. Sustained advocacy of such a transformation by stakeholders outside CIDA, especially in civil society, would be essential in driving such a multi-party effort.

NOTES

1 The Standing Senate Committee on Foreign Affairs and International Trade, *Overcoming 40 Years of Failure: A New Road Map for Sub-Saharan Africa* (Ottawa: The Senate, February 2007), x and xiii.
2 All data on the global architecture of development assistance are from A. Bhattacharya, "The Role of Aid in a Changing World," paper presented at the CIDA/North-South Institute "Does Aid Work Conference," Ottawa, Canada, 17–18 June 2008. Available at www.nsi-ins.ca; accessed 25 September 2008. Many of the same data are also recorded in the conference report, North-South Institute, *Conference Report: Does Aid Work?* (Ottawa, 2008).
3 Bhattacharya, "The Role of Aid."
4 Adam Chapnick, "Canada's Aid Program: Still Struggling After Sixty Years," *Behind the Headlines* 65, no. 3, (2008): 10.
5 Canadian International Development Agency, *Statistical Report On Official Development Assistance, Fiscal Year 2005/06*, (Ottawa, Canadian International Development Agency, May 2008), Tables D-1, D-2 and D-4.

6 Chapnick, "Canada's Aid Program," 8.
7 Stephen Brown, "'Creating the world's best development agency'? Confusion and Contradictions in CIDA's New Policy Blueprint," *Canadian Journal of Development Studie* 28, no. 2 (2007): 223.
8 Brown, "'Creating the World's Best Development Agency'?" 223.
9 Roger C. Riddell, "The Impact of Aid on Development Objectives: Current Evidence and Thinking and Key Issues for the Future," paper presented at the CIDA/North-South Institute "Does Aid Work Conference," Ottawa, Canada, 17–18 June 2008, 2–4. Available at www.nsi-ins.ca; accessed 25 September, 2008. A more detailed discussion is contained in Roger C. Riddell, *Does Foreign Aid Really Work?* (Oxford: Oxford University Press, 2007).
10 Riddell, "The Impact of Aid," 4–10.
11 David R. Black and Rebecca Tiessen, "The Canadian International Development Agency: New Policies, Old Problems," *Canadian Journal of Development Studies* 28, no. 2 (2007): 206.
12 Chapnick, "Canada's Aid Program," 1.
13 Black and Tiessen, "CIDA," 192.
14 Brown, "Creating the World's Best Development Agency?" 213. Two other recent academic discussions of CIDA, both of which echo these assessments, are Danielle Goldfarb and Stephen Tapp, "How Canada Can Improve its Development Aid: Lessons from Other Countries," *CD Howe Institute Commentary 232* (April 2006) and Jennifer Welsh and Ngaire Woods (eds.), *Exporting Good Governance: Temptations and Challenges in Canada's Aid Program*, (Waterloo: Wilfred Laurier Press, 2007).
15 Robert Greenhill, *Making a Difference? External Views on Canada's International Impact*, (Toronto: Canadian Institute of International Affairs, 2005), 25.
16 Chapnick, "Canada's Aid Program," 18.
17 Brown, "Creating the World's Best Development Agency?" 215.
18 Benu Schneider, "Aid and Other Development Finance: From Accra to Doha," paper presented at the CIDA/North-South Institute "Does Aid Work Conference," Ottawa, Canada, 17–18 June 2008. Available at www.nsi-ins.ca; accessed 25 September 2008.
19 Cited in Black and Tiessen, "The Canadian International Development Agency," 194.
20 Organization of Economic Cooperation and Development, *Paris Declaration on Aid Effectiveness*. Available at www.oecd.org; accessed 10 October 2008.
21 Accra High Level Forum. Available at www.accrahlf.net; accessed 10 October 2008.
22 Paolo de Renzio, Lindsay Whitfield and Isaline Bergamaschi, "Reforming Foreign Aid Practices: What Country Ownership Is and What Donors Can Do to Support It," Global Economic Governance Programme Briefing Paper. Available at www.globaleconomicgovernance.org; accessed 10 October 2008, 2. The full research is published in Alistair Fraser and Lindsay Whitfield (eds.), *The Politics of Aid: African Strategies for Dealing with Donors* (Oxford: Oxford University Press, 2008).
23 David Booth, "Aid Modalities and Governance: Where the Paris Agenda Goes Wrong," paper presented at the CIDA/North-South Institute "Does Aid Work Conference," Ottawa, Canada, 17–18 June 2008. Available at www.nsi-ins.ca; accessed 25 September 2008.

24 North-South Institute, *Conference Report: Does Aid Work?* (Ottawa, 2008), 9. Available at www.nsi-ins.ca; accessed 25 September 2008.
25 Brown, "Creating the World's Best Development Agency?" 226.
26 Black and Tiessen, "CIDA," 192.
27 Quoted in Chapnick, "Canada's Aid Program," 6.
28 Black and Tiessen, "CIDA," 193/4.
29 Black and Tiessen, "CIDA," 205.
30 Black and Tiessen, "CIDA," 205.
31 Chapnick, "Canada's Aid Program," 9.
32 John Cameron, "CIDA in the Americas: New Directions and Warning Signs for Canadian Development Policy," *Canadian Journal of Development Studies* 28, no. 2 (2007): 231–7.
33 Prime Minister's Office, "Prime Minister Harper signals Canada's renewed engagement in the Americas." Available at www.pm.gc.ca; accessed 10 October 2008.
34 Lee Berthiaume, "CIDA Program Foreshadows Move Away From Africa, Poorest Countries," *Embassy*, 21 May 2008, 3 and "World Bank Applauds Canada's Americas Focus," *Embassy*, 25 June 2008, 3.
35 CIDA. Available at www.acdi-cida.gc.ca; accessed 13 October 2008.
36 Greenhill, *Making a Difference?*, 26.
37 Lee Berthiaume, "A Clear View of Power, a River Running Through It," *Embassy*, 18 June 2008, 1.
38 Greenhill, *Making a Difference?*, 25.
39 Black and Tiessen, "CIDA," 195.
40 "NGOs Applaud Adoption of 'Better Aid Bill'," *Issue Update* 4, no. 5 (30 May 2008).
41 Black and Tiessen, "CIDA," 206.
42 CIDA, *Statistical Report 2005/06*, Table D-2.
43 Minister of Public Works and Government Services, *Independent Panel on Canada's Future Role in Afghanistan* (Ottawa: Ministry of Public Works and Government Services, 2008), 25.
44 Minister of Public Works, *Independent Panel on Afghanistan*, 28.
45 Matt Waldman, *Falling Short: Aid Effectiveness in Afghanistan* (Kabul: Agency Coordinating Body for Afghan Relief, 2008), 5.
46 Waldman, *Falling Short*, 2.
47 Erin Simpson, "From Inter-Dependence to Conflation: Security and Development in the Post-9/11 Era," *Canadian Journal of Development Studies* 28, no. 2 (2007): 264.
48 Brown, "Creating the World's Best Development Agency?" 226.
49 Senate Committee, *40 Years of Failure*, 97.

7 Federal Gas Tax Transfers: Politics and Perverse Policy

ROBERT HILTON
AND CHRISTOPHER STONEY

In Budget 2008, the Harper Conservative government committed to providing municipalities with a permanent transfer of $2 billion annually from revenues derived from the federal excise tax on gasoline. This new initiative was intended to succeed an existing fixed term federal transfer program known as the Gas Tax Fund, launched by the Martin Liberal government in 2004 with a total contribution of $5 billion over four years. Following the election in 2006, the Harper government supplemented the Gas Tax Fund, increasing it by $8 billion and extending its duration for another four years beginning in 2010. While local politicians are always eager to receive "free cash"[1] from the federal government, municipal associations, mayors and councillors across the country continued to complain about the lack of permanence in the funding that was available through Ottawa's various infrastructure programs. With its annual budgetary surpluses after 1999, the federal government had created a myriad of limited duration municipal programs as a convenient means of channelling treasury funds into local projects. However, as with the "economic stimulus" package announced recently in Budget 2009, questions were being raised about accountability and the political nature of the programs. As the Federation of Canadian Municipalities observed, "it is ad hoc and unpredictable short-term funding that muddies accountability and obscures objectives because of short-term political considerations ..."[2]

The Harper government's commitment to provide a "permanent" share of gas tax revenues was designed to address these criticisms and to deflect arguments from local governments that, while the federal government enjoyed budget surpluses, municipalities were facing a massive fiscal shortfall as they attempted to cope with the significant demands of infrastructure replacement and renewal.[3] For the Harper Conservatives, the new initiative was marketed as a significant departure from traditional short-term funding for infrastructure. Through this policy, the federal government was sending a clear message acknowledging that it has an ongoing responsibility to supplement the financial resources available to municipal governments. In order to meet its "obligations" in this respect, Ottawa was now committing to indefinitely share a portion of its revenues for local infrastructure.

The position taken by the Harper Conservatives was surprising given their espoused commitment to "open federalism" and sharply contrasts from that expressed twenty years earlier by the Progressive Conservative government led by Brian Mulroney. The Mulroney government categorically refused to provide *any* federal funds for municipal infrastructure. Tom Macmillan, Mulroney's Minister of the Environment, stated at the time that, "the Government of Canada cannot at this time re-launch multi-billion dollar national programs ... that according to the *Constitution* and the provinces themselves, are not in the federal jurisdiction."[4]

Since the roles and responsibilities assigned under the *Constitution* have not changed during the past two decades, what would persuade the Harper Conservatives to commit to permanently sharing a portion of federal revenues with local government? In this chapter we explore the origins of this shift in federal policy and what it portends for future demands from local governments and the provinces for more permanent revenue transfers from the federal treasury. First, we provide some background that briefly traces the evolution of federal transfers for municipal infrastructure and outlines how these financial arrangements changed over time. We then examine the origin of the federal excise tax on gasoline and the recent decisions to share a portion of these revenues through the creation of the Gas Tax Fund. Next, we present some observations on the rationale underlying the policy for the Fund and provide our views on the impact of launching a permanent fiscal arrangement that transfers $2 billion annually to municipal governments for infrastructure: does this continue to "muddy accountability" for the expenditure of tax dollars? We also consider whether this policy creates a precedent that strengthens arguments calling on the federal government to transfer to municipal governments *other revenue sources* such as personal and corporate income tax.

FEDERAL INVOLVEMENT IN FUNDING MUNICIPAL INFRASTRUCTURE

The development and maintenance of local infrastructure in Canada falls solely under the jurisdiction of the provinces and their municipal governments. Section 92 of the *Constitution Act* (1867) sets out the exclusive powers of provincial legislatures in sixteen areas, with section 92 (8) giving the legislature of each province total responsibility for making laws relating to that province's municipal institutions. Local governments are not recognized under the *Constitution* as a separate order of government, and are often referred to as "creatures" of the provinces, legally subordinate to them and dependent on provincial legislation for defining the parameters of their authority and sources of revenue.

Despite the parameters set out in the *Constitution*, during the decades after World War I until the early 1980's the federal government occasionally provided municipal governments with financial assistance that took the form of loans and grants for a variety of local public works projects. Ottawa's financial assistance was intended to be short term rather than ongoing, targeting economic and social problems resulting from high unemployment, housing shortages, urban decay and environmental degradation. As Wolfe observed, many of these public crises can be traced to federal government actions – policies related to immigration, housing development, and transportation – or inaction, such as the failure to anticipate the effects of demobilization following World War II.[5] The federal response to these crises was reactive, driven by demands that the senior level of government intervene by providing cash to help alleviate these problems.

In its responses to these crises, the federal government acted very much like a bank, augmenting the financial resources available to provincial and municipal governments. Federal participation was temporary and arms-length, limited to creating programs that provided either loans (requiring repayment), unconditional transfers of funds (grants) or alternatively, conditional payments (contributions that provided a share of costs matched by the municipal and provincial government). As Hilton observes, "Regardless of the broader nature of these public problems, the federal government's solution invariably involved the creation of short-term programs that were designed as national policy responses to address local problems or needs."[6]

The role of the federal government was limited to providing a financial stimulus that allowed local governments and the provinces to take necessary action. For example, federal funding through the Sewer Treatment Program (1961 to 1974) provided $979 million in loans and $131 million in grants to local governments to address the shortage of serviced land, which was a major impediment to expanding residential construction. The Municipal Winter Works Incentive (1958 to 1968) provided $267 million to boost employment by supporting fifty per cent of direct payroll costs in municipalities. The *Municipal Development and Loan Act* established a $400 million fund during 1963–66 to stimulate employment by providing loans to local government that encouraged them to accelerate and expand their capital works. Programs such as these were designed to provide municipalities with temporary injection of cash, most of which was repayable to the federal government.

With the election of the Chrétien Liberal government in 1993, a new era in federal funding for municipal governments began. Despite the daunting $42+ billion deficit in the federal treasury, a severe drop in federal revenues and increased spending on employment insurance benefits caused by a severe recession, the Liberals sought to stimulate a recovering economy by adjusting monetary and fiscal policies that included new federal spending through a new infrastructure program. The Canada Infrastructure Works Program (CIWP) – with initial funding of $2 billion that was subsequently increased by an additional $400 million – was intended originally as a short-term means of stimulating the economy through job creation in the construction industry, much like those from previous decades. However, the CIWP, which ran over two phases during 1994–1999, morphed into something quite different. It called for a "partnership" among the three levels of government to jointly deal with a variety of public policy needs that could be addressed through investment in local infrastructure. The federal government would now provide its own "share" of the costs of municipal infrastructure projects, up to a maximum of one-third.

The Liberal's election platform in 1993 (Red Book I) had outlined four objectives for a tri-partite "shared cost, two-year $6 billion infrastructure program, to upgrade transportation and local services."[7] The new program was intended to help create employment rapidly over a two-year period, build infrastructure that "support(ed) economic growth," develop infrastructure that "enhance(d) community liveability," and demonstrate to the public that the federal government could work cooperatively with other levels of government. While spending to help spur job creation was the main driver behind the policy, there was a much more significant and enduring legacy of the Canada Infrastructure Works Program (CIWP): it established the concept of a "tri-partite shared cost" for municipal infrastructure that has helped to shape arguments calling for a realignment of the fiscal framework for the nation.

Since the CIWP, the federal government has launched a series of other "partnership" infrastructure programs, notably the Canada Infrastructure Program ($2.05 billion), the Municipal-Rural Infrastructure Fund ($1.2 billion) and the Canada Strategic Infrastructure Fund ($6 billion). While the first two were "bottom-up," requiring local governments to apply for matched funding from their province and the federal government, the third appeared more politically motivated. Unlike previous infrastructure programs, there was no application and vetting process for the Canada Strategic Infrastructure Fund (or for another program, the Border Infrastructure Fund). As Hilton observed, "Rather than basing (federal funding) decisions on public policy interests, the selection process became very much enmeshed in politics."[8]

Representatives from municipal and provincial governments seeking federal funding through these programs carried out extensive campaigns to curry favour in the Prime Minister's Office (PMO), Privy Council Office (PCO) as well as ministers" offices, particularly those of regional ministers. The political nature of CSIF was reinforced by the significant amount of potential federal "investment" in infrastructure projects: the federal share of costs involved tens and, in some cases, hundreds of millions of dollars. As well, the allowed maximum federal funding had now risen significantly to fifty (50) per cent of eligible project costs. Since spending in these programs was discretionary, there was considerable latitude both in choosing recipients and the amount of funding they received. The political capital derived from making funding announcements of this magnitude presented an irresistible opportunity for federal politicians.

The policy rationale underlying federal infrastructure programming also evolved. Projects receiving funding were ostensibly intended to have a positive impact, improving the economy, the quality of life in communities, and the environment. A myriad of vaguely defined objectives for each program served to justify federal largesse, providing the narrative for press releases and speeches announcing (or, as was often the case, re-announcing as often as possible) federal funding for local infrastructure projects. Even very small infrastructure projects were heralded by federal politicians for their contribution to "improving national, provincial and local economic competitiveness," "supporting long-term economic growth," "improving economic opportunities," "improving the quality of life," and "promoting improved environmental quality."[9] In reality, however, by providing funding for thousands of municipal infrastructure projects – sprinkling cash across the country – the federal government was using a standard ploy of distributive politics, creating as many opportunities as possible to allow government MPs to engage in "retail politics" from coast to coast to coast.

The funding announcements and signage at construction sites were intended to provide the federal government with a visible presence in many rural and urban communities. Signage at construction sites large and small were, in effect, "billboards" used as a means of trying to convince citizens that the federal government was relevant and played active role in improving the quality of life in communities. The demand to promote "federal visibility" ramped up soon after the near death-referendum crisis in Québec in 1995 and the negative fall-out across the country following announcements of severe reductions in federal programming in order to reduce the deficit (cuts in spending resulting from "Program Review"). The federal presence in communities had started to wane through efforts to curb spending, which included significant reductions in various social transfer programs to the provinces. Through its infrastructure programs, the federal government was endeavouring to "show the flag" in communities across the country. At the same time, the federal government began to assume a far greater share of infrastructure costs and demanded – except in Québec – a greater role in the administration of program spending.[10]

Despite these efforts and the significant overhead costs associated with "communications" activities in infrastructure programs, a poll conducted by the federal government in 2004 revealed disappointing results: "This poll revealed that Canadians did not see the role of the federal government in communities. This finding heavily influenced the development of the communications annex of the GTF agreement (Infrastructure Canada) was to sign with each Province and Territory."[11] As a self-proclaimed "partner" in building local infrastructure, the federal government began to demand greater recognition for its involvement, requiring the recipients of federal largesse to follow "communications protocols" outlining how media events and activities would ensure the participation of federal Ministers and government MPs. Particularly for the Canada Strategic Investment Fund (and the Border Infrastructure Fund), recipients were required to be accountable to Ottawa not only for the how the funds were spent but also for progress reports at a *project level*. The federal government was now much more than a banker – it was becoming an active partner involved in project management.[12]

The launch in 2006 of the Public Transit Fund,[13] which sprinkled $400 million to communities across the country, and the curious funding instrument known as the Public Transit Capital Trust (PTCT) – a $900 million transfer to a trust company which in turn cut cheques to "beneficiaries," viz. the provinces and territories – was further evidence that the federal government was assuming a greater share of costs for local infrastructure: by now there was no requirement for recipients to match federal funding. Budget 2008 topped up the funding available under the PTCT with an additional $500 million "to support capital investments." In the Harper Conservatives' 2006 Budget, the rationale in establishing the Trust was presented as part of a broader agenda: federal resources would be transferred to municipal governments in order to "*restore fiscal balance.*" This commitment was also to be realized through Budget 2008 which committed to making permanent the transfer of a portion of revenues from the federal excise tax on gasoline. However, the initiative to share federal revenues from the Gas Tax did not begin under the Conservatives; rather, it was a carryover from the Martin Liberal government's "New Deal for Communities." Before exploring how this policy came into being, however, we first provide a brief history of revenues derived by the federal government from fuel taxes.

ORIGIN OF FUEL TAXES

The federal government started to impose a tax on gasoline more than thirty years ago. On 23 June 1975, John Turner – then federal minister of Finance – announced to the House of Commons that the government was introducing "a special excise tax on gasoline for personal use."[14] At the time, the rate was set at ten cents per gallon and was expected to generate $350 million for the federal treasury during the first year. Together with increases in the price of domestic oil prices, the measures introduced in Budget 1975 were intended to "encourage motorists to make their driving habits more efficient in terms of saving gasoline ... (and) encourage the use of public transportation, thereby helping to relieve the growing congestion in our cities."

The gasoline tax was increased to 8.5 cents per litre, a rate that remained unchanged until 1995.[15] As part of a deficit reduction measure, it was then increased to ten cents per litre. At present, the federal excise tax on gasoline remains at a flat rate of ten cents per litre. The federal tax on diesel fuel (in effect since 1987) is also a flat rate, applied at four cents per litre. While furnace oil, natural gas and propane are exempt from this tax, the Goods and Services Tax (GST) or Harmonized Sales Tax (HST) is applied to all petroleum products. With respect to gasoline, therefore, considerable government revenues are obtained both from the flat tax rate and as the percentage of the retail price (*ad valorem*) when the GST/HST is applied. In addition to federal taxes on fuel, provincial governments and some municipalities levy taxes on gasoline and other petroleum products:

- In Newfoundland and Labrador, Nova Scotia and New Brunswick, the GST and the provincial retail sales tax are combined to levy the 14 per cent Harmonized Sales Tax, applicable to all retail petroleum products.
- Provincial taxes range from 6.2 cents per litre (Yukon) to 20.4 cents per litre (Prince Edward Island).
- Special provincial taxes collected on gasoline are allocated to three municipalities: Montreal (1.5 cents per litre); Vancouver (6.0 cents) and Victoria (2.5 cents).
- Alberta and Ontario also share provincial sales tax revenues with their municipal governments.

Totalling $11.2 billion in 2005–06, road fuel taxes (including gasoline and diesel) are the most important component of federal, provincial and territorial government tax revenues from transportation. Total fuel taxes made up seventy-five per cent of total revenues by transport users.[16] Estimated road fuel tax revenue for the federal government is over $4.3 billion (2005–06). In addition to the excise and sales taxes levied on gasoline, a carbon tax on gasoline was recently levied in B.C. and Québec. The impact of these taxes is as yet unknown, particularly those imposed in BC as the provincial government committed to making them "revenue neutral," offsetting the carbon tax by reducing by an equivalent amount personal income taxes. From the perspective of the consumer/taxpayer, the complexity and costs involved in administering the revenues from the myriad of fuel taxes and levies raised by all three levels of government must seem perplexing.

Despite the considerable revenues obtained from its excise tax on gasoline since 1975, the federal government has chosen not to view these funds as consumption tax earmarked for specific spending, e.g., reinvesting these revenues in transportation infrastructure. Rather, gasoline and diesel taxes have been deposited along with other revenues to the Consolidated Revenue Fund, a general pool of money to be applied to government spending. The Canadian Taxpayers Federation (CTF) has been highly critical of this practice, particularly the federal government's failure to apply the annual "windfall" of revenues from gasoline and diesel to support of highway and roadway construction.[17] In a report issued in 2007 as part of its Gas Tax Honesty Campaign, the CTF recommended that "the federal government transfer and dedicate five cents per litre of federal gasoline tax revenues (equivalent to 50 per cent of gas tax revenues) to municipalities for roadway development and maintenance."[18] Rather than applying the share of gas tax revenues only for municipal roads, however, the federal government had already signed agreements with the provinces and municipal governments in 2005 to transfer a share of its gas tax revenues for a much broader purpose. As the CTF complained, the revenues were "tossed into the abyss of 'green infrastructure projects.'"[19]

SHARING FEDERAL REVENUES FROM THE GASOLINE TAX

When annual surpluses started to mount in the federal treasury in the years following 1999, the mayors of Canada's largest cities began to lobby strongly for a greater share of government revenues. Their arguments for more cash were strengthened following the tabling of a report by the Prime Minister's Caucus Task Force on Urban Issues. Jean Chrétien had created the Task Force in May 2001, which his party described "as a key part of fulfilling the commitment made in Opportunity for All, the 2000 Liberal election platform…"[20] Composed only with members of the Liberal caucus (MPs and Senators), this group was given the mandate by the PM "to engage in a dialogue with citizens, experts and other orders of government on the opportunities and challenges facing our urban regions."

The rationale given to the Task Force for focusing exclusively on urban issues was unequivocal: "it is clear that strengthened partnerships will be required to sustain and enhance the quality of life in our large urban areas." As a senior bureaucrat in the Privy Council Office explained shortly after the "Task Force on Urban Communities (*sic*)"[21] was formed, money for *urban* governments – or rather a lack thereof – was recognized by the federal government as a major issue: "Regardless of size or region, cities are clearly expressing the opinions that they do not have the fiscal flexibility to meet (the) challenges (facing them)."[22]

For the big city mayors – who were expecting to see the Task Force recommend a lot of federal cash for the "large urban areas" – receiving a share of federal revenues from the gas tax was considered a good place to start. To their chagrin, the Chrétien Liberal government rejected this option. As minister of Finance, Paul Martin initially sided with his Cabinet colleagues on the issue.[23] However, he appeared to experience an epiphany a short time later – in May 2002 – when he delivered his controversial "New Deal for Cities" address at the FCM Annual Conference. Significantly, his speech outlined a policy platform that radically differed from that of the PM and the rest of the Chrétien cabinet and was the catalyst that led to him being ousted as Minister of Finance. In particular, he declared that, "Canada was in need of a New Deal for municipal governments… (and needed to) shed conventional wisdom …mov(ing) beyond the tyranny of inertia that lies behind the objection, 'But that's the way it's always worked'" (Martin, 2003). Part of the New Deal also proposed sharing the federal excise tax on gasoline with municipal governments, but Jean Chrétien and his Cabinet colleagues at the time were not prepared to "shed conventional wisdom."

While Paul Martin sat on the sidelines on the government side of the House of Commons, the PM's Task Force set out to develop an "urban strategy" for the nation. In November 2002 the Task Force tabled its final report, entitled "Canada's Urban Strategy: A Blueprint for Action" although it is more popularly known as the Sgro Report.[24] The document focused on the "three pillars of the new urban strategy for the federal government: affordable housing; transit/transportation/ and sustainable infrastructure. While the report recommended "long term sustainable funding for public transportation systems" as well as other infrastructure, there was no mention of sharing revenues from the Gas Tax.

In a speech delivered in June 2003 – shortly before the end of the Chrétien regime – the Deputy prime minister and minister of Finance curtly outlined the pervading arguments against sharing the gas tax with municipalities: "I do not favour the suggestion that the federal government vacate the fuel tax. First, it is not necessary for the federal government to do so in order for the provinces to grant fuel tax authority to municipalities. Second, it is not a solution that meets the needs of small and rural municipalities. Third, it is foregone revenue without accountability. And fourth, it undermines the vital partnership that we must foster between and among levels of government."[25] In order to get a share of the Gas Tax, the big city mayors had to bide their time until Paul Martin rejoined the front benches of the government as leader of the Liberal Party and prime minister. What they had hoped for was a continued emphasis by the government on large urban areas. They were soon disappointed.

NEW DOLLARS IN THE NEW DEAL

Once Martin was sworn in as prime minister in December 2003, he quickly launched his plan to develop the "New Deal" although the scope of his policy initiative had broadened significantly, shifting from a need to address the concerns of "cities" to now include "communities." This was a deliberate political manoeuvre aimed at addressing complaints from his caucus that the proposed focus on more federal cash for cities was too narrow. A remarkably candid federal government document entitled "Tracing the Development of the Gas Tax Fund" reveals the turmoil behind the decision to broaden the eligible recipients who would receive a share of federal gas tax revenues:

> During the GTF policy development process there was significant disagreement in the media and within the Government as to whether the GTF should have been focused on larger urban centres, or shared among all municipalities ... In discussions with senior level bureaucrats and the Minister, the Prime Minister acknowledged the need to help all Canadian communities, but suggested that a first focus (*sic*) should be the 27 Census Metropolitan Areas (CMAs). Consequently, the rural caucus fiercely protested the idea that the NDCC (New Deal for Cities and Communities) have a strictly urban agenda. The Government in turn developed a new holistic approach, described by the Prime Minister as, "no hamlet too small."[26]

Paul Martin created an External Advisory Committee on Cities and Communities chaired by former mayor of Vancouver and NDP premier of B.C., Mike Harcourt. The Committee's mandate was guided by the following principles: "The new deal for municipalities has three components: reliable, predictable, long-term funding; a new relationship among orders of government; and looking at federal activities through an urban lens. This means respecting provincial jurisdiction and bringing cities and communities to the table."[27] Further, the Committee was responsible for creating an urban policy for the federal government, "develop(ing) a long-term vision on the role that cities should play in sustaining Canada's quality of life by looking at such issues as the environment, competitiveness and social cohesion." It was hardly a coincidence that, while Chrétien had launched an *internal*, Liberal Party driven exercise (the PM's Caucus Task Force on Urban Issues) Martin launched a broader exercise led by a former big city mayor and premier.

The Martin government's "New Deal for Cities and Communities" was ostensibly intended to address the need to enhance the fiscal capacities within cities and smaller communities and to address the infrastructure deficit in a meaningful and sustained fashion. In its first budget, the Martin government committed "to share with municipalities a portion of the revenue from the federal excise tax on gasoline to help fund local environmentally sustainable infrastructure." Under the heading of "A Greener, More Sustainable Canada" the budget outlined further dimensions to the New Deal for Cities and Communities, most notably the requirement that "at least half of the new revenues to be transferred through the gas tax (would) will be dedicated to sustainable infrastructure."

Soon after the Gas Tax agreements were launched, the Martin Liberals were defeated during a general election and replaced by the Harper Conservatives in 2006. During their first budget, the Conservatives committed to retain the GTF over five years, and in the Budget 2007 extended the GTF by another four years with an additional $8 billion. The Speech from the Throne endorsed his initiative as part of a "historic investment of more than $16 billion over seven years in infrastructure – bringing federal support under a new long-term plan for infrastructure to a total of $33 billion, including the funding provided in Budget 2006."[28] In Budget 2008, the government committed to launching a "permanent" transfer of gas tax revenues to municipal governments: $2 billion annually. The Conservative government's rationale for making permanent a Liberal policy initiative was explained as follows:

The Government recognizes the need for long-term funding for infrastructure to help drive economic growth and productivity, to achieve our environmental goals, and to build strong, competitive communities ... In response to ongoing requests for stable, long-term funding, the Government announces that the Gas Tax Fund will be extended at $2 billion per year beyond 2013–14 and become a permanent measure. This will allow all municipalities, both large and small, to better plan and finance their long-term infrastructure needs.[29]

In the next section, we will explore the policy rationale underlying the GTF and the claim made in Budget 2008 that a permanent GTF "will help put in place the world-class infrastructure Canada needs." Despite the bold claims, however, it can be seen as an extension of the distributive politics that appear to have underpinned previous infrastructure programs?

SMART POLITICS: BAD POLICY

Much of the Martin Liberal government's rhetoric about the purpose of the gas tax transfer was based on the purported need to build "sustainable infrastructure" in communities. The Harper Conservatives have nuanced this by calling for "investments in infrastructure ... (that) help in the achievement of environmental goals." Unlike previous programs, however, municipalities receive their federal cash in advance – not for specific projects – but for *intended* capital spending. Rather than being reimbursed by the federal government for the costs of an approved capital project that the local government has already incurred and paid, an annual allocation of funding is provided in advance. As a document from Infrastructure Canada reveals, this approach was viewed as anathema by the Treasury Board Secretariat (TBS), the guardians of the public purse: "TBS fought hardest against the issue of flexibility in GTF agreements. They were concerned about providing funds upfront to a municipal association or a city because this created accountability and reporting issues, notably regarding federal due diligence and federal liability."[30]

The proliferation of infrastructure programs was identified as another concern by the central agencies of the federal government. While Infrastructure Canada endeavoured to get Martin's political dream of sharing the gas tax into operation, "(b)oth Finance and TBS expressed concerns over the GTF duplicating existing infrastructure programs in terms of target audience and objectives." As well, the Intergovernmental Affairs unit within the Privy Council Office also "had concerns regarding the uniqueness of the GTF from existing infrastructure programs." As Infrastructure Canada explained, "(t)hey were concerned that the involvement of municipal associations could lead to a lack of accountability, which in turn could put the federal government at risk."[31]

Another area of concern raised by PCO pertained to the proposed requirement that recipients of federal funding under the program develop a long-term plan for sustainability within the first five years of receiving gas tax funds. The Integrated Community Sustainability Plans (ICSPs) were intended to be a "long term plan, developed in consultation with community members, for the community to realize sustainability objectives it has for the environmental, cultural, social and economic dimensions of its identity (sic)."[32] PCO recognized that the federal government was dangerously traversing "jurisdictional boundaries." As Infrastructure Canada explains: "IGA [Inter Governmental Affairs]felt that ICSPs and municipal planning should be left to the provinces and territories. INFC [Infrastructure Canada]argued that an integrated approach to community planning would have the ability to reap national benefits and meet shared national objectives."[33] The argument that the federal government is somehow in a position to lead "an integrated approach to community planning" is specious. Apart from jurisdictional concerns – which PCO correctly identified from the outset – the greater concern is that bureaucrats in Ottawa would be passing judgement on the quality of community planning in cities, towns and villages across the country. As will be discussed below, such efforts by the federal government to target communities with free cash as a means of redefining its role within municipal affairs is a significant concern.

The allocation formula for the GTF betrays the program's rhetoric about the need to focus on "building environmentally sustainable infrastructure," "helping to drive economic growth and productivity" and "putting in place world-class infrastructure." By deciding to spread federal cash around the country – a policy described by Martin as "no hamlet too small" – the distributive politics underlying the GTF is revealed. As Infrastructure Canada acknowledged, "It was widely recognized that the larger city-regions had the greatest ability to affect environmental change and therefore their investments should be very focused." The failure of the federal government to concentrate program funds on those areas of the country generating the greatest revenues from gasoline taxes – cities and city-regions – signals the real focus of the GTF. As was evident in previous infrastructure programs, the need to generate a maximum number of opportunities for federal politicians to engage in retail politics trumped good public policy.

PROBLEMS OF ACCOUNTABILITY: MEDDLING OR MUDDYING?

What is the role of the federal government in funding municipal infrastructure? In a speech delivered in May 2001, Stéphane Dion – then president of the Privy Council and minister of Intergovernmental Affairs in the Chrétien Cabinet – outlined arguments for the federal government to engage in a more "collaborative role" in large urban centres. As a recognized expert on the *Constitution*, Dion was the author of the *Clarity Act* which spelled out the terms for Québec separation. Unfortunately, there was little evidence of clarity in his description of the role of the federal government in its relationship with municipal governments:

> While it is clear that the federal government has no role to play in municipal affairs, and that it is not its place to decide on the specific roles, powers or organization of municipal governments, it is equally clear that the federal government's activities in the areas of the economy, immigration, foreign affairs, employment and so on have a profound impact on our cities and towns. So an important distinction needs to be made between *municipal affairs* – which are absolutely not under federal jurisdiction – and *rural and urban issues* in a broader sense – which the federal government needs to address through its activities.[34]

Liberal and more recently Conservative governments in Ottawa have identified municipal infrastructure as well as community planning as *bona fide* issues of federal interest. However, despite efforts to nuance the federal role as a means of staying clear of constitutional turf wars, decisions about community planning as well as municipal infrastructure and how to fund it are much broader than "issues;" rather, they go to the heart of "municipal affairs" that set out the accountability of local governments to their residents and to the provincial government.

While federal politicians are quick to cite federal infrastructure programs as "the best example(s) of federal-provincial-municipal cooperation,"[35] their descriptions of the role that municipal governments play in these programs are particularly troubling: "For the Government of Canada, it was essential that *municipalities be partners* in this program, because experience has taught that it is difficult to make the right decisions on these matters without including local decision-makers."[36]

Referring to the need for a "partnership role for municipalities" and a "shared accountability" in program administration underscores the perversity of the policy driving the federal government's programming agenda. Municipal infrastructure is, after all, constructed to provide services to local residents who are required normally to pay not only the entire capital construction costs of these assets but also for their maintenance, repair and eventual replacement. Those in municipal government who make decisions in this regard are accountable to their taxpayers for these expenditures, not to Ottawa. The federal infrastructure programs, which provide "free cash" to local governments to build municipal infrastructure, have distorted this relationship.

Nowhere else is the incongruous nature of federal infrastructure policy better described than in the document entitled "Tracing the Development of the Gas Tax Fund," produced by Infrastructure Canada (INFC), the government department responsible for administering the Gas Tax Fund as well as other infrastructure programs. In describing the consultation process used with stakeholders during the development of the GTF, the document reveals that, "the Prime Minister told the big city mayors that he wanted them to limit their GTF spending to one or two of the eligible project categories."[37] Bureaucrats followed the PM's lead in this regard: "INFC placed restrictions on investments in roads and bridges. Municipalities with populations of over 500,000 *were not allowed to invest in roads and bridges* as such investments were not deemed to lead to positive environmental impacts."[38] This edict from bureaucrats did not go down well with some city governments: "The Mayor of Winnipeg pushed strongly against the restrictions on the use of funds for roads and bridges and this dispute received heavy media attention from the outset ... The Government of Canada *denied Winnipeg's demands to use the money on roads and bridges*. The solution required multiple deputy minister level meetings and heavy involvement from Minister Godfrey and his staff."[39]

The arrival of the Harper Conservatives eventually put an end to the bickering with the decision to allow Winnipeg to invest in roads with gas tax funding. Nevertheless, these examples illustrate that the federal government has increasingly assumed the role of a *dirigeant* in decisions about what infrastructure is needed for local government. This is a significant evolution in a role that began many decades ago when the federal government provided repayable loans and grants to local governments during times of crises.

OPTIONS FOR "PERMANENT TRANSFER"

We now outline our views on the impact of making the Gas Tax transfer a permanent fiscal arrangement. Given the number of concerns about the GTF from a policy perspective, are there any alternatives? Is there another approach to a permanent fiscal arrangement that transfers a share of federal revenues to municipal governments for infrastructure that does not "muddy accountability" for the expenditure of tax dollars?

It is clear that making the GTF "permanent" will not address the underlying concerns about the program. While the issue of insufficient resources for municipal governments – and in particular those needed in large cities and city regions – remains problematic; any solution that involves three levels of bureaucracy to administer a transfer of funds from one level of government to another is equally problematic.[40] The federal government acknowledged in Budget 2006 for a need to *restore fiscal balance*. Towards this aim, the Conservative government committed to transferring additional resources to assist local governments with their capital program for infrastructure. Despite the rhetoric from the Harper government that these transfers provide "stable, long-term funding," these programs do not offer the structural changes that are needed to address the shortage of revenues for Canadian municipalities and large cities in particular. As Harry Kitchen points out, "(t)he federal government's recent initiative to provide grants to municipalities from federal gas tax revenues is a form of revenue sharing and not a municipal fuel tax because the municipalities do not set fuel tax rates and have no say over the tax base."[41]

Rather than continuing to "share" its revenues from the excise tax on gasoline and transferring this annually to municipal governments – and maintaining a permanent bureaucracy to administer it – the federal government has a better option: tax point transfers. Through agreements with the provinces, the federal government could "vacate" half of the excise tax (five cents per litre) and allow specific cities and city-regions (e.g., Metro Vancouver) to impose, under new provincial legislation, an equivalent amount as a municipal fuel tax. As Kitchen notes, "earmarking" the revenues from municipal fuel taxes provides additional benefits:

> Municipally set fuel taxes may be viewed as benefit-based taxes where the revenues are earmarked for funding local roads and public transit. A municipal fuel tax could raise the cost of road usage to direct beneficiaries and lower the costs on others. Not only could the application of a municipal fuel tax raise the price paid by road users to a level that is more in line with the marginal social cost (production costs plus environmental costs) of providing roads, it would provide funds for improving and reconstructing local roads and public transit and lead to a more efficient use of local roads.[42]

Rather than creating new administrative structures, Kitchen suggests that the municipal fuel tax could be "piggy-backed" onto the provincial fuel tax. The creation of municipal fuel taxes would provide clearer accountability for the use of these revenues: locally imposed and locally collected, and incorporated within the ongoing financial resources available to local government.

SHARING MORE FEDERAL REVENUES

What are the consequences of the decision to permanently transfer federal revenues to municipalities? Does this create a precedent that would lead to more demands from municipalities for more cash from the federal government? Since the federal government has already committed to "permanently transferring" a share of revenues from the excise tax on gasoline, the mechanism used to make these resources available to municipalities is particularly important. As we have argued, the creation of a city or city region gas tax equal to that which is vacated by one-half of the federal government's excise tax – thereby creating "tax room" – is a better option that the existing GTF. A city or city-region gas tax would respect provincial jurisdiction since creating it would require provincial legislation. As well, an agreement between the federal government and the provincial government would be required, committing the federal government to providing "the tax room" while prohibiting the provincial government from "clawing-back" these revenues from municipalities.

While this approach would be a positive step towards increasing the fiscal capacity of local government, it is unlikely to prevent calls from municipalities for additional shares of government revenues. One of these sources – income tax – may be of particular interest to the cities and city-regions. Historically, income tax was a key revenue source for municipalities. The provinces and municipalities levied income taxes more than 80 years before the federal government starting accessing these revenues in 1917. After 1941, however, the revenues from income tax were withdrawn from municipalities in accordance with the Wartime Tax Rental Agreements.[43] These revenue sources were never restored to municipal governments. During the past sixty years, while municipal governments have experienced a severe drop in their share of government revenues, they have faced an extensive and growing burden with respect to their responsibilities for providing public services and building the associated capital stock that is necessary to build them.

At present, only the province of Manitoba shares a portion of its revenues from income tax with its municipalities. While this involves a revenue sharing agreement rather than a municipal income tax, the province has nevertheless taken a positive step towards broadening the source of revenues for municipal governments. Manitoba transfers a portion of the revenues from provincial-levied personal and corporate income taxes to its municipalities as unconditional per capita grants (two per cent and one per cent respectively). While Manitoba is the only jurisdiction in the country to share its revenues from income tax, the arrangement nevertheless is a "transfer" of revenues rather than a permanent sharing of tax points that would permit the municipalities to levy their own income taxes.

On the heels of providing tax room for cities and city-regions to create a municipal fuel tax, pressure may begin to mount on the federal government to expand its share of income tax revenues as well. Given the significance of city and city-regions both in terms of population and political clout during federal and provincial elections, we are likely to see increasing demands for a greater share of these government revenues and the federal and provincial governments would do well to consider these calls. While we are not able to pursue this idea in detail within this chapter, providing tax room to allow city and city-regions to create a municipal income tax – piggy-backed on existing tax collection administration – would have the potential to put Canada's larger cities on a more equal footing with the large urban centres around the world, including the US. However, as Slack, Bourne and Gertler point out, restoring municipal income tax does not require a pan-Canadian, universal approach: "It is not appropriate to give more taxing authority to all municipal jurisdictions in the province. Large cities and city-regions are best suited to take advantage of new taxing authority; smaller cities are unlikely to be able to raise sufficient revenues from some of these sources to make the effort worthwhile."[44]

Taking these steps would finally address the structural weakness in the fiscal framework for the nation by correcting the fiscal imbalance facing municipal governments and allowing them to better plan for growth, price their services and generate needed revenues. As Silver observed, such an approach would be consistent with the principles of accountability and subsidiarity, allowing municipal governments to raise revenues "derived from the people who live and work in the municipality and who, presumably, have the primary responsibility for the financing of municipal services, (and) bear the political burden of having to do so."[45]

NOTES

1 By free cash we refer to the money municipalities receive from the federal government, as opposed to local taxation, and for which there is no requirement to demonstrate specific needs.
2 Massimo Bergamini, Director of Policy, FCM, letter to the editor, *Ottawa Citizen*, 11 March 2007.
3 A survey carried out by McGill University on behalf of the Federation of Canadian Municipalities and reported in November 2007 concluded that the current municipal infrastructure deficit was $125 billion.
4 Cited in Caroline Andrew and Jeff Morrison, "Canada Infrastructure Works: Between 'Picks and Shovels' and the Information Highway," in *How Ottawa Spends 1995–96: Mid-Life Crises*, Susan D. Phillips, ed., (Ottawa: Carleton University Press, 1995), 109.
5 Jeanne M. Wolfe, "A national urban policy for Canada? Prospects and Challenges," *Canadian Journal of Urban Research* 12, no. 1 (Summer 2003), 1–21.
6 Robert N. Hilton, "Building Political Capital: The Politics of 'Need' in the Federal Government's Municipal Infrastructure Programs, 1993–2006," Carleton University, 25 April 2007.
7 Liberal Party of Canada, 1993, "Creating Opportunity" The Liberal Plan for Canada" (Red Book 1), 6.
8 Hilton, 91.
9 Objectives of the municipal infrastructure programs are outlined in Hilton, table 6, 124.

10 The government of Québec remained adamant is this regard, arguing that the provinces were solely responsible for the *maitre d'ouevre* in administering program funds. While Québec was quite willing to accept federal cash for municipal infrastructure projects, provincial legislation prohibited municipal governments from dealing directly with Ottawa.
11 Infrastructure Canada, Cities and Communities Branch, "Tracing the Development of the Gas Tax Fund," Revised Final Version, 17 January 2007. The poll was conducted by Infrastructure Canada together with "several other federal departments to perform a survey on the quality of life in Canadian cities."
12 Agreements spelling out the conditions of federal funding included the need to establish "Management Committees" and "Oversight Committees" that included representatives of the federal government. In Québec, as can be expected, the federal role was limited in accordance with the province's demand that it be solely responsible for the *maitre d'oeuvre* of infrastructure projects.
13 Funding was provided to *any* municipality that currently operated public transit regardless of size or effectiveness, and was allocated proportionally, based on their public transit ridership as reported by the Canadian Urban Transit Association.
14 The government clarified that the tax applied to "gasoline used in private automobiles, in pleasure boats, motorcycles, snowmobiles, and so on." It did not apply to diesel fuel or aviation fuel, heating fuels or other similar products used to produce heat or light (Budget Highlights and Supplementary Information, 35).
15 The metrification of gasoline and diesel fuel in 1981 assisted the federal government in increasing its revenues accordingly.
16 Transport Canada, "Government spending on Transportation," *Transportation in Canada*, 2006.
17 According to the CTF, during the 2006–07 fiscal year, Ottawa collected $5.2 billion in gasoline and diesel taxes (excluding GST revenues).
18 Canadian Taxpayers Association, "Roadway Spending Up, But Ottawa Still Gouging Families," May 2007, 2.
19 Ibid., 6.
20 Liberal Party of Canada Press Release, 9 May 2001.
21 The policy thinking which helped to shape the Task Force is outlined in a document from the Institute on Governance, CityScapes: "Federal Perspectives on Urban Communities," Notes on a seminar presentation by Claire Morris, deputy minister, Intergovernmental Affairs, Privy Council Office, 18 September 2002.
22 Ibid.
23 A. Mohammed, "Martin says no to mayors on gas tax: Collenette, finance minister disagree over plan," in the *Ottawa Citizen*, A-1, 19 February 2002.
24 The report was named after the chair of the Task Force, MP Judy Sgro.
25 John Manley in a speech delivered to the Federation of Canadian Municipalities, 1 June 2003.
26 Infrastructure Canada, "Tracing the Development of the Gas Tax Fund," 1.
27 PMO News Release, 14 February 2003.

28 Department of Finance, *Budget Plan: Budget 2007* (Ottawa: Department of Finance Canada, 2007), chapter 5.
29 Department of Finance, *Budget Plan: Budget 2008* (Ottawa: Department of Finance Canada, 2008, chapter 3.
30 Infrastructure Canada, "Tracing the Development of the Gas Tax Fund," 16.
31 Ibid., 11.
32 Ibid., 9.
33 Ibid., 16–17
34 Stéphane Dion, address to the Annual General Meeting of the Federation of Canadian Municipalities, Banff Alberta, 26 May 2001 (original emphasis).
35 Ibid.
36 Ibid., emphasis added.
37 Infrastructure Canada, "Tracing the Development of the Gas Tax Fund," 14.
38 Ibid., 14
39 Ibid., 24, emphasis added.
40 The extent of the overhead involved in federal transfers was evident in the number of departments and agencies involved in the administration of infrastructure programs. In Infrastructure Canada alone, the bureaucracy included more than 240 employees managed by a top heavy executive (deputy minister and five assistant deputy ministers).
41 Harry Kitchen, "A State of Disrepair: How to Fix the Financing of Municipal Infrastructure in Canada," *CD Howe Commentary* No. 241, 8–9.
42 Ibid.
43 The federal government "rented out" the revenues collected from personal and corporate income taxes as a means of supplementing revenues to pay for the war effort.
44 Enid Slack, Larry S. Bourne, and Meric S. Gertler. "Vibrant Cities and City-Regions: Responding to Emerging Challenges." Paper prepared for the Panel on the Role of Government, 13 August 2003.
45 Sheldon Silver, "The Feasibility of a Municipal Income Tax in Canada," *Canadian Tax Journal* 16, no. 5 (September-October, 1968).

8 How Ottawa Spends and How Canadians Save: "Asset-Based" Approaches in Uncertain Times

JENNIFER ROBSON, RICHARD SHILLINGTON, AND PETER NARES

INTRODUCTION

The recent collapse of the US housing and financial markets reminds us of the precariousness of household finances and the broader economic consequences when things go awry. The housing collapse is now going beyond subprime and into the mainstream housing market with more than two million US homeowners entering the foreclosure process in 2008, an average of more than 6,000 per day and so many that the Obama administration has had to force a moratorium on foreclosures as part of its economic stimulus plan.[1] For many of these homeowners, even a good income is not enough to hang on to their largest asset when they've been so over-leveraged. The problem was not just the debt-to-income ratio in these households, but also the debt-to-asset ratio. Across the US, but particularly in Florida and California, enticed by questionable financial products, homeowners entered into housing arrangements where they actually owned very little of their own house. Housing remains one of the most powerful individual and family assets but when financing is done badly or with duplicity, the consequences are stark. Financial markets that had invested in mortgage-backed securities are now in a crisis of historic proportions and the bailout and stimulus packages are expected to cost US taxpayers more than a trillion dollars. If the Reganomics model of "trickle-down" wealth creation has been largely discredited, perhaps its inverse a "trickle-up" model of financial insecurity may hold some weight.

The spill-over effects of the US crisis are being felt as consumer spending slows, commodity prices fall and the shockwaves ripple through global financial markets. As far away as New Zealand, household net worth is estimated to have fallen by an average of (NZ)$6,000 in the first quarter of 2008 alone, due in large measure to the turmoil in US financial markets.[2] Here in Canada, while national net worth rose in first half of 2008 to $111B or $174,300 per capita,[3] housing prices have fallen across the country and unemployment has risen. The slump in housing and significant volatility in financial markets now means that household net worth is almost certainly lower than before. Personal bankruptcies had grown by 50 per cent by the end of 2008, an increase attributed to job losses and increasingly strict lending conditions.[4] According to the Bank of Canada, it also means that while Canadians are not as leveraged as their US neighbors, they are more leveraged than they have been in the last 18 years.[5] Households in Canada now have roughly 19.6 cents of debt for every dollar of net worth and more than $1.30 of debt for every dollar of personal disposable income. A report from Merrill Lynch Canada[6] suggests that Canadians are not entirely immune to the same hollow largess that is now leading to economic and financial implosion south of our border. They note that Canadian households are also balancing precariously on a precipice of housing equity and consumer debt.

In Canada, as in the US, this precarious balance has been encouraged both indirectly and directly by public policy, particularly at the national level in shaping incentives for households. As the table below makes clear, Canadians are actually more dependent on housing as a source of wealth than are Americans, proportionally speaking. So too, debt plays a slightly higher role in household portfolios in Canada than in the US, particularly when (as was the foundation of so much borrowing in the US) it is secured against assumed housing equity.

Canada doesn't share the US "ownership" ethos with quite the same fervour. Neither does our public policy yet reflect such a strong bias towards ownership over capital. According to the Corporation for Enterprise Development, the U.S. federal government spends more than $335 billion in direct and tax expenditures to reward private savings and ownership.[7] In 2004, that was nearly the same as the US national defence budget. What Canada does share with the US is a pattern of federal spending to encourage savings and ownership that arise out of multiple programs with little or no policy coherence or coordination and almost no public scrutiny.

Public support for private capital accumulation is nothing new to Canada. From our earliest days as a country, Canada's colonial and later national government used public policy instruments to encourage individual and family asset-holding. In the 18th and 19th centuries, land, the main source of wealth, was distributed to millions of immigrants, helping to settle and shape the Canada we know today. During, but especially following World War II, the Veterans' Charter had an enormous impact in promoting homeownership and access to education to the thousands of men and women who had fought in the war. Registered Retirement Savings Plans were introduced in 1957 and

Table 1
Household Portfolio Composition (percentage share of total assets), Canada and the US

	Canada	US
NON-FINANCIAL ASSETS	78	62
Principal residence	64	45
Real estates	13	17
FINANCIAL ASSETS	22	38
Deposit accounts	9	10
Bonds	1	4
Stocks	7	15
Mutual funds	5	9
TOTAL ASSETS	100	100
DEBT	26	21
of which: home secured	22	18
NET WORTH	74	79

Source: Eva Sierminska, Andrea Brandolini and Timothy M. Smeeding, "Comparing Wealth Distribution Across Rich Countries: First Results from the Luxembourg Wealth Study", Luxembourg Wealth Study, Working Paper no 1. August 2006. Available on-line at: http://www.lisproject.org/publications/lwswps/lws1.pdf; accessed 2 September 2008.

Registered Education Savings Plans in 1974, followed by a variety of housing initiatives in the 1970's that all encouraged individual savings among Canadians through tax-benefited instruments. Today's array of asset-based instruments still includes these registered vehicles as well as targeted grants, but particularly tax expenditures that should be examined quite differently from other social spending.

In Canada we have been blessed with certain public goods and services that directly transfer human, physical, and financial capital to citizens. We enjoy, for example a universal and public system of healthcare as well as primary through secondary education. Canada also has in place a quasi-universal system of seniors' benefits that guarantees a minimum income to all seniors who meet the residence test to receive their entitlements and includes a public pension plan that acts in many respects as a mandatory retirement savings plan for Canadian workers. These and other public goods and services have helped to ensure a basic level of well-being for Canadians and have generated economic and social returns for the country as a whole. These collective forms of capital also provide a critical platform from which individual ownership of productive assets becomes, at least in theory, more readily accessible to Canadians. Having said this, however, they cannot, on their own, guarantee that all Canadians have equal and fair access to the various forms of capital that are so critical to well-being over the life course.

The purpose of this chapter is to begin to shed some light on the nature and level of Ottawa's spending that directly (such as the Canada Education Savings Grant), or more often indirectly (through tax expenditures on capital gains or registered accounts) supports the accumulation of individual or household financial and tangible assets. It begins with a brief overview of current federal direct and indirect (in the form of forgone taxes) federal spending that subsidizes the costs of individual or household ownership over capital. A summary description of these various measures is included as Appendix 1 at the end of this chapter. The chapter then attempts to provide some quantitative measure of this spending in recent years and to initiate a discussion on the potential impacts of these public expenditures in the context of current trends in income and wealth distribution. Finally, we consider possible future policy directions, whether the stripe of the governing party will matter much in this regard and potential areas for future research and discussion.

METHODOLOGY

The present chapter builds on a 2004 review of federal expenditures and compares the results with figures for 2007 expenditures and 2008/2009 projections. We include spending from all federal departments and agencies, including crown corporations (namely Canada Mortgage and Housing Corporation), and include direct as well as indirect expenditures as reported in public federal sources including the 2008 Budget, the Department of Finance annual tax expenditure report, departmental reports on performance and expenditure estimates.

The past year proved to be an exceptional year for federal spending. A spring 2008 budget was followed by a fall election replete with campaign promises, followed by a fall economic update, followed by a political crisis and the January 2009 budget. While the 2009 budget was released very late into the preparation of this chapter, it is discussed towards the end of the chapter as part of the forwarding-looking discussion.

Broadly speaking, it might be helpful to group productive assets into the following categories:

- Human capital (such as education and employment skills or even healthcare);
- Physical capital (including housing, transportation, business or other goods);
- Social capital (social networks and connectedness); and
- Financial capital (including retirement or other savings).

For the purpose of this study, we are primarily interested in measures that may affect personal net worth through financial or tangible assets such as investments and housing equity. Other forms of capital, particularly social capital and human capital, are simply too difficult to quantify or to relate directly to public spending. For example, governments at both the federal and provincial levels collectively invest billions in post-secondary education. However, the rates of return to individual students, in the form of life-time earnings, show a very wide variation,[8] likely far too wide to enable any discussion of the impacts of transfers to provinces and institutions on individual net worth. Investments, whether direct or indirect, in social and human capital or in public assets (such as universal health care) are extremely important in determining well-being and in shaping the equity of outcomes in Canada. However, for methodological reasons, they are simply outside the scope of the present study. We do however include those measures that may aim to support certain forms of capital (for example Canada Study Grants intended to support human capital development) where the instrument offers a benefit that is fungible, in other words where the cash value can be used or moved around by qualifying recipients largely as they see fit.

We also exclude income support instruments (such as the Canada Child Tax Benefit or non-taxation of provincial social assistance benefits) and income insurance programs (such as Employment Insurance) from the notional total as the focus is on savings and assets. Information on a selected number of these (those available to working age adults outside contributory premiums like EI or CPP) is presented for the purpose of comparing federal expenditures in the stocks or pools of household financial resources with investment in flows. Finally we, develop notional totals for overall expenditure and by the form of asset or capital (housing, registered, unregistered, etc).

It is also important to emphasize that the numbers presented are a notional total only because tax and program expenditures interact with each other so are not cumulative. The tax expenditure estimates are obtained by estimating the revenue impact of eliminating each tax preference in isolation; that is, while keeping all other aspects of the tax system fixed. This is because the elimination on one tax expenditure will affect the marginal tax rates of Canadians and consequently the cost of the remaining tax expenditures. Estimating the combined cost of two or more tax expenditures would require a completely new analysis. For example, if RRSPs were eliminated then marginal tax rates would increase and then the tax impact of eliminating a second tax preference, say the exemption from capital gains for principal residences, would be higher. This is because the taxes that would be paid on the capital gain are determined by the marginal tax rate, which would itself be higher if RRSPs were also eliminated. A reduction in the marginal tax rate can only be contemplated with an assumption of behavioral change either on the part of individual tax payers (who might adjust their behavior in accordance to new budget constraints or changed preferences when taxes are changed) or on the part of governments (which might adjust other forms of taxation to maintain revenues at constant or comparable levels). However, federal income tax expenditure calculations assume no behavioral effects. Usually the cost of the combined effect will be greater than that sum of effects because some will increase marginal tax rates.

Where possible, all figures have been collected for fiscal years 2004–05 (actual expenditures), 2007–08 (actual expenditures) and 2008–09 (projected expenditures). However certain agencies, such as Canada Mortgage and Housing Corporation, report on calendar years but the difference in real expenditure is expected to be negligible.

Finally, to develop some benchmark of the degree of progressiveness in the expenditure (in addition to whatever level of progressiveness the use of the income tax system may or may not provide) we also identify those initiatives that are income-tested and provide either higher levels of benefits to household with lower incomes (and presumably less fiscal capacity to save) or benefits targeted only to lower income households. However for at least one program, the Canada Education Savings Grant, we are only able to estimate the actual proportion (using the same ratio as the 2004–05 projections) that is income-tested from the universal basic amount as the reporting system in implementation does not differentiate these two cost streams for the managing department, Human Resources and Skills Development Canada.[9]

KEY TYPES OF POLICY INSTRUMENTS

In addition to differentiating between social, human, financial and tangible types of assets, it may be helpful to briefly discuss different types of policy instruments that are currently used by the federal government to subsidize individual or household asset accumulation. Each of these instruments comes with its own set of constraints and advantages for policy making. When we later discuss the distribution of the benefits of current federal spending, it becomes clear that the interaction between these instrument types and the types of assets selected by policymakers for public subsidy creates in a sense a double whammy for low and modest income Canadians.

Tax deductions and non-refundable credits

One broad category of policy instrument comes in the form of tax deductions and non-refundable credits. Deductions reduce the income on which tax is calculated and as such offer the greatest benefit to those taxpayers with larger taxable incomes. Non-refundable credits reduce the income tax already owed, giving a credit based on the lowest possible taxation rate but where a reduction in taxes owed can't lead to a tax refund. These offer more benefit to those with the largest tax liabilities.

Refundable tax credits and cash transfers

A second broad category of policy instrument is in the form of refundable credits and cash transfers. Refundable credits, for example the Goods and Services Tax Credit, are paid to households or individuals with eligible (ie:

very low) taxable incomes and are usually paid out to recipients over the course of the following fiscal year. Cash transfers to individuals may include measures such as grants (paid for example to eligible postsecondary students in the form of Canada Study Grants), as non-repayable loans (paid for example as forgivable assistance to elderly homeowners under the Residential Rehabilitation Program), or as transfers payable as a match to an individual deposit (paid for example on eligible deposits to a Registered Education Savings Plan through the matching Canada Education Savings Grant).

Tax exemptions

A third broad category of policy instrument is in the form of forgone taxes. In this case, the government has chosen to set aside its own far-reaching definition of income and has labeled certain forms of real or imputed income as being exempt from taxation. The critical idea here is that, under the strict definitions of the federal *Income Tax Act*, these resources could be taxed. Perhaps the best-known example is the exemption for capital gains on the sale of primary residence. While the sale of most assets, such as a business, leads to a tax liability, any gains are not taxed when the sale involves a primary home. In the case of this and other forgone taxation, the benefit only goes to those who already hold the favored form of capital. The benefits of foregone taxes on capital gains on a primary residence, for example, aren't available to those who don't already own their home.

RESULTS: FEDERAL EXPENDITURES

Canada's income tax system is based on the principle that a tax can be applied to income earned on all sources, including employment, business and property and that a tax is also applicable to a capital gain. When government policy precludes or delays the application of a tax on particular types or amounts of income, or on certain capital gains, these exceptions create tax expenditures. Each year, the Department of Finance publishes data on federal tax expenditures, calculating the amount the government could have raised in tax revenues save for tax credits, exemptions or deductions.

THE LARGEST EXPENDITURES: SUBSIDIZING HOUSING AND PENSIONS THROUGH TAX EXEMPTIONS AND DEDUCTIONS

In the economic sphere, there are three major tax expenditures for savings that cut across both the types of assets and the types of policy instruments outlined earlier in this chapter.

- Capital gains for a principal residence are generally not taxable contrary to other capital gains.
- Contributions to employer sponsored pension plans are tax deductible, and the returns on capital inside a pension plan are not taxed until withdrawn.
- In a similar fashion, funds in Registered Retirement Savings Plans (RRSPs) receive the same preferential treatment as pension plans (tax deferral until retirement). For RRSPs there is an additional positive feature in that RRSP spousal plans can be used to aid in income-splitting between spouses. Higher income spouses can contribute to a lower-income spouse's RRSP to even their respective incomes at retirement. New pension splitting provisions similarly allow spouses to duplicate this benefit when drawing down RRSP funds during retirement.

Perhaps the best known (and certainly the largest) of these is the foregone federal tax on individual Registered Retirement Savings Plans (RRSPs) and employer-sponsored Registered Retirement Plans (RPPs). Eventually the funds in the plans are subject to tax, the original contribution and the return on investment (the accumulated interest and/or dividend income and growth in capital). Therefore, the impact of these preferences on tax revenue changes over time; early on there is a loss in tax revenue but later on the funds are taxed and so later on the tax on withdrawals may equal or exceed the tax lost on contributions and tax deferred on the current investment return.

The impact of the federal treasury can change over time. The advantage to the individual from RRSPs and pensions though is clear. As is well known to the financial industry, far greater returns are possible when funds are sheltered and the taxes deferred even after considering that they are subject to tax at retirement. For savers who expect to see their incomes decline in retirement and will not rely on income-tested support in retirement (such as the Guaranteed Income Supplement or Old Age Security), the tax sheltering increases the rate of return on savings and investments considerably.[10] However, because withdrawals from pension and RRSPs are treated as income, working-age Canadians with low and modest incomes who will eventually need income-tested support in retirement are likely to find that claw-backs of benefits and tax rates offset totally any tax advantages for RRSPs and pensions, or worse still, they may find that the clawbacks result in a net loss for having saved and contributed to a tax-benefited retirement plan.

One other tax preference relates to capital gains on the principal residence. When the value of a principal residence increases and is sold there is no capital gains tax (the exemption does not apply to vacation or other second properties). This tax expenditure is currently valued at about $8 billion. This implies that some portion of the equity that Canadians have in their home is accumulated because of this preferential tax treatment. Economists also identify another tax expenditure which also benefits home-owners which is not quantified here; this is the non-taxation of what economists refer to as 'imputed rent'. Imputed rent refers to the 'consumption' of owner occupied homes. Essentially there is an inequity in that rent is paid out of after-tax income whereas home-owners occupy, utilize or consume their capital, the home equity, tax-free. To illustrate, if two individuals take $200,000 and one buys a home while the other invests the funds and rents an identical home out of the investment income, the renter will be forced to pay income taxes on investment income, which provides their accommodation. The home-owner pays no income tax on these funds.

In addition to tax expenditures, the Government of Canada also directly transfers financial assistance for certain assets through a handful of programs, often but not exclusively linked to a tax-benefited instrument. These are grants, forgivable loans or matched contributions to personal savings. For example, the Canada Learning Bond and Canada Education Savings Grant (see also Appendix 1 for a description on these and other programs referenced in this chapter) are direct transfers to individuals to support savings for post-secondary education but are only payable into tax-benefited Registered Education Savings Plans. The newly announced Registered Disability Savings Plans will similarly have associated direct transfers available to participating families. In addition to the tax expenditures in support of homeownership, the Government of Canada also provides direct transfers to individual owners through the mortgage insurance program at Canada Mortgage and Housing Corporation and a portion of the Residential Rehabilitation Assistance Program (RRAP). RRAP is generally offered as a program repayable assistance for owners of residential housing (either rental or owner-occupied) to enable them to upgrade or adapt the housing for health, safety or accessibility. Table 2 includes only the repayable portion available for owner-occupied housing.

Using the notional totals, table 2 organizes the expenditures by the kinds of capital that federal expenditures are favoring rather than by whether they are tax or direct expenditures. This is because a more nuanced understanding is only possible by looking both across and within the two main forms of subsidies to individual wealth creation. The vast majority (more than 80 per cent) of the notional total is related to foregone taxes. This heavy reliance on the income tax system for delivery of asset-based instruments very much determines the distribution of benefits across low, middle and upper income households. When the tax benefits are directly related to the amount of money saved, for example deductions for RRSPs, those households with more financial flexibility will benefit more. Direct transfers are not immune to this design feature however governments (both Liberal and Conservative) have tended to make these income-tested and somewhat progressive. The income tax system does, as a whole, provide some progressive income redistribution

Table 2
Federal Tax and Direct Spending on Individual Assets

Category and Measure	2004/05			2007/2008			2008/2009			Income-tested?
	Annual Expenditure ($000s)	Notional Totals ($000s)	% of Notional Total	Annual Expenditure ($000s)	Notional Totals ($000s)	% of Notional Total	Annual Expenditure ($000s)	Notional Totals ($000s)	% of Notional Total	
Education savings		796,000	2.73		881,100	1.93		985,000	2.10	
Net forgone tax on RESPs	135,000			180,000			225,000			No
CESG	401,000			436,320			475,104			No
Enhanced CESG	95,000			103,680			112,896			Yes
CLB	85,000			25,000			34,000			Yes
Canada Study Grants	80,000			136,100			138,000			Yes
Housing and homeownership		5,880,000	20.18		9,455,000	20.71		9,600,000	20.50	
Foregone capital gains taxes on principal residences	4,770,000			8,400,000			8,570,000			No
GST rebate on eligible new housing purchases	1,015,000			960,000			935,000			No
Homeowner RRAP (forgiveness assistance)	44,000			49,093			49,093*			Yes
Net mortgage insurance claims	51,000			51,000*			51,000*			No
Private retirement savings		19,260,000	66.09		28,185,000	61.74		28,850,000	61.62	

Table 2
Federal Tax and Direct Spending on Individual Assets (Continued)

Category and Measure	2004/05			2007/2008			2008/2009			Income-tested?
	Annual Expenditure ($000s)	Notional Totals ($000s)	% of Notional Total	Annual Expenditure ($000s)	Notional Totals ($000s)	% of Notional Total	Annual Expenditure ($000s)	Notional Totals ($000s)	% of Notional Total	
Net deductions and foregone taxes on RRSPs	7,720,000			11,235,000			11,595,000			No
Net deductions and foregone taxes on RRPs	11,540,000			16,950,000			17,255,000			No
Private savings and investment		2,620,000	8.99		6,214,000	13.61		6,344,000	13.55	
Tax-Free Savings Accounts	NA			NA			5,000			No
Investment tax credits	35,000			57,000			58,000			No
Deductions on employee stock options	350,000			1,070,000			1,090,000			No
Foregone capital gains taxes on gifts of cultural property	7,000			5,000			5,000			No
Five year deferral of capital gains	33,000			22,000			21,000			No
Foregone taxes on partial inclusion of capital gains	2,195,000			5,060,000			5,165,000			No
Self-employment and small enterprise		585,000	2.01		890,000	1.95		925,000	1.98	

$500,000 lifetime capital gains exemption for farm property	255,000		375,000		390,000	No
$500,000 lifetime capital gains exemption for small business shares	320,000		490,000		510,000	No
Deduction for tradespersons' tools	NA		15,000		15,000	
Apprentice mechanics' tools deduction	10,000		10,000		10,000	
Disability			25,300	0.05	115,000	0.25
Registered Disability Savings Plans and related grants and bonds	NA		25,000		115,000	
Notional total	29,141,000	29,141,000	100.00	45,650,100	45,650,100	46,819,000	46,819,000
Percentage income tested		304,000	1.04		308,780	0.68	328,896	0.70

* Data not available for the year in question. Figures presented are conservatively held constant to the most recent annual expenditure reported.

Figure 1
Sources of Household Wealth in Canada, 1999 and 2005

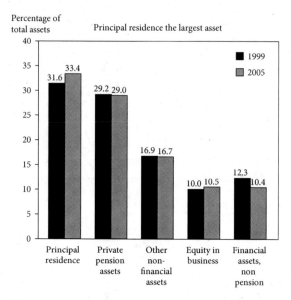

Figure reproduced from Statistics Canada, "Survey of Financial Security," *The Daily*, Thursday, 7 December 2006.

but on savings, continuing to rely on deductions and non-refundable tax credits (which make up the bulk of the net tax expenditures in table 2) mean that taxpayers with low or modest incomes who have little or no tax liability draw proportionally less (and sometimes no) real benefit from the same instruments as middle and upper income earners.

Federal policy can also shape what forms of capital are accumulated. For the last several decades, the largest sources of household wealth in Canada have been housing equity and retirement savings.

Looking at the notional totals, more than 80 per cent of the federal expenditures are directed towards encouraging the two main forms of wealth accumulation in Canada – housing and retirement savings. Within these, the largest single expenditure is for employer-sponsored pension plans which cover a declining number of working-age Canadians.[11] The net cost of RRSPs comes in at a close second. RRSPs are increasingly used as multi-purpose accounts, sometimes encouraged by tax-sheltered withdrawals for housing purchase or adult education, other times used by working-age Canadians to make ends meet when other resources run short. In other words, the policy to spend so much to encourage Canadians to save for their own retirement may in practice be subsidizing all kinds of other capital acquisitions or household transactions. Regardless lower and modest income households who use RRSPs

Figure 2
Distribution of Home Equity and Retirement Savings by Income, Canada

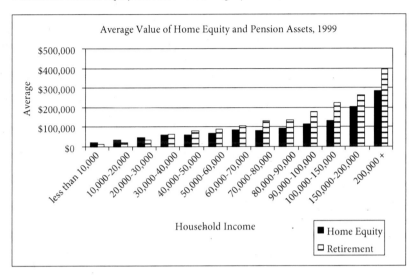

Source: Statistics Canada (1999) Survey of Financial Security.

in working age – whether to save for retirement, to purchase a house or for any other reason – are drawing little if any net benefit over their total life course. This is because when the claw-backs to other sources of retirement income are considered, then the tax deductions and deferrals of RRSPs are outweighed by the longer-term costs of lower public transfers in retirement.

In considering the distribution of the federal tax expenditures, it's important to consider not just the annual expenditure flows but also the value of the tax benefits to the accumulated wealth that accrue over time. When the tax-favored forms of assets are examined in light of a) the income distribution of those Canadians who hold those assets and b) attention to the form of tax measures that grow with tax liability, it becomes clear that a disproportionate share of the real benefit of the tax expenditure on homeownership and retirement savings is flowing to higher income and higher wealth Canadians.

As illustrated in figure 2, average home equity and retirement assets grow with household income. In the context of tax subsidies to savings, this also strongly suggests that the tax advantages associated with home ownership and retirement savings go disproportionately to those with higher incomes. On this basis, we estimate that the top 10 per cent wealthiest households received nearly 30 per cent of all the financial benefit of federal tax expenditures in support of housing and retirement wealth in 2004–05. It is to some degree a chicken and egg problem – which came first, Canada's pattern of wealth inequality or the inequitable distribution of public expenditures to foster private wealth accumulation? Steve Kerstetter has opined that public expenditures, and more specifically tax expenditures, in favor of private wealth accumulation, have directly contributed towards the concentration of household wealth in this country.[12]

Already the wealthiest 20 per cent of Canadians now own nearly 70 per cent of all net worth in Canada and have an average net worth nearly 4 times that of even the next richest 20 per cent of Canadians.[13] Lars Osberg has also recently examined the concentration of income and wealth in Canada over the last quarter century.[14] He suggests that incomes, on an after tax basis rose by more than $10,000 for the richest ten per cent of Canadians between 1981 and 2006 while the incomes of the lowest ten per cent barely grew at all during the same time. The picture on wealth is even more stark. Between 1984 and 2005, the wealthiest ten per cent of Canadians nearly doubled their net worth, while the poorest ten per cent saw little if any gain and remained in net debt. As the incomes and assets of the wealthiest Canadians grow, so too will their share of public expenditures on tax deductions, exemptions and non-refundable tax credits that favor the forms of savings and asset accumulation they are already best able to engage in.

Another way to consider the problem of wealth distribution is to consider the position of Canadian households at the very lowest end of the spectrum. For example, René Morissette[15] has proposed a measure of "financial vulnerability" defined as being both in low-income and having insufficient financial assets to liquidate and raise the total income above the Low Income Cut-Off. Using this measure, about one in ten Canadians are financially vulnerable. Another possible measure could be the widely-used financial adage that we should all have at least three months current living expenses in liquid financial assets. Kerstetter found that the poorest 20 per cent of Canadians have less than half that and could only replace five weeks of lost income out of their savings.

OTHER POLICY OPTIONS: FAVORING SMALLER SAVERS, OTHER FORMS OF WEALTH AND USING MORE PROGRESSIVE INSTRUMENTS

If public policy wants to have an impact on the financial security of these families, then new instruments will be needed that are better suited to Canadians with little tax liability and perhaps different preferences in saving and asset accumulation. The federal government continues to introduce new tax measures to favour saving but do these even begin to redistribute the overall expenditures towards poorer households? Our estimates suggest that the share of federal dollars going to small savers (through income-testing) has actually declined in recent years and is now less than 1 per cent of the notional total. That fact is less than encouraging but also should be evaluated in light of at least three recent policy developments.

CHANGES TO RESPS, THE CANADA EDUCATION SAVINGS GRANT, INTRODUCTION OF THE CANADA LEARNING BOND
Perhaps one of the first developments in the current era of asset-based policy development came with a package of changes to post-secondary education (PSE) savings in 2004/5 and again in 2006/7. RESPs, as noted earlier, have been around for decades. In the mid 1990's, as part of series of changes to PSE funding, the Canada Education Savings Grant (CESG) was introduced as a 20 per cent annual capped grant to reward Canadian families who used the registered instruments to save for the children's future higher education costs. While successful in increasing RESP participation and savings, evaluations of the program soon revealed that the overwhelming majority of families were in the upper middle and upper income quintiles.[16] The Canada Learning Bond (CLB), advocated by Social and Enterprise Development Innovations (SEDI) among others, was viewed as at least a partial solution in providing a benefit targeted to lower and modest income families regardless of whether they contributed funds of their own to an RESP. Concurrent with the CLB, changes were made to the CESG to provide higher (but still capped) proportional grants to families with lower and middle income who made even small contributions to an RESP. While these initiatives of the then Liberal government enjoyed the support of the Conservative opposition, more recent directions from the Conservative government have been primarily aimed at larger savers by increasing the annual ceiling on RESP contributions eligible for tax-exemptions and government matching grants. In other words, the more an RESP holder can save, the better off they are.

Uptake on the CLB continues to be low at just over ten per cent of eligible households.[17] Critics of asset-based approaches for lower income families have cited this as evidence that these policy instruments simply don't work for families with little or no income left-over for saving after bills are paid and basic needs are met. However this criticism overlooks at least two fundamental issues. The first is that few if any households save by using "extra" income when other bills are paid. Instead, most of us tend to rely on payroll deductions for a pension plan and the forced savings imposed by mortgage payments. Traditional economic understandings of household saving tend to dominate policy discourse and development when in fact behavioural economics may have more useful information and ideas on why people do what they do with the resources they have and where policy can have an influence. The second fundamental issue is that in fact the Canada Learning Bond does not require any savings deposits by low income families at all. It is a straight grant conditional only on the opening of a recognized RESP product. The problem instead, based on anecdotal but compelling reports from financial institutions and voluntary sector organizations involved in its implementation, is more likely related to issues of financial inclusion and the use of the RESP instrument which may be deterring lower income parents. Making large financial decisions, even to receive "free" money is never high on the day to day agenda for most of us but lower and modest income families, the very targets of the Canada Learning Bond, may also face barriers to participating in the financial mainstream (such as ID requirements, credit ratings and minimum deposits). RESPs are necessarily part of the financial mainstream so unless a family is willing and able to navigate the sometimes murky waters of choosing an RESP provider and product, they won't see a dime of the Canada Learning Bond. If the flexibility and portability of RESP products were improved, if the administrative and application process for families and investing were simplified and if more and better measures to provide impartial information and personalized assistance to families who are eligible for the bonds, uptake might improve. It remains to be seen whether any RESP providers or political parties, particularly those who first embraced the idea of a progressive asset-based instrument, will take the actions necessary to ensure it succeeds. Even the best policies implemented in the least enabling environments are unlikely to prove successful. It also remains to be seen whether the modest costs of the Canada Learning Bond might yield some significant returns in the educational performance and persistence of children born to lower income families in Canada. The data on that question are at least some 20 years out.

REGISTERED DISABILITY SAVINGS PLAN,
AND ASSOCIATED GRANT AND BOND

Another new measure is the Registered Disability Savings Plan or RDSP. Introduced in the 2007 Conservative budget, it was developed after a lengthy consultative process of policy design outsourced from the Department of Finance to an external panel on the tax treatment of disability savings. The design has been heavily influenced by the RESP model by treating deposits as tax pre-paid and attaching a matching savings grant and income-tested bond to encourage savings. Given the important increases in the life expectancy of children with disabilities, the RDSP is intended to provide a better option for parents and caregivers to plan ahead for a time when their child outlives them but still needs significant support. It's not a simple product given the complex rules around withdrawals, interactions with provincial disability benefits, private disability insurance and the complexities (like any savings plan) of choosing investment vehicles and managers. It's also somewhat of a niche policy aimed at only those families caring for children with disabilities. But these families are among some of the highest need of all Canadian household, often suffering large financial hardships to meet the day-to-day needs of their dependent children, not to mention the strain of worrying about the future. In adulthood, persons with disabilities have some of the highest rates of poverty and some of the greatest depths of poverty among any at-risk group in Canada. For the families of Canadians with disabilities, particularly those with very young children today, the RDSP and its associated grants and bond may have some real impact in helping them bear the financial burden of care. In their most recent election platform, the Conservatives also pledged to make the plans (not even yet available on the market) more flexible by permitting direct rollovers from RESPs. This measure would involve a relatively small cost in the short-term but could increase longer-term costs to the public purse by reducing the taxes eventually paid on RRSP deposits and converting a portion of "tax-deferred" savings (savings that will eventually be taxed, but at a presumed lower rate) into "tax-prepaid" savings (savings that are presumed to be from after-tax income). Again, for so long as the current trends continue (and we expect they will), it will be primarily the families in middle and upper income brackets who have the diversity in their portfolios to convert savings from one form to another.

THE TAX-FREE SAVINGS ACCOUNT

The theme of shifting savings within a portfolio is perhaps a very good segue way to discussing the Tax Free Savings Account (TFSAs). Announced in the 2008 budget by a Conservative Finance Minister but informed by a consultation launched in the 2003 budget by a Liberal Finance Minister, the TFSAs were first offered as of January 2009. Canada is joining several other countries, including the United Kingdom where Individual Savings Accounts (ISAs) have been among the most popular financial product since they were first offered in the 1990s. The policy logic behind the TFSA is that:

a) It is better to tax consumption than earning and saving;
b) It is costly to the public purse in the short and long-term to offer generous tax deductions on current stored income and then recoup taxes at lower rates when the savings are drawn down as retirement income;
c) It is more efficient to simply forgo the shell game of tax deferral and treat savings on an after-tax basis.

In contrast to the RRSP, the TFSA doesn't offer a handsome tax deduction for annual deposits. It does shelter deposits and eligible investment earnings from annual taxation. It includes an annual contribution limit of $5,000 but no lifetime limit.

The TFSA also exempts future withdrawals from being included as "income" for either tax purposes or in determining eligibility for the Guaranteed Income Supplement or Old Age Security. What this means for low and modest income Canadians is that they finally have an alternative to the RRSP and its costly clawbacks. This is no small thing. While some shifting from

RRSPs to TFSAS is likely, particularly among the very wealthiest Canadians who have already maxed out their lifetime RRSP room, shifting among lower and modest income Canadians who have diligently been contributing to RRSPS may be highly desirable if it increases their eligibility for income-tested seniors benefits. For the growing share of the Canadian workforce without an employer sponsored pension of any kind (whether defined benefit or defined contribution) the TFSAs offer another way to build some stores for the retirement that will surely come whether by force or by desire for the self-employed, dependent contractors and other non-standard workers.

Within the life course, retirement is really only one of many savings goals. Along the way, and particularly for lower income households, there are many, many lumpy costs that cannot necessarily be borne out of income flows alone. In his 2008 budget remarks, Minister Flaherty named vacations and home purchase as among these shorter or medium term goals, clearly speaking to a mostly middle-class audience. For lower income households, sometimes the goal is more modest or practical like buying a new washing machine, saving up for next Christmas, or just having a little emergency nest-egg in case the car breaks down again. These households have less access to consumer credit than do middle and upper income households and, by definition, far more constrained income flows so their alternatives are vastly more constrained. The TFSA has all the potential to offer a good vehicle for a broader range of asset accumulation that may appeal to lower and modest income Canadians than the current array of publicly subsidized savings accounts. But for Canadians with a very limited relationship with or limited trust in mainstream financial institutions, a cookie jar or mattress may be a more attractive option (despite the lost interest) if TFSA providers don't find a way to make the product simple to buy, simple to use and truly accessible to segments of the market who have more limited relationships with and lower trust in financial service providers. It's also not clear that removing a barrier is enough to create incentives for formal, structured and mainstream forms of saving for those with few assets. Drawing from the example of the RESP and RDSP, an up-front cash incentive aimed at lower income savers may do much more to improve the redistribution and well-being impacts of the TFSA.

It is also not yet clear how TFSA savings and interest income will be treated by the patchwork of provincial and territorial rules on child care and housing subsidies, income assistance and public drug plans – all essential programs on which low and modest income families rely to make ends meet. If the example of the Canada Learning Bond is at all instructive (despite the problem with take-up) or at least inspirational, there may be reason for optimism. Whatever its challenges in implementation, the Canada Learning Bond did have an extremely important impact in shining a much needed light on the treatment of savings in provincial programs and led to a coast-to-coast exemption of education savings for dependent children from provincial means-tests. A broader lens on the treatment of savings and assets in Canada – a perspective that would require some expansion on the present study – might in fact find that Canada has a two-tiered welfare system: clawbacks for low income small savers and generous tax breaks for higher income big savers. Is this really the best approach?

WHERE ARE WE HEADED?

South of our border, measures to increase savings and asset accumulation have enjoyed bi-partisan support for years but the focus of the recent economic stimulus package is aimed almost exclusively at stimulating consumer spending while providing more traditional forms of welfare state support – wage loss insurance and more accessible post secondary education.. A notable and laudable exception is the package of measures President Obama has now introduced to reverse the swell of mortgage defaults and home foreclosures. The consequences to the US, both economically and socially, of failing to help families stay in their homes would be nothing short of catastrophic.

Across the pond in the UK, New Labour distinguished itself from old in part by embracing capital and the ethos of ownership that had been so symbolic of Thatcherism but now finds itself similarly preoccupied with rising unemployment, nationalizing financial institutions and similarly trying desperately to stimulate consumer spending like so many other developed nations.

So too here in Canada, savings and asset-based policies cannot be readily identified as either Conservative or Liberal. Liberals have, as noted above, been the architects of many of the current instruments. Conservatives have supported these when introduced by Liberal governments, enhanced existing instruments when they took over power and have, in 2 and half years, introduced 2 brand new and significant federal tax-benefited savings instruments. Outside of these two parties, interest in savings and asset seems to be lukewarm at best. The NDP continue to favour policies to increase income flows wherever possible. Their 2008 election platform included proposals to introduce a national minimum wage, increase the availability of subsidized housing and to increase financial support to students in higher education. The BQ similarly favours increases to Employment Insurance benefits and Guaranteed Annual Income benefits. The Green Party made income splitting a centrepiece of its social policy and pointed to reviews of employer pensions and publicizing public income benefits as the keys to retirement security. None of these measures is antithetical to savings and asset-based measures but they do signal a very different emphasis on flows of household resources rather than on stocks of household resources.

Now in the current recession, policymakers appear to be nearly schizophrenic on the balance between trying to motivate saving and spending. On the one hand, there is a preoccupation with greasing the wheels of credit markets and cutting taxes to get consumers spending again as the major engine of economic growth. The risk, according to this point of view, is that households will simply pocket the income, forgoing consumption to save for potentially harder times ahead. On the other hand, the 2009 federal Budget included several measures that will, in the longer term, lead to an increase in the value of housing equity, already the most valuable asset for most Canadians:

- The time limited Home Renovation Tax Credit, at a cost of $3 billion over the next two years offers homeowners a tax credit on renovations paid for in 2009 or 2010 only and costing more than $1,000. The credit will be a windfall for those homeowners who had planned to do a renovation and have the cash in hand or access to credit to afford it. When housing markets recover, they will have seen an increase in the value of their homes subsidized by Canadian taxpayers.
- Withdrawal limits have been increased from $20,000 to $25,000 for the Home Buyer's Plan that lets first time homeowners borrow, tax-free, from their RRSP to make a down payment on a home. The net cost to the federal treasury will be an additional $15 million per year. It's not likely that this measure will make homeownership more affordable for low and modest wealth Canadians. Only those with larger RRSP savings will reap much benefit.
- The Conservatives also made good on their election promise to introduce a First Time Home Buyer's Tax Credit that gives a non-refundable tax credit of up to $5,000 (or $750 net) for eligible first time home buyers. Because the credit is non-refundable and can only be claimed after the purchase has been made, it will (like so many other policy instruments) proportionally reward Canadians with higher incomes (and higher tax liabilities) and the cash or credit on hand to afford the front-end cost of buying a home. These are the same Canadians who likely would've bought a home anyway.

If it difficult to conclude whether policymakers would prefer that Canadians spend or save, there are at least two other conclusions we can draw. The first is that we still are sorely lacking asset-based policy instruments that can distribute more of the benefit to lower wealth and lower income Canadians. There are important exceptions in the Canada Learning Bond and TFSA discussed above, but we remain stuck in a general pattern of rewarding ownership most heavily for those with more private resources. The second conclusion is that those Canadians who had more assets coming into the current recession will be the ones who manage best in getting through it. Prime Minister Harper was roundly criticised in the fall 2008 for suggesting he saw some excellent buying opportunities on the market for investors.[18] Whether or not it was sound economic advice, it certainly revealed an underlying and flawed assumption about the financial resources of average

Canadians and that's an assumption that all parties have been guilty of at one time or another.

One somewhat surprising announcement in the 2009 Budget was the announcement of new National Financial Literacy Task Force, to be comprised of experts who will be charged with developing a national strategy to boost the financial literacy of Canadians. A good and timely thing too. Given the historic number of financial products consumer must now chose from on the market, given the different incentives for different forms of capital accumulation in public policy and given the complex interactions of different tax and other policy instruments, it would be no wonder if many Canadians simply felt overwhelmed, confused and mystified at where their money goes and what to do with it.

Tax policy has a real and legitimate role to play in shaping individual behaviour and choices in how financial resources are used or stored up. It usually makes sense to tax less when people do "good" things like saving money for "good" uses and to tax them more heavily when they consume more. In this respect, the tax expenditures to support retirement savings, home ownership and savings for education, among others, are entirely warranted. These expenditures have likely helped thousands of Canadians to save more for retirement, to buy and maintain a home and to develop a financial cushion in liquid and fixed assets that is so important for well-being and inclusion. However, the principle of vertical equity (that those with more money should pay more taxes) has largely not been preserved. Having incrementally put in place such a system – and we do argue that these tax expenditures should be viewed as forming a kind of system to support household asset-building – it is unlikely that the biggest and more popular measures (capital gains exemptions on primary residences and deductions for RRSPs) can or should be scrapped. In any case this area of inquiry is still too new and too little is known to be able to suggest wide-scale change. But changes to the existing measures, even at the margins, could have significant and important impacts on vertical equity and make a difference to those households with less money on hand to save.

First, we need to begin to look at public expenditures on savings and asset accumulation as constituting a form of welfare in parallel with the public expenditures (such as EI, social assistance and the Canada Child Tax Benefit) to support household incomes and transfer income support to those who need it most. Previous studies in the US by CFED[19] and Howard[20] and in Ireland by Callan, Walsh and Coleman[21] have suggested that much more and systematic scrutiny should be paid to how governments spend through the tax system. Canada does not have a statutory requirement for government to publish annual tax expenditure data but does so by convention. Unfortunately the way in which the information is reported makes it difficult, without the kind of effort and time required by a study of this kind, to see patterns in the expenditures or track its distribution or impacts among Canadians. But the need for scrutiny also needs to apply to the direct expenditures that favour certain forms of asset accumulation for certain Canadians but not others. Tax expenditures are by far the largest but by no means the only ways that the federal government encourages Canadians to save and build wealth, or conversely to dis-save and spend more. And together these tax and program expenditures interact with provincial measures to test wealth or build it. All of these phenomena need to be better understood, better described and better analyzed in a systematic approach.

In the meantime there may be small but important changes that can be made to key policy instruments to make them more progressive and also responsive to the ways in which Canadians actually do save and build assets in practice.

First, the new Tax-Free Savings Account should be subject to a lifetime limit to keep a disproportionate amount of the benefit from flowing to those high wealth Canadians who have already maxed out their RRSP room. Second, the TFSA should also be exempted from provincial means tests so that when low income Canadians turn to temporary income support, they aren't stripped of all their assets and left more susceptible to future financial crisis. Savings made by low income earners can and should be bolstered by governments through a refundable credit or a direct program transfer – instruments that can have a real benefit for lower income savers where non-refundable credits and deductions fail. Third, more could be done to increase the very modest progressiveness of some current measures. For example, the matching rates on RESP savings by low and modest income families could be accelerated. Finally, attention should be paid to the ways that instruments are designed and implemented. Where choices have to be made among multiple options, among multiple products and among multiple providers, governments have a role to play to inform consumers and enable them to make the best choices for themselves and their families. Virtually any policy to increase household saving and wealth will necessarily require Canadians to interact with mainstream financial service providers so, particularly for the segments of the population who rely on payday lenders and cheque cashers, attention needs to be paid too to financial inclusion and financial literacy.

Real progress on the distribution of wealth in Canada is only going to be made if households with less money get more support to save and build assets. Critics will suggest that attending to the savings needs of low income Canadians is an exercise in futility because they presume that these Canadians just don't save. This isn't true. They save but differently than middle and upper income Canadians. Upper income Canadians save under the guidance of their advisors and with careful attention to their portfolio mix of liquid and illiquid assets as well as implications for their tax liabilities. Middle income Canadians tend to save through semi-automated measures like building housing equity as they paid down a mortgage or payroll deductions for an employer sponsored pension or RRSP. Low income Canadians can and do save. In fact almost one million Canadians with incomes under $20,000 report Dividend Income.[22] Furthermore, almost half of households aged 55–64 with incomes under $30,000 had retirement savings (amounts in RRSPs averaged about $40,000). Programs such as learn$ave (a demonstration developed and implemented by SEDI) are demonstrating that even households on social assistance will save when given the opportunity. But compared to middle and higher income Canadians, households with less money to set aside save smaller amounts, they save it less regularly (in small lump sums when they can instead of regular monthly amounts) and they may favor a much wider range of uses – for example saving for a modest used car, purchasing appliances or covering other household medium or even short-term needs that can't be afforded out of income alone. Unfortunately, our public policy approach has tended to favor the ways and reasons that wealthier Canadians save. Moving to a more progressive and inclusive approach to supporting household wealth comes with risks that are not negligible but there are significantly greater risks to continuing to ignore the growing polarization of wealth. The current economic crisis illustrates some of the problems with staying an outdated course and, hopefully, creates an opportunity for a real dialogue about doing things differently.

APPENDIX: GLOSSARY OF SELECTED FEDERAL MEASURES DISCUSSED IN THE CHAPTER

CANADA EDUCATION SAVINGS GRANT (CESG)

The Canada Education Savings Grant (CESG) is a transfer deposited into eligible Registered Education Savings Plans (see below) where the beneficiary is under age 17. To receive the CESG, a plan owner must make deposits and the CESG is added as a matching credit. The basic rate is 20% on the first $2,500 saved annually, or $500 per year, but families with lower incomes can receive a higher matching rate on the first $500 saved each year. The maximum lifetime amount of CESG for each child is $7,200. The grant is deposited directed into an RESP and is included in eligible withdrawals once the beneficiary starts post-secondary education. If the plan is ended early or the beneficiary does not go on to post-secondary education, the CESG and any investment income earned on the public grants are returned to the federal government.

CANADA LEARNING BOND (CLB)

The Canada Learning Bond (CLB) is a transfer deposited into eligible RESPs where the child's caregivers are receiving the National Child Benefit Supplement, an income-tested child benefit aimed at low-income families. In the first year, the bond is $500 and for each subsequent year the child is eligible (up to age 15), it is worth $100. The maximum lifetime amount of CLB that can be paid to RESPs for an individual child is $2,000. Unlike the CESG, the CLB does not require that RESP owners first deposit their own money in the account.

CANADA STUDY GRANTS

Canada Study Grants are bursaries payable to eligible high needs post-secondary students with disabilities or with dependants. To be considered, students must apply and be eligible for federal and provincial student loans.

CAPITAL GAINS

A capital gain is made when property is sold for more than the cost of maintaining or selling the property. The gain is defined as taxable income under the *Income Tax Act* and is reported as such (after adjustments) on the income tax return. The definition excludes any gains from a residential property that has been the primary home of the taxpayer. If a taxable gain is incurred on other sales of property (including other real estate, business property, etc.), the gain can be deferred so that the payment is only received and taxed over time. As of 2008, only 50% of the capital gain is taxable. There is a lifetime limit of $750,000 that can be exempted. Taxable amounts may be eligible for a deduction of up to $375,000.

HOMEOWNER RESIDENTIAL REHABILITATION ASSISTANCE PROGRAM (RRAP)

The Homeowner Residential Rehabilitation Assistance Program (RRAP) is a financial program offered by Canada Mortgage and Housing Corporation. The program offers fully forgivable loans to low-income homeowners who live in housing that requires major repairs to its structure, heating, fire safety, etc. Both the household income and the value of the home must be below CMHC established thresholds. The amount of assistance depends on the cost of needed repairs and the region where the house is located. The loan does not have to be repaid as long as the owner continues to live in the home for the five years after the loan is made.

Investment tax credits

NET MORTGAGE INSURANCE CLAIMS

Canada Mortgage and Housing Corporation provides insurance for eligible mortgages where the owners have made a downpayment of less than 25% of the purchase price of a home. Premiums are paid, as part of the closing costs of the home purchase, depending on the size of the downpayment (larger downpayments incur proportionally smaller interest). A claim of 100% of the outstanding mortgage and costs is made on CMHC when the owner defaults on the mortgage. The net amount of the claims is the total claim less revenues from mortgage insurance premiums.

REGISTERED DISABILITY SAVINGS PLAN (RDSP)
The Registered Disability Savings Plan (RDSP) is similar to the RESP (see below) in that it is a registered savings account (regulated under the *Income Tax Act*) that allows an owner to save, in a tax-deferred way, for a dependent child. In this case, the dependent child must have a disability and be eligible for the Disability Tax Credit. The lifetime limit that can be saved is $200,000 in plans for an individual child. Annual contributions are matched, similar to the CESG, through the Canada Disability Savings Grant. The match rate is between $1:$1 and $3:$1, depending on family income, up to an annual maximum of $3,500. Low and modest income families are also eligible for an unmatched grant, similar to the CLB, through the Canada Disability Savings Bond, worth up to $1,000 annually. Contributions are permitted into the account until the dependent child is 59 years of age.

REGISTERED EDUCATION SAVINGS PLAN (RESP):
A Registered Education Savings Plan (RESP) is a registered savings account (regulated under the *Income Tax Act*) that allows an owner (referred to as a "subscriber") to save, in a tax-deferred way for a beneficiary's post-secondary education. Normally the beneficiary is a child. Providers (referred to as "promoters") of RESPs are financial institutions and include banks, trust companies and scholarship funds. Contributions made by the subscriber can't be deducted from total income (like RRSP contributions) but earnings on such contributions are held in a tax-exempt trust. There is no annual limit on contributions however no more than $50,000 can be held in one or more RESPs for one beneficiary. Investment earnings on RESP funds grow tax-free until they are paid out to the plan's beneficiary and are then included in his or her income and taxed accordingly. Because recipients of the funds are expected to be full-time students, their taxable incomes are projected to be very low and the net tax payable on the RESP is expected to be negligible.

REGISTERED RETIREMENT SAVINGS PLAN (RRSP)
A Registered Retirement Savings Plan (RRSP) is a registered savings account (regulated under the *Income Tax Act*) that allows an owner or their spouse (including common-law partner) to save in a tax-sheltered account toward their retirement. Any investment income earned within the plan is not taxed so long as the money remains in the plan. Contributions, subject to annual and lifetime maximums, can be deducted from total income before tax is calculated. RRSP owner cannot contribute to their RRSP after they turn age 71 and in that year funds in an RRSP must be transferred into another financial product, such as an annuity or income fund.

Early withdrawals are taxed as regular income (and tax is deducted at source), unless the withdrawal is made under the Lifelong Learning Plan or the Homebuyer's Plan. Both measures permit RRSP owners to borrow, tax-free, from their RRSP to finance eligible full-time education and home purchases respectively. The limit for withdrawals under the LLP is $20,000 and for the HBP it is $25,000. The funds must be repaid back to the RRSP within 15 years or unpaid amounts will be subject to tax.

TAX-FREE SAVINGS ACCOUNT (TFSA)

The Tax-Free Savings Account (TFSA) is a registered account that enables an owner to save in an account (regulated under the *Income Tax* Act) for any purpose. The contributions are not eligible for any deductions or credits. However investment income is not taxable, nor are withdrawals from the account, regardless of the time or reason for the withdrawal. Account owners must be aged 18 or older. Contributions are limited to $5,000 per year for each individual owner however contribution space can accumulate over time. There is no lifetime maximum on TFSA contributions.

NOTES

1 Mortagage Bankers Association (2009), data from the National Delinquency Survey, February 2009.
2 Marta Steeman, "World Turmoil Hits Kiwi Savings," *The Press*, Wednesday, 17 September 2008. Available online at http://www.stuff.co.nz/thepress/4695637a6430.html; accessed 17 September 2008.
3 Statistics Canada, "National Balance Sheet Accounts," *The Daily*, Monday, 15 September 2008.
4 Reuters Canada "Personal Bankruptcies Up 50 Per Cent in December," February 2009.
5 Ottawa Citizen, "What's a Canadian Worth? $174,300 StatCan Says," Monday, 15 September 2008. Available online at: http://www.canada.com/ottawacitizen/news/story.html?id=aae81348–f09f-4bca-9a88–3e6ec91f04cb; accessed 17 September 2008. And Reuters Canada 2009.
6 The Canadian Press, "Canada Could Face Housing Woes, Merrill Warns," 24 September 2008.
7 Corporation for Enterprise Development, "Hidden in Plain Sight: A Look at the $335 Billion Federal Asset-Building Budget," 2004. Available on-line at: http://www.cfed.org/think.m?id=112&pubid=130; accessed 20 September 2008.
8 Daniel Boothby and Geoff Rowe, "Rate of Return to Education: A Distributional Analysis Using the LifePaths Model," Working Paper 02–8E, Applied Research Branch, Human Resources and Social Development Canada.
9 Personal communication with officials in the Canada Education Savings Branch, Human Resources and Social Development Canada, September 2008.
10 Shillington, Richard (1999) "The Dark Side of Targeting: Retirement Saving for Low-Income Canadians," C.D. Howe Institute, *Commentary 130*, September 1999.

11 Tomagno, Edward (2006) "Occupational Pension Plans in Canada: Trends in Coverage and the Incomes of Seniors," Caledon Institute of Social Policy, Ottawa.
12 Steven Kerstetter, "Rags and Riches: Wealth Inequality in Canada," Canadian Centre for Policy Alternatives, 2002.
13 Statistics Canada, "The Wealth of Canadians: An Overview of the Survey of Financial Security," Catalogue no. 13F0026MIE — No. 001, 2008.
14 Lars Osberg, "A Quarter Century of Economic Inequality in Canada: 1981–2005," Working Paper 2007-09, Dalhousie University, October 2007.
15 René Morissette, "On the Edge: Financially Vulnerable Families," *Canadian Social Trends* 67 (2003): 3–17.
16 HRSDC (2003) Program data.
17 HRSDC (2008) Program data.
18 CBC (2008) "Dion, Layton Slam Harper's 'Opportunities' Advice Amid Dropping Markets," 8 October 2008.
19 CFED 2004
20 Christopher Howard, *The Hidden Welfare State: Tax Expenditures and Social Policy in the United States* (Princeton: Princeton University Press).
21 Tim Callan, John Walsh and Kieran Coleman, "Tax Expenditures" in Callan, Doris and McCoy. (eds) *Budget Perspectives 2006* (Dublin, ESRI, 2005).
22 Canada Revenue Agency web-site; http://www.cra-arc.gc.ca/agency/stats/interim-e.html.

9 Communication by Stealth: The New Common Sense in Government Communication

KIRSTEN KOZOLANKA

INTRODUCTION

Communications in government and by government has received little scholarly examination, especially in the context of Canadian politics. With its relatively small budgets compared to other government functions, communications was seen in the past as an adjunct, but not integral, to public policy. Over time, however, this has changed dramatically. The sponsorship scandal that helped topple the Liberals from power in 2006 and the investigation of the 2006 election advertising of the Conservatives both serve to emphasize the increasing profile and power of not just traditional communications, but also public relations and political marketing, in structuring the work of politics. Moreover, changes to media systems and practice have transformed the media-politics relationship into an ongoing, high-stakes struggle to define issues and inform the public. A previous edition of *How Ottawa Spends* acknowledged the shift in the status of communications by devoting a chapter to public opinion research in the federal government.[1] Although budgets remain small relative to other government activities, communications has gained in influence to the point that it has often been said to lead policy. The entry of sophisticated communication-based strategies into a central position in governing and campaigning blurs the difference between the two, as well as the line between the political and the administrative arms of government.

This chapter lays out the different approaches to communications taken by recent Liberal governments (1993–2006) and the current Conservative government. While the Liberal governments blatantly utilized communications to achieve their political and policy goals, the Conservative government has a deep strategy of strictly managed, hidden and incremental change.² The paradigm-changing scuffle with the Parliamentary Press Gallery that took place at the beginning of their mandate aside, the Conservatives' backdoor strategy of implementing its policies also extends to its handling of communications, which I call "communication by stealth." This is an extension of the phrase "policy by stealth" coined by the Caledon Institute to describe the backdoor policies of Brian Mulroney in the 1980s.³ I use it here to describe how the Conservatives decentralized their media management strategies, closed down channels of information flow and tightly controlled their communications strategies centrally, especially but not exclusively in their first year in power.

The difference in how the two parties communicated while in government is rooted in their overall ideological purpose. While the Liberals no doubt felt that their hegemony was firmly established, given their record of having been in government for most of the twentieth century and for the thirteen years previous to the Conservative win, the new government had a different gameplan. Overall, the Conservative government's project is to "shift thinking and make their priorities the new common sense."⁴ This new common sense borrows its socially conservative political philosophy from the former Reform Party, the New Right government of Mike Harris in Ontario, the US Republicans and the Howard government of Australia. Its strategy illustrates what has been called the "permanent campaign,"⁵ that is, the discipline and high stakes of an election campaign extended throughout the mandate with the help of political marketing to secure continued public consent. The Liberals utilized sophisticated public relations as well, but they did so visibly, secure in their belief that the "liberal" public would be supportive; their task was not to gain consent, but to maintain it.

Under both governments, the cost and apparatus to support the permanent campaign has reached new heights, giving rise to the view that governments in Canada, the US and the UK, if not in other industrialized nations, have fostered a "modern publicity state."⁶ Key to the success of the publicity state is the continuous packaging of politics for media and public consumption.⁷

A pivotal question is how both approaches serve democracy and the public. There is justifiable concern that communications from governments preoccupied with image politics and political marketing – whether visible or by stealth – have a detrimental impact on citizens' ability to make deliberative decisions regarding government and public policy when the permanent campaign provides information that increasingly is neither transparent nor inclusive, but intended to persuade. In their research on the growing strategic communications power of elite groups in policy making, Bennett and Manheim (2001) describe conditions that could well describe the overall political process:

Policy organizations all across the political spectrum have learned to use communication technologies to target the smallest audiences likely to be helpful to their political aims, and to deliver information that is designed not to promote informed, deliberative engagement on the part of those selected citizens. Rather, information is typically publicized to mobilize and demobilize segments of the population to serve narrow strategic objectives.[8]

Bennett and Manheim suggest publics have been transformed into "exclusive target audiences," which challenges "the democratic ideal of publics as inclusive deliberative bodies."[9] This chapter will also assess how the communications efforts of the current government might have an impact on a Canadian public already concerned about what has been called the "democratic deficit." As Baier, Bakvis, and Brown have written in a previous edition of *How Ottawa Spends*, there is "surprisingly strong consensus" from academics, the public and the political level of Canadian society on this deficit and the need for reform.[10]

BACKGROUND

The Conservatives' strategy of communication by stealth within the publicity state is also a product of political and media environments that mutually constitute each other and that have in recent years undergone transformative change.

Over the 1980s and 1990s, the federal government environment changed dramatically as a result of the strengthening of the New Right political project. In a prolonged process that started with the Mulroney government, the administrative state was decentred and delegitimated. Ongoing retrenchment in the public service culminated in massive cutbacks under the Chrétien Liberals in 1995. The significance for political communication was the swift rebound of the communication apparatus in government, which was needed to sell policies of restraint. While other occupational groups experienced cutbacks, the information services group in government, which had already increased substantially in the late 1980s, rose by seven per cent between 1991 and 1999.[11]

In tandem with the shrinking of the state apparatus was the establishment of new management ideologies borrowed from the private sector with the goal of running government as a business, and with citizens in a new relationship with government as their clients.[12] Another unexpected outcome of a delayed and smaller public service was the loss of checks and balances for accountability, which opened up possibilities for abuse of process as well as politicization of the administrative arm of government. Both accountability and politicization came together in the sponsorship scandal that contributed to the defeat of the Liberals in 2006.

More broadly across industrialized nations and over several generations, political participation has been in decline, especially among younger citizens, with widespread voter disenchantment. There is less party loyalty, and political parties have fragmented and multiplied. The political information available to citizens is abundant, but much of it is negative, divisive and viewed suspiciously or ignored. Overall, according Bennett and Manheim, pluralist democracy has been transformed.[13]

In the media environment, media institutions now are more concentrated and converged corporate entities, with increased market presence, while CBC, the public broadcaster, is hampered in fulfilling its public interest mandate by chronic underfunding. As corporate entities, privately owned media also heed the bottom line, with newsrooms a common casualty to cost cutting. Journalists turn to "information subsidies" in the form of news releases and other material provided by governments and other sources with their own interests to promote in order to meet deadlines without costly research. Technology has exacerbated this by making possible a 24–hour news cycle that prizes the first news out of the starting block, rather than the most complete or accurate news.

Traditional media are experiencing a decline in audiences, while new media have given rise to new forms of political communication with greater but as yet unproven potential for citizen access and information, such as blogging and podcasting. New media have also contributed to the need for visuals, which enhances the reliance in political communication on image and political marketing. Media practice has also changed, as journalists feed the public's thirst for news that entertains, such as satiric "fake news" programs like *The Daily Show*. American conservative media such as Fox News and talk radio programs have been influential in promoting the idea of a "liberal bias" in the media.

Within political journalism, a prevailing attitude of "gotcha" journalism in which the media seem to seek out scandal is much debated, with the media defence that politicians provide much to be "got." Press galleries may be one of the casualties of this environment, as there is little desire by politicians to have the media on their doorstep and a checkered history in which political press corps have often been seen to collaborate and legitimate the government.[14] In any event, many believe technology precludes the need for a geographical presence at legislatures.

THE LIBERALS IN GOVERNMENT: L'ÉTAT, C'EST LIBÉRAL

A major factor in the election of the Conservatives in 2006 was the culture of accountability that was the fallout from the sponsorship scandal. In 2005, the Gomery Inquiry confirmed the concern expressed by the auditor general in her reports that the Liberal government had misused millions of dollars sponsoring events by promoting the Canada brand, mostly in Québec, channeled through advertising firms that had done little or nothing for the money and some that had also paid kickbacks to the Liberal Party of Québec.[15] The Conservatives made accountability one of their five priorities in the 2006 election campaign.

Usually overlooked in the scandal is the fact that the sponsorship program was a communications initiative that flowed out of the promotional activities of Communication Canada, an entire department devoted to communications that was forged by the Liberals. The department began as the Canada Unity Information Office for political purposes to fight Québec separatism and grew over the years to coordinate and centralize communications across government.[16] Other strategic, persuasive communications activities centralized by the Liberals included fairs and exhibits, advertising, householder booklets, public opinion research and sponsorships. In effect, the Liberals institutionalized and normalized the use of persuasive communications that blurred the difference between the interests of the government at large, which has the right and responsibility to communicate with its citizens, and the political purposes of the party in power.[17] Before the sponsorship program's activities came to light, Savoie had warned of a widening breach in the traditional politics-administration relationship, referring to it evocatively as "breaking the bargain" and "the glue ... coming unstuck."[18] In terms of the power of communications inside the public service, this process culminated in the misuse of government money through the sponsorship program.

A publicity-oriented state depends on the strength of its internal capacity to communicate. As communication activities in the 1990s expanded in government, it was matched by a rise in numbers of communications officers in the public service, this despite the stringent overall cost-cutting exercises instituted by the Liberals. By 2003, there were 2,102 employees in government communications branches, an increase of 28 per cent from two years earlier.[19] Up to 427 (24.8 per cent) of them were engaged in corporate communications or marketing activities in 2001. The cost of communicating also rose. Spending on public opinion research, which stood at $12 million in 1993, rose to $29.1 million in 2004. Advertising hit a high of $111 million in 2003 and the government committed to a three-year plan to lower advertising costs. Success at cutting advertising costs was helped considerably by two election periods, during which times government advertising is suspended and political parties pay for their own advertising.[20]

All of this occurred within the Liberals' highly visible approach to communication, undertaken within the comfortable space of long-held power, as well as the strength of their conviction on their message of national unity. Over time, although providing information to Canadian citizens continued, much communication in the public service took on the distinct aura of promotion of a political party instead of information to citizens on what their government was doing.[21]

THE CONSERVATIVES IN GOVERNMENT: SPINNING INTO CONTROL[22]

Politically, the Conservatives came to power in 2006 as a party dominated by the social conservatism of its former Reform and Alliance elements.[23] Their overall strategy was influenced by former campaign chair Tom Flanagan, whose "10 commandments" for Conservative success in government mentioned communication prominently.[24] A key tool was the idea of incrementalism, a major departure from the "communications offensives"[25] undertaken by the New Right government of Mike Harris in Ontario and which caused considerable and ongoing backlash from social justice and labour groups.[26] Yet the new government also inherited several former Harris cabinet ministers, who took up key posts in the Harper cabinet, indicating a difference in tactics, but not in ideology. Incrementalism was a strategic tactic born of the necessity of getting elected and then managing a minority government, but it also was a political opportunity for the government to demonstrate to doubting Canadians and the "liberal" media that it could govern.

After their loss in the election of 2004, the Conservatives fought the next election with a tightly disciplined strategy of centralized messaging and an announcement a day to focus the media on the party's message. Learning from the 2004 defeat, the party held a convention in Montreal in 2005 from which emerged, according to Paré and Berger, a strictly pared-down platform without the controversial hot-button policies that had the potential to throw party messaging off-track.[27] The policy convention identified the five issues that the party would use as its next election platform. More importantly, it emerged from the conference with a rebranded party, a rebranded leader and a tightly controlled political marketing strategy.[28] In effect, the Conservatives rebuilt their party from the ground up, much the same as the Harris Conservatives in Ontario did before gaining power in 1995.[29] In tandem with a superior ability and capacity to segment the voting populace learned from the US Republicans and the Howard government of Australia,[30] political marketing allowed the Conservatives to offer "short-term and personal-gain proposals" that would appeal to different sets of voters.[31]

Immediately after its win, the Harper government took steps to limit the perceived power of the press gallery, viewing it as an elite group and a direct component of a "wider 'permanent Liberal government.'"[32] Harper held press conferences and appeared at media scrums rarely, his office personally selected friendly journalists for interviews and private briefings, he held unannounced cabinet meetings and his office approved national media interviews for his Cabinet ministers. Further, he tried to achieve an American presidential ambience by having his own staff manage press conferences by controlling who got to ask questions, instead of the press gallery. At one point, it was revealed through an Access to Information request that the government planned to set up its own media centre, although those plans were later dropped.³³ In effect, Harper acted to "decertify" the media by bypassing them.³⁴ Over time, after the initial furor, the press gallery resigned itself to less access to the prime minister and his Cabinet. What is notable about this approach to media is that staff in the Prime Minister's Office, which already had considerable control over ministers, also controlled media access to them.

The scuffle with the press gallery should be seen as a key moment in the new government's media management. It was important because it was a rare example of a visible and head-on communication strategy and also because it was intended to demonstrate leadership, a new way of doing business that left behind the cozy relationship that the Conservatives perceived the press gallery had with the previous government. As long-time Conservative strategist Tom Flanagan has written, "[t]he media are unforgiving of conservative errors, so we have to exercise strict discipline."³⁵

Instead, the Conservatives preferred to give access to local, regional and international media, far from the usual domination of Ottawa-led news making. They showed a preference for granting interviews on local supper-hour newscasts on privately owned stations, usually CTV and Global rather than the public broadcaster, CBC. In addition to the dispersed, outside-Ottawa strategy, they confined minister availability to targeted popular political programs such as *Mike Duffy Live*, and their priority for print media was the *Globe and Mail* and the *National Post*, Canada's two high-profile, conservative daily newspapers. They also favoured communicating directly through appearances on radio talk shows and participating in blogging on conservative-friendly sites.³⁶ In addition, the prime minister had a podcast that was frequently accessed. Wiseman summed up the Harper media strategy as "intended to compel the media to respond to the Harper logic and pace, not theirs."³⁷ Wiseman said Harper either goes over the head of the media to be able to control communication or flies below the media by using direct and unmediated communication to targeted segments of the public. In this way, Harper avoided the traditional media gatekeepers and constructed an under-the-radar incremental communication strategy that was to play a key role in December 2008 in saving his government against a proposed Liberal-NDP coalition.

Although the media management strategy relied primarily on decentralized opportunities, both it and the Harper government's communication strategy were centralized within the Prime Minister's Office and relied specifically on the prime minister himself. No doubt mindful of the 2004 election campaign and other times when Conservative candidates brought up controversial issues that were off-message, the prime minister "exercised some of the tightest communication control in recent memory, especially over his Cabinet."³⁸ In a media interview, political science professor Alan Tupper pointed out that it is a signal of the importance of communications in modern-day politics that the blame or the credit for a public policy are both believed to rest on the success of the communication surrounding it, obscuring the actually worth of the policy.[39] Central control, as well as the stealth approach to communication, was also evident in how government members of Parliament handle their day-to-day work. Opposition members learned in May 2007 that the Conservatives had prepared a manual to instruct Conservative MPs how to obstruct Parliamentary committee meetings "when the debate turns hostile" to the government.[40] The problem with a media and communications strategy that rests completely on the prime minister is that he leaves himself personally exposed to criticism while implying that he doesn't trust his Cabinet ministers.[41]

The government also put its stamp on communication within government in various ways. Early in its mandate, it directed that it be referred to in official public communication as "Canada's New Government," a rebranding intended to set it apart from the departing Liberals.[42] It also rebranded government departmental websites, whose home pages now sport Canadian landscapes that are heavy on Tory-blue skies and seas, in addition to the ubiquitous Liberal-red maple leaf. The main government website attempts to link Conservative values to governance through the use of a phrase taken from the national anthem as a slogan: "The True North Strong and Free." The Conservative party ads that attacked then-new Liberal leader Stéphane Dion in 2007 echoed messaging used by the US Republicans, here as "A stronger, safer, better Canada."

Beyond expected cosmetic changes, however, the government exerted a tight hold over the substance of communications activities within the public service, starting with the Privy Council Office. A leaked document from PCO, the nonpartisan office that liaises with the Prime Minister's Office and administers the public service, revealed a speech module that refers openly to "our party" and urged voters to contact their MPs to say they "support our agenda."[43]

Another aspect of communications that has changed under the Conservative government involves the flow of information, what one journalist has called the government's belief that "fewer communications is seen as better."[44] The silence extends to a chill over the public service. Where public employees were once able to speak to the media or members of Parliament directly on their areas of expertise, now such requests for information must go through, not the deputy minister, their titular boss, but the minister's office.[45] This information muzzling extended to the 2008 election campaign. The Privy Council Office issued a directive to public employees to shut down their public activities so as not to risk having an impact on the election. Critics with expertise in senior management in the public service called the move "unprecedented" and "dramatic."[46]

The Harper government has also used the law to close down issues that would almost certainly otherwise become negative media stories. One example is the lawsuit launched by the Conservatives against the Liberal Party for comments made about election expenses violations alleged by Elections Canada; another is the suit for libel against the Liberals regarding Harper's alleged knowledge of an alleged bribe in return for the vote of Chuck Cadman in a key non-confidence motion.[47] As a strategy, legal action tends to keep issues out of the public eye, but it also discourages criticism and, more importantly, prevents open and transparent information sharing with the public on issues of potential concern. This truncated information flow is also evident in the lack of resources provided in the public service to deal with access to information requests,[48] a problem Roberts has identified in many provincial governments as well as the federal government.[49] Changes to such legislation have meant a serious decline in requests for information from private citizens. Roberts said message and information control is not just a preoccupation of the Canadian Conservatives; other governments are also struggling to keep control of the public domain.[50]

In tandem with the closing down of information channels and the centralization of control on communication, the Harper Conservatives have exhibited a tendency in messaging to marginalize scientific knowledge with which they don't agree ideologically. In diverse matters such as policy on safe-injection sites, the elimination of the position of national science advisor and safety of backup nuclear systems, they have rejected advice and policy based on research. In the case of the safe-injection sites, even *The Globe and Mail* expressed concern in an editorial, as have medical journals, that the government is treating research that consistently shows the same results as just another opinion that can be ignored.[51]

This behaviour may seem like a retreat from the publicity state. After all, without communication, there is no publicity. The key is that the Harper government insists on setting the media and communication agenda itself. Its goal is to foster a new common sense, to use the phrase made popular by the Harris government in Ontario. This does not, however, keep the government from using the extensive communications apparatus set up by the Liberals. Although Communication Canada as the nucleus of communication activity in government no longer exists, considerable investment and strength in communications remain. The 2007 Paille report on public opinion research indicates that the Conservatives spent $31.2 million on 548 polling contracts during their first full fiscal year in office, more than any previous government.[52] The government continues to rely on public opinion research for gauging the views of the public, although the prime minister said in 2002 before coming to power that they would not take a stand based on such "vagaries" of public opinion.[53] In addition to this financial outlay, the government proposed changing the contracting rules to allow the minister of a department to approve polling projects, raising questions about potential politicization.[54]

Moreover, the current capacity of the public service to fill the communications' needs of the government is still extensive, despite the sponsorship scandal identified by the Auditor General and investigated in the Gomery Report. In 2008, there were 3,758 approved positions in communications branches across government, an increase of 44.1 per cent since 2003. In the same five-year period, the public service overall only grew by 15.8 per cent. In addition, budgets in communications branches totaled $324 million, an increase of 46.1 per cent in the same period of time.[55] This by no means represents a post-sponsorship pullback in communications capacity.

When it feels it is warranted, however, the government engages in visible communications. It did so in March and April 2008 when it spent $3.4 million of the House of Commons budget on printing and mailing small householder newsletters called "ten percenters" (they go to ten percent of a riding) to millions of Canadians in ridings not held by the Conservatives, rather than to their own constituents.[56] The other three parties also produced householders for non-constituents, but not to the same extent; together, they spent only $4.1 million. The householders were the kind of unmediated, direct-to-citizen communication favoured by the Conservatives. Ontario premier Mike Harris used public money in the same way in the spring of 2003, prior to an expected election in Ontario.[57] The Harper householders were criticized for their partisanship, as they clearly attacked the Liberals, particularly their leader, Stéphane Dion. Given the saturation the party could achieve without paying for it, it must have seemed worth the inevitable criticism. In fact, the householder splash might be considered the end – at least of this phase – of the Conservatives' communication by stealth, as they began the overt lead-up to the next election.

A second, but more high profile, example of visible communications is the advertising campaign the Conservative Party mounted against the new Liberal leader. In effect, the party used to advantage the surprise win of the relatively unknown Dion to mount a national advertising campaign that framed an unmediated image of Dion as "not a leader" and "not worth the risk." Starting immediately after the Liberal Party leadership convention, the Conservatives ran six sets of ads in English and French over a period of 15 months. By the time the country began to prepare for the Fall 2008 election, polls confirmed the impact of the campaign to delegitimate Dion and "define [him] as a leader before he had a chance to define himself."[58] From a high of 38 per cent support for the Liberals immediately following the December 2006 leadership convention, the party was at 24 percent the day before the September 2008 election call.[59]

For all its disciplined management of media and communication, however, the control did not prevent the government from becoming embroiled in another communication-related government scandal. In April 2008, the RCMP raided Conservative Party headquarters to seize documents related to the advertising conducted by the national party in the 2006 election. Elections Canada believes the Conservatives contravened the Election Finance

Act when they transferred money from their central campaign to local candidates, transferred it back and purchased national campaign advertising with the "local" money. The local candidates then claimed rebates available under the election law and the central campaign stayed within allowable spending limits. For a government that came to power on the heels of an accountability scandal vowing transparency, this is a major embarrassment.

CONCLUSION: COMMUNICATING FOR POWER

In power for thirteen years, the Liberals were comfortable with overt and visible media and communication strategies. They even created a self-standing centralized department, Communication Canada, to house the apparatus for their communications activities. The new Conservative government of Stephen Harper took on a key battle with the Parliamentary Press Gallery to establish its control, after which it preferred a stealth approach to communication. Instead of providing an easy target for criticism through an institution for strategic communications such as Communication Canada or by relying on Ottawa-based journalists, the Conservatives undertook diverse and localized media and communications strategies that reached targeted voters directly or privately without the mediation of the national media. The strategy denied the broader public its right to participate in matters of national importance and denied the media the ability to engage in both their official (through the press gallery) and non-official roles as guardians of the public interest and democracy.

The Liberals operated openly from the perspective of what could be called hegemonic confidence, but they used the same tactics of strategic communication within a pragmatic politics in which citizens become target audiences for promotional messages. The Conservatives elevated their political marketing strategies prior to the 2006 election, but this can be considered part of our usual political history in which one party develops new communications tactics that are used subsequently by the other parties. In addition, as Paré and Berger point out, the political marketing they used, in which they micro-target voters and then match them to "personal-gain" election platform planks, is a tactic that may work best only when a party is coming from opposition.[60] For example, the extensive and targeted public opinion research needed in political marketing was used successfully by Mike Harris in Ontario in 1995 to build short-term alliances on hot-button issues that moved different segments of the electorate to vote for the Conservatives.[61] What is virtually certain is that we will see more political marketing from both parties as the permanent campaign intensifies and becomes more sophisticated. Moreover, political marketing will also be used by challengers from other political parties and from non-party but not non-partisan organizations that seek to have influence over public policy and who have the resources to communicate for power.[62]

The control tendency of the prime minister, however, should not be forgotten. At stake is the rare opportunity in Canadian political history for the party of the right to achieve the hegemonic status once enjoyed by the Liberals. As Gramsci theorized, those who wish to form a hegemonic bloc need time to establish themselves, begin the shift in ideology and consolidate their support – a strategy for which Harper's backdoor stealth strategy is well suited.[63] Moreover, the party in power is able to leverage its communications tactics by making use of the publicity apparatus of government. As I have demonstrated, strategic communications capacity in government remains extensive, a considerable power that cannot be taken lightly. Golding has written about the growth in government communications and the decline in government information to the public, concluding that "[w]here the institutions of public information are expressly intended to act as a check and balance on the undue concentration of power in the state, then the growth of that state as itself an information machine of formidable power is bound to pose a threat to the free and diverse distribution of information."[64] Thus, institutions of public information that are intended to act as a check and balance articulated and disseminated in the public interest can be transformed into information that could be said to represent narrow party interests. Although Golding was writing at the beginning of the Thatcher era in Great Britain, a key moment in the shift to more politicized communication by governments and in government, his analysis clearly is relatable to the current situation in Canada.

The effectiveness of the current government's media, communications and information strategies on the public are difficult to assess; in politics, election victories or losses are usually the bottom line. When a government has a long-term strategy of not only coming to power but also establishing itself as a new political force, however, perhaps different standards for success apply. The public opinion research company Ekos Research Associates has been asking Canadians the same question about their values orientation annually for fifteen years: do they see themselves as small "l" liberal, small "c" conservative or neither? In 2008, for the first time, those respondents reporting a small "c" outlook outnumbered the small "l" outlook.[65] The meaning of this result is disputed. Vancouver writer Murray Dobbin has rejoined: "It's not Canadians" values that have changed – it's their expectations."[66] Dobbin draws attention to other findings in the Ekos poll that speak to underlying issues troubling the public. For example, he pointed out that the survey also showed "increased receptivity to the need for government to play a role in addressing problems in our collective life."[67]

As important as assessing the success of the Conservatives' communications strategies is assessing their impact on democratic discourse and the public. The democratic deficit represents a level of disappointment felt by the public when its expectations of good governance are not being met, or the gap between expectation and reality.[68] (Dobbin's comment on lowered expectations here comes into sharper focus.) This is worrisome because reduced expectations lower public confidence in government and politicians, and can discourage voting and political involvement. The Conservatives came to power on a platform that included open and accountable government as one of its five election platform planks and, indeed, followed up with an *Accountability Act*. Other than that, there are few clues as to how the Conservatives see the public's role in politics. In his struggle with the press gallery, however, Harper did suggest that breaking the gallery up would be "helpful for democracy."[69] For the new government's first budget in 2006, public consultation consisted of soliciting e-mail feedback directly from Canadians on Finance Canada's website.[70] Another hint was when the government passed a law designating fixed election dates, an idea that is seen as a way of taking the politics out of picking election timing – but then the government called the election a year early.

For over two years, the media have highlighted the prime minister's secretive style and his tendency to control all messaging and decision-making for his ministers. Given this and the government's seeming inability to articulate a more complete policy agenda to deal with the democratic deficit, it is not surprising that survey results in mid-2008 showed that 45 per cent of Canadians believed the government was doing a poor job at being open and honest, and 43 per cent thought it was poor at being accountable to citizens for public spending.[71] In an earlier poll, 58 per cent said they were unhappy with how the Conservatives informed the public about their policies and 50 per cent said they were secretive.[72]

As the government headed into the general election in September 2008, media scrutiny of all parties was fierce, and the Conservatives found themselves pushed off-message in situations in which the prime minister could not control all activities on multiple fronts across the country. Somewhat unusually, and perhaps demonstrating that Canadians were still uncertain about the Conservatives, public opinion was volatile and divided amongst the other political parties, and political advertising was negative from the outset. The outcome of the election – a continued Conservative minority – appeared to satisfy no one. Citing lack of action by the Conservatives on the impending international economic crisis, the Liberal and NDP, supported by the Bloc Québécois, attempted to form a coalition government.

It is here that communication by stealth – nearly two years of bypassing national media and the press gallery, and targeting regional and sympathetic media – reaped a further calculable reward for the prime minister beyond the delegitimation of Stéphane Dion. In the days following the fledgling coalition's announcement of its intentions, Harper and his government mounted a public relations campaign to stir Conservatives to action, urging them to contribute to a Facebook page, go to rallies, call in to talk shows, sign petitions and write their MPs to express their opposition.[73] The Prime Minister's Office sent out an e-mail to its members of Parliament urging them to "use every single tool and medium at our disposal," tools that included an attached package of communications products of "our key messages, talking points for use with local media, talk radio scripts for your local activists, a letter to the editor for local media and two "Just the Facts" documents..."[74] The communications tactics had two elements in common: they bypassed the media and were aimed directly at the grass-roots. The campaign included the prime minister speaking directly to Canadians in a televised address on December 3 that framed the coalition option as not democratic and stressing that it included "separatists." (The issue framing was reminiscent of the Liberals' use of national unity as a rationale for the sponsorship program.) A poll taken the next day showed an increase in support for the Conservatives back to their election-day support amid mixed support for the idea of a coalition.[75] By December 5, another poll showed the government had support of 46 per cent of the public.[76] Television coverage of rallies showed some participants waving Canadian flags in response to the Conservatives' framing of the coalition as a threat to national unity. Although it was unclear from the poll why those polled supported the government over the coalition, the question asked was situated as a "coalition led by Stéphane Dion," a leader whose reputation had already withered under the Conservatives' advertising campaign the year before. Governor General Michaëlle Jean granted Harper permission to prorogue his two-week-old Parliament and break for seven weeks, giving the Conservatives further time to consolidate support.

In fact, the Harper government's public relations response to the threat of losing power may give us insight into how the Conservatives see democracy and the democratic deficit. As was cited at the beginning of this chapter, Bennett and Mannheim suggest that such targeted mobilization as is used by the Conservatives, "typically serves narrow strategic objectives" and is "designed not to promote informed, deliberative engagement on the part of those selected citizens." Given the use of highly charged language such as "socialists" and "separatists," as well as the invocation of a threat to national unity in the prime minister's televised address, it is difficult to see Canadians under a Harper government participating in the rational dialogue that is usually cited as the bedrock of citizen–government interaction on public policy. Altogether, the increased capacity within government to communicate with citizens, the ability of the Conservatives to mount targeted and ongoing communications campaigns directly to citizens, and the will of the prime minister to centralize and control communications provide formidable tools to mobilize public opinion on behalf of their own strategic objectives. The promising strategy of communication by stealth – which is turned on and off at will – might yet capture the hearts and minds of Canadians for Stephen Harper's Conservatives.

NOTES

1 Andrea D. Rounce, "Ottawa's Spending on Public Opinion Research" Implications for Governance," in G. Bruce Doern, ed., *How Ottawa Spends, 2006–2007: In From the Cold – The Tory Rise and the Liberal Demise* (Montreal: McGill-Queen's University Press, 2006), 138–61.
2 Tom Flanagan, "Harper's Learned the Liberal Art of Managing a Minority," *Globe and Mail*, 29 June 2007, A15.
3 Gratton Gray, "Social Policy by Stealth," *Policy Options* 11, no. 2 (1990): 17–29.
4 Chris Dornan, "The Cool on the Hill," *Globe and Mail*, 20 October 2007, F3.
5 Robert Everett and Frederick J. Fletcher, "The Mass Media and Political Communication in Canada," in Craig McKie and Benjamin D. Singer, eds., *Communications in Canadian Society*. 5th edn. (Toronto: Thompson Educational, 2001): 165–78.
6 Jay G. Blumler, "Elections, the Media and the Modern Publicity Process" in Marjorie Ferguson, ed., *Public Communication: The New Imperative*. (London: Macmillan, 1990): 101–13; Peter Golding, "The Mass Media and the Public Sphere: The Crisis of Information in the 'Information Society,'" in Stephen Edgell, Sandra Walklate, and Gareth Williams, eds., *Debating the Future of the Public Sphere: Transforming the Public and Private Domains in Free Market Societies*. (Aldershot: Avebury. 1995): 25–40.
7 Bob Franklin, "'A Good Day to Bury Bad News'? Journalists, Sources and the Packaging of Politics," in Simon Cottle, ed., *Media Organization and Production*. (London: Sage, 2003): 45–61.
8 Here, "communication technologies" can be taken to mean, for example, public opinion research and refined voter targeting processes. Lance Bennett and Jarol B. Manheim, "The Big Spin: Strategic Communication and the Transformation of Pluralist Democracy," in W. Lance Bennett and Robert M. Entman, eds., *Mediated Politics: Communication in the Future of Democracy* (Cambridge: Cambridge University Press, 2001): 280.
9 Bennett and Manheim, "The Big Spin: Strategic Communication and the Transformation of Pluralist Democracy," 2001, 280.
10 Gerald Baier, Herman Bakvis, and Douglas Brown, "Executive Federalism, the Democratic Deficit, and Parliamentary Reform," in G. Bruce Doern, ed., *How Ottawa Spends, 2005–2006: Managing the Minority* (Montreal: McGill-Queen's University Press), 163.
11 Kirsten Kozolanka, "The Sponsorship Scandal as Communication: The Rise of Politicized and Strategic Communication in the Federal Government," *Canadian Journal of Communication* 31, no. 2 (2006): 350.
12 Allan Tupper, "New Public Management and Canadian Politics," in Janine Brodie and Linda Trimble, eds., *Reinventing Canada: Politics of the 21st Century* (Toronto: Prentice Hall, 2003): 231–42.
13 Bennett and Manheim, "The Big Spin: Strategic Communication and the Transformation of Pluralist Democracy," 2001.
14 This has been borne out by many studies, beginning with the Watergate scandal in the 1970s, notably the Mark Hertsgaard account of the White House press corps in the

Reagan administration in the US, *On Bended Knee: The Press and the Reagan Presidency* (New York: Farrar, Straus, Giroux, 1988).

15 Promoting the Canada brand often consisted of little more than plastering the Canada wordmark and logo on the boards of a sporting arena. Canada, *Commission of Inquiry into the Sponsorship Program and Advertising Activities. Who is Responsible? Phase 1 report.* (Ottawa, ON: Government of Canada, 2005).

16 Kozolanka, "The Sponsorship Scandal as Communication: The Rise of Politicized and Strategic Communication in the Federal Government," 2006.

17 Ibid.

18 Donald Savoie, *Breaking the Bargain: Public Servants, Ministers, and Parliament* (Toronto, ON: University of Toronto Press, 2003); Donald Savoie, "The Public Service: The Glue is Coming Unstuck," *Policy Options* (March/April 2005).

19 Canada, *Benchmarking Review of Federal Government Communications Branches*. Review conducted by Likely Communication Strategies Ltd. for PCO on behalf of DGs of Communication, 2001; Canada, *2003 Benchmarking Review of Federal Government Communications Branches*. Review conducted by Likely Communication Strategies Ltd. for the Communications Community Office, Fall 2003.

20 Canada. Public Works and Government Services, Sustained Commitment – Annual report on Government of Canada Advertising Activities 2005–2006. 1–17. http://www.pwgsc.gc.ca/adv/text/raar05-06-e.html; accessed 12 April 2008.

21 Kozolanka, "The Sponsorship Scandal as Communication: The Rise of Politicized and Strategic Communication in the Federal Government," 2006.

22 "Spinning into control" is a phrase used by Jerry Palmer in his book of the same name, *Spinning into Control: News Values and Source Strategies* (London: Leicester University Press, 2002).

23 John Ibbitson, "This Time It's the Liberals Who Keep Losing the Luggage," *Globe and Mail*, 9 June 2004, A4.

24 Tom Flanagan, "Thou Shalt Not Lean too Far to the Right." *Globe and Mail*, 22 September 2007, A1.

25 Peter Golding, "Communicating Capitalism: Resisting and Restructuring State Ideology." *Media, Culture and Society* 14, no. 4 (1992): 503–22.

26 Kirsten Kozolanka, *The Power of Persuasion: The Politics of the New Right in Ontario*. (Montreal: Black Rose Books, 2007).

27 Daniel J. Paré and Flavia Berger, "Political Marketing Canadian Style? The Conservative Party and the 2006 General Election," *Canadian Journal of Communication* 33 (2008), 49.

28 Paré and Berger, "Political Marketing Canadian Style? The Conservative party and the 2006 General Election," 51.

29 Kozolanka, *The Power of Persuasion: The Politics of the New Right in Ontario*, 2007.

30 Jeffrey Simpson, "Tories" Down-home Campaign Raiding Down Under Down-South Ideas," *The Globe and Mail*, 18 September 2008, A17.

31 Paré and Berger, "Political Marketing Canadian Style? The Conservative party and the 2006 General Election," 56.

32 Robin V. Sears, "Harper vs. the Press Gallery: The Frog and the Scorpion." *Policy Options*, (July-August 2006), 6.
33 CBC News. "Harper to Create Government-Run Media Centre: Report," *CBC News*. http://www.cbc.ca/Canada/story/2007/10/15/media-pm.html?ref=rss; accessed 15 October 2007.
34 Ira Basen, "Spin Class: Harper's Attempt to Exorcize the Press Corps," *CBC News*. 26 May 26, 2006, 1–3. http:www.cbc.ca/includes/printablestory.jsp; accessed 5 May 2007.
35 Flanagan, "Thou Shalt Not Lean too Far to the Right," A1.
36 Simon Doyle, "PMO Clears Media Requests, Some Cabinet Ministers Not Allowed to Talk," *Hill Times*, 5 November 2007, 1.
37 Nelson Wiseman, "Media: The Message and the Messengers," *Hill Times*, 10 December 2007, 11.
38 Simon Doyle, "PM's Tight Control on Government 'Weird' Strategy, Say Some Experts." *Hill Times*, 28 January 2008, 1.
39 Doyle, "PM's Tight Control on Government 'Weird' Strategy, Say Some Experts," 1.
40 Gloria Galloway, "Manual Called Proof of 'Control Fetish,'" *Globe and Mail*, 19 May 2007, 4.
41 Deirdre McMurdry, "Harper's Rigid Grip on Government has Started to Cause Problems." *Ottawa Citizen*, 25 July 2007, A5; Chris Dornan, "Harper Versus the Parliamentary Press Gallery." *Media*, Spring (2006), 6.
42 McGregor and May, "Tories Rebrand Government to Reflect Change of Guard," The Ottawa Citizen, 6 September 2006, A1.
43 Paul Samyn, "'Non-partisan' Privy Council Spouts Tory Lines." *Winnipeg Free Press*. 17 September 2006, A5.
44 Doyle, "PM's Tight Control on Government 'Weird' Strategy, Say Some Experts." 28 January 2008.
45 Tim Naumetz, "Harper Tactics: Powerful, but Disturbing,' *Ottawa Citizen*, 12 March 2007, A5.
46 David Pugliese and Kathryn May. "PCO Tightens Muzzle on PS for Campaign," *Ottawa Citizen*, 20 September 2008, A1.
47 Glen McGregor, "That's All You'll Hear About the Cadman Affair Until After the Election," *Ottawa Citizen*, 18 September 2008, A5.
48 Jack Aubry, "Access Program Overwhelmed, Report Says," *Ottawa Citizen*, 28 March 2008, A3.
49 Alastair Roberts, "Retrenchment and FOI: Recent Experience under Federal, Ontario and B.C. Law." *Canadian Public Administration* 42, no. 4 (1999), 422–51.
50 Kathryn May, "Harper's Gag on Ministers Breaks Vow," *Ottawa Citizen*, 18 March 2006, A3.
51 Peter McKnight, "When Science Runs Into an Ideological Wall; The Canadian Government Has Been Taken to Task for Its Lack of Support for, or Knowledge of, Scientific Research," *Vancouver Sun*, 1 March 2008, C5; *Globe and Mail*. "Safe-Injection Sites Appearance of Bias," editorial, 5 May 2008, A14; During the 2008 election,

scientists called for the end of politicization of science by the Harper government: Margaret Munro, "Researchers Call For End to Political 'Subverting' of Science," *Ottawa Citizen*, 10 October 2008. A4.
52 The report also recommended that public opinion research prior to 1999 not be audited, depriving the public of the opportunity to uncover more about the Liberals' use of such research. Canada. Public Works and Government Services, *Public Opinion Research Practices of the Government of Canada*. Independent Advisor's Report to the Minister of Public Works and Government Services. Ottawa, 2007, 6.
53 Rounce, "Ottawa's Spending on Public Opinion Research" Implications for Governance,"158.
54 Glen McGregor, "Polling Firms Fear Political Influence," *Ottawa Citizen*, 15 February 2008, A1.
55 Figures for approved positions in 2008 are taken from Access to Information requests submitted by the author. Note that all approved positions may not necessarily be filled by an actual person on staff. The calculation based on approved positions is used to provide a comparison with the figures from a study commissioned by the government itself in 2003. Canada, 2003. Figures on number of employees overall in the public service are from the Public Service Commission. Canada, 2008. "Overall Hiring and Staffing Activities to and within the Public Service by Type and Tenure." http://www/psc-cfp.gc.ca/arp-rpa/2008/st-ts/tbl01/tbl16-eng.htm; accessed 9 December 2008.
56 Bea Vonduangchanh, "Tories Abusing 'Ten Percenters' Free Mailing, Say Federal Liberals. *Hill Times*, 21 April 2008, 1.
57 Kozolanka, *The Power of Persuasion: The Politics of the New Right in Ontario*, 2007.
58 Chris Cobb, "How the Tories Hijacked Stéphane Dion's Image," *Ottawa Citizen*, 27 September 2008.
59 Mark Kennedy, "Liberal Popularity Peaking with Dion," CanWest News Service, 8 December 2006. http://www.canada.com/components/print.aspx?id=95c9d866–89ac-46fa-83ba-d1; accessed 14 December 2008; "Public Opinion Polls on Political Parties, as of Sept. 26, 2008," *The Hill Times*, 29 December 2008, 27.
60 Paré and Berger, "Political Marketing Canadian Style? The Conservative Party and the 2006 General Election," 57.
61 Kozolanka, *The Power of Persuasion: The Politics of the New Right in Ontario*, 2007.
62 Bennett and Manheim, "The Big Spin: Strategic Communication and the Transformation of Pluralist Democracy," 2001.
63 Antonio Gramsci, *Selections from the Prison Notebooks*, trans. by Geoffrey Nowell Smith (London: Lawrence and Wishart, 1971), 79.
64 Peter Golding, "Media Research and the New Communications Map: The Twin Crises of European Communications," *Nordicom Review* 1 (1994), 7–16.
65 Frank Graves, "Canada: The Next Generation." *Globe and Mail*, 6 May 2008, A13.
66 Murray Dobbin, "Canadians More Conservative? Evidence Doesn't Add Up" *Toronto Star*, 29 September 2008, AA8.

67 Dobbin also points to another finding in the Ekos report to support the view that Canadians are not becoming more small 'c' in outlook: "We are also seeing a fairly strong rejection of trickle-down economics," Dobbin, AA8.
68 Peter Aucoin and Lori Turnbull, "The Democratic Deficit: Paul Martin and Parliamentary Reform," *Canadian Public Administration* 46, no. 4 (2003): 436.
69 Simon Doyle, "'I Have More Control Now' Over Media, Says Prime Minister." *Hill Times*, 10 July 2006, 7.
70 Deirdre McMurdry, "Plenty of Unknowns as Harper's Secretive Style Spreads to Budget," *Ottawa Citizen*, 2 May 2006, A5.
71 Andrew Mayeda, "Only 29% Believe Government Is 'Open, Honest.'" *Ottawa Citizen*, 4 June 2008, A3.
72 Richard Brennan, "Tories Seen as Secretive, Arrogant; 58% Unhappy with How Government Informs Public about Policies," *Toronto Star*, 30 May 2008, A19.
73 Mike De Souza, "Canadians on the Potential Liberal-NDP-Bloc Coalition Government: 'A Slap in the Face to All Voters,'" *Ottawa Citizen*, 4 December 2008, A4.
74 Joan Bryden, "Tories Reverse Decision on Political Subsidies," *Canadian Press and Globe and Mail Update*, 29 November 2008. http://www.theglobeandmail.com/servlet/story/RTGAM.20081129.wtories_message1129; accessed 29 November 2008.
75 Ekos Research Associates, "A Deeply Divided Public Ponders Prorogation," 5 December 2008. 10. http://www.ekoselection.com/wp-content/uploads/poll-results-dec-5-final.pdf; accessed 14 December 2008.
76 Norma Greenaway, "Majority of Canadians Want Harper to Lead Nation: Poll," *Ottawa Citizen*, 5 December 2008, A1.

10 Framing the Harper Government: "Gender-Neutral" Electoral Appeals While Being Gender-Negative in Caucus

MELISSA HAUSSMAN
AND L. PAULINE RANKIN

The Harper coalition came to power in January 2006 with both fiscally and socially conservative wings. Similar to many Conservative governments in the US and Canada since the 1980s, the main interest of those elected was to pass economic reforms to keep fiscal conservatives happy (mainly, corporate tax cuts and balanced public-sector budgets) while claiming also to represent social conservatives. The Harper coalition appears to have gained the benefit of electoral experience of New Right contacts in the US. The Harper government, advised by some consultants who also worked with President George W. Bush, emphasized its "incremental nature" and its "Prairie roots of small government" from Harper's previous days (1997–2001) as President of the National Citizens' Coalition.[1] Balancing the coalition halves is necessary to keeping power, particularly in the minority government situation in which the Conservatives have found themselves since January 2006. Keeping the two elements of the coalition together also involves selling different things to different people, since the fiscal conservatives appear to be mainly a "bottom-line" bunch, interested in numbers such as tax rates and reduction in government spending, while the social group often invokes other-worldly types of examples and rarely has a hard-numbers argument on its side. This discussion is first one about "How Ottawa Prioritizes" under the Harper governments and then turns to budgetary issues. Throughout the discussion, it is interesting to bear in mind that despite acting negatively towards women on both social and economic issues, the Conservative caucus was the only one to increase its number of women MP's in the 2008 election (from 16 to 23).

The number of Conservative MP's who could be classified as "social conservatives" based on their publicly recorded views against abortion has fluctuated somewhat between the elections of January 2006 and October 2008.

Before the 2008 election, there were 95 members of the 127–member Conservative caucus identified as pro-life (75 per cent). After the 2008 election, the absolute number of pro-life members went up to 98, but made up a smaller percentage of the overall caucus (68 per cent), which increased to 143 total members. As stated on the Abortion Rights Coalition of Canada website, the pro-life designation is given to those who have supported pro-life legislation in the House or made public speeches at pro-life organizations' events. The Liberal party went from 26 of its 95–member caucus identifying as pro-life after the January 2006 election (27 per cent) to 19 of 77 after the October 2008 election (25 per cent). Both Independent members in 2006 and 2008 identified as pro-life, while 56 (18 per cent) members' stances were unknown after 2006, which changed to 64 (21 per cent of the House) after 14 October 2008. Overall, the number of pro-choice members across the parties in the House remained the same, at 125 for a total of 41 per cent of the House.[2] While the overall numbers of pro-choice House members comport relatively well with an Angus Reid poll on abortion of 20 June 2008, showing that almost 50 per cent of men and women supported abortion access in Canada, it is clear that the Conservative caucus is still heavily skewed toward a publicly identified pro-life stance.[3]

Stephen Harper seems a strong player in electoral gamesmanship, shown while helping to negotiate the creation of the new Conservative party from the fragments of the Reform, Alliance and Progressive Conservative caucuses. He has continued this pattern in steering a divided conservative coalition to (a minority) victory twice since 2006. Much of the electoral task has been performed by controlling the message from the PMO but also in playing some semantic games in campaign statements and particularly at the 2005 party convention. For example, Stephen Harper has continuously assured voters that they had "nothing to fear" from a Conservative government on social issues, such as abortion.[4] The bulk of this discussion is concerned with showing how the Conservative government has worked at keeping its pro-life caucus majority happy without actually having enacted any legislation that it favors. The main tactic used has been to allow the multiparty Parliamentary Pro-Life Caucus (PPLC), comprised of many backbenchers and opposition members, a fairly free reign in introducing items but then in blocking final passage of those items. One pre-election comment by an adviser concerning the "orangutans" in the caucus, necessitating Harper's constant vigilance to keep them off the front newspaper pages, exemplifies the views of the different blocs.[5]

CONVENTION POLITICS

In March 2005, the Conservative Party adopted a resolution at their convention (by a vote of 55 per cent to 45) that "a Conservative government will not initiate or support any legislation to regulate abortion." The January 2006 campaign was one in which Stephen Harper as leader of the Conservative party simultaneously told voters different stories on his government and anti abortion policies. On 11 January, Harper insisted he would not reopen the abortion debate. "A Conservative government will not be bringing forward, will not be supporting, and will not be debating the abortion laws in this country. I've been clear on that ..." On 17 January, in response to Dr. Henry Morgentaler saying that he didn't trust Harper's promise to not re-introduce the abortion issue, Harper maintained that: "The Conservative government won't be initiating or supporting abortion legislation, and I'll use whatever influence I have in Parliament to be sure that such a matter doesn't come to a vote. ... I will use whatever influence I have to keep that off of the agenda, and I don't see any likelihood of that in the next Parliament."[6] On the other hand, he did not specifically disavow letting private members introduce legislation on the topic. Campaign Life Coalition, a pro-life group which has been active since the 1980s and which publishes the daily lifesitenews.com, noted with disapproval that on 9 January 2006, many Conservative Party candidates were refusing to answer questionnaires from pro-life groups. "About 200 MPs and candidates from all parties have turned in completed questionnaires to CLC or responded in some other form to the questionnaire, but of that total, only 72 were from Conservative candidates. The survey has nine questions related to abortion, same-sex marriage, euthanasia, and research on human embryos." A few days later, CLC reported that Conservative candidates have told them that they were actually *forbidden* to answer the group's questionnaire. "Several candidates sent in an unsigned memo from party headquarters saying that answering questionnaires was not allowed."[7]

Illustrating the internal party tension over the prominence of social conservative stands in the platform is the fact that the December 2008 party convention moved rightward in certain ways. While the post-election timing may have provided the basis for the convention's bravado, it is important to highlight the difference in language from 2005. First, the more aggressive convention declared that the strategy of "incrementalism" (on social issues) "is dead."[8] In addition, Resolution P-207 was passed, incorporating the language of Bill C-484, which had died after second Reading in the House prior to the election. The Resolution stated that "the Conservative Party supports legislation to ensure that individuals who commit violence against a pregnant woman would face additional charges if her unborn child was killed or injured during the commission of a crime against the mother."[9]

As an "electoral ballet" of sorts, it is interesting to draw out the tensions within the party organization, formed from its historically disparate elements of Prairie social conservatives and Ontario fiscal conservatives. For the purposes of this analysis, it is also crucial to relate these tensions to actions of the anti-choice or pro-life members of Parliament, particularly from the Conservative party, since 2006.[10]

PARLIAMENTARY PRO-LIFE CAUCUS ACTIVITIES

According to his website (Mauricevellacott.ca), MP Maurice Vellacott was co-chair of the Party Parliamentary Pro-Life Caucus for eight years, until 2008. A former pastor, he was first elected to the House as a Reform Member for Saskatoon in 1997, and has more recently been an Alliance member. His frequent legislative co-sponsor, Senator Stanley Haidasz, was a Liberal MP from 1957–58 and then 1962–78 from the Toronto area (first Trinity and then Parkdale); in 1978 Prime Minister Trudeau appointed him to the Senate. Other prominent members of the pro-life coalition in the House have been MP Garry Breitkreutz, an "original" Reform MP elected in 1993 (and a fellow Saskatchewan representative to MP Vellacott) who also originated the "Unborn Victims of Crime Act" in 2001 that was re- introduced by Conservative MP Ken Epp in 2008 as Bill C-484. Garry Breitkreutz was the sponsor of eight pieces of Private Member's legislation to restrict abortion, from the opposition side of the Chamber, from 1997–2004.[11] The newest Co-Chair of the caucus, Conservative MP Rod Bruinooge (Winnipeg), wrote in an opinion piece in the 29 December 2008 *National Post* that "Canada has one of the most permissive abortion laws in the world" and that he planned to reintroduce private member's legislation to change this. Once again, this elicited a public denial from Prime Minister Harper.[12]

According to an article by Lloyd Mackey and found on the website canadianchristianity.com (reprinted in the *Hill Times*, 18 October 2004), the Parliamentary Pro-Life Caucus has "been around for nearly a decade." Members identified in the article include the MP's mentioned above as well as Prime Minister Stephen Harper, former Justice Minister Vic Toews, House Leader Peter Van Loan and former Foreign Affairs Minister Peter McKay. MP Rob Nicholson, current Justice Minister, was not identified in the article as being a caucus member.[13]

The main strategies employed by the PPLC (Parliamentary Pro-Life Caucus) have been very similar to those used by the Congressional Pro-Life Caucus (and other prominent pro-life groups, such as the American Life League) in the US. Due mainly to the different structures of political power in the two countries, particularly the party-based nature of voting and lack of unilateral Presidential powers for the Prime Minister, these strategies have not succeeded as well in Canada. As with the US movement, the anti-abortion movement in Canada has tried to pursue options to make it more difficult for a woman to access abortion services. This emphasis includes successfully reducing the number of facilities and personnel to perform abortion; trying to move forward the statutory or constitutional definition of when "life" is said to begin (so far unsuccessful in both countries); and trying to implement the "Band-Aid" approach of raising the legal consent age to sexual intercourse and promoting sexual abstinence. What the latter approaches have in common is the belief that somehow unplanned pregnancy (and abortion) rates are higher among the under-18 and unmarried populations, for which there are no data.[14] While "abstinence-based" programs sponsored by the US government and the Conservative caucus' attempts to raise the age of sexual consent in Canada have been implemented, neither one has had any proven results regarding reduction in sexual activity, unplanned pregnancies or abortion rates.

The first area of pro-life strategizing has been on the issue of "conscience legislation," to increase the scope of individuals and institutions who may decide not to participate in abortion procedures. On 16 April 2008 MP Vellacott re-introduced, for the third time, his Private Member's Bill, C-537, to "protect the conscience rights of Canada's health care workers." The bill sought to ensure "that health care providers will never be forced to participate against their will in procedures such as abortions or acts of euthanasia. Vellacott added: "Canada has a long history of recognizing the rights of freedom of religion and of conscience in our country. Yet health care workers and those seeking to be educated for the health care system have often been denied those rights in medical facilities and educational institutions. Some have even been wrongfully dismissed."[15] As with all other legislation sponsored by the caucus, its progress stopped when the election writ was dropped in September 2008.

A comparative note is that the "conscience clause" requirement has been an extremely effective tool of U.S. social conservatives to restrict access to abortion-providing facilities in the US. Based on the 1973 "Church Amendment" sponsored by Sen. Frank Church shortly after *Roe v. Wade* was handed down, 47 states and the District of Columbia have passed similar laws.[16] They have a broader impact than their title implies, not only allowing doctors and nurses opposed to abortion to eschew participation, but also for corporations and hospital board members to take decisions to generally prohibit institutional access. Canada does not have such "conscience clause" legislation in place, which was why MP Vellacott was attempting to get it passed. There have been examples of certain Canadian hospitals which have had limited "conscience clause" policies in effect to address individuals, but the only ones found at the institutional level exist in Catholic Church-owned hospitals.

The key organization speaking for the "conscience clause" position in Canada is the "Protection of Conscience" Project, founded in 1999 as a project of the Canadian group, Physicians for Life (itself affiliated with the US-based and globally-affiliated Physicians for Life). There are similar organizations for nurses in the US, Canada and elsewhere. On the organization's website, consciencelaws.org, may be found its ethical statement, excerpted as follows:

"…(the conduct of) physicians has been guided by the Hippocratic Oath, which states, in part:" *…I will neither prescribe nor administer a lethal dose of medicine to any* *patient even if asked nor counsel any such thing nor perform an act or omission with direct intent deliberately to end a human life. I will maintain the utmost respect for every human life from fertilization to natural death and reject abortion that deliberately takes a unique human life.*" Would the public expect those of us who respect the Oath to ignore our consciences and sacrifice our professional integrity?[17]

A description of the legislative history of Bill C-537 is available on the Conscience Project's website:

Bill C-422 (originally Bill C-461) is a copy of Senator Haidasz's Bill S-7 that was introduced in the Senate. C-461 passed first reading in the House of Commons and secured the 100 signatures necessary for second reading. It was re-introduced in October, 1999 as Bill C-207, but denied a vote in the Commons by the decision of a parliamentary sub-committee the following month. It was re-introduced as Bill C-422, but died on the order paper when Parliament was dissolved for the Canadian federal election in 2000. On February 2nd, 2001, Mr. Vellacott again brought the bill forward as C-246 in the 1st session of the new parliament, and reintroduced it to the second session on 30 October, 2002. The present version of the bill, Bill C-537, was introduced in April, 2008 (where it was given first reading).[18]

The "conscience clause" strategy of the PPLC may be shown to have at the very least a strong theoretical connection to tactics of the Congressional Pro-Life Caucus. This caucus has been co-chaired since its (unnamed) founding date by Representative Chris Smith, Republican of NJ, first elected to the US House at 27 years old (two years older than the legal minimum) in 1981. As the Caucus is referenced in a 1985 journal article, it appears to have been formed early on in Rep. Smith's career.[19] The Caucus has been active on many of the same issues as its Parliamentary counterpart, particularly on restricting abortion, the mandate of courts and gay rights. A group that works with the Caucus is the legal group Americans United for Life, which puts out a manual each year to provide model legislation for states on abortion and general hot-button issues, and has aggressively litigated in court in the US to protect the "conscience rights" of health-care workers to refuse to participate in either abortion or euthanasia procedures. AUL describes itself as the "oldest pro-life organization in the US," since it was formed in 1971 prior to *Roe v. Wade*.[20] It is also related to both the Alliance Defense Fund and the Christian Legal Society.

One of the AUL Directors, Professor Lynn Wardle of Brigham Young University's Law School, is also a director of the (Canadian) Conscience Project. The Conscience Project supported MP Vellacott's legislative proposals on freedom of conscience for health-care workers, lamenting that "Canada is one of the few countries in the world without such legislation."[21] On the other hand, it appears that many workers at Canadian hospitals or clinics that provide abortion are exercising certain "conscience" rights by either incorrectly reporting or refusing to provide information on the services offered by the institution. In a national study conducted by Canadians for Choice in 2006, in which all 791 hospitals across Canada were sent a written questionnaire and asked if they provided abortion services (followed up by phone interviews whether a written response was returned or not), thirty one hospitals of the 183 returning the questionnaire said they provided abortion services, a figure of 16 per cent (down from 18 per cent in 2003). More seriously, 41 per cent of those contacted at these hospitals said they either did not know whether the hospital performed abortion services or would/could not refer to an institution that did provide these services.[22] Canadians for Choice has urged the CMA and College of Physicians and Surgeons to adopt directives countering the Conscience Project's "freedom to refuse" interpretation of the Hippocratic oath with one affirming the duty of doctors to perform constitutionally legal services, so far to no avail.

Another tactic of PPLC members has been to support "Crisis Pregnancy Centres" (which do not provide counseling on pro-choice options), modeled on their spread across the US. Among the institutional supporters of such centers are CareNet, the largest funder of "crisis" pregnancy centers in North America and Focus on the Family of Colorado, the parent organization of the Canadian affiliate. One example is that MP Maurice Vellacott lists himself as a founding member of "Real Choices Crisis Pregnancy Center" in Saskatoon and as a supporter of both the Evangelical Fellowship of Canada and Focus on the Family Canada.[23] The Saskatoon Center was formed in 2000 and contains links to the "Canadian Association of Pregnancy Support Services" (CAPSS) founded in 1997. A visit to that link says that any pregnancy crisis center that has an "approved affiliation to CAPSS" (as the Saskatoon center presumably does) also confers "the option of dual or triple affiliation with CareNet or Heartbeat (international), with the related benefits of both organizations."[24]

In the US, one of the major funders of the "Crisis Pregnancy Centers" has been the "abstinence based" anti-sex education program, begun by President Reagan in 1981 (and passed by a Democratic House and Republican Senate), and expanded under the "welfare reform" law supported by President Clinton in 1996–97 (passed by Republican majorities in both Houses). The welfare reform law was part of the Contract with America, supported by the Republican Congress starting in 1994. The pollster and adviser on the Contract was Frank Luntz (who advised Prime Minister Harper in Spring 2006). Finally, "abstinence based" education and other programs have been expanded even further by President Bush from 2000 onward, passed enthusiastically by a Republican-dominated Congress until 2000 but only grudgingly extended by the Democratic-dominated Congress since January 2007.

The funding for the "abstinence-based" program which was a centerpiece of the Contract with America's "Personal Responsibility and Work Opportunity Reconciliation Act" of 1996 was made available through Title V of the

Social Security Act. This funding scheme provided a $4 federal match for every $3 that a state government authorized for participation in the program, "up to 87.5 million annually."[25] Other studies have shown that since 2000, under a presumably pro-life President, approximately $1.5 billion has been expended on abstinence-based education in the US, with about one-tenth of that amount, $157 million, going to Crisis Pregnancy Centers.[26]

One way in which the Bush Administration has channeled this funding is through the presidential tool of the Executive Order, by which the Executive can unilaterally make policy affecting executive branch agencies. Through this strategy, the president set up "Faith-Based and Community Initiatives" offices in the White House just after his 2001 Inauguration and in five other Executive agencies within his first month.[27] The Department of Health and Human Services has been a major "funnel" by which money has been distributed to states and their abstinence-based programs, including the crisis pregnancy centers.[28]

While direct funding from the US government has been shown to flow to crisis pregnancy centers in the US, such an option has not yet been developed in Canada. One of the main reasons is the lack of a mechanism such as a unilateral Executive Order available to a prime minister. On the other hand, the co-chair of the Parliamentary Pro-Life Caucus has been a founding member of such a center, linked to CareNet which is the biggest umbrella organization for such centers. It is possible that the parliamentary Pro-Life Caucus has been acting as a similar internal advocate as the Faith Based and Community Initiatives offices in the US executive agency structure.

In Canada, while the "abstinence-only" program aimed at minors has had less of an institutional toehold than in the US, the PPLC successfully got behind a similar measure, that of raising the age of sexual consent. It was passed in 2007, and raised the age of sexual consent from 14 to 16.

A third key strategy of the PPLC, seemingly mirroring that of its US counterparts is that of enhancing the charges for killing a pregnant woman to include those related to "fetal homicide." The most recent example was that of Conservative MP Ken Epp basically reintroducing the Breitkreutz legislative proposal of 2001 as Bill C-484 in Spring 2008, to make killing a pregnant woman a double crime. While it died on the Order Paper when the writ was dropped for the October 2008 election, it had gone through second reading in the House in March 2008. M.P. Epp's proposed legislation (based on that of MP Breitkreutz) mirrors the "Unborn Victims of Violence" Act passed by the Republican-dominated Congress and signed by President Bush in 2004. This US federal legislation itself followed the passage of similar laws in 29 states.[29]

Justice Minister Rob Nicholson has been inconsistent on to the issues dear to the PPLC, pointing perhaps to a varied mandate given to him by the PMO. On one hand, the Minister voted in 2008 for both Bill C-484 and Resolution P-207 at the party convention. On the other, just before Parliament was dissolved for the 2008 election, he held a press conference in late August, to distance the government from Bill C-484. At that time, he promised to introduce legislation that would make pregnancy an aggravating circumstance in an assault on a woman, and leaving no room for the introduction of fetal rights. "Let me be clear. Our government will not reopen the debate on abortion."[30]

Another strategy used by the Harper Conservative Government to keep its social conservative voting base supportive has been through its appointment strategy to some federal boards and offices. One example relevant to this discussion was the public condemnation by scientists, physicians and representatives of the community interested in fertility and reproduction issues on the politicization of appointments to the Board of the Assisted Human Reproduction Agency of Canada.[31] The agency was set up in January 2006, following the long and contentious passage of Bill C-6 by the Senate in March 2004. This legislation, "Respecting Human Reproductive and Related Research" (or the "Assisted Human Reproduction Act" came out of the Royal Commission on Reproductive Technologies, struck by the Mulroney government in 1989, requiring three different attempts at legislative passage prior to 2004.[32] Ten appointments to the 13–member Board were announced during the December parliamentary recess of 2006, and four of those included people who had either made public statements on behalf of or been associated with the social conservative position on reproduction, stem cell technology and abortion in the past.

Objections to circumstances surrounding the agency's creation were based on at least three points. The first was the highlighted oddity of the appointment procedure, given that the legislation had been passed during a period of Liberal government and Conservative opposition. A list of names for appointment to the Board had been drawn up in 2005 and only two of the people on that list, including the ultimate Chair, John Hamm (former Nova Scotia Premier and a physician), made it through the Conservative vetting process. Other concerns related to the appointments announced in December 2006 were that Board members representing potential clients of the procedures were not included. The more serious charge was that a number of members had made pro-life and specifically anti-embryonic stem cell comments in public fora, and this was troubling, given that part of the agency's remit is to make stem-cell research policy. On the other hand, this emphasis followed the 2006 Conservative platform opposing embryonic stem-cell research (and imposing a three-year moratorium).[33]

The agency's mandate is rather broad and somewhat innocuous. It may be found on its website, www.ahrc-pac.gc.ca.[34] It is also probably of little comfort to those wishing to avail themselves of its services that the parent agency, Health Canada, is headed by a woman MP first elected in October 2008. In a journal article from the end of 2007, Professor Samantha King writes that according to Dr. Abby Lippman, Chair of the Board of the Canadian Women's Health Network, the Assisted Reproductive Health Agency is a "toothless paper dragon." Professor King concurs in saying that the 2004 legislation still has not been implemented.[35] Part of this may be due to the social conservative influence on the Board to essentially "do nothing" in this controversial area. Dr. Lippmann also cites the fact that Québec is claiming competing jurisdiction over much of the reproductive technology area and this may have been viewed as an unaffordable electoral cost to the Harper coalition.[36] On these fronts, giving the agency any kind of enforcement teeth may be viewed by the Conservative government as having too high a price.

FISCAL CONSERVATISM AND "INCREMENTALISM" AS PROVIDING ELECTORAL COVER

Simply put, fiscal conservatism and a calming allusion to "soundness" in economic policy is what draws in the marginal votes (including women) to a Conservative coalition. These votes are crucial for balancing those who would be scared off by the socially-conservative agenda, and getting the government elected. The Harper campaigns of 2006 and 2008 were very much of this mold, as has been seen, in that they both claimed that the "Government" would not attempt to legislate on abortion (while allowing virtually everyone else to introduce such proposals).

Luntz and Thomas Flanagan, key adviser (and former academic colleague) to Prime Minister Harper, were on the "same page" when they spoke of "incrementalism" in terms of the slow, careful steps that a Conservative government would take to put Canada on a solid economic footing. Running on a platform of reducing taxes is not unique or new; most candidates on the mainstream-to-right part of the spectrum allude to taxes quite frequently. George W. Bush campaigned on his "Big Six" themes in 2000, as did Stephen Harper in 2006. The first one implemented by each was a tax cut, since that is the usually the "easy" fix on which to gain legislative support. Some of the pointers dispensed by Frank Luntz when he visited Ottawa in May 2006, four months after the Conservative victory, included the following. During his speech, entitled Massaging the Conservative Message for Voters, Luntz

"drew a communications roadmap to bring the Conservatives to a majority government, a roadmap that Harper's government already appears to be following in several respects. Focus on accountability and tax relief, said Luntz. Images and pictures are important. Tap into national symbols like hockey. If there is some way to link hockey to what you all do, I would try to do it." Much of that lies in personalizing the message for voters and the choice of words the party uses to describe what it wants to do, Luntz said. Luntz hinted at a division between economic conservatives and social conservatives in the Conservative party, urging them to set aside their differences and work together. "We are all one family."[37]

Undoubtedly, Prime Minister Harper has taken the statements of his Canadian and US advisors to heart in forging a coalition across the social and economic conservative divide since 2006. The downside is that while the 2008 election returned the Conservative government to power, it was returned based on the lowest federal election turnout recorded in Canadian history.

While the public seems not to support the pro-life position as strongly as the Conservative caucus, some women will vote for Conservatives even when the government's fiscal package contains nothing for them. This shows the interesting nature of campaigning and forging an electoral and parliamentary coalition of diverse views. Prime Minister Harper has been successful on this if on nothing else. Lacking the tools of his US Presidential counterpart such as executive orders and the power of independent agency rulemaking (constitutionally as strong as legislation), he has had to try to balance the rather vocal pro-life part of his caucus by trying to reassure the public that his government has no intention of legislating on abortion even while allowing backbenchers some wins on the issue (and the 2008 party convention as well). The bulk of the campaign statements in both 2006 and 2008 have clearly been based on the fiscal conservative side, which at least provides Stephen Harper with the votes he needs to retain office. However, neither set of activities speaks to the majority of women in Canada, who are pro-choice and work outside the home.

Fiscal Conservatism and Gender Equality

Not surprisingly, given the Conservatives' electoral strategy of knitting together a viable fiscal and social conservative coalition, candidate Stephen Harper avoided addressing specific questions about gender equality in the 2006 federal electoral campaign, although he did go on record as assuring Canadian women that, if elected, he promised to "take concrete and immediate measures, as recommended by the United Nations, to ensure that Canada fully upholds its commitments to women." [38] Perhaps lulled into complacency by the Tories' campaign rhetoric, women's groups across the country experienced significant shock when on 25 September 2006 the self-described "new" Conservative government announced "efficiency savings" [39] of $5 million to Status of Women Canada, the federal government agency which since 1976 assumed responsibility for coordinating federal action to address Canadian women's equality concerns. With SWC's total administrative budget totaling a modest $13 million, however, the cuts to the operating budget constituted a devastating 38.5 per cent reduction, effectively handcuffing the agency's potential for future effectiveness. The government introduced these cuts as an extension of the $2 billion in spending cuts announced in its first budget, thus squarely situating the decision as one motivated by fiscal responsibility rather than as evidence of a socially-conservative driven rollback on women's rights.

In a dramatic move one week later, however, then-Minister Responsible for the Status of Women, Beverley Oda, announced that the Women's Program (the grants and contribution fund that had provided funding for women's organizations and equality-seeking groups since 1973) no longer would fund women's groups that engaged in advocacy, lobbying or general research. In fact, as the minister explained, the Women's Program would focus not on ensuring equality, but rather on "supporting the full participation of all Canadian women in the economic, social and cultural life of Canada,"[40] a subtle but critically important distinction. All references to the Women's Program as targeting improvements in women's political and legal status were expunged. For the first time in the Program's history, funding criteria were redrafted to allow for-profit organizations to submit proposals. Arguably even more profound, however, was the erasure of the word "equality" from the Program's mandate which, in effect, reversed swc's longstanding objective of aiding women's groups to participate fully in the public policy process and increasing Canadians' understanding of women's equality needs. Another prong of swc's restructuring involved closing twelve of sixteen regional offices, a move the Minister justified by insisting that "[w]e don't need to separate the men from the women in this country."[41] As a consequence of the cuts, swc's total staff dropped to 70 from 131.[42] This reorganization also involved terminating the swc's Policy Research Fund which since 1993 had generated independent research studies on a diverse range of equality-related topics. Instead, swc merged its Research, Policy and Gender-Based Analysis directorates. When Minister Oda appeared before the Parliamentary Standing Committee on the Status of Women two days after this second announcement, she defended the government's actions, assuring citizens that "Canada's new Government fundamentally believes that women are equal."[43]

Following an outcry from women's groups across the country, the word 'equality' was reinstated into the Women's Program and on International Women's Day in March, 2007 the Government of Canada allocated additional funding to the Women's Program. The new funding regime, however, divided the Women's Program into a "Women's Community Fund," the focus of which includes grants and contributions aimed to increase awareness among women in identifying and removing barriers to their participation in their communities and the "Women's Partnership Fund" which prioritizes collaborative projects designed to enhance women's economic security, economic prosperity and leadership development. The new resources significantly increased the Women's Community Fund to $12.3 million and the Women's Partnership Fund to $3.0 million, with the total funding growing from $10.8 million in 2006 to $15.3 million in 2007.[44] The government boasted that the overall budget increases for the Women's Program represented a dramatic expansion of opportunities to enhance women's equality, and that now the Women's Program would promote more concrete action in the lives of women. In a later appearance before the Standing Committee on the Status of Women in 2007, Minister Oda acknowledged the continued concern over the changes to the Women's Program and the removal of advocacy from the mandate, admitting that "[a]dvocacy does have a role to play, but Canada's new government believes that now is the time to act...Instead of wasting more time discussing the issues, our government is looking at tangible ways we can make a difference now."[45] Nevertheless, funding for "domestic advocacy activities and lobbying of federal, provincial and municipal governments," remained strictly ineligible.[46] This retreat from funding women's advocacy and research organizations, a feature of the Canadian system since the mid-1970s, triggered a quick succession of closures of long-established feminist research and advocacy organizations, among them the well-respected Canadian Research Institute for the Advancement of Women. One further pillar of the Women's Program, the provision of funding to targeted vulnerable populations, also quietly ended in 2008–9 when SWC policy changed such that it "no longer identifies priority populations (Aboriginal, seniors, ethnic and immigrant minorities); it works to bring about the advancement of all women in Canada."[47] This significant recasting of the "Canadian woman" as race, class and age-neutral aligns perfectly with citizenship ideals that underpin neo-liberal principles and negate the need for social policy sensitive to diversity and difference.[48]

Brodie and Bakker argue that the Harper government's "delegitimization, dismantling, and disappearance of gender equity as a goal of public policy"[49] derives from the particular coalition that merged to create the Conservative Party, including "neo-liberals, devotees of Leo Strauss, libertarians, the religious right and advocates of 'family values,'" all of whom were hostile to gender equity.[50] Despite the cover provided by arguments around fiscal responsibility, however, they point to the on-line campaign against Status of Women Canada launched by the right-wing, social conservative group, REAL Women, which encouraged readers during the summer of 2006 to lobby the Prime Minister and MPs "to offset this national feminist effort to protect feminist control of Canada" and then heaped praise on the government for the funding cuts leveled later that same year.[51] Brodie and Bakker conclude that even though the Harper government justified its restructuring of SWC in terms of economic efficiency rather than anti-feminism, the move still succeeded in cutting "the transmission lines that had been cultivated between the women's movement and the federal state."[52]

The incrementalist strategy of systematically dismantling the 'women's state' by appealing to a 'common sense' approach to enhancing fiscal accountability rather than through an overt social conservative attack on feminist goals extended to dismantling gender policy units and downgrading gender mainstreaming activities throughout much of the federal government. In 1995, following the Beijing UN Fourth World Conference on Women, the Liberal government adopted *Setting the Stage for the Next*

Century: The Federal Plan on Gender Equality outlining Canada's vision of gender mainstreaming and introducing a required vetting of all programs and policies from federal departments and agencies to assess their gender impact. Mounting such a strategy was highly significant, as it constituted a more systematic approach to pursuing gender equality through public policymaking than had ever been attempted previously in Canada. With its promise of generating efficient policy design and outcomes, gender mainstreaming was deemed an appropriate vehicle for governments to maintain their commitments to gender equality while ensuring cost-effective and efficient public policy tailored to the new Canadian realities.[53]

At this time, Status of Women Canada was charged with furnishing other departments with gender analysis tools, training materials and procedures, as well as monitoring the overall implementation of gender mainstreaming through the federal state. SWC's new role included the promotion of GBA externally through interdepartmental committees, reviewing and commenting on Cabinet submissions and Ministerial and departmental presentations to Standing Committees of the House of Commons and the Senate, and developing training seminars for use across the public service. Much of this work in the late 1990s and early 2000s involved liaison both with long-established gender policy units within departments such as Human Resources Development Canada and the Canadian International Development Agency and a network of newer gender policy units within departments such as Health Canada, Foreign Affairs and International Trade, and Indian and Northern Affairs Canada. Although the efficacy of Gender-Based Analysis in achieving more gender-equitable policy outcomes is highly debatable, this short period did mark one in which gender analysis gained visibility and some measure of legitimacy in particular departments.[54]

By 2005, however, the Standing Committee on the Status of Women found that GBA lacked sufficient mechanisms for accountability and sustainability and recommended concrete measures to ensure its implementation across government. In the last year of the Liberals' tenure, Status of Women Canada allocated $6.2 million specifically to Gender-Based Policy Analysis.[55] But by 2007, one of Canada's most vocal feminist coalitions, the Feminist Alliance for International Action, characterized the state of gender mainstreaming within Canada as a "veritable abyss" given the quiet closure of several gender policy units, the Harper government's failure to craft a new coordinating framework for gender equality following the end of the previous Agenda for Gender Equality (2000–05) and the Conservative government's mantra that gender equality has already been achieved in Canada.[56]

Within SWC, a shift from "individual to institutional capacity building to ensure the sustainability of GBA across government" began in 2006 with the decision to concentrate GBA efforts in central agencies, specifically in conjunction with the Privy Council Office, the Treasury Board Secretariat and the Department of Finance.[57] The 2006–07 estimates show that the status of SWC's Gender-Based Analysis and Accountability Directorate was downgraded significantly as the budgetary commitment to gender-based policy analysis dropped precipitously to $1.1 million with the emphasis now placed squarely on departments to manage gender analysis themselves.[58] More recently, the Gender-Based Analysis and Accountability Directorate was renamed the Gender-Based Analysis Support Services, indicative of its narrowed focused on a "Train the Trainer program" designed to support domestic and international training on GBA and the new philosophy emphasizing a concentration on offering support for central agencies in building their GBA capacity. SWC's 2008–09 Plans and Priorities outlines a further drift away from the agency's previous orientation towards a focus on: building strategic partnerships, particularly with central agencies; funding specific projects through the Women's Program; developing accountability mechanisms to monitor and measure progress; and strengthening the organizational structure of the Department to ensure its accountabilities mesh with overall Government of Canada accountabilities.[59] The message is that individual departments and agencies must now assume responsibility for their own gender work, but the absence of even modest funding and any meaningful progress on accountability mechanisms leaves little chance for any further substantive progress on gender-sensitive policymaking at the departmental level. Given that SWC itself noted in 1998 that successful gender mainstreaming requires "…a national machinery with a clearly defined role, mechanisms to support gender equality with other government departments, intergovernmental collaborative mechanisms and mechanisms for information exchange and collaboration"[60] it appears that the conditions necessary for institutional leadership in gender mainstreaming by SWC have evaporated, particularly in light of the Harper government's dismissal of gender issues (at least domestically) as anachronistic in an 'already-equal' Canadian society.

Despite the 2006 campaign assurances about honouring Canada's commitments to gender equality, within two years the Harper government faced harsh and embarrassing criticism from the United Nations Committee on the Elimination of All Forms of Discrimination against Women (CEDAW) and Canada's country ranking had tumbled from 14th in 2006 to a disappointing 31st in the 2008 Global Gender Gap Report published by the World Economic Forum. In the case of the UN's response to Canada's periodic report on CEDAW, the Committee expressed serious concern about Canada's record on human rights, particularly with respect to cuts in social assistance that disproportionately affect vulnerable populations, and appealed to the Canadian government to "urgently carry out thorough investigations of the cases of aboriginal women who have gone missing or been murdered in recent decades."[61] The World Economic Forum, in turn, cited losses in educational attainment and political empowerment as responsible for Canada's poor showing.[62]

This erosion of Canada's substantive policy commitments to women's equality during the Harper years and the attention drawn to that dismal record in global fora counterpoints a trend of consistent attention to, and, arguably, an expansion of, "taking gender on the road" as an integral element of Canada's promotion of good governance abroad. As Claire Turenne Sjolander observes: "Canada has prided itself on the leadership role it has shown in moving forward the agenda for gender mainstreaming in international policy and practice ... the Canadian commitment to gender mainstreaming has been – to say the least – rhetorically robust."[63] Similarly, the Liberal-appointed Expert Panel on Accountability Mechanisms for Gender Equality that reported in December 2005, just prior to the first Harper electoral victory, drew attention to the gap between Canada's rhetorical commitment to promoting gender equality abroad and the fact that although our "foreign aid policies derive strength from gender-based analysis, there is no comparative action across the domestic policies of the Government of Canada."[64]

What is noteworthy is that even as it relies on arguments about sound fiscal management to ignore internationally-voiced concerns about Canada's declining record on gender equality, the Harper government continues to position itself as a champion of gender equality on the global stage while radically re-drawing the boundaries of the relationship between women's equality groups and the state in domestic politics. In fact, the rhetoric of gender equality as already achieved "at home," facilitates its deployment "on the road" within foreign policy agendas for other purposes; most overtly at the moment to support our military campaign in Afghanistan.

Canada's foreign aid program, administered through the Canadian International Development Agency, systematically supported women's role in development as early as 1976 when CIDA first released guidelines on Women and Development. A gender unit and a policy advocating the "integration of Women in Development" in all programming" followed in 1984.[65] In 1999, CIDA adopted its current policy on gender equality, explicitly linking gender equality to sustainable international development. Over the course of the last three decades, in fact, Canada's reputation as a major "exporter" of gender equality and, more recently, its explicit mandate of prioritizing gender equality as a "cross-cutting theme" across the departmental priorities of governance, health, education, private sector development and environmental sustainability enhanced its reputation on the global stage. The 2005 International Policy Statement released after an extensive foreign policy review identified gender equality as a key initiative: "Canada has been a leader among donors in promoting gender equality, both as a global issue and as a practical matter in implementing programs and projects. Across all five sectors, gender equality will be systematically integrated into programming. The focus will be on equal participation of women as decision makers, on their full human rights and on their equal access to and control over community and household assets."[66]

The IPS went on to add that gender equality "reflects the values and interests of Canadians, as well as being [an]area in which Canada has the experience and expertise to make a difference."⁶⁷ Between 1998 and 2005, for example, CIDA disbursed funds totaling $792.8 million for initiatives that had equality between women and men either as the principal objective and result ... or had equality between women and men as one of its objectives." ⁶⁸ Currently, Canada funds close to 200 international projects containing a gender equality component.

Given its dismal domestic record on gender equality, it is interesting that the Harper government continues its strategic reliance on gender equality in certain foreign policy areas.⁶⁹ For example, almost immediately following the Conservative government's announcement of cuts to Status of Women Canada in September 2006, Canadians saw television images of then-Minister for International Cooperation, Josée Verner, visiting Kabul, Afghanistan to announce government spending of $14.5 million on a girls' education initiative and pledging additional funding towards micro-credit initiatives to help women establish their own businesses selling and growing fruits and vegetables.⁷⁰ Upon her return to Canada, Verner explained: "I have spoken with Afghan women in Ottawa, as well as in Montréal... I met the Minister of the Status of Women in Kabul. I met the Director of the Status of Women in Kandahar. All of these women are asking us to continue our involvement in Afghanistan. These women need international aid and they need Canadian aid. And this aid cannot reach them, particularly in the south, without the security provided by our soldiers."⁷¹

Later, once Verner and Oda switched their portfolios and Verner assumed the position of as Minister Responsible for the Status of Women, she reiterated that "Canada has brightened the future for over two million girls in a country where equality remains an urgent goal. It is a point of pride, that, thanks to Canada's financial aid, women's centres have opened throughout the country. The women, their families and their communities depend on our continued aid and support."⁷² Indeed, Stephen Harper himself has deployed the discourse of women's equality as a rationale for Canada's continued involvement in the NATO mission. Harper highlighted the plight of the Afghan women and Canada's commitment to Afghanistan on International Women's Day 2008, for example, when he met with a visiting delegation of Afghan women parliamentarians and Canadian women active in Afghan women's rights initiatives.⁷³

Canada continues to highlight Afghan women's equality struggles and CIDA's 2008–9 Estimates, for example, flags small loan and saving services for over 280,000 Afghan women as one of the agency's major achievements in 2006–7.⁷⁴ But despite the fact that Afghanistan now constitutes Canada's largest aid program with 1.2 billion over ten years, ⁷⁵ the specific commitment to Afghan women is, at best, limited. By 2006, Ottawa's pledged assistance to

Afghan women earmarked only $2 million of its total funding directly for women.[76] And despite the high profile announcements about aid for women, some Canadian programs have already been discontinued, including the Vancouver-based IMPAC project supporting women's radio stations and a CARE Canada project that fed and employed 10,000 widows in Kabul. CIDA was forced to reinstate this latter program for one year, after women marched in protests through the streets of Kabul.[77]

Cindy Hanson exposes the irony of this situation in her research about the pressure on the short-staffed Gender-Based Analysis unit of Status of Women Canada to respond to increasing international requests for training because Canada's reputation in the area of gender mainstreaming remains strong, despite the hollowing out of SWC and GBA initiatives.[78] Such deployment of gender equality talk by the Conservatives to shore up support for controversial foreign policy decisions is, in turn, equally effective as a strategy to cast Canadian women's movements' demands for increased funding to address gender inequality at home as excessive when compared with the life situations of women in the developing world. In short, the Harper government's success to date in appeasing its social conservative wing, using fiscal arguments to advance its incremental approach to dismantling women's policy machinery, and simultaneously invoking women's rights struggles abroad to support its military priorities is a skillful balancing act that is eroding hard-fought gender equality gains in Canada.

NOTES

1 Elizabeth Thompson, "American Strategist Teaches Tories Tips on Keeping Power," Canwest News Service, Montreal Gazette, 6 May 2007, accessed through Canada.com, 12 December 2008.
2 Table on the Abortion Rights Coalition of Canada website, www.arcc-cdac.ca, accessed November 2008. Specific names of caucus members in the different categories are listed here.
3 "Canadians Uphold Abortion Policy, Split on Health Care System's Role," released 20 June 2008, www.angus-reid.com; accessed 8 December 2008.
4 This mantra was repeated throughout the 2006 campaign; check the Abortion Rights Coalition of Canada website, arcc-cdac.ca, for reprints of news stories on this.
5 The quote cited from a *Globe and Mail* story published before the election was, "Part of the control mentality comes from having a caucus with orangutans in it. In Mulroney's time, we could send MPs off on some fact-finding mission and keep them busy, but with a minority they're around all the time." The author added his own comment that "the subject was abortion, an issue that refuses to go away." Geoffrey Stevens, "Harper Finds Himself Handcuffed with Minority Status," *Guelph Mercury*, opinions, 12 January 2009, accessed at http://news.guelphmercury.com/Opinions.

6 All references in this paragraph are drawn from the Abortion Rights Coalition of Canada website, arcc-cdac.ca, "Conservative Minority Poses a Danger to Abortion Rights," 23 June 2006, website accessed 11 December 2008.
7 Ibid, citing the Campaign Life Coalition's newsletter, www.lifesitenews.com, 9 January 2006.
8 ARCC website, www.arcc-cdac.ca; accessed 10 December 2008.
9 Joyce Arthur, ARCC, "Expect a Bill C-484 Clone Soon," 2 December 2008, posted on www.arcc-cdac.ca; accessed 11 December 2008.
10 The designation of anti-choice or pro-life clearly reflects the political stance of those making the description. The side of Canadian social movements and politics that supports the 1988 *Morgentaler* decision increasing women's access to legal abortion across Canada terms itself pro-choice, and the other side wishing to restrict that access anti-choice. The side of the question interested in reducing what it sees as the "easy" access to contraception and abortion in Canadian society terms itself the pro-life side. Obviously, each side of the issue sees the labeling as highly contested and seeks to have control over its own designation.
11 ARCC, "Conservative Minority Poses a Danger to Abortion Rights," 23 June 2006, www.arcc-cdac.ca; accessed 11 December 2008.
12 John Jalsevac, "Canadian Prime Minister Again Promises He Won't Re-open Abortion Debate," www.lifesitenews.com, 5 January 2009.
13 Lloyd Mackey, "Ottawa Watch: Cross-Party Faith Groups for All Tastes," dated 18 October (no year), www.canadianchristianity.com; accessed 11 December 2008.
14 See the Guttmacher Institute, www.guttmacher.org, for statistics on abortion in the US and Canada across age groups, and the Abortion Rights Coalition of Canada website for Canadian data, www.arcc-cdac.ca.
15 MP Maurice Vellacott, quoted on LifeSitenews.com 16 April 2008, reprinted by Abortion Rights Coalition of Canada, www.arcc-cdac.ca the same day.
16 "Refusal Clauses: Dangerous to Health," Issue Brief released 2 July 2008 by ProChoice America, www.ProChoiceAmerica.org: accessed 12 August 2008.
17 Protection of Conscience Project (Canada), www.consciencelaws.org; accessed 9 December 2008.
18 Protection of Conscience Project, accessed 10 December 2008.
19 Susan W. Hammond, "Informal Congressional Caucuses and Agenda-Setting," *Western Politics Quarterly* 38, 4 (December 1985): 583–605.
20 Americans United for Life, www.aul.org, accessed 11 December 2008.
21 www.conscienceproject.ca, accessed 12 December 2008.
22 Canadians for Choice, "Access Denied," 2006, p. 50; www.canadiansforchoice.ca, accessed 10 December 2008.
23 www.mauricevellacott.ca; accessed 11 December 2008.
24 www.capss.com and www.saskatoonpregnancy.com, accessed 11 December 2008.
25 Barbara Devaney, Amy Johnson, Rebecca Maynard, and Chris Trenholm of Mathematica Policy Research inc, "The Evaluation of Abstinence Education Programs Funded under Title V Section 510: an Interim Report" (no year given), submitted to

Meredith Kelsey, Office of the Assistant Secretary for Planning and Evaluation, U.S. Department of Health and Human Services, http://aspe.hhs.gov/hsp/abstinence02; accessed 11 December 2008.

26 Thomas B. Edsall, "Grants Flow to Bush Allies on Social Issues," *Washington Post*, 22 March 2006, A01, www.washingtonpost.com; accessed 11 December 2008.

27 The five Cabinet agencies were: Attorney General (Justice Department), Education, Labor, Health and Human Services and Housing and Urban Development.

28 Community HIV/AIDS Mobilization Project (CHAMP), "HHS Watch," November 2006, www.champ.org, accessed 5 January 2009.

29 www.guttmacher.org; accessed 11 December 2008.

30 Ibid.

31 Ibid.

32 Samantha King, "Designer Babies, Stem Cells and the Market for Genetics: The Limits of the Assisted Human Reproduction Act," *Canadian Journal of Communication* 22, no. 3–4, (2007): 613–21.

33 Laura Eggertson, "New Reproductive Technology Board Belies Expert Selection Process," *Canadian Medical Association Journal* (online) 7 February 2007, www.cmaj.ca, accessed 10 January 2009.

34 From Assisted Human Reproduction Canada, "Assisted Human Reproduction Canada (AHRC) was formally established by an Order in Council on 12 January 2006. AHRC's function is to administer the *Assisted Human Reproduction Act* (*An Act Respecting Assisted Human Reproduction and Related Research*, S.C. 2004, c. 2) on behalf of Canada's Minister of Health. Its mission is to protect and promote the health, safety, dignity and rights of donors, patients and offspring born of AHR technologies, and to foster the application of ethical principles in relation to assisted human reproduction. It will do this by becoming a centre of expertise in administering a comprehensive legislative and regulatory framework governing acceptable controlled activities in Canada." Part of the agency's remit as described on the website is to oversee "controlled activities" which were defined in the Assisted Human Reproduction Act, such as those relating to in vitro fertilization and the "keeping and handling of gametes, genomes and embryos", www.ahrc-pac.gc.ca; accessed 12 January 2009.

35 Samantha King, "Designer Babies, Stem Cells and the Market."

36 Abby Lippman and Jeff Nisker, "Health Canada Delay Endangers Women," June 2006, Canadian Center for Policy Alternatives, www.policyalternatives.ca; accessed 14 December 2008.

37 Elizabeth Thompson, "American Strategist Teaches Tories Tips on Keeping Power," *Montreal Gazette*, 7 May 2006; accessed on Canada.com, 12 December 2008. In addition to meeting with Prime Minister Harper, Luntz spoke at this conference, the Civitas Society, an organization which Thompson describes as "having close ties to Harper." Both Tom Flanagan and Ian Broadie, chief Harper advisers, were either founders or directors of the organization. Two active Parliamentary Pro-Life Caucus members were there, Maurice Vellacott in attendance and Garry Breitkreutz on the program (about gun ownership). According to Thompson, other topics discussed at

the meeting were: euthanasia, judicial activism by the Supreme Court, "the Moral Justification for War," electoral reform and the future of Canadian cities.

38 Cited in M. Young, "Women Let Down: Government Cuts to Status of Women Canada Budget Betray Our UN Commitments and Harper's Words," *Vancouver Sun*, 7 December 2006, A17.
39 Status of Women Canada, *2006–07 Departmental Performance Report*, (Ottawa, 2007), 3.
40 Minister Beverley Oda, *Evidence of the Standing Committee on the Status of Women*, Meeting No. 15, Thursday, 5 October 2006.
41 "Tories Shutting Status of Women Offices" CBC News, Thursday, 30 November 2006, www.cbc.ca/canada/story/2006/11/29/status-women.html. The Minister's announcement that twelve of sixteen regional offices were closing is somewhat misleading in that the national Ottawa office also serves as the Ontario regional office. In fact, there are only three regional offices still open, located in Moncton, Edmonton and Montreal.
42 SWC, *2006–7 Departmental Performance Report*, (Ottawa, 2007), 7.
43 Minister Beverley Oda, *Evidence of the Standing Committee on the Status of Women*, Meeting No. 15, Thursday, 5 October 2006.
44 SWC, *2006–07 Departmental Performance Report*, 7.
45 Speaking Notes for the Honourable Beverley J. Oda for an appearance before the Standing Committee on the Status of Women, www.swc-cfc.gc.ca/med/spe-dis/2007/0201-eng.html; accessed 1 February 2007.
46 Status of Women Canada, *Women's Partnership Fund Information Guide* (2008), 7.
47 SWC, *2008–9 Report on Plans and Priorities*, 10.
48 On this point, see Alexandra Dobrowolsky, "Interrogating 'Invisibilization' and 'Instrumentalization': Women and Current Citizenship Trends in Canada" *Citizenship Studies* 12, 5 (2008) 465–79.
49 Janine Brodie and Isabella Bakker, *Where Are the Women? Gender Equity, Budgets and Canadian Public Policy* (Ottawa: Canadian Centre for Policy Alternatives, 2008), 113.
50 Ibid.,115.
51 Ibid., 116.
52 Ibid., 117.
53 For a discussion of the implications of gender mainstreaming for women's movements in Canada, see L. Pauline Rankin and Krista D. Wilcox, "De-gendering Engagement?: Gender Mainstreaming, Women's Movements, and the Canadian Federal State" *Atlantis* 29, 1 (Fall, 2004), 52–60.
54 One often-cited example of a Canadian policy 'success story' using gender mainstreaming is the example of Citizenship and Immigration Canada's GBA legislation. On this point and for a fuller assessment of gender mainstreaming, consult Olena Hankivsky, "Gender Mainstreaming in Canada and Australia: A Comparative Analysis" *Policy and Society* 27 (2008), 69–81.
55 SWC, *2005–06 Report on Plans and Priorities*.
56 Presentation by Executive Director of FAFIA to Bangladesh Delegation, Policy Leadership and Advocacy for Gender Equality Project, Ottawa, 23 November 2007.
57 SWC, *2006–07 Report on Plans and Priorities*, (Ottawa, 2006), 7.

58 Ibid., 9.
59 SWC, *2008–09 Report on Plans and Priorities* (Ottawa, 2008), 6.
60 SWC, *Canadian Experiences with Gender Mainstreaming* (Ottawa 1998), 2.
61 United Nations, Committee on the Elimination of Discrimination against Women, Forty-second session 20-October – 7 November 2008, *Concluding Observations of the Committee on the Elimination of Discrimination Against Women – Canada*, 7.
62 Ricardo Hausmann, Laura D. Tyson, Saadia Zahidi, *The Global Gender Gap Report* (Geneva, World Economic Forum, 2008), 54.
63 Claire Turenne Sjolander, "Canadian Foreign Policy: Does Gender Matter?" *Canadian Foreign Policy* 12, 1 (Spring 2005)19, 20.
64 Canada, Expert Panel on Accountability Mechanisms for Gender Equality, Final Report, *Equality for Women: Beyond the Illusion*, (Ottawa, December 2005), 15.
65 Lucie Bazinet, Tamara Sequeira, and Julie Delahanty, "Promoting Institutional Change: CIDA's Framework for Assessing Gender Equality Results" *Development* 49, 1 (2006), 104.
66 Canada. *Canada's International Policy State: A Role of Pride and Influence in the World* (Ottawa, Government of Canada, 2005), 25.
67 Ibid., 24.
68 Canada. Canadian International Development Agency, *2006–07 Report on Plans and Priorities* (Ottawa, 2006).
69 CIDA's Equality between Women and Men Policy is scheduled for a major evaluation in 2008–9.
70 "Josée Verner Visits Afghanistan Amid Violence" *Ottawa Citizen*, 22 October 2006.
71 Speech of the Honourable Josée Verner, Minister of International Cooperation, International Cooperation Days, www.acdi-cida.gc.ca/CIDAWEB/acdicida.nsf/En/RAC-1030163913–TE3; accessed 31 October 2006.
72 Speech for the Honorable Josée Verner, Standing Committee on the Status of Women, www.swc-cfc.gc.ca/med-spe-dis.2008/0205–eng.html; accessed 5 February 2008.
73 During this same visit, however, the Prime Minister's Office cancelled a training session on gender mainstreaming for the Afghan delegation (which they had requested) when the PMO learned that the seminar would be facilitated by representatives from the Feminist Alliance for International Action, a coalition highly critical of the government's role in Afghanistan.
74 Canada, Canadian International Development Agency, *Estimates 2008–09 Part III: Report on Plans and Priorities* (Ottawa, 2008), 3.
75 Ibid., 1. Also see the chapter in this volume by Brown and Jackson.
76 Susan Riley, "Helping Afghanistan?" *Ottawa Citizen*, 25 October 2006, A16.
77 Lauryn Oates, "The Plight of Afghan Women for Security and Democracy" *Horizons* 20, 1 (Summer 2006), 21.
78 Cindy Hanson, "Canadian Gender-Based Analysis Training in South Africa," *International Feminist Journal of Politics* 9, 2 (June 2007), 201.

11 Where Is VIA Going? A Case Study of Managing a Commercial Crown Corporation

MALCOM G. BIRD

For most of its history, traveling by train was the only viable means to move about Canada's vast and sparsely populated landscape. Prior to the Second World War – and even well into the postwar era – there simply were few suitable or affordable alternatives to train travel. Canada's paved, pan-national networks of roads, its air travel system, and widespread private car ownership system are relatively recent, postwar developments. Train travel and railroad development more generally, then, have a critical place in the development of this nation. Not surprisingly, state involvement in both the construction and operation of the country's two largest railroads, privately owned Canadian Pacific Railways (CP) and the former Crown Corporation, Canadian National (CN), likewise, have also been integral to our nation's history. Whether it was through the provision of land grants to complete the transcontinental line in 1886 or the outright public ownership of CN for most of the last century, governments have always played key role in the railway sector.[1] Although CN was privatized in 1995, the federal government still owns and operates a passenger service provider, VIA Rail. Over the last forty years, however, few Canadians have chosen to travel by train, opting instead to use cars or, for long distances, planes. The slow, steady decline of train travel on VIA Rail is no accident, but rather is the result of deliberate action – or often inaction – by successive federal governments to undermine VIA's attractiveness as viable method of transportation.

This chapter will focus on VIA Rail.[2] It will argue that VIA Rail is an organization beset by problems, and that these troubles have limited its ability to provide a high quality transportation experience to its customers. The net result is slow and steady decline of this organization over its thirty-year history. This is not to fault VIA itself, since its management is restricted by a number of factors and interests that are largely outside of its control. Its status is principally due to actions of its former parent, CN, and especially, the federal government, each of which has a vested interest in a marginally operated VIA Rail. Political interference in VIA's operations as well as institutional neglect are the two fundamental problems facing Canada's passenger rail service. Its problems, and potential solutions to these problems, interestingly, have been examined in a number of research projects over VIA's thirty-year lifespan, making much of this chapter's policy findings unoriginal; what is unclear, however, is why VIA continues to exist at all in its current form and why successive governments have treated it with such indifference.[3] VIA Rail is an institution that has been cast adrift by its political masters. Only fundamental change in both the governance and financing structures of VIA can rectify its problems. Until that happens, Canadians will continue to be served by a marginal passenger rail service.

The chapter will be organized in the following manner. The first section will provide a brief historical sketch of VIA Rail. It will outline VIA's historical roots, its thirty-year life and its contemporary state of affairs. It will also provide a number of reasons why VIA continues to be publicly owned. The next section will articulate the reasons why VIA is a marginal transportation provider, and demonstrate that fault lies with the federal government and CN, both of whom have a vested interest a marginal VIA. The final section will elucidate some potential solutions to VIA's problems by examining the fate of the Liquor Control Board of Ontario (LCBO), explaining how that Crown Corporation evolved as an organization and, more specifically, how it was able to influence its fate at the hands of its own political masters, demonstrating that some important insights can be gleaned from its evolution. A few concluding remarks will complete the chapter.

VIA AT 30: ITS HISTORY AND CURRENT CONDITION

Via was created in 1977 as an amalgamation of both CP and CN's passenger rail services and equipment. CP had largely removed itself from the passenger service business by the mid-1970s. Accordingly, most of VIA's business and equipment came from CN which, at the time, was carrying five times as many passengers as its private sector counterpart. The decision to create VIA was partly due to a reorientation of CN towards increasing profit levels, but both it and CP were eager to dispose of their money-losing passenger enterprises. Through much of the postwar period, passenger operations had only been possible by virtue of significant subsidies from the federal government. Even with subsidies, CN and CP claimed that they did not adequately cover the costs associated with providing passenger service.

For much of its early life, VIA essentially operated as a division of the publicly owned CN, emulating its corporate structure, including its patronage-appointed board of directors.[4] Its capital and operational budgets were (and still are) subject to scrutiny by Treasury Board. Initially, it had no statutory basis. It was officially made a Crown Corporation in 1978 by an order-in-council.[5] Over the next ten years or so, VIA acquired other infrastructure associated with its business, such as railway stations and employees, from both CP and CN.[6] Accordingly, from its inception VIA Rail was comprised of an eclectic collection of old equipment and staff from two companies that were no longer interested in providing the services it was undertaking to provide.

While an order-in-council created VIA Rail in the late 1970s, this does not mean that those who created it had a clear conception of VIA's function or role in Canada's transportation plan. Specific enabling legislation was never introduced for it, and VIA itself, for all intents and purposes, does not have a definitive and consistent mandate from its political masters as to what – exactly – its purpose is and how to go about fulfilling it. The nebulous nature of its existence is, in fact, at the heart of its problems: no government – Liberal or Conservative – has expressed a long-term, holistic vision for what it would like to see happen at VIA Rail. Few public agencies would make the following comment in their annual report nearly twenty years after their inception: "But VIA cannot fulfill that role, or take advantage of the opportunities for growth, unless we – as a country – are ready and able to pursue new and innovative ways of delivering passenger rail services. To grow, there must be some major changes: a clear mandate for VIA Rail, an appropriate legal and corporate environment, fair access to the rail infrastructure, and access to private sector investment for new equipment."[7] As will be explained shortly, without a clear mandate, VIA is subjected to political interference in its operational and strategic decisions that hinder its ability to efficiently allocate its resources to provide high-value passenger rail service to Canadians.

Any criticism of an organization requires some sort of benchmark to which to compare it. Ideally, with respect to passenger rail service, such a benchmark would be VIA Rail providing Canadians with relatively cheap, reliable and frequent service within the central Canadian corridor. (It would also continue to provide service to remote communities and would provide some sort of transcontinental service, targeting the tourist market, but the frequency of service might need some sort of review). Focusing on corridor service makes sense, given that the central Canadian corridor is the only place in the country where there is sufficient population densities and infrastructure to make transit by rail competitive with other means of travel, principally travel by plane, bus or automobile. Currently, VIA's service in the corridor, as will be explained, is relatively lacklustre. Traveling between central Canadian cites by rail would be a viable option for average Canadians – perhaps even their first choice – were service improved. Instead, today, flying, or even renting a car and driving, are more economical and convenient ways to move about within central Canada. High-speed rail, like that which is available in continental Europe and Japan, would perhaps be the most ideal mode of rail transport for this purpose, but the probability of its development in Canada (despite countless government feasibility studies) is near zero. Given that the federal government has shown itself unwilling to provide VIA Rail with a clear and concise mandate or the necessary funding to carry out its tasks, it is almost certain that the political will to spend the multiple billions of dollars required to build a high-speed rail network in central Canada would likewise be absent.

Why Public Ownership?

There are a number of reasons why VIA continues to be a publicly owned and operated entity. As a mode of energy-efficient transport, VIA provides intercity travel in the Windsor-Quebec City corridor. This service segment accounts for approximately 70 per cent of its business. It also provides year-round, coast-to-coast service across Canada on its intercontinental trains. These train routes, as well as much of the corridor train travel, are popular with tourists, many of whom come from places with sophisticated train networks, the lack of which in Canada could be seen as a bit of a national embarrassment. Very importantly, VIA also provides access to nine remote communities that otherwise would not have a year-round land-based transportation link, and where road construction is not economically feasible. These are the main transportation related reasons for VIA Rail's continued existence, and that fact that the objectives it must meet are so disparate (corridor travel, coast-to-coast service, remote community service) continues to militate in favour of VIA being kept in public hands. There are other more ephemeral, yet equally important rationales that support the continued public ownership of VIA.

Despite criticisms to the contrary,[8] VIA provides service that is accessible to the disabled and the elderly, and traveling by train is a relatively energy efficient means of transportation. More people on trains, in theory at least, implies that fewer people are using less energy efficient and more pollution-producing modes of transportation such as cars and planes, both of which require accompanying highway and airport infrastructure. VIA, accordingly, provides a certain amount of congestion relief for other means of transportation. It also serves an important national unity purpose in that it links the country from coast to coast (to coast) and, in the corridor, connects English and French Canada. It is a fully bilingual organization and its head office is in Montreal.

VIA Rail is the last vestige of passenger rail service in Canada, and trains, in general, and travel by train, in particular, have a strong and loyal historical or 'heritage' pull for among many Canadians – especially older ones. Soldiers went off to war by train and many immigrants saw this land for the first time from inside a rail car. This strong emotional attachment to rail travel, while not necessarily supported by individual consumers purchasing rail tickets, remains a key reason why passenger rail remains publicly provided.

Perhaps, as well, VIA continues to be a Crown Corporation because privatizing or altering the passenger rail market would require too much political capital for relatively little political gain. Governments, after all, only have a limited amount of time and energy to dedicate to solving issues proactively, and successive governments might well have chosen to direct their resources elsewhere. As mentioned previously, VIA provides ground transportation to a number of remote communities that otherwise would not have a viable transport link; if VIA were to disappear, the federal government would still be charged with providing some sort of ground transportation service. Transcontinental service, while relatively marginal, still provides many cities with train service that they would not have otherwise. In its current form, VIA's more lucrative corridor routes subsidize services provided elsewhere. (A similar argument applies to Canada Post, which provides postal services to the entire nation, regardless of cost or utilization rates). Obviously, VIA exists today, but it is not entirely clear how it has managed to survive the past thirty-years in its current form. As will be explained a little later in the chapter, the array and political power of its foes are significant and, in some respects, appear to overwhelm efforts that support a publicly-funded passenger rail service.

VIA: The Last Thirty Years, 1978–2008

VIA's thirty-year history is one of institutional deterioration. Its decline has not, however, been on a constant, linear trajectory. It is better described as a downward sloping line with marked upward and downward oscillations due to sharp government cutbacks followed by the occasional injections of new capital. When evaluated over a thirty-year period, the portrait of VIA Rail as a transportation organization is not a positive one. An examination of key operating statistics tells most of this story (see the appendix to this chapter). In 1980, for example, VIA served 7.6 million passengers and carried those individuals 1.928 billion miles. To do this it received $320.1 million as an annual operating subsidy and $94.6 million to fund its capital acquisitions from the federal government. Twenty years later, in 2000, VIA provided transport for 3.96 million passengers and moved those passengers a total of 942 million miles. To help fund these services, it received $164.4 million as an annual operating subsidy and $45.9 million for capital improvements. The decline in passenger volumes has been dramatic, and is the result of reductions in train frequencies as well as in cities served by rail service; such reductions, not surprisingly, are causatively related to the nominal and real decline in both VIA's operational and capital cash allocations from its political masters. Since 2000, little has changed. In 2007, VIA carried 4.18 million passengers a total of 874 million miles while receiving $200.4 million as an annual operational subsidy, and a paltry $12.4 million for capital expenses.

Note, as well, that during a number of years in this period, VIA's capital and operational subsides were dramatically reduced year-over-year. In 1983, the government provided a total of $597 million in operational and capital funding. The next year, the funding was reduced to a total of $473 million. While it received $631.6 million from the federal government in 1985, from that point monies received from the government decrease considerably. Total payments, for instance, from the government in 1993 were $332.8 million. Payments fell to $212.4 million in 1997 a mere four years later. Take note that in 1985 VIA employed 4,178 people, and then in the following year, almost 1,200 people were added to the payroll, despite the fact that VIA received $125 million less in subsidies from the federal government in 1986. These employees were transferred from CN and CP's passenger operations, but regardless where they came from, few corporations – public or private – experience such a drastic increase in employment levels while, at the same time, having their income reduced considerably year-over-year. This is just one of many unique circumstances this corporate entity has had to manage over the course of its lifetime.

Shrinking operational subsidies are one major problem VIA faces. However, a bigger problem is scant or erratic funds provided for capital expenditures, like new rolling stock or track improvements. Since 1997, for instance, operational subsidies have averaged $174.8 million per year, but average funding from the federal government for capital expenses has been $39.37 million (most of this funding was received between 2000 and 2004). It is important to note, as well, that in 1998, 1999 and 2006, VIA received no capital funding from the government whatsoever.[9] Significant reductions in VIA's capital and operational subsidies from the federal government are probably the most tangible indicators of the neglect it has received, as an organization, from its political masters. An analysis of VIA's operating statistics illustrates that moving people around Canada by rail is not a priority for any federal governments.

Mediocre Service

Limited operating and capital subsidies as well as indifference on behalf of the government, not surprisingly, constrains VIA's ability to provide a high-value consumer experience. This is particularly apparent on its corridor service. If you are not a student, senior or have not purchased your ticket two-weeks in advance, taking VIA is quite expensive. Travel times are also restricted. On a weekday, between Canada's two largest cities, Montreal and Toronto, VIA offers only six departure trains. In comparison, Air Canada has 23 daily flights, WestJet has eight flights and Porter Airlines (a luxury upstart airline that operates from Toronto's downtown island airport) has ten flights, while Greyhound has seven daily bus departures. An additional annoyance is that fact that there are no continuous trains that pass through the two major cities, Toronto and Montreal. Traveling directly from London, Ontario, to Montreal or from Ottawa to Quebec City on one train, for example, is impossible. Instead passengers must get off in Toronto or Montreal, wait (sometimes for extended periods of time) before boarding the train to their final destination.

Other matters also impede an easy traveling experience. Passengers must line up to board their trains, and boarding is often delayed with little or no explanation. The LRC (Light, Rapid, Comfortable) cars used on many corridor routes are well over twenty years old, show their age and are prone to breakdown – the new Renaissance-class cars provide for a much improved passenger experience, but are used mostly on routes east of Montreal. Union station in Toronto is a beautiful, historic building, but it, like much of Toronto's transit infrastructure, has suffered from years of neglect and as a result, the station has a tired look to it. While not a direct responsibility of VIA (Union Station is owned and operated by the City of Toronto) its condition detracts from one's traveling experience. Baggage service is also limited on VIA's network. This means that passengers are responsible for moving their own baggage, which may not be a problem for many, but limits the extent of travel on its network for those who choose to travel with their pets or those who may have difficulty managing their own luggage. When ordering train tickets online, tickets can be picked up from the station for free, but a $15 fee is required to have them mailed directly to one's address. Customer interfacing and staff quality are acceptable, but hardly exemplary.

However, the biggest factor impeding VIA's ability to provide for a high-quality consumer experience is the tardiness of its trains. VIA's trains are late far more often than not. In 2005, for example, only 36 per cent of its trains were exactly on time.[10] Holdups are sometimes due to weather or mechanical problems (the former being relatively understandable, given Canada's inclement weather, while problems with the latter are causatively related to VIA's relatively old rolling stock), but the vast majority of delays are due to the fact that CN privileges the timely arrival of its own freight trains over those of VIA. Delays are perhaps the most frustrating part of traveling with VIA Rail. Overall, VIA's customer experience is relatively weak. This weakness is made particularly apparent when its service is compared to one of its rivals, Porter Airlines, which provides an excellent traveling experience.

Too Little, Too Late: VIA's Capital Funding

In October 2007, the federal government announced a new capital-funding package for VIA Rail. A close examination of the five-year, $692 million agreement, illustrates, however, that it will not be enough transform this organization. Much of this new money will be spent on improving infrastructure in the corridor (upgrading tracks, sidings and signals and the like) as well as refurbishing 53 F-40 General Motors locomotives and 98 LRC cars, both of which are over twenty years old. The refurbishment of the LRC cars and engines will cost approximately $100 million each ($200 million total). An estimated $200 million will be spent on the track upgrades in the corridor. Station refurbishment, as well as retrofitting 40 of VIA's Renaissance class cars (in order to comply with 2007 ruling from the Supreme Court of Canada, favouring the Council of Canadians with Disabilities over VIA Rail) will, in conjunction with the rolling stock and track upgrades, mean that $516 million of this money is already spoken for. The remainder of the money, $175.9 million, will be directed towards VIA's operating subsidy, and will augment the approximately $169 million per year VIA currently receives from the federal government.[11]

While the new funding from the government has been welcomed by travelers, rail enthusiasts and VIA's management, and will be allocated to improve service in VIA's most important corridor market with the potential to increase on time performance, reliability and track capacity, it will not, by itself, lead to a significantly improved organization. The refurbishment of locomotives and cars, again, are important developments, but refurbishment is very much of a second-best option when compared to the purchase of new equipment. When compared to VIA's past levels of capital (and operational) subsidies, these funds constitute a relatively limited amount of money. When analyzed in light of VIA's tenuous thirty-year lifespan (again, see the appendix) the amount allocated to VIA by the Harper Conservatives will allow VIA to continue operating, but the funds appear as small positive blip on an otherwise downward sloping institutional trajectory.

VIA: Doing Its Best, Given the Circumstances

The purpose of this chapter is to explore the context and condition of VIA Rail, not simply to engage in unjustified criticism of a public institution. Its central aim, in fact, is to demonstrate the extent to which externally imposed constraints are limiting the ability of this organization to properly fulfill its mandate. In light of the limited and erratic funding provided to it, as well as the political interference in its business decisions experienced by it, coupled with hostility it receives from a number of powerful interests, VIA is forced to follow a survival strategy. Within the confines of these external constraints, it does its best to provide transportation services to Canadians. Special attention, then, needs to be paid to the special circumstances that VIA faces externally.

For instance, VIA has markedly increased its efficiency levels. Evidence for this, like its slow decline, can be found in its operating statistics. Despite aggregate reductions in subsidies and ridership numbers, in terms of output per unit cost, VIA has made some remarkable improvements. The best indicator of this is to be found in its increasing yields, which are measures of its passenger revenues per passenger mile (measured in cents per passenger mile). The yield measure captures a number of variables, and shows that VIA is earning more income from passenger fares than it has in the past, and is correspondingly less dependent on government operational subsidies for its revenue. VIA is also making more general improvements in efficiencies by moving more people with fewer expenditures of resources. VIA's yield has grown steadily over the course of its life, from a paltry 7.1 cents per passenger mile in 1980 to a more respectable 30.5 cents per passenger mile in 2007. Reducing service on routes with less ridership is one contributing factor to the growth of its yield factor; however, the other important contributing variable is the fact that VIA has raised fares at levels that exceed the rate of inflation. Doing so has helped VIA to improve its cost recovery record. Unfortunately, such increases have resulted in expensive fares that have reduced VIA's appeal as a means of travel. VIA has also reduced its staffing levels, from roughly 4,500 in 1990 to fewer than 3,000, in 2000.

The creation of VIA's Asset Renewal Fund (ARF) is a good example of its senior management's attempts to increase VIA's degree of self-sufficiency and independence from the government. The ARF was created in the early 1990s when VIA sold off a number of its properties and buildings, such as unused train stations and accompanying land. These assets were no longer required, since VIA had reduced its service areas. The ARF is used to cover budget shortfalls, capital expenses and other discretionary costs associated with VIA operations. VIA's senior management ardently supported its creation of this fund and their right to control it, against strong opposition from within both the Treasury Board Secretariat and the Ministry of Finance. The ARF provides VIA's management with a small pool of capital that it can use to fund small capital projects and cover budgetary shortfalls. Unfortunately, the value of the ARF has shrunk considerably, at the same time as the government has limited the funding it provides to VIA, and VIA has been forced to use its savings to cover capital costs, as well as budget and pension obligation shortfalls. Like VIA's efficiency gains, the ARF provides an example of efforts made by VIA's management to operate this organization within the limiting confines set by its political superiors.

VIA has also made a number of visible improvements to its service. For example, the 140 Renaissance cars, acquired by VIA in 2000, represent a vast improvement over the older LRC cars. These cars have are equipped with one row of double seats and one row of single seats, are well designed and provide for a comfortable travel experience. The purchase of 21 General Electric P42 Genesis locomotives in 2001 is noteworthy as well, since these locomotives are fuel efficient, powerful, and much more reliable than older locomotives. In addition, VIA now offers a travel-miles program and internet access on specific routes, and, as of very recently, it is now possible to purchase better quality food on VIA trains while watching the scenery pass by. Having said this, however, these efforts, while well intentioned, do not provide a solution to the structural problems that VIA faces. This is because the source of these problems lies outside of this Crown Corporation.

OUT OF ITS HANDS: CN, THE FEDERAL GOVERNMENT AND VIA'S FATE

Most of the problems that VIA faces stem from the actions or, more accurately, the inactions of its two major stakeholders: CN and the federal government. The latter's relations with VIA embody a paradoxical mix of political interference combined with general neglect of the Crown Corporation, while the former views VIA trains as a significant burden hindering its own freight operations. It is important to remember, however, that distinctions between VIA and CN for much of VIA's early years were not clear. While officially created in 1978, VIA only gradually assumed responsibility for passenger service, infrastructure, employees and costs from CN over the succeeding ten years (It is important to note, as well, that until CN was privatized in 1995, both it and VIA were federally owned Crown Corporations based in Montreal). What is unclear, however, is whether the hostility faced by VIA comes from within the federal government itself (VIA faces significant hostility from some parts of Transport Canada and Treasury Board, for instance)[12] or whether it is pressure brought about on the federal government by privately owned CN to influence it to adopt rail policies that meet its corporate interests, and thus maintain the status quo in regards to the limited priority given to passenger trains. What is clear is that regardless of the specifics of the source of the enmity to VIA, these two entities limit VIA's ability to provide high-value to the rail traveling public.

The role of the federal government in determining the fate of VIA can be characterized as a mixture of general neglect of, and political interference in, its operations. The indifference shown by the federal government, as discussed earlier, is most evident in the small and inconsistent operational and capital funding it provides this organization, both of which have shrunk considerably over the course of VIA's existence. Such neglect also extends to general failure of the government to ensure that VIA's trains run quickly and arrive on time, and its failure to provide VIA with a legislative mandate, which could give it more authority to pressure CN to provide VIA with some form of priority on the tracks.

The many problems that VIA faces have been well documented and researched, yet no concrete actions to ameliorate them have been taken by any federal government. VIA's issues with late trains, equipment deficiencies and a convoluted governance structure, for example, have been thoroughly examined by a number of academic experts and parliamentary committees. All have arrived at similar conclusions regarding how best to resolve these problems.[13]

The recommendations often include providing VIA with enough resources to update its equipment, as well as some system to prioritize passenger trains *vis-a-vis* freight trains (or, alternatively, some kind of effective incentive structure to motivate CN to work towards improving train reliability) and granting VIA's management more control over operations and business decisions. Even VIA itself, in a submission to a panel reviewing the *Canada Transportation Act* in 2000, argued that "legislation for VIA Rail [should]be enacted to address governance and other issues and to clearly articulate the objectives of the Government of Canada with respect to passenger rail."[14] Despite this, nothing has yet been done to address these relatively basic problems that it faces.

In a somewhat paradoxical twist, at least some of VIA's troubles have resulted from an overly interventionist approach by the federal government towards this entity. Indeed, the government is involved in many of its corporate decisions, and makes them not with the best interests of the organization in mind, but instead with its own political considerations in the foreground. The areas of the country that VIA services, for example, as well as train frequency on routes, are choices made by the government, and are decisions that are often influenced by political or partisan considerations. They are not made on sound transport or financial bases. These problems have beset VIA through much of its history. Reductions and additions to VIA's service area, for instance, are often made for political gain. Cuts made to VIA in the mid-1980s, for example, were made in an arbitrary manner by the Minister responsible for VIA, with little regard for the effects of the cutbacks on service. (Some relatively well-used lines were scrapped while ones with lower use were retained. The result was higher-than-proportional loss of passenger numbers with regards to the passenger-mile reductions).[15] Since then, cuts to and restoration of train service often follows partisan constituency boundaries with the latter often occurring to opposition ridings, and the former to government-held seats. The fact that VIA still provides year-round transcontinental service, for instance, is another example of the government prioritizing political considerations and partisan interests; specifically, the interests of the constituencies that the lines run through. Requiring VIA to provide service to remote communities is likewise directly related to political considerations, since train service to these communities is the only viable means of ground transportation, but this concern is perhaps a more legitimate one, and a more legitimate use of political pressure on VIA than, say, requiring VIA to providing train service on the prairies in the middle of winter merely to preserve transcontinental service.

A recent announcement by the Harper Tories graphically illustrates that this government still views train service as an instrument of partisan politics. In February of 2008, federal Finance Minister Jim Flaherty announced that commuter service would be restored between Peterborough and Toronto. It is not clear, however, whether VIA is to be responsible for providing this service, or if the service will instead be provided by the provincially owned and operated GO Transit. Such a service, if it were created, might be a welcome addition to the Greater Toronto Area's transit system, but what was important to note is that announcement was made by the government (not VIA Rail) and that the decision appears to have been made with political, rather than transportation, concerns in mind. Peterborough and its surrounding constituency, it is worth noting, was recently won by a young Conservative MP, Dean Del Mastro, after being held by the Liberals since 1993. The proposed line will run through Mr. Flahery's riding as well. Provincial transport officials were not privy to the discussions surrounding this announcement before it was made.[16]

The federal government also bears responsibility for VIA's poor train-times and its inability to provide timely service, problems that have occurred as a result of CN trains having priority on the rail lines. (This problem is also somewhat attributable to the fact that VIA has been given insufficient funds for capital expenditures, as additional sidings could help to alleviate some of the most critical pinch points). The biggest problem facing VIA is that CN has little interest or incentive to ensure that VIA's trains arrive on time. The rail-sharing contract between CN and VIA contains no incentives to ensure that this occurs, and the federal government has not brought any pressure to bear on CN to motivate it to change its behaviour. The federal government has a number of policy levers that it could use to motivate CN to prioritize VIA's trains (relations between a large railway and the federal government that regulates it intertwine enough to ensure this), but the government chooses not to use them. If there was sufficient political will, the government could legislate a well functioning passenger service as an important public policy priority, and take the necessary steps to ensure that this policy is fulfilled.

Unsurprisingly, CN has an active incentive to ensure that VIA Rail is marginally run. For example, if VIA trains were to provide more timely service, rail would be a much more attractive mode of travel. This, in turn, would mean more passenger trains on CN's rail lines. More trains could potentially impede CN's ability to maximize its profits. Think, for a moment, about the interests of the profit maximizing CN. CN would certainly want to prioritize the arrival of its own hundred car freight train, carrying multiple millions of dollars of products, over the arrival of a VIA rail train that would be carrying a few hundred individual passengers at best. To compound matters, CN, of late, appears to be increasingly unresponsive to VIA's needs and deaf to the public good aspect of its role in providing efficient passenger rail service. The optimal outcome for CN would be if VIA Rail disappeared altogether.

What is important to note is that the inability of VIA to run its trains on time is a result of a lack of political will to ensure that this is done. Late trains are not a result of technical problems. Elizabeth May, the leader of the Green Party, embarked on a cross-Canada rail tour on a VIA Rail train during the

2008 federal government election campaign, and while her train was an hour late on its first stop in Kamloops, BC, for the remainder of the tour the train was – miraculously – on time. Having a leader of a national party, accompanied by a coterie of reporters, must have motivated both VIA and CN to ensure that her train, if no-one else's, arrived in a timely fashion as it made its way across the country.[17]

CN is a large and extremely profitable corporate entity, one that is able to extract monopoly rents from its client base given the structure of the market that it operates in – rail service in Canada is, for the most part, an oligopoly dominated by CN and CP. In 2006, for instance, CN reported revenues of $7.7 billion and a net income of $2.01 billion for a profit on its sales of 26 per cent.[18] To provide some context, the Liquor Control Board of Ontario (LCBO), a provincially-owned and operated liquor board, which also operates in an oligopolistic market and is specifically intended to return monopolistic rents for the Ontario government (and includes a "sin" tax component of the profit), earned $1.2 billion on sales of $3.66 billion for percentage profit on sales of almost 33 per cent.[19] Protecting such a privileged position in the rail sector specifically, and the transportation arena more generally, almost certainly requires CN to operate an effective government relations corporate division, in order to insulate the firm from calls (and actions) that would threaten its enormous profit margins. CN must, in other words, protect its market share in the political sphere, as well as in the marketplace. This assertion implies that it is CN that is influencing the actions or, again, inactions, of the federal government with regard not only to VIA Rail, but also with regard to limiting competition in their particular sector.

Other Interests Critical of VIA Rail

There are a number of other interest groups that oppose increased state funding for VIA, and support, more generally, its marginal operation. Alternative modes of transportation such as cars, planes and buses, and the accompanying coterie of firms and organizations that support or are involved in these other means of transportation, like automobile and car part manufacturers, those connected to road construction, airlines, airports and so forth, do not support the fact that VIA rail continues to be publicly owned, and certainly do not like the fact that it receives public monies. The politically well-connected bus transport industry, in particular, resents having a publicly funded competitor. Central Canada is the home of much of Canada's automobile parts suppliers and all of its car-manufacturing plants, and likewise resents competition the VIA's corridor service provides.

Much of the criticism of VIA Rail coming from these entities revolves around the direct nature of the subsidies it receives from the federal government, and the fact that passenger rail systems must be publicly owned and operated monopolies in order to operate effectively. Although there are no examples of efficient privately operated rail systems throughout the world, the subsidies VIA receives and the structure of the market place required for effective passenger rail service – a public monopoly – make VIA an easy target for criticism from competing firms. On a more ideological note, these factors also make VIA susceptible to criticism from ardent supporters of competitive markets generally, and those critical of state interventions and subsidies in any form. These individuals view unimpeded markets as the optimal method to solve collective action problems. The highly visible nature of the intervention in the passenger rail sector and the less visible "subsidies" other sectors receive compound this problem for VIA. The principal trouble with such views is that they ignore the historic subsidies provided to other means of travel – in Canada, roads, highways and airports were likewise constructed using public funds – as well as the negative externalities associated with car and plane travel, the most significant of which is relatively high levels of energy used by cars and planes, and the pollution that emanates from using these forms of travel.

CONCLUSIONS: OUT OF PLACE: REMAINING CROWNS AND VIA RAIL

Crown Corporations Today: Rationalized or Privatized

Examining the evolution of a number of other Crown Corporations might help provide some insights into the problems VIA faces and how it might be reformed. A number of provincial and federal governments have chosen to privatize government-owned Crowns. The federal government chose to privatize CN, Air Canada and Petro-Canada in the 1990s. A number of provincially owned Crowns, notably, BC Rail in 2003 and the Alberta Liquor Control Board (ALCB) in 1993, have also been privatized. However, a number of Crowns have remained in public hands, and have drastically reformed not only their internal operations to provide much improved customer value, but also, more interestingly, their structures through which they are governed. Most critically, some of these Crowns have significantly altered the nature of their relationship with their political masters, to their benefit. The evolution of the Liquor Control Board of Ontario (LCBO), in particular, provides some important policy prescriptions with respect to the types of changes needed at VIA Rail. While a direct comparison is difficult since selling alcohol – and earning lots of revenue for the provincial government – is an easier task than providing efficient and effective passenger service, there are a number of important lessons that can be derived from the reforms seen at the LCBO.[20]

The LCBO was created in 1927 as a response to outright prohibition, and was charged with distributing alcoholic products throughout the province. Its history, for our purposes, is marked by two distinctive phases. The first of these phases, the period from its inception until 1985, is notable for its poor function, by today's standards. During this period, the LCBO's stores were dingy and poorly located, and its staff was, for the most part, surly and disinterested in providing good customer service. Product selection was poor and what the LCBO did sell was relatively expensive. In short, the LCBO provided low overall consumer value (Viewed in another way, however, the LCBO's poor customer service was directly correlated to its mandate, which was to "control" the sale and consumption of alcoholic beverages). The LCBO's internal structures were likewise archaic. The LCBO had no effective marketing, accounting, logistics or information technology departments. Product movement information, for instance, took six months to reach senior management. The organization was also hopelessly overstaffed, and the LCBO had many patronage appointees working in its stores and head office. Finally, decisions as to where stores should be located and other business decisions were often made with political, personal or partisan considerations of the ruling government in mind. There were no defined boundaries between the LCBO management and the government.

The second phase of the LCBO's evolution started in 1985. The sorry state of the LCBO was an embarrassment to David Peterson's newly elected Liberal government. The Peterson government embarked on a process of "modernizing" the LCBO, starting by removing its entire board of directors and almost all of its senior executives. Peterson's hand picked reformers, Len Pitura and Jack Ackeryod, then went about hiring both a new board and executives with private sector retailing experience. This new board, however, imposed conditions of its own on the government. It agreed to undertake the monumental task of reorganizing this institution only on condition that the government refrain from interfering in the LCBO's operations. This meant an end to patronage-based appointments, as well as to all other forms of interference with respect to how the LCBO conducted its day-to-day operations. The government could set the overall direction of the modernization process, but it could not dictate how the LCBO managed its retail operations.[21]

The LCBO's modernization process continued for 15 more years and received a significant boost when the government of Mike Harris gave the LCBO significant amounts of capital to rebuild its store network and logistics systems. As a result of these efforts and this cash infusion, the LCBO is now an efficient and very effective retailer that provides a superb shopping experience to consumers. Its remittances to the government have correspondingly grown, and it is regarded as the market leader among other provincially owned alcohol retailers. Reforms made at ATB Financial, a bank that is owned and operated by the Alberta government, followed a remarkably similar path to the one charted by the LCBO. When ATB Financial was reformed in the late 1990s, one of the reform measures was to create clear and definite lines between the role of the government and the bank's board members and executives. Interference in its operations from the political sphere for short-term partisan gain is no longer tolerated at ATB Financial.

There are three key lessons that the LCBO's evolution teaches. The first, and most significant finding, is that it is important to clearly delineate between the government's role in a Crown Corporation and the role played by management. If the Crown is to be successful, all political and partisan-based interference, particularly the making of operationally based micromanagement-type decisions by the government, must come to an end. It is true that the federal government is the principal "shareholder" of VIA. It is also true that the fact that the government provides operational and capital funding to it entitles the government to make demands of its subordinate entity. However, when such demands impede VIA's ability to provide quality service and amount to little more than politically tinged micromanagement of this organization, these decisions must cease. Other publicly funded entities that receive their funding either in part or in whole from the government, such as police services, universities and hospitals, are, by specific organizational design, sufficiently insulated from potential meddling stemming from the political sphere. The old axiom "he who pays the piper, calls the tune" can apply to general policy direction, but not day-to-day or operational decisions of public institutions. The respective roles played by the Crown Corporation's management and the government do not have to be set in stone, and will, of necessity, relate to the specifics of the organization and its function, the needs of the government and the like. However, once the roles have been clearly defined and once established, they must be adhered to.

Second, because effective reforms require changing the governance structure within which the Crown exists, change, at least initially, must come from the political sphere. With respect to VIA, this means that the Minister responsible for it, or more likely, the Prime Minister's Office, must have the will to alter VIA's governance structure. VIA can try to shape decisions made regarding its fate, but ultimately, the political will to make VIA work effectively and to provide the initial impetus for real – structural – change must occur at the executive level of government. The privatization of a Crown Corporation does, by definition, require clearly defined roles for the government and the corporate entity, principally because privatization severs most links between them, thus resolving, for the most part, the problem of political interference in the former Crown Corporation's operations. However, this change in governance structure has also occurred in many of the Crowns that have been retained in public hands, regardless of their function or the sector in which they exist, like the LCBO and ATB Financial, and such change has resulted in these Crowns becoming increasingly successful in their delivery of services. VIA Rail has not gone through such a set of reforms, nor has it been privatized. There has been no will, thus far, at the executive level, to change its governance structure. Accordingly, VIA has been largely left to operate with a dysfunctional governance model.

Finally, the LCBO's evolution illustrates the importance of hiring competent employees and providing them with adequate amounts of capital for equipment, training and the like. These are additional key factors for the successful reform of a Crown Corporation. None of these suggestions are particularly novel, nor would they be particularly difficult to carry out with respect to VIA Rail. It is not a matter of technical or policy feasibility, but rather one of political will which stands in the way of effective reforms at VIA Rail.

CONCLUSIONS

The federal government's 2009 budget contained some good news for VIA Rail. VIA is set to receive $407 million in additional capital funding. Much of the money is earmarked to improve the rail tracks between Montreal, Ottawa and Toronto, in order to allow two additional express trains to travel between Montreal and Toronto. This will have the effect of reducing the travel times by thirty minutes between both Toronto and Montreal, and Toronto and Ottawa. Money will also be spent to improve train stations in Toronto, Montreal, Vancouver, Hamilton, Bellville and Windsor. Additional funds will also be spent on improvements to two First Nations railways, level crossing upgrades and a number of rail safety initiatives.[22] If this money materializes and is spent improving passenger rail infrastructure, it will, like the infusion of cash the Harper Conservatives provided to VIA in 2007, improve VIA's ability to provide high quality rail service in central Canada. However, these funds will not solve systemic problems with VIA's governance structure, and will not reduce CN's hostility towards it as an organization. Additional funds will not result in a change in the structural nature of the relationship between VIA Rail and its political masters, which is what it would be required to really make this Crown a success.

APPENDIX

All figures were derived from annual reports or other documents from VIA Rail. Figures start in 1980 since VIA did not take over all passenger service from CN until 1979. Yield (passenger revenue per passenger mile in cents) figures were derived from annual reports when available, but note that some early years did not include passenger miles from tour travel in the calculations. The author calculated data for years 1990 to 1998 and he was not able to distil tour miles from regular passenger miles, and so calculations are slightly higher than if tour miles were excluded (approximately by 4% –5%). Total government contributions do not include "reorganization" charges paid by government from 1990 to1997 and in 2000. Numbers include deposits into the Asset Renewal Fund (ARF), but do not include withdrawals from fund. "Restated" figures further complicated data analysis and calculations.

Year	1980	1981	1982	1983	1984	1985	1986	1987	1988	1989	1990	1991	1992	1993	1994	1995	1996	1997	1998	1999	2000	2001	2002	2003	2004	2005	2006	2007
Number of Passengers (thousands)	7,586	8,009	7,223	6,730	6,960	7,034	6,286	5,865	6,415	6,457	3,536	3,633	3,601	3,570	3,586	3,597	3,666	3,765	3,646	3,757	3,957	3,865	3,981	3,789	3,887	4,097	4,091	4,181
Passenger miles (millions)	1,928	1,936	1,577	1,533	1,556	1,543	1,405	1,300	1,428	1,517	785	820	817	820	834	859	892	884	856	931	942	921	948	857	851	888	874	874
Operational Subsidy ($ millions)	320.1	399.8	449.1	451.2	397.8	523.6	462	452.3	509.2	470.9	350.3	328	331.3	321	262.1	222.3	205.3	196	178.4	0	0	45.9	151.7	103.4	82.4	20.2	0.7	0
Capital Subsidy ($ millions)	94.6	109.4	103.8	135.1	153.6	108	44	84	126	60.6	31.5	40.1	44.7	11.8	25.3	39.6	20.7	16.4	0	0	0	315	257.1	263.5	197.7	169.9	169	12.4
Total Government Funding ($ millions)	414.7	509.2	552.9	597	473	631.6	506	536	636.6	530.9	381.8	368.1	375.9	332.8	287.4	261.9	226	212.4	178.4	170	210.3							213
Employees	4,200	4,135	3,640	3,474	3,653	4,178	5,370	5,726	6,873	6,594	4,525	4,402	4,478	4,131	3,718	3,178	3,000	2,969	2,952	2,909	2,958	3,013	3,054	3,051	3,027	3,059	3,003	3,017
Yield (revenue cents per passenger mile)	7.1	8.3	9.9	11.3	11.7	12.7	14.1	14.5	14.7	15.3	18.2	18.3	19.1	20	21.2	20.4	20.7	21.6	23.4	22.6	24	25.3	26.6	26.8	28	28.6	30.3	30.5

VIA Rail Statistics: 1980–2007

NOTES

1 A brief history of Canada's transportation system and government involvement in its development see: *Directions: The Final Report of the Royal Commission on National Passenger Transportation*, volume 1, Louis D. Hyndman, chair (Ottawa: Ministry of Supply and Service, 1992), 13–15.
2 This chapter is based on a number of interviews with senior personnel within VIA Rail and Transport Canada, as well as number of primary and secondary sources. Names and positions of participants, however, will remain anonymous for this chapter.
3 See for example: Kenneth A. Mozersky, Michael Parry, and Serge Pepin *Report of the Inquiry into the On-Time Performance of* VIA *Rail Canada Inc.* (Hull: Canadian Transportation Commission, 1984); David McQueen, *Aspects of Rail Passenger Policy in Canada* (Hull: Canadian Transportation Commission, 1985) and House of Commons Standing Committee on Transport, *The Renaissance of Passenger Rail in Canada*, Raymond Bonin, Chairman, June 1998.
4 Garth Stevenson, "Canadian National Railways and Via Rail" in *Privatization, Public Policy and Public Corporations in Canada,* Allan Tupper and G. Bruce Doern, editors (Halifax: The Institute for Research on Public Policy, 1988), 81–4.
5 Stevenson, "Canadian National Railways and Via Rail," 84.
6 Pierre A.H. Franche, "A Year of Goals Reached for VIA," in *Annual Report 1985*, VIA Rail Canada Inc. (Montreal: VIA Rail, 1985) 6.
7 Terry W. Ivany, "President's Message" in *VIA Annual Report 1997* (Montreal: VIA Rail, 1997) Available at: http://www.viarail.ca/corporate/ar/1997/en.info.1997.mes2.html (accessed 11 Feb 2009).
8 The Supreme Court of Canada recently ruled against VIA Rail in a case between the Crown corporation and the Council of Canadians with Disabilities. The Court ruled that VIA Rail was obligated to renovate its Renaissance cars to accommodate physically disabled individuals. The estimated cost of the refurbishment is between $48 million and $92 million. Tracey Tyler, "All Aboard with VIA Verdict: Supreme Court Orders Costly Overhaul of Railcars for Disabled Access," *The Toronto Star*, 24 March 2007, A4. Despite this legal conflict, VIA Rail does make accessibility of its service a key part of its operational mandate.
9 During years of little or no funding from the federal government, VIA drew upon moneys in its Asset Renewal Fund. For instance, it withdrew $28 million in 2005 and $10.5 million in 2006 (when it received only $700,000 from the federal government) to help fund capital improvements. After 2006 the fund has been depleted. VIA Rail, *Summary of the Amended 2005–09 Corporate Plan and 2005 Operating and Capital Budgets* (Montreal: VIA Rail, 2005) 4.
10 Only once a train is 15 minutes past its scheduled arrival time is it considered "late" by VIA. Using such a criteria 81per cent of its trains in 2005 were "on time." VIA Rail Canada, Summary *of the 2006–10 Corporate Plan and Operating and Capital Budgets* (Montreal: VIA Rail Canada, 2006) 3.
11 Transport Canada, *Canada's New Government Revitalizes Inter-City Passenger Rail Service in Canada* (Ottawa: Transport Canada, 11 October 2007) Available at: http://

www.viarail.ca/investmentprogram/pdf/en_transport_media.pdf (accessed 16 Feb 2009)
12 Stevenson, "Canadian National Railways and Via Rail," 84.
13 Mozersky et al, *Report of the Inquiry into the On-Time Performance of VIA Rail Canada Inc.;* McQueen, *Aspects of Rail Passenger Policy in Canada*; House of Commons Standing Committee on Transport, *The Renaissance of Passenger Rail in Canada.*
14 VIA Rail Canada, VIA *Submission: CTA Review Panel*, December 2000. Available at: http://www.reviewcta-examenltc.gc.ca/submissions-soumissions/Txt/Viaper cent20Railper cent20Canada(1).txt (accessed 29 October 2008)
15 Stevenson, "Canadian National Railways and Via Rail," 84.
16 VIA Rail's executives, it is worth noting, accept that the federal government has the right, as the "shareholder," to prescribe to VIA where and when it provides train service. It is difficult, if not impossible, in such a circumstance, for VIA's executives to act any differently since bureaucrats are obligated to follow the orders of their political masters. This is one reason why real reform to VIA Rail can only come from the political sphere and must include some sets of mechanisms to limit political and partisan interference in its rail operations.
17 Sandro Contenta, "Red Eyes on the Green Train," *The Toronto Star*, 24 September 2008.
18 CN, *Annual Report 2007* (Montreal: CN, 2007) available at: http://www.cn.ca/ documents/Investor-Annual-Report-Archive/2006–annual-report-en.pdf (accessed 28 October 2008) 2.
19 LCBO, *Annual Report 2005–06* (Toronto: LCBO, 2006) available at: http://www.lcbo.com/aboutlcbo/annual/2005_2006.pdf (accessed Oct. 28, 2008) 4.
20 Malcolm G. Bird, *The Rise of the Liquor Control Board of Ontario and the Demise of the Alberta Liquor Control Board: Why Such Divergent Outcomes?* (Unpublished PhD dissertation, Carleton University, School of Public Policy and Administration, 2008).
21 For example, the government gave directions to the new board and its executives to increase the revenues that the LCBO returned to the government, but stipulated that this could not be accomplished by selling higher volumes of alcoholic products. The government did not want to be seen to be pushing alcohol onto the consuming public. Their solution, interestingly, was to promote higher-value alcoholic products that would return more revenue to the government without selling more alcohol.
22 Department of Finance, *Budget 2009 – Canada's Economic Action Plan* (Ottawa: Department of Finance, 2009), chapter 3. Available at: http://www.budget.gc.ca/2009/plan/bpc3d-eng.asp (accessed 16 Feb 2009)

APPENDIX A
Canadian Political Facts and Trends

1 FEB 2008
The Royal Bank of Canada opens its first office in India. The CEO says "India is showing an increasing demand for areas in which RBC has competitive strengths."

1 FEB 2008
The House of Commons resumes debate on Bill C-3 – designed to replace immigration security legislation the Supreme Court struck down last year – with just a few weeks to go before the old legislation essentially expires. The debate carried on against the backdrop of two separate court appearances in Ottawa by men who have become public faces of Canada's security-certificate controversy.

4 FEB 2008
Peter Miliken celebrates seven years as House Speaker.

9 FEB 2008
Prime Minister Stephen Harper and Premier Jean Charest agreed at a private meeting in Quebec City to work on a deal to speed up the province's share of a fund to help struggling industries.

11 FEB 2008
In the Throne Speech, the Harper government promised a new water strategy to block exports of water in bulk.

12 FEB 2008
CAW head Buzz Hargrove says he told Prime Minister Harper that Ford and GM will be bankrupt in 10 years if nothing is done about trade with Asian countries.

12 FEB 2008
Harper vows compromise on Afghan mission: Election over Afghanistan less likely as PM promises to seriously consider Liberal amendments to Conservative confidence motion; Dion wants end to combat by 2009, leading to full withdrawal by 2011.

12 FEB 2008
Newfoundland Grits delay leadership convention: Party hopes delay until spring of 2010 will give party chance to rebuild, pay down debt.

26 FEB 2008
Budget 2008 released: Planned debt reduction is $10.2 billion in 2007–08, $2.3 billion in 2008–09 and $1.3 billion in 2009–10. The federal tax burden, measured by total revenues as a share of the economy, is projected to decline from 16.3 per cent in 2006–07 to 15.3 per cent in 2009–10 – the lowest level in nearly 50 years. Finance Minister Jim Flaherty's budget allocates a miserly $50-million a year, for five years, to the auto companies. "Grossly inadequate ... a baby step," sniffed the CAW chief, who was hoping for something grander: $1-billion, right away.

28 FEB 2008
Canada's international travel deficit – the difference between spending by Canadians abroad and spending by foreigners in Canada – reached a record deficit of $10.3-billion, substantially more than the previous high of $6.7-billion in 2006.

25 MAR 2008
The McGuinty government hopes to prop up Ontario's flagging economy with an immediate infusion of $1-billion in infrastructure spending, large investments in skills training, and a modest set of business income tax cuts in a budget overshadowed by the war of words it has provoked with Ottawa.

28 MAR 2008
The Conservative government resolved a record number of native land-claim disputes this year in a bid to improve relations with Canada's aboriginals and spur economic development on reserves. Indian Affairs Minister Jim Prentice caused a stir in his department last year when he quietly ordered public servants to conclude at least 50 specific land-claim disputes for the 2007–2008 fiscal year ending Monday.

21 APRIL 2008
2008 North American Leaders' Summit – Prime Minister Stephen Harper travels to New Orleans, Louisiana, for the 2008 North American Leaders' Summit. April 21–22.

23 APRIL 2008
Canadian banks cut interest rates dramatically after the Bank of Canada slashed its main rate by half a percentage point and warned that a serious economic slowdown was only just beginning.

23 APRIL 2008
With oil prices at historic highs, the Alberta Progressive Conservative government announces another double-digit spending hike to cover a record $37-billion tab for everything from fighting climate change to modest tax relief.

6 JUNE 2008
Athletes village to get $100-million loan: City of Vancouver has already advanced nearly $30-million to rescue financially troubled Olympic project.

9 JUNE 2008
Government of Canada apologizes on behalf of all Canadians to residential school victims.

15 AUG 2008
Canadian dollar hits par with US dollar.

20 AUG 2008
Tories slashing $44.8-million in arts spending: Canadian Heritage programs hit hardest.

9 SEPT 2008
Conservatives call for federal election for October 14th.

20 SEPT 2008
Harper rejects notion of Canadian bailout for banks: Stephen Harper says there is no need for a bailout of Canada's chartered banks and he is urging Canadians not to panic in the face of the U.S. financial crisis.

4 OCT 2008
Tories promise $300-million for economic development: Conservatives unveil part of economic plan and hope to convince voters they're the best choice to lead Canada through a time of 'global economic uncertainty'.

14 OCT 2008

Election Day: Harper is pleased with a stronger minority, however, voter turnout dropped to 59.1 per cent of Canadians – a record low in the history of confederation.

15 OCT 2008

Premier's 'Anything But Conservative' campaign shuts out Tories in Nfld.: The Conservatives were shut out of Newfoundland and Labrador yesterday, losing their three seats in the province after a rancorous blocking campaign run by Premier Danny Williams. The losses leave the party facing the prospect of forming a government without any representation from the increasingly wealthy province.

18 OCT 2008

Leadership convention set for Fredericton, with at least four satellite voting centres around province for N.B. Tories to pick new leader.

5 NOV 2008

Opposition MPs, including Liberals who have worked on justice issues, say they would plunge the country into another federal election before agreeing to a slate of Conservative proposals that would see convicted criminals treated more harshly.

15 NOV 2008

The Assembly of First Nations suggests expanding the residential schools Truth and Reconciliation Commission to five members in an effort to extricate the panel from the mess left by Mr. Justice Harry LaForme's resignation.

19 NOV 2008

Throne Speech, Protecting Canada's Future: Under the leadership of Prime Minister Stephen Harper, the Government of Canada will follow a five-pronged plan to protect Canada's economic security.

21 NOV 2008

Parliament: Budget Office Forecasts a deficit of $3.9 bilion for 2009–2010.

24 NOV 2008

Flaherty vows project spending: Finance minister says Ottawa will move quickly to get infrastructure projects up and running.

25 NOV 2008

OECD forecasts 0.5 per cent Canadian contraction: Predicts rising unemployment and government deficits.

27 NOV 2008
Economic and Fiscal statement 2008: In 2009–10, Canadians and Canadian businesses will pay $31 billion less in taxes – or almost 2 per cent of gross domestic product – as a result of tax reductions implemented by the Government since 2006.

27 NOV 2008
Opposition takes hit as Tories move to cut $27-million subsidy for parties: The Harper government is proposing to end a $27-million subsidy for political parties in today's fiscal and economic update – a measure taken in the name of federal belt-tightening that also threatens to hit opposition parties especially hard in the wallet.

28 NOV 2008
Tory minority in jeopardy as opposition talks coalition: Stephen Harper's six-week-old minority government is already in danger of falling, with the Liberals warning that the Prime Minister has four days to change "unacceptable" elements of yesterday's economic fiscal package.

1 DEC 2008
Liberals, NDP firm up deal to topple Tories: The Liberals and NDP reach a deal to bring down the federal Conservative government and form an unprecedented coalition to take its place that would last 30 months and include cabinet seats for both parties.

04 DEC 2008
Parliament shut down till Jan. 26: PM obtains governor-general's consent to prorogue in face of bid to topple his minority government; opposition complains he's "throwing the locks on" and "running away."

6 DEC 2008
Detroit 3 seeking $6-billion from Canada: Canadian taxpayers are being asked to provide at least $6-billion to the Detroit Three auto makers – and the two most troubled companies say they need a big chunk of the money immediately.

11 DEC 2008
Ex-MP Emerson to lead economic council: Former Conservative foreign affairs minister David Emerson will be heading a BC economic advisory council.

11 DEC 2008
U.S. braces for $1–trillion deficit: The United States is on track to post a record-setting deficit of more than $1–trillion (U.S.) this year amid the mounting cost of bank bailouts and easing the pain of recession.

11 DEC 2008
Ottawa broke law in financing EI: Supreme Court says Liberal governments of Jean Chrétien and Paul Martin collected employment insurance contributions illegally 2002–05.

12 DEC 2008
Stelmach plans oil sands strategy as spending slows: Premier Ed Stelmach is looking to spur investment in Alberta's oil sands as two more oil and gas producers announced they are slashing capital spending budgets for next year.

12 DEC 2008
Ontario mayors urge auto action: Mayors of Ontario's motor cities called on the Harper government to follow the lead of the United States and bail out the Canadian operations of the Detroit Three auto makers.

13 DEC 2008
Flaherty asks for time to consult on stimulus: Finance Minister Jim Flaherty is asking for a little breathing room to come up with an economic stimulus package. Canada's economy retains enough life to allow for some "thoughtful consideration" of how to proceed, said Mr. Flaherty, rejecting critics who say he is taking too long to develop an economic stimulus plan.

15 DEC 2008
Tories set to add forestry, mining to bailout list: After pledging more than $3-billion to rescue the auto sector, the Harper government is now poised to offer similar aid to the struggling mining and forestry industries in next month's budget.

16 DEC 2008
PM's economic flip: "I've never seen such uncertainty": Stephen Harper has delivered his bleakest forecast yet for the Canadian economy, warning the future is increasingly hard to read and conceding the possibility of a depression. "The truth is, I've never seen such uncertainty in terms of looking forward to the future," the Prime Minister told CTV News in Halifax.

22 DEC 2008
Harper names 18 new senators: Conservatives are on pace for a Senate majority by 2010 as Prime Minister Stephen Harper drops his objection to Senate appointments and fills all current vacancies before Christmas. By making the appointments now, Harper sought to prevent a potential Liberal-NDP coalition government from getting the opportunity to fill the seats.

23 DEC 2008
Ottawa books $600-million deficit in October: Federal government posts third consecutive month of shortfalls; surplus for first seven months now just $200-million.

24 DEC 2008
U.S. falls deeper into recession: Number of people filing unemployment claims reaching a 26–year high and consumers cutting spending for the fifth successive month.

13 JAN 2009
Battle erupts over securities watchdog: Finance Minister Jim Flaherty is pushing ahead with the creation of a long-debated national securities regulator, igniting a battle with Quebec and Alberta just as Ottawa is seeking the provinces' help in reviving Canada's flagging economy.

14 JAN 2009
Nortel granted bankruptcy protection: CEO rejects talk company will be sold off in pieces: "A break-up is not a top priority for the business."

16 JAN 2009
19.4 per cent drop in the value of Canadian energy exports between October and November: Canada's energy exports fell by $2-billion in just one month, to $8.4-billion in November from $10.4-billion in October. While the plunging oil price was a big factor, a softening of world demand for petroleum products made the situation worse. Even the seemingly insatiable appetite for oil in the United States – our biggest customer – declined as the world economy spiralled into recession.

16 JAN 2009
U.S. inflation lowest since 1954: Recession, energy's plunge send 2008 price rate to 0.1 per cent.

17 JAN 2009
Vancouver looks to borrow $800-million: The City of Vancouver has entered discussions that would see it borrow an estimated $800-million to consolidate funding around the problem-plagued Olympic athletes village.

19 JAN 2009
Aluminum price drops more than 4 per cent: Metal hits lowest level since September 2003, as warehouses bulge with supply.

19 JAN 2009
Oil falls below $35 a barrel.

26 JAN 2009
Throne Speech: The economic stimulus plan is the plan of action.

27 JAN 2009
Budget Speech: Budget 2009 is Canada's Economic Action Plan.

APPENDIX B
Fiscal Facts and Trends

Figure B.1
Sources of Federal Revenue as a Percentage of Total, 2007–08

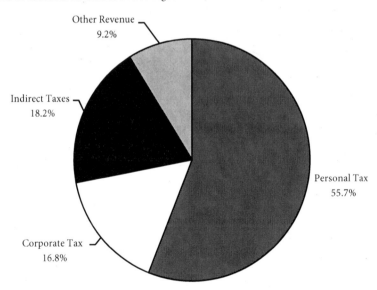

Source: Department of Finance, *Fiscal Reference Tables 2008*, Table 3.

Figure B. 2
Federal Expenditures by Ministry 2008-09 Estimates

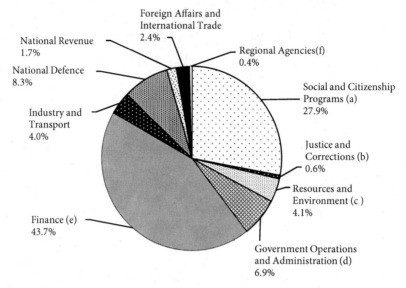

(a) Social Citizenship programs include departmental spending from Canadian Heritage, Citizenship and Immigration, Human Resources and Social Development, Veterans Affairs, Health, and Indian Affairs and Northern Affairs
(b) Justice and Corrections includes spending from the Department of Justice
(c) Resources and Environment includes departmental spending from Agriculture and Agri-Food, Environment, Fisheries and Oceans, and Natural Resources
(d) Government Operations and Administration Spending includes that from Public Works and Government Services, the Governor General, Parliament, the Privy Council, and the Treasury Board
(e) Finance expenditures include but are not limited to, spending on public interest charges and major transfers to the provinces.
(f) Regional Agencies includes Western Economic Diversification, the Atlantic Canada Opportunities Agency and the Economic Development Agency of Canada for the Regions of Quebec

Source: Treasury Board Secretariat, *Main Estimates, Budgetary Main Estimates by Standard Object of Expenditure*, Part II, 2008–2009

Figure B.3
Federal Budgetary Expenses by Type of Payment 1999-2000 to 2007–08

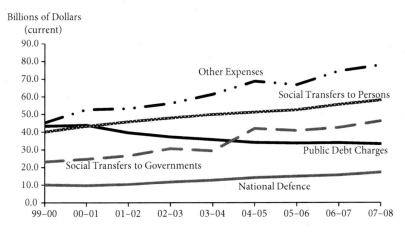

Source: Department of Finance, *Fiscal Reference Tables 2008*, Table 7.

Figure B.4
Federal Revenue, Program Spending, and Deficit as Percentages of GDP 1999–2000 to 2009–10

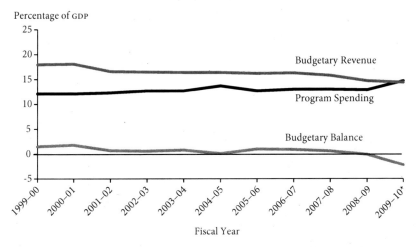

Source: Department of Finance, Fiscal Reference Tables 2008, Table 2; Department of Finance, Budget, Jan. 27, 2009

Note: Budgetary revenue and program spending are based upon fiscal years, while GDP is based on the calendar year. Revenues, program spending, and the deficit are on a net basis. Program spending does not include public interest charges. GDP is nominal GDP.
* Estimates

Figure B.5
Federal Revenue, Expenditures and the Deficit 1999–00 to 2009–10

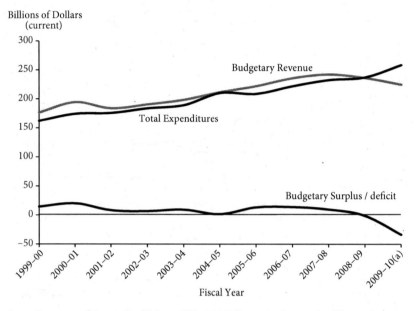

Source: Department of Finance, *Fiscal Reference Tables 2008*, Tables 1 and 3; Department of Finance, *Budget*, Jan. 27, 2009

Note: Expenditures include program spending and public interest charges on the debt.

(a) estimates

Figure B.6
Growth in Real GDP 1997–2007

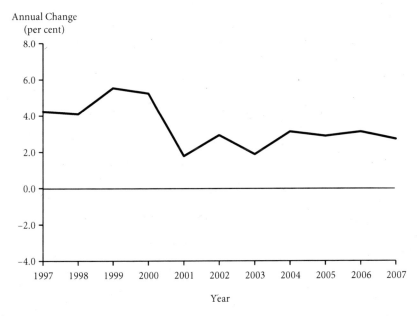

Source: Statistics Canada, *CANSIM*, Table 380–0017: Gross Domestic Product (GDP), expenditure-based, annual (Constant 2002 Prices).

Figure B.7
Rate of Unemployment and Employment Growth 1998–2008

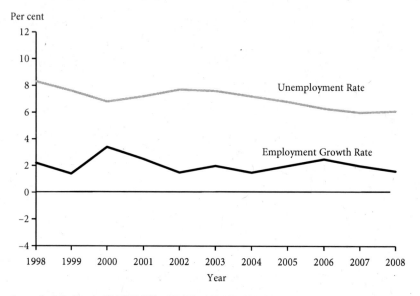

Source: Statistics Canada, *CANSIM*, Tables 109–5004, 109–5304, 281–0023.
Note: Employment growth rate and the unemployment rate apply to both sexes, 15 years and older.

Figure B.8
Interest Rates and the Consumer Price Index (CPI) 1998–2008

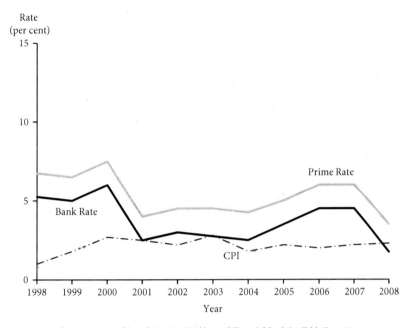

Source: Bank of Canada, *Bank of Canada Review, Banking and Financial Statistics*, Table F1, various years; Statistics Canada, *CANSIM*, Table 326-0021.
Note: The Prime Rate refers to the prime business interest rate charged by chartered bank, and the Bank Rate refered to the rate charged by the Bank of Canada on any loans to commercial banks.
Note: The Prime Rate and Bank Rate are rates effective at year end.
Note: The Trend line for the CPI shows annual percentage change in the index.

Figure B.9
Productivity and Costs 1997–2007

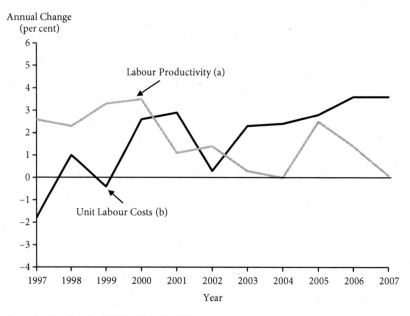

Source: Statistics Canada, *CANSIM*, Table 383–0008

(a) Labour Productivity is the ratio between real value added and hours worked in the business sector. This trend shows the annual percentage change in the index.

(b) This is a measure of the cost of labour input required to produce one unit of output, and is equal to labour compensation in current dollars divided by real output. This trend shows the annual percentage change in the index.

Figure B.10
Balance of Payments (Current Account) 1997–2008

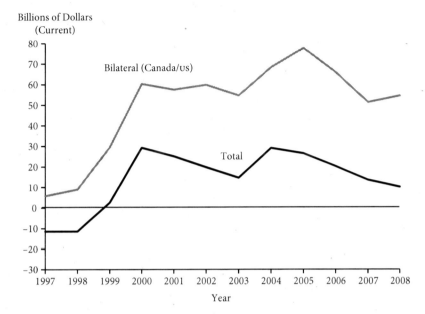

Source: Statistics Canada, cat.# 67-001, various years.

Figure B.11
Growth in Real GDP Canada and Selected Countries 1998–2010

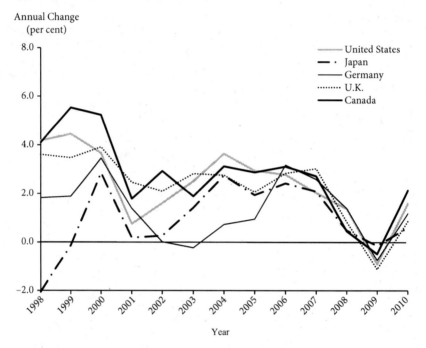

Source: Organization for Economic Cooperation and Development (OECD), Economic Outlook, no.84, Nov. 2008, Annex Table 1.

Figure B.12
Standardized Unemployment Rates Canada and Selected Countries 1998–2010

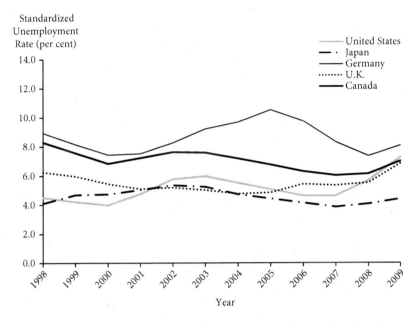

Source: Organization for Economic Cooperation and Development (OECD), Economic Outlook, no.84, Nov. 2008, Annex Table 13.

Figure B.13
Annual Inflation Rates Canada and Selected Countries 1998–2010

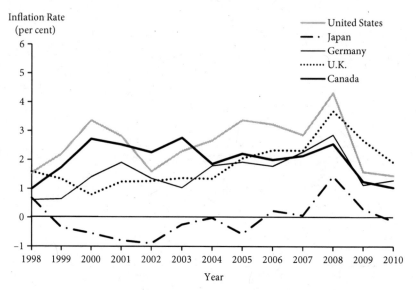

Source: Organization for Economic Cooperation and Development (OECD), Economic Outlook, no.84, Nov. 2008, Annex Table 18.

Figure B.14
Labour Productivity Canada and Selected Countries 1998–2010

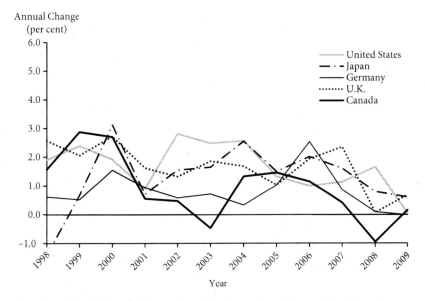

Source: Organization for Economic Cooperation and Development (OECD), Economic Outlook, no.84, Nov. 2008, Annex Table 13.
Note: Labour productivity is defined as output per unit of labour input.

Table B.1
Federal Revenue by Source 1997–98 to 2007–08

	As a Percentage of Total					
Fiscal Year	Personal Tax[a]	Corporate Tax	Indirect Taxes[b]	Other Revenue[c]	Total Revenue	Annual Change (%)
1997–98	59.8	13.2	19.4	7.7	100.0	7.3
1998–99	59.9	12.8	19.2	8.1	100.0	2.9
1999–00	60.3	12.5	18.9	8.3	100.0	6.6
2000–01	58.8	14.6	18.4	8.2	100.0	10.2
2001–02	58.5	13.2	20.2	8.2	100.0	-5.4
2002–03	58.1	11.7	21.7	8.6	100.0	3.6
2003–04	57.2	13.8	20.8	8.1	100.0	4.2
2004–05	56.4	14.1	20.2	9.3	100.0	6.7
2005–06	56.1	14.3	20.8	8.8	100.0	4.8
2006–07	56.0	16.0	19.2	8.8	100.0	6.2
2007–08	55.7	16.8	18.2	9.2	100.0	2.7

Source: Department of Finance, *Fiscal Reference Tables 2008*, Table 3 and 5. Revenue by Source is on a net basis.
(a) Employment Insurance and other income taxes are included in the total.
(b) Consists of total excise taxes and duties.
(c) Consists of non-tax and other tax revenue

Table B.2
Federal Deficit/Surplus 1996–97 to 2009–10 in billions of dollars (current)

Fiscal Year	Budgetary Revenue	Total Expenditures	Budgetary Deficit/Surplus	As % of GDP
1997–98	160.9	157.9	3.0	0.3
1998–99	165.5	159.7	5.8	0.6
1999–00	176.4	162.2	14.3	1.5
2000–01	194.3	174.5	19.9	1.8
2001–02	183.9	175.9	8.0	0.7
2002–03	190.6	183.9	6.6	0.6
2003–04	198.6	189.4	9.1	0.8
2004–05	211.9	210.5	1.5	0.1
2005–06	222.2	209.0	13.2	1.0
2006–07	236.0	222.2	13.8	0.9
2007–08	242.4	232.8	9.6	0.6
2008–09[a]	236.4	237.5	-1.1	-0.1

Source. Department of Finance, Fiscal Reference Tables 2008, Tables 1 and 2; Department of Finance, Budget Plan, January 2009

Note: While revenue, expenditures, and deficit categories refer to fiscal years, nominal GDP is based upon a calendar year. Total expenditures include program spending and public debt charges.
a) Figures for this year are estimates

Table B.3
International Comparisons 1998–2010, Percentage Change from Previous Period

	1998	1999	2000	2001	2002	2003	2004	2005	2006	2007	2008	2009	2010
Growth in Real GDP													
Canada	4.1	5.5	5.2	1.8	2.9	1.9	3.1	2.9	3.1	2.7	0.5	-0.5	2.1
U.S.	4.2	4.4	3.7	0.8	1.6	2.5	3.6	2.9	2.8	2.0	1.4	-0.9	1.6
Japan	-2.0	-0.1	2.9	0.2	0.3	1.4	2.7	1.9	2.4	2.1	0.5	-0.1	0.6
Germany	1.8	1.9	3.5	1.4	0.0	-0.2	0.7	0.9	3.2	2.6	1.4	-0.8	1.2
U.K.	3.6	3.5	3.9	2.5	2.1	2.8	2.8	2.1	2.8	3.0	0.8	-1.1	0.9
Unemployment Rates													
Canada	8.3	7.6	6.8	7.2	7.6	7.6	7.2	6.8	6.3	6.0	6.1	7.0	7.5
U.S.	4.5	4.2	4.0	4.8	5.8	6.0	5.5	5.1	4.6	4.6	5.7	7.3	7.5
Japan	4.1	4.7	4.7	5.0	5.4	5.3	4.7	4.4	4.1	3.9	4.1	4.4	4.4
Germany	8.9	8.2	7.4	7.5	8.3	9.2	9.7	10.5	9.8	8.3	7.4	8.1	8.6
U.K.	6.3	6.0	5.5	5.1	5.2	5.0	4.8	4.8	5.4	5.4	5.5	6.8	8.2
Labour Productivity													
Canada	1.6	2.9	2.7	0.6	0.5	-0.5	1.3	1.5	1.1	0.4	-1.0	0.1	1.5
U.S.	1.9	2.4	1.9	0.9	2.8	2.5	2.6	1.3	1.0	1.1	1.6	0.0	1.1
Japan	-1.4	0.7	3.1	0.7	1.5	1.6	2.5	1.5	2.0	1.6	0.8	0.6	0.8
Germany	0.6	0.5	1.5	0.9	0.6	0.7	0.3	1.0	2.5	0.9	0.1	0.0	1.4
U.K.	2.6	2.1	2.7	1.6	1.3	1.9	1.7	1.0	1.9	2.3	0.1	0.7	2.8

Source: Organization for Economic Cooperation and Development (OECD), *Economic Outlook*, no. 84, Nov. 2008, Annex Tables 1, 12, 13.

Contributors

MALCOLM G. BIRD earned his PhD from the School of Public Policy and Administration in 2008.

CHRIS BROWN is an associate professor in the Department of Political Science at Carleton University.

G. BRUCE DOERN is professor of Public Policy and Administration, Carleton University, Ottawa, and joint professor, Department of Politics, University of Exeter.

MELISSA HAUSSMAN is an associate professor of Political Science at Carleton University.

ROBERT HILTON is an adjunct research professor of Public Policy and Administration at Carleton University.

RUTH HUBBARD is senior fellow of the University of Ottawa's Graduate School of Public and International Affairs as well as its Centre on Governance, and a senior partner of Invenire – a firm that specializes in governance and stewardship.

EDWARD T. JACKSON is associate dean (Research and Graduate Affairs) in the Faculty of Public Affairs at Carleton University, where he teaches in the School of Public Policy and Administration.

KIRSTEN KOZOLANKA is an assistant professor at School of Journalism and Communication, Carleton University.

EVERT LINDQUIST is director and professor of the School of Public Administration, University of Victoria, British Columbia.

ALLAN M. MASLOVE is a professor of Public Policy and Administration at Carleton University and the former dean of Carleton's Faculty of Public Affairs and Management.

PETER NARES is the founding executive director of Social and Enterprise Development Innovations (SEDI) and an Ashoka Senior Fellow.

GILLES PAQUET is professor emeritus at the University of Ottawa, a senior research fellow of its Center on Governance, an associate with its Graduate School of Public and International Affairs, and the editor-in-chief of www.optimumonline.ca

L. PAULINE RANKIN is an associate professor of Canadian Studies at Carleton University and the associate dean of Research and Graduate Affairs for Carleton's Faculty of Arts and Social Sciences.

JENNIFER ROBSON is a PhD candidate at the School of Public Policy and Administration, Carleton University.

ROBERT P. SHEPHERD is an assistant professor of Public Policy and Administration at Carleton University specializing in Canadian public management and federal program evaluation.

RICHARD SHILLINGTON is a senior associate with Informetrica Limited.

CHRIS STONEY is an associate professor of Public Policy and Administration at Carleton University and Director of the Centre for Urban Research and Education (CURE).

The *How Ottawa Spends* Series

How Ottawa Spends 2008–2009: A More Orderly Federalism?
Edited by Allan M. Maslove

How Ottawa Spends 2007–2008: The Harper Conservative – Climate of Change
Edited by G. Bruce Doern

How Ottawa Spends 2006–2007: In From the Cold – The Tory Rise and the Liberal Demise
Edited by G. Bruce Doern

How Ottawa Spends 2005–2006: Managing the Minority
Edited by G. Bruce Doern

How Ottawa Spends 2004–2005: Mandate Change in the Paul Martin Era
Edited by G. Bruce Doern

How Ottawa Spends 2003–2004: Regime Change and Policy Shift
Edited by G. Bruce Doern

How Ottawa Spends 2002–2003: The Security Aftermath and National Priorities
Edited by G. Bruce Doern

How Ottawa Spends 2001–2002: Power in Transition
Edited by Leslie A. Pal

How Ottawa Spends 2000–2001: Past Imperfect, Future Tense
Edited by Leslie A. Pal

How Ottawa Spends 1999–2000: Shape Shifting: Canadian Governance Toward the 21 Century
Edited by Leslie A. Pal

How Ottawa Spends 1998–99: Balancing Act: The Post-Deficit Mandate
Edited by Leslie A. Pal

How Ottawa Spends 1997–98: Seeing Red: A Liberal Report Card
Edited by Gene Swimmer

How Ottawa Spends 1996–97: Life Under the Knife
Edited by Gene Swimmer

How Ottawa Spends 1995–96: Mid-Life Crises
Edited by Susan D. Phillips

How Ottawa Spends 1994–95: Making Change
Edited by Susan D. Phillips

How Ottawa Spends 1993–94: A More Democratic Canada…?
Edited by Susan D. Phillips

How Ottawa Spends 1992–93: The Politics of Competitiveness
Edited by Frances Abele

How Ottawa Spends 1991–92: The Politics of Fragmentation
Edited by Frances Abele

How Ottawa Spends 1990–91: Tracking the Second Agenda
Edited by Katherine A. Graham

How Ottawa Spends 1989–90: The Buck Stops Where?
Edited by Katherine A. Graham

How Ottawa Spends 1988–89: The Conservatives Heading into the Stretch
Edited by Katherine A. Graham

How Ottawa Spends 1987–88: Restraining The State
Edited by Michael J. Prince

How Ottawa Spends 1986–87: Tracking The Tories
Edited by Michael J. Prince

How Ottawa Spends 1985: Sharing the Pie
Edited by Allan M. Maslove

How Ottawa Spends 1984: The New Agenda
Edited by Allan M. Maslove

How Ottawa Spends 1983: The Liberals, The Opposition & Federal Priorities
Edited by Bruce Doern

How Ottawa Spends Your Tax Dollars: National Policy and Economic Development 1982
Edited by Bruce Doern

How Ottawa Spends Your Tax Dollars: Federal Priorities 1981
Edited by Bruce Doern

Spending Tax Dollars: Federal Expenditures, 1980–81
Edited by Bruce Doern